The Kinship of Jesus

The Kinship of Jesus

Christology and Discipleship in the Gospel of Mark

KATHLEEN ELIZABETH MILLS

Foreword by Warren Carter

◥PICKWICK *Publications* • Eugene, Oregon

THE KINSHIP OF JESUS
Christology and Discipleship in the Gospel of Mark

Copyright © 2016 Kathleen Elizabeth Mills. All rights reserved. Except for brief quotations in critical publications or reviews, no part of this book may be reproduced in any manner without prior written permission from the publisher. Write: Permissions, Wipf and Stock Publishers, 199 W. 8th Ave., Suite 3, Eugene, OR 97401.

Pickwick Publications
An Imprint of Wipf and Stock Publishers
199 W. 8th Ave., Suite 3
Eugene, OR 97401

www.wipfandstock.com

PAPERBACK ISBN: 978-1-4982-3031-5
HARDCOVER ISBN: 978-1-4982-3033-9
EBOOK ISBN: 978-1-4982-3032-2

Cataloguing-in-Publication data:

Names: Mills, Kathleen Elizabeth | other names in same manner

Title: The kinship of Jesus : christology and discipleship in the Gospel of Mark / Kathleen Elizabeth Mills.

Description: Eugene, OR: Pickwick Publications, 2016 | **Includes bibliographical references.**

Identifiers: ISBN 978-1-4982-3031-5 (paperback) | ISBN 978-1-4982-3033-9 (hardcover) | ISBN 978-1-4982-3032-2 (ebook)

Subjects: LCSH: Bible. Mark—Criticism, interpretation, etc. | Jesus Christ—Person and offices. | Christian life—Biblical teaching.

Classification: BS2585.52 M4 2016 (paperback) | BS2585.52 (ebook)

Manufactured in the U.S.A.   10/06/16

For Ryan, John, and Helen

Contents

Foreword by Warren Carter | ix
Acknowledgments | xi
Abbreviations | xiii

1 Scholarly Approaches to Christology and Discipleship in the Gospel of Mark | 1

2 Methodology | 35

3 Mark 1:1—8:30 | 82

4 Mark 8:31—16:8 | 168

5 Conclusion | 253

Bibliography | 261
Ancient Document Index | 275

Foreword

SCHOLARS HAVE LONG PUZZLED over Mark's presentation of Jesus. They have noted Mark's interest, for example, in secrecy, in titles, and in the interaction of Jesus' displays of both power and weakness across the Gospel. Scholars have also noticed Mark's distinctive construction of non-comprehending disciples more often choosing fear than faith and have offered various theories to explain the origin and function of this presentation. They have read disciples as representatives of a community and its struggles, as well as literary constructs.

But rarely, as Kathleen Mills argues in this important study, have scholars wrestled with the interactions of Mark's constructions of Christology and discipleship. Are these two entities connected and if so how?

It is this question concerning how the Gospel's Christology intersects with the Gospel's presentation of discipleship that provides both the central concern of this study as well as its leading contribution. Employing social-science, literary and imperial-critical approaches, Mills argues that it is the notion of kinship that provides the nexus between Mark's Christology and discipleship. She argues that Mark constructs Jesus as the most honored divine Son who even through the circumstances of his death by crucifixion remains faithful to his task of manifesting God's empire. Throughout his public activity, Jesus establishes a kinship group of disciples through hospitality and welcome, creating a family or household of brothers and sisters who are charged to do the will of God and in various circumstances struggle to do so. Moreover, she sets this kinship group in the larger context of the Roman imperial world arguing that in places the Gospel's notion of kinship imitates and in other places contests Roman structures.

Mills makes her argument by demonstrating this nexus through a commentary on the whole Gospel. Fundamental to this analysis is a new construction of the Gospel's plot. She surfaces the extensive use of kinship terms in the Gospel and identifies the various interactions between Jesus the son with his family of disciples and an extended kinship network. Kinship provides the nexus between the Gospel's Christology and discipleship.

The contributions of Mills' compelling work are multiple. In addition to her main argument concerning the intersections of Christology and discipleship, she provides a new analysis of the plot of the Gospel, she constructs and employs a multivalent methodology comprising narrative, social-science and imperial critical approaches, and she adds to studies on the Gospel's interaction with Roman power.

This is a sophisticated, insightful, and well-written study. In terms of both method and argument, it carefully engages previous studies of Mark's Gospel, and positions itself thoughtfully so as to make a significant contribution to the ongoing conversation.

Warren Carter
Brite Divinity School

Acknowledgments

THE SEEDS OF THIS study have their roots primarily in a sermon on Bartimaeus in the Gospel of Mark that Gordon Lathrop preached in the Chapel of the Lutheran Theological Seminary at Philadelphia. Subsequent to that sermon and many conversations with Dr. Lathrop, I wrote a paper under the advisement of Erik Heen on the "Son of God" in Mark and its connections to the Roman Empire. When I told Carolyn Osiek about this paper, she thought it was "interesting," and offered me an opportunity to study at Brite Divinity School. I am grateful to her and to David Balch for introducing me to social-scientific approaches to the Bible and for their wisdom, support, and encouragement during my coursework at Brite. I must also thank Francisco Lozada who served as a reader and offered helpful suggestions on another paper that served as a catalyst to this project. I am grateful to Shelly Matthews for her service as a reader and her careful reading, suggestions, and challenges. My most profound thanks go to Warren Carter, my doctoral adviser and dissertation director. He accepted me as his graduate student assistant when he arrived at Brite and has worked with me since my exams. I am grateful for the instruction I received not only in constructing this project, but in how to be a better writer and a better scholar. He helped me to develop my earlier ideas about sonship in the Gospel of Mark, incorporating narrative, social-science, and imperial critical approaches to the Bible. Dr. Carter offered endless guidance and constantly reminded me that I had a good argument, for which I will be forever grateful.

I must also thank three Lutheran congregations and their members that have supported me through my doctoral journey. My home congregation of Prince of Peace Lutheran Church in Augusta, Maine offered financial support and much prayer. Hope Lutheran Church in Springtown, Texas served as my first call when I was ordained to the ministry in 2008. Not only did the congregation employ me, but they encouraged me in my studies, were proud of me, and were patient as I tried to balance all of my responsibilities. I also give thanks for the congregation of Trinity Evangelical Lutheran Church in New Haven, Connecticut which has welcomed me as the pastor's wife, but also as a leader in my own right. They sat through many Bible studies where I shared this project with them.

Finally, I thank my family. First and foremost, I am grateful to my husband, Ryan, and my children, John and Helen. They have loved me, encouraged me, distracted me, and spent lots of time elsewhere as I completed this project. I must also thank my parents, Liz and Bill Burgess, and my in-laws, Carol and Andrew Mills, for their constant love and support and for providing many hours of childcare. I am grateful to my extended family of brother, sister, in-laws, aunts, uncles, and cousins and their love and support as well. There are so many more people who have played a part in the success of my doctoral program, and I will always be grateful.

Abbreviations

AB	The Yale Anchor Bible
AnBib	Analecta Biblica
Ant.	Josephus, *Jewish Antiquities*
BAGD	Bauer, W., W. F. Arndt, F. W. Gingrich, and F. W. Danker. *Greek-English Lexicon of the New Testament and Other Early Christian Literature.* 3rd ed. Chicago, 2000.
BibInt	Biblical Interpretation
BICS	Bulletin of the Institute of Classical Studies
BIS	Biblical Interpretation Series
BMW	The Bible in the Modern World
BSac	Bibliotheca Sacra
BTB	Biblical Theology Bulletin
CBQ	Catholic Biblical Quarterly
GBS	Guides to Biblical Scholarship
HTR	Harvard Theological Review
HvTSt	Hervormde teologies studies
Int	Interpretation
JBL	Journal of Biblical Literature
JETS	Journal of the Evangelical Theological Society
JR	Journal of Religion
JRT	Journal of Religious Thought
JSNT	Journal for the Study of the New Testament
JSNTSup	Journal for the Study of the New Testament Supplement Series

JTS	*Journal of Theological Studies*
JTSA	*Journal of Theology for Southern Africa*
LCL	Loeb Classical Library
NovT	*Novum Testamentum*
NRSV	New Revised Standard Version
NTL	New Testament Library
NTS	*New Testament Studies*
NTTS	New Testament Tools and Studies
PRSt	*Perspectives in Religious Studies*
RevExp	*Review and Expositor*
SBLDS	Society of Biblical Literature Dissertation Series
SemeiaSt	Semeia Studies
SNTSMS	Society of New Testament Studies Monograph Series
SP	Sacra Pagina
Suet.*Cl.*	Suetonius, *Caligula, Lives of Caesars*
Suet.*Tit.*	Suetonius, *Titus, Lives of Caesars*
Suet.*Vesp.*	Suetonius, *Vespasian, Lives of Caesars*
ThR	*Theological Review*
TJ	*Trinity Journal*
USQR	Union Seminary Quarterly Review
War	Josephus, *Jewish War*
WUNT	Wissenschaftliche Untersuchungen zum Neuen Testament

1

Scholarly Approaches to Christology and Discipleship in the Gospel of Mark

IN THIS BOOK I will argue that structures of honor and kinship serve as a nexus between Christology and discipleship in Mark's gospel. While previous work has examined the Gospel's "Son" language (of God, of Man, of David) in its history-of-religions, titular, and narrative contexts, it has largely neglected attention to the language and social structures of kinship to which "Son" language belongs. Moreover, while previous scholarship has noted kinship language in Markan discipleship, it has not sufficiently attended to the function of kinship language and structures in drawing Christology and discipleship together, and to its contribution to, and role in, the imitative and contestive interface between the community of disciples and the Roman imperial world.

I will bring together two of the most important aspects of Markan scholarship in an analysis of the language of sonship and kinship pertaining to both Jesus and disciples. The intersection of Christology and discipleship will come plainly into view by way of a multidisciplinary approach that will center on a narrative methodology through a lens of imperial negotiation with a focus on honor and kinship. My argument is that Mark's use of sonship language for Jesus functions to ascribe honor to him as chosen by God to be the authorized agent of God's will and to establish a kinship community (brothers, sisters, sons, daughters, mothers, and children) that will further God's will. This community acquires honor through service and suffering with other followers of Jesus. This realignment of conventional kinship roles in terms of service and suffering will be viewed as a means by which Mark's gospel negotiates its Roman imperial context–a context which prized kinship and the gaining of honor as central cultural practices.[1]

In this chapter, I analyze various methodological approaches to Markan Christology and discipleship. The discussion of approaches to Christology in Mark follows its historical development, including history-of-religions, titular studies, and narrative approaches. The discussion of scholarly approaches to discipleship in Mark includes the identification of the twelve as a literary construct serving as a corrective to Mark's historical community, historical-critical approaches, narrative approaches, and sociohistorical approaches. I also address a few works that have attempted, though inadequately, intersections of Christology and discipleship. In addition, I review three contributions to Mark and its Roman imperial context because they provide a foundation for the imperial critical lens through which Christology and discipleship intersect.

Many studies in discipleship and Mark reflect solely on the role of the twelve disciples of Jesus. However there are those that recognize that the concept of discipleship belongs to all those who follow Jesus, including the crowds, the women, and the recipients of the Gospel of Mark.[2] For this study, it is better not to limit the concept of discipleship to the twelve, though in order to understand the major discussions and methodological approaches to discipleship, the majority of studies addressed do focus primarily on the twelve disciples in Mark.

CHRISTOLOGY

Christology–History of Religions

Christology and discipleship are two central themes in the Gospel of Mark. The history of scholarship pertaining to these themes has largely moved along two diverging tracks with little explicit connection between the two. The spectrum of discussions of Christology in Mark has ranged from history-of-religions to titular studies to the narrative context. In order to gain a firm foothold on Christology and discipleship in Mark, it will be necessary to survey the major contributions that scholars have made to these themes.

---

1. For a helpful summary of the concept of honor in ancient Mediterranean culture, see Plevnik, "Honor/Shame," 106–15.

2. For studies limited to discipleship and the twelve, see Weeden, *Mark*; Best, *Disciples and Discipleship*. For studies that have a broader focus on discipleship, Donahue, *Theology and Setting of Discipleship*; Malbon, *In the Company of Jesus*; Schüssler Fiorenza, *In Memory of Her*, 105–59.

The history-of-religions method finds the definition and origin of Christology in Mark and other early Christian documents in their Near Eastern and Greco-Roman literary predecessors. In the quest to determine the form and source of the gospels, scholars considered that they were partly made up of a collection of miracle stories akin to collections about Hellenistic gods, divinized men, and magicians called *aretologies*.[3] In his analysis of Mark 3:7–12, for example, Leander Keck concludes that Jesus is a *theios aner*,[4] a type of divine-human religious hero or holy man in Hellenistic literature that demonstrates his divinity through miracles and healings.[5] His analysis of Mark 3:7–12 becomes significant for the whole gospel because the stream of miracles Keck derives from the *theios aner* tradition defines Jesus over and against the natural world. The miracles Jesus performs "are direct manifestations of the Son of God, and in a particular way–the θεῖος ἀνήρ."[6]

Based on several pericopes in Mark that he deems pre-Synoptic, Hans Dieter Betz also suggests that Jesus could be seen as a *theios aner*. The pericopes (Mark 1:32–34; 3:7–12; 6:53–56) follow the profile of the *theios aner*: nature miracles, healings, exorcisms, and raisings from the dead.[7] The implication then is that the gospel writers utilized such *theios aner* stories in their works to aid in their depiction of Jesus as a miracle-working holy man. While concentrating on depictions of Jesus' power, these studies, however, did not adequately take into account other dimensions of the presentation of Jesus, such as suffering, and so cannot give an adequate account of the gospel's Christology.

In his critique of the *theois aner* influence on Markan miracle stories, Barry Blackburn provides false correspondences between Judaism and Hellenism when he argues that the *theios aner* concept cannot be limited to Hellenistic sources, but must draw on Old Testament and Jewish sources as well.[8] Based on the writings of Artapanus, Philo, and Josephus, Blackburn contends that the tradition surrounding Moses defines him as a *theios aner*.[9] This work is a significant contribution to the study of *theios aner* illuminating the significance of christological sources for Mark. Unfortunately, he

---

3. For a helpful analysis and summary of this scholarship see, Smith, "Prolegomena," 174–99.
4. Keck, "Mark 3:7–12," 341–58.
5. Definition from Blackburn, *Theios Anēr*, 1.
6. Keck, "Mark 3:7–12," 350.
7. Betz, "Jesus as Divine Man," 114–33.
8. Blackburn, *Theios Anēr*.
9. Ibid., 59.

overstates his argument to the point that he suggests some sort of artificial bifurcation between Hellenism and Judaism, when in reality it is necessary to consider both.[10] Blackburn also ignores the significant role of suffering in Mark's christological presentation.

Scholars have also suggested a connection between the gospel's designation of Jesus as "Son of God" and the emperor's title. Adela Yarbro Collins provides a brief outline of the Greco-Roman texts that may influence the gospel's depiction of Jesus as "Son of God."[11] The study focuses on a textual analysis and comparison between the gospel's Son of God language and how the specific title υἱός θεοῦ functions in the Greco-Roman literary world and within the imperial cult. Although she does acknowledge that cultural context and traditions would have influenced how early believers understood "Son of God," she does not investigate the impact of such a link of understanding the gospel as a whole, nor in relation to other aspects of Christology, nor on the requirements of discipleship.[12]

The history-of-religions method in Markan Christology limits itself to a study of some of the possible sources of Mark's Christology. While it is very important to understand the background and context of Christology in Mark, it is also imperative to see how these sources were used within the context of Mark as a whole and in the presentation of the person and character of Jesus. As biblical criticism developed in the twentieth century, these issues were taken into account.

Christology–Titular Studies

A focus on developing ecclesial traditions was central to mid-twentieth-century discussions of titles used for Jesus in the gospel. Scholars understood Christology as a developing confessional response to the history and person of Jesus of Nazareth expressed primarily through titles whose meaning developed as the church expanded from Palestinian Judaism into the worlds dominated by Hellenistic Judaism and Hellenism.[13] Probably one of the most distinguished analyses in Christology from this time period is by Ferdinand Hahn.[14] In these ecclesial contexts, he treats each of the major

---

10. For example, see Hengel, *Judaism and Hellenism* for a comprehensive study of the relationship between Judaism and Hellenism during the third and first half of the second centuries BCE.
11. Collins, "Mark and His Readers," 85–100.
12. Ibid., 100.
13. Fuller, *Foundations of New Testament Christology*.
14. Hahn, *Titles of Jesus*.

titles of Jesus and provides a history of the use of the titles in Hebrew scripture and tradition and their subsequent use in the New Testament. Within each of the christological titles for Jesus, Hahn utilizes the biblical texts to obtain the developing understandings of each title in the changing cultural contexts. Hahn's method, however, precludes adequate attention to the way titles function in the gospel narratives, and it ignores non-titular presentations of the significance of Jesus including intersections of Christology and discipleship.

Of particular interest to titular-focused Christology in Mark is the title "Son of Man." A majority of scholars are concerned with the "Son of Man" sayings and their origins in the Gospel of Mark. While some focus on a particular origin like Dan 7 and its influence,[15] over time, multiple theories for the "Son of Man" references in Mark have been accepted. Casey concludes that not all of the Son of Man references in Mark can be based on Dan 7, but rather there arose a general ancient "Son of Man" concept that allowed those who knew the Septuagint to grasp this description of Jesus and subsequently link "together the Jesus of history in the Aramaic-speaking Jewish world with the Christ of faith as he was eventually perceived among the Greeks."[16] In a more recent work, Casey provides an analysis of the "Son of Man" references in the canonical gospels based upon the idiomatic use of the Aramaic phrase (א)נשׁ(א) בר.[17] He concludes that the idiom has both a specific level of meaning when it refers to the speaker and a general meaning referring to human beings. Casey traces the development of the saying through the gospels from its idiomatic use to a title for Jesus. The gospels could not support the ambiguous meaning of the Aramaic idiom in the title ὁ υἱός τοῦ ἀνθρώπου and thus the phrase moved from idiom to a specific title for Jesus. Casey then designates the authentic and inauthentic "Son of Man" sayings of Jesus by determining if they can be traced back to the Aramaic idiom.

Barnabas Lindars criticizes the work of Casey by suggesting that the general, ancient concept "Son of Man" was in reality a myth created by modern critical scholarship.[18] Significant for our discussion is that Lindars holds that Mark's use of "Son of Man" must be considered in addition to Jesus' historical use of the title. He divides the "Son of Man" sayings into three categories: the present, earthly position of Jesus; passion predictions; and future coming of the Son of Man. Lindars asserts that Mark has a christological

---

15. Casey, *Son of Man*.
16. Ibid., 239.
17. Casey, *Solution to the 'Son of Man.'*
18. Lindars, *Jesus Son of Man*, 8.

concern that "leads him to build on the sayings tradition in such a way as to bring home to the reader essential aspects of the confession of faith."[19] Unfortunately, Lindars is so concerned with differentiating what is original to Jesus and what is original to Mark that this significance is somehow lost. Though the information is about the Christology in Mark, he provides no perspective on the implications for the use of the Son of Man in Mark aside from his brief mentions of the title in Mark.

In an historical overview of the Son of Man debate, Delbert Burkett has traced several lines of the debate from the patristic period until 1996.[20] These lines of debate include the use of the phrase as a genealogical reference. He surveys the scholars who search for the origin of the phrase which gave rise to the Son of Man as an expression of Jesus' humanity, as a messianic title derived from Dan 7:13, and as a nontitular idiom by which a man can refer to himself (p. 4). Other strands of the debate include the specific reference to the phrase and which "Son of Man" sayings are authentic. Burkett ultimately concludes that there never has been, and probably never will be, a consensus on the Son of Man debate. However, "the bulk of scholarship is now divided between two basic alternatives, each with several variations: (a) the Christian Son of Man tradition originated with Jesus in the use of *bar enasha* as a nontitular idiom (circumlocutional, generic, or indefinite); (b) it originated as a messianic title applied to Jesus either by himself or by the early church" (p. 122). Burkett suggests that the debate is a demonstration of the limitations of New Testament scholarship (p. 124). Not only can scholars find no consensus of the phrase "Son of Man" and its use, origin, and definition in the gospels, but the debate has largely ignored its particular use in each gospel narrative or in the context of other christological attributes of Jesus.

Another important though ultimately unsatisfactory aspect of scholarship involving titular-focused Christology is the notion that the various titles in Mark's gospel reflect and counter competing christological understandings in the Markan community. Theodore Weeden argued that the Christology asserted in Mark's gospel was intended to correct a false Christology that may have been threatening his community. "For one or more adduced reasons, [Mark] regarded the title 'Son of God' (with which 'Messiah,' too, is aligned) as defective for conveying the true meaning of the person of Jesus."[21] So, Mark wrote his gospel with an intentional focus upon a theology of the cross and the use of the title "Son of Man." Mark "takes

---

19. Ibid., 113.
20. Burkett, *Son of Man Debate*.
21. Kingsbury, *Christology of Mark's Gospel*, 25.

his opponents' christological title, *Son of God*, empties it of its *theios-aner* connotation, and associates it with the suffering Son-of-man Christology, thereby turning it into a title appropriate for his own theology."[22] The difficulty with such an approach is that the questionable transparent reading of Mark assumes an antithetical relationship among the titles and remains distant from the discussion of discipleship. We will return to an evaluation of transparent reading strategies of discipleship below.

Narrative Christology

The atomistic and speculative nature of titular-based christological discussion brought a reaction from those who argued that this approach was flawed because it ignored much relevant material in the gospel narratives. Markan scholars began to focus on the person of Jesus as a character within the story that Mark presents. In a 1979 article, Robert Tannehill argued that it is necessary to take seriously the narrative form of the gospel in its presentation of Jesus.[23] If this is done, then one can see the narrative development of Mark's Christology in the relationships Jesus has with his disciples; with the scribes, Pharisees, and Jerusalem leaders; with those who seek him for healing, and with the demons.[24] These relationships and encounters contribute to the presentation of Jesus by means of his speech, actions, and attributes. As these encounters function within the story Mark presents, the narrative features of Mark give rise to Mark's Christology.[25]

Consistent with Tannehill's approach, Jack Dean Kingsbury utilizes a narrative methodology to address Christology and titles for Jesus throughout the narrative of Mark.[26] Through this approach, Kingsbury demonstrates how the titles for Jesus function within the gospel narrative. Kingsbury distinguishes between Son of God and Son of Man. He posits that Son of God relates to Jesus as the Davidic Messiah and thus has royal connotations, whereas Son of Man functions more as a public title rather than as definitive title for Jesus' christological identity. Kingsbury shows the significance of reading Mark as a narrative whole and understanding Christology within

---

22. Weeden, *Mark*, 165. See also Achtemeier, *Mark*; Betz, "Jesus as Divine Man;" Perrin, "Creative Use of the Son of Man," 357–65.

23. Tannehill, "Gospel of Mark," 57–95.

24. Ibid., 63.

25. For a significant and helpful contribution to the discussion of Christology and narrative methodologies, see Keck, "Toward the Renewal of New Testament Christology," 362–77.

26. Kingsbury, *Christology of Mark's Gospel*.

the narrative; however his distinction between Son of Man and Son of God continues the questionable antithetical relationship among the christological titles that was exhibited in the above-mentioned titular studies (such as Weeden's). His focus on Christology neglects interactions with other important dimensions of the gospel such as its presentation of discipleship.

Richard Horsley addresses Markan Christology in his narrative approach to the gospel in *Hearing the Whole Story*. Horsley is highly critical of the pursuit of Christology, especially titular studies, suggesting that focusing on isolated passages about Jesus and titles for Jesus in Mark is problematic because it "diverts attention from the dynamics of the overall story and obscures the more complex ways in which the story may be rooted in Israelite tradition."[27] Horsley nevertheless concludes that the Markan portrayal of Jesus is one of a prophetic leader "engaged in the renewal of Israel over against the rulers."[28] But Horsley seems to go too far the other way. While his note of caution is important to consider regarding the pursuit of Christology, it is not possible to completely ignore the "titles" for Jesus as this diminishes the presentation of Jesus and any relationship to the presentation of the disciples.

In a more recent contribution, Elizabeth Struthers Malbon attends to Christology in Mark utilizing characterization within the narrative itself. She summarizes her work as a "multilayered Markan narrative christology."[29] Malbon divides the characterization of Jesus into five categories: what the narrator and others say about Jesus (projected christology), what Jesus says in response to what other say to and about him (deflected christology), what Jesus says about himself (refracted christology), what Jesus does (enacted christology), and what others do in response to what Jesus says and does (reflected christology). This methodology is significant because Malbon endeavors to remain completely within the context of the Markan narrative. Malbon contends that defining the character of Jesus in Mark as the historical Jesus and defining the narrator as the author of Mark is epistemologically inappropriate. Other scholars have used these designations as a way to deal with the tension that is created between the narrator and Jesus. But, Malbon argues this tension is not a problem to be resolved, "but a narrative christological confession offered by the implied author to the implied audience as a challenge and a mystery."[30] She acknowledges the historical and

27. Horsley, *Hearing the Whole Story*, 232–33.

28. Ibid., 253.

29. Malbon, *Mark's Jesus*, 231. Malbon purposefully does not capitalize Christology because hers is not a discussion in the usual sense as a branch of theology, but rather narrative christology within Mark (5).

30. Ibid., 258.

social contexts out of which Mark arises, but she maintains that a narrative approach to Christology must remain within the bounds of the text itself and so she gives little attention to influence from or interaction with sociohistorical factors. Malbon is critical of the titular approach to Christology and yet she ends up addressing the titles of Jesus as particularly significant within the context of projected and refracted christology.[31] In addition and of note, Malbon addresses discipleship in terms of "reflected christology." By a metaphor of a mirror, Malbon demonstrates how the disciples and others who interact with Jesus relate to him and how Jesus relates to God. The focus of her discussion is primarily christological, but this reference to "reflected christology" is quite significant for my study.

Assessment

Instead of drawing such a strong distinction between a titular focus in Christology and narrative Christology in Mark, it is important for this study to recognize that the two aspects augment one another. Mark purposely defines Jesus with various titles throughout his narrative as well as by various other means such as actions and teachings to demonstrate his character, his function within the narrative, and his interaction with those he encounters. Conversely, the presentation of his character, interaction with other characters, and function through the narrative define the titles. The work of Elizabeth Struthers Malbon will be particularly useful, though in this work it will be necessary to draw on the historical and social contexts of the narrative as much as the narrative itself to help us understand Christology in the Gospel of Mark. A significant aspect of my contribution will be to emphasize that Christology exists in relation to discipleship; who Jesus is defines who the disciples are and how they follow Jesus.

DISCIPLESHIP

Within the arena of discipleship, Markan scholarship has adopted four dominant approaches to the presentation of the disciples and others who follow Jesus: their roles as literary constructions, as representatives of community factions, as characters in the gospel story, and as depicting family or household models of discipleship.

---

31. Ibid., chapters 2 and 4.

Disciples as Literary Constructs

Probably the most significant study for twentieth-century scholarship is the work of William Wrede. In *The Messianic Secret*, Wrede focuses upon the possible "messianic self-consciousness" of Jesus, trying to discern if Jesus himself was aware of his messianism or if it is the work of the gospel writers. Although the work centers largely upon the person of Jesus as he is portrayed, Wrede comes to some significant conclusions about the portrayal of the disciples. Wrede posits that the disciples are the authenticated recipients of Jesus' secret messianic teaching, but he then asks the questions: "Why then do they not understand Jesus?"[32] Wrede sees Mark utilizing the incomprehension of the disciples in a three-fold manner. Historically, it makes sense that the disciples would react to predictions of Jesus' suffering and death. However, the disciples are actually a postresurrection construct, that is, they cannot fully understand the meaning of Jesus' suffering and death until the resurrection. This post-resurrection construct subsequently acts as instruction for later followers of Jesus. Wrede concludes that the disciples must not receive a negative interpretation for their lack of understanding, but rather the lack of understanding further highlights the role of the messianic secret. In this way, the disciples serve to define who Jesus is, but Wrede does not see the presentation of Jesus in Mark as serving to define who the disciples are.

Paul J. Achtemeier makes a similar claim in his article, "Mark as Interpreter of the Jesus Traditions." He posits that discipleship as a major theme in the gospel is one hermeneutical key to Mark's understanding of the Jesus tradition. Central to this is the disciples' inability to comprehend. "It is abundantly clear, first of all, that the disciples cannot understand Jesus prior to his cross and resurrection."[33] The disciples' lack of comprehension leads those later disciples to realize that they cannot fully follow Jesus unless they follow him to the cross. In this case the disciples and discipleship are constructs that are used to point to the central aspect of Mark's gospel, the cross and resurrection. Again, the disciples serve as a tool to define who Jesus is, but discipleship is limited to following Jesus to the cross and only after the resurrection reveals the efficaciousness of the cross.

---

32. Wrede, *Messianic Secret*, 231.
33. Achtemeier, "Mark as Interpreter," 347.

Disciples as Representatives of Community: Reading Transparently–Historical-critical Approaches

As noted above, Theodore J. Weeden argues that the christological titles reveal community disputes. Likewise, others have argued that the presentation of disciples reflects disputes within the Markan community. Mark's portrayal of the disciples with a lack of understanding and with incomprehension is one way to articulate this argument. Joseph Tyson, in his article "The Blindness of the Disciples of Mark" explains that Mark wanted to call "attention to the fact that the disciples did not understand what was to be their own relationship to the community."[34] For Tyson, Mark stands in opposition to the Jerusalem church, represented by the twelve disciples in the gospel, who awaited the triumphant return of the royal Messiah, Jesus. Mark believes that the suffering and death of Jesus are significant to his messiahship. The conflict that Tyson describes draws on the understanding the twelve disciples have of Jesus as a royal messiah. Tyson also suggests the notion of discipleship is not defined by Jesus in Mark. Ironically, it is the Christology of Jesus that affects the description of the disciples; but it is their misunderstanding of that Christology that Mark is criticizing. Christology and discipleship are, strangely, set in antithetical relationship.

Another work that denotes a struggle between the community of Mark and the Jerusalem church is *The Formation of the Gospel according to Mark* by Etienne Trocmé. Rather than a struggle over Christology as in Tyson's approach, Trocmé's approach is ecclesiological. He sees that Mark separated himself from the Jerusalem church and "launched out into a large-scale missionary venture among the common people in Palestine and in so doing felt that it was obeying the command of the risen Christ and at the same time following his earthly example."[35] The disciples appear to have a more positive portrayal in Trocmé's interpretation, but his interpretation centers itself on the conflict between Mark and the Jerusalem church. Based on his treatment of James and the family of Jesus and his admonishments to Peter, James, and John, Mark indicates a conflict over authority and status among the disciples. Jesus is the Lord and teacher and he creates a new family, but it does not appear that the identity of Jesus affects the identity of the disciples as this new family. One problem in reading Mark this way is that it is not clear which transparencies, that is, which conflicts, an interpreter is establishing as governing the text.

---

34. Tyson, "Blindness of Disciples in Mark," 264.
35. Trocmé, *Formation of the Gospel*, 214.

In response to Tyson and Trocmé, David Hawkin seeks to determine what "set of purposes governed Mark's thematic presentation of the incomprehension of the disciples."[36] Through his redaction-critical approach, Hawkin seeks a more nuanced view of the conflict he argues is at work in Mark's community. He states that the incomprehension of the disciples is central to the gospel, and yet at the same time he seeks to lift up the distinction of the disciples from the crowd in order to make a claim about Mark's community. "The disciples are made to be figures representative of the church, and the crowds are made to be figures representative of Israel."[37] In the redaction, Hawkin sees the distinction between the disciples and the crowd as helping to elucidate the messianic secret and why Israel as a whole did not accept Jesus as the messiah. The mystery of the incomprehension of the disciples becomes the mystery into which the church of Mark's community can enter. The incomprehension motif is a pedagogical tool used by Mark for instruction to his community. "Only by understanding what the disciples failed to understand can the catechumen be initiated into the mystery of Christ."[38] Hawkin draws Christology and discipleship closely together in his assessment of the incomprehension of the disciples. Yet his discussion is limited in that he identifies Jesus solely as an Israelite messiah and the incomprehension motif only as a pedagogical tool by Mark. Any broader understanding of discipleship is lost.

Theodore J. Weeden picks up on the theme of incomprehension in his literary approach to the gospel, *Mark: Traditions in Conflict*.[39] He notices the ambivalent manner in which Mark portrays the disciples. On the one hand they are Jesus' closest companions and recipients of his teaching. Yet, on the other hand, they are unperceptive, misconceive messiahship, and ultimately reject Jesus. Weeden is of the opinion that Mark is utilizing a polemic against the disciples, but rather than a polemic that pits Jesus against the disciples and the Jerusalem church and what it means to be a follower of Jesus, it is a conflict of Christology. Mark defines Jesus as a suffering Son of God rather than as the disciples see him, as a powerful Son of God. Again, a connection between Christology and discipleship is made in Mark, and yet their connection is one of conflict rather than an interdependent connection where they mutually define each other.

Though Werner Kelber may dispute that his work falls in the realm of historical-critical approaches, it is best placed here for it is a response

---

36. Hawkin, "The Incomprehension of the Disciples," 491.
37. Ibid., 497.
38. Ibid., 500.
39. Weeden, *Mark*.

and reflection of historical-critical approaches to the disciples in Mark. In *The Oral and Written Gospel*, Kelber has demonstrated the need to respond to the reality that the written biblical texts began as oral traditions. Kelber concludes and designates "the written gospel as a counterform to, rather than extension of, oral hermeneutics."[40] Because the gospel was originally an oral manifestation, he sees in its textualization Mark's repudiation of its very orality, and subsequently the repudiation of those who follow and represent the oral tradition, including the disciples. For Mark, the failure of the disciples, their inability to enact the gospel, provides the reason and necessity for transferring the oral gospel to a written text. "By highlighting the failure of the oral representatives, this gospel writes its case on behalf of its technological innovation."[41] While a seminal and critical work, Kelber has been criticized for overstating his theories. In the end, even as Kelber required those who came before him to complicate the connection between orality and textuality, so too should Kelber's approach also be tempered and nuanced. Kelber creates as much a distinction between orality and textuality as his predecessors, so much so that he limits and downplays the continuity between the oral and written forms of the gospel.

Disciples as Characters–Narrative Approaches

A different approach does not read Mark transparently but as a narrative in which disciples are characters. Robert C. Tannehill's 1977 article, "Disciples in Mark: the Function of a Narrative Role"[42] sees the narrative function of the disciples pastorally in relation to the reader for whom Mark wrote the gospel.[43] This is the reason that Mark portrays the disciples positively in the first part of the gospel, so that readers may identify positively. Then in the latter half of the gospel, as the disciples come into a more negative light in their relationship with Jesus, the reader can judge his or her own relationship with Jesus. In this way, Mark acts pastorally. Even though it appears that the disciples fail at the end, Mark assures the community of its continuity in the promise at the resurrection.

Jack Dean Kingsbury utilizes a narrative approach and studies the characters and storylines of Mark with the premise that conflict and resolution

40. Kelber, *Oral and Written Gospel*, 184–85.
41. Ibid., 98.
42. Tannehill, "Disciples in Mark," 386–405.
43. Tannehill does not differentiate between implied or real reader, but he indicates the reader for whom Mark was originally written, that is, the implied reader, à la Chatman, *Story and Discourse*, 150.

drive the plot.⁴⁴ Of the three storylines he posits, the story of the disciples is third. Kingsbury describes the conflict in this storyline as between Jesus and the disciples. "It revolves around the disciples' remarkable lack of comprehension and their refusal to come to terms with either the central purpose of Jesus' ministry or the true meaning of discipleship."⁴⁵ The significance of this conflict lies in the definition of Jesus' ministry and what that means for discipleship. Kingsbury concludes that the resolution of this storyline concludes beyond the actual text of Mark with the implication that Jesus and the disciples are reconciled in the resurrection.⁴⁶ Kingsbury's approach is typical of those who position Markan discipleship only as a response to or an incomprehension of Jesus whereas I will make clear that there is an intersection or nexus between discipleship and Jesus (Christology).

In an analysis and critique of Werner Kelber, Elizabeth Struthers Malbon discusses the role of the disciples in the Gospel of Mark.⁴⁷ Malbon is concerned mainly with the interaction of text and context. In the interpretation of a biblical text, how does one negotiate the internal or "literary" context of a text and its external or "historical" context?⁴⁸ Although she is limited to her own analysis of the disciples in the Gospel of Mark, Malbon asks two significant questions about them vis-à-vis Kelber: (1) "Does not a reading of Mark with primary reference to its own 'internal' relations suggest (for example) that two of the narrator's critical decisions must be interpreted together–the decision to end chapter 16 with questions about the disciples' future actions unanswered and the decision to include in chapter 13 Jesus' description of the disciples' future actions?"⁴⁹ She suggests that the polemical interpretation (based on an "historical" context) Kelber reads between the oral and written gospel creates a polemical relationship between the disciples and readers of Mark's gospel. The disciples are viewed as failures and the readers of Mark's gospel are the true followers of the gospel. Rather, if one focuses upon the internal context of these two aforementioned chapters, then Kelber's interpretation is put in check. Malbon further asks: (2) "In terms of the internal relations of the text, are not the disciples more closely related to the other Markan characters and to the readers than

---

44. Kingsbury, *Conflict in Mark*.

45. Ibid., 89.

46. For other contributions of narrative approaches to discipleship in Mark, see Best, *Following Jesus*; Melbourne, *Slow to Understand*; Shiner, *Follow Me!*

47. Malbon, "Texts and Contexts," 81–102.

48. Ibid., 82.

49. Ibid., 91.

Kelber suggests?"⁵⁰ There is a close connection between the disciples and the crowd. Malbon again highlights the polemic created by Kelber's interpretation; not only are the disciples at odds with Mark's readers, but they are also at odds with other characters in the text. Malbon believes that there is rather a complexity to Mark's characterization of the disciples and they are interconnected with the crowd that follows Jesus. It is unfortunate that Malbon is unable to provide a more thorough analysis of the disciples in Mark, but nevertheless, her contribution is significant to this study. Her critique of Kelber's work highlights the need for interpreters to "advocate" for a text, to provide expertise, and to keep the text at the center of interpretation, but also to "complicate"⁵¹ existing understandings of a text, demonstrating the need for continuous interpretation as new contexts are revealed.

Discipleship and Context–Socio-historical Approaches

In a chapter on the first-century Jesus movement and discipleship in her seminal feminist work, *In Memory of Her*, Elisabeth Schüssler Fiorenza has highlighted the Jewish context within the larger Roman context in which Jesus established his community of disciples. "The praxis and vision of Jesus and his movement is best understood as an inner-Jewish renewal movement that presented an *alternative* option to the dominant patriarchal structures rather than an oppositional formation rejecting the values and praxis of Judaism."⁵² Schüssler Fiorenza draws on Jewish wisdom literature and designates Jesus as Sophia or the child of Sophia, the feminine aspect of the Israelite God. In so doing, Schüssler Fiorenza demonstrates Jesus establishing a community of "discipleship of equals" where patriarchal structures are eliminated.⁵³ Mark 3:31–35 and Mark 10:30 provide the basis of the elimination of patriarchy where there are no references to earthly fathers. She recognizes that both men and women are welcomed into the community and function as disciples of Jesus. Schüssler Fiorenza concludes that the new "family" of equal disciples absent of fathers "implicitly rejects their power and status and thus claims that in the messianic community all patriarchal structures are abolished."⁵⁴ Designating Jesus as Sophia/Child of Sophia removes his particular identification as the Son of God and fails to recognize that, even in the significant contribution that discipleship is open

50. Ibid., 92.
51. Ibid., 97–98.
52. Schüssler Fiorenza, *In Memory of Her*, 107.
53. Ibid., 135.
54. Ibid., 147.

to both men and women, the patriarchal structures continue in the father-son relationship between God and Jesus, at least in the Gospel of Mark. She does recognize the "fatherhood" of God, but views it as a subversion of patriarchy rather than legitimizing patriarchal structures. Patriarchal structures are necessary, however, insofar as Jesus receives his authority from God the father and disseminates it to his disciples. Jesus and the disciples do not reject patriarchal structures but reorient them within the community of discipleship of equals.

In a more sociological approach to family and discipleship, Stephen Barton provides an analysis of family ties in Mark and Matthew.[55] He utilizes a multidisciplinary approach of form, redaction, literary, and sociological criticisms. Barton suggests that there is a subordination of family and household ties in the Gospels of Mark and Matthew that also exists in Jewish and Greco-Roman sources. Barton, however, would also qualify the subordination of family ties in Mark and Matthew, not as hostile, but as a devaluation. "And this devaluation has to do specifically with missionary discipleship of Jesus as an alternative, transcendent focus of identity, allegiance and role."[56] Unfortunately, Barton does not define what he means by kinship or family ties and what those relationships are in order to support the gospel's devaluation of family ties. In reference to Mark, Barton concludes that household and family ties are relativized because Jesus comes as the Son of God to establish a new covenant community, an eschatological family that is obedient, not to blood ties, but to the will of God.[57] Barton does, significantly, acknowledge that discipleship in Mark is kinship related, but as he sees Mark subordinating kinship ties, Barton himself subordinates kinship ties in discipleship. He briefly acknowledges Christology as a significant concern for the gospel, but he does not connect discipleship to it at all.[58]

Jack Elliott has supplied a very helpful survey of household and family structures and language in the Gospel of Mark tied to discipleship and Christology. Elliott states that, contrary to the notions that Jesus is establishing an egalitarian, antifamily community in Mark, Jesus leads an alternative family to which disciples belong. In this case, Christology defines discipleship. "As Jesus is the obedient son of God, so believers who do the Father's will are God's children and constitute collectively the family of

---

55. Barton, *Discipleship and Family Ties*.
56. Ibid., 21.
57. Ibid., 122.
58. Ibid., 124.

God."⁵⁹ Elliott's broad understanding of discipleship as those who follow Jesus and sociolinguistic analysis of family and household in Mark will provide a helpful resource to inform this study of Christology and discipleship in Mark. Elliott focuses his essay specifically on the language of kinship in Mark but stops short of exploring the implications of this language for the intersection between Christology and discipleship.

Assessment

These analyses of discipleship have been extremely helpful in discerning the communal and functional nature of discipleship in Mark. The variety of approaches to discipleship has elucidated the roles of the disciples within Mark's narrative and perhaps within the sociohistorical context of the gospel. There is, though, still an inadequate connection with Christology; discipleship generally remains a separate category and rests largely on role and function as opposed to identity in relationship with Jesus. Also neglected in all of these discussions, with the exception of Schüssler Fiorenza and her discussion of discipleship, is the language of kinship for disciples and for Jesus. The fact remains that Jesus is designated as *Son* of God and *Son* of Man and *Son* of David; the disciples are defined in familial terms in connection with Jesus. Who Jesus is as a son defines and interprets who the disciples are as a family who follow Jesus.

ATTEMPTS AT THE INTERSECTION OF CHRISTOLOGY AND DISCIPLESHIP

There have, nevertheless, been several attempts to formulate the intersection of Christology and discipleship in the Gospel of Mark. In these attempts, scholars see the connection of Jesus as teacher of disciples[60] and Jesus who leads those who follow him "on the way."[61] Given that this is a central concern of this study, there are four works that require more detailed discussion in order to locate the contribution of the present study: Howard Clark Kee's *Community of the New Age*; John R. Donahue's *The Theology and Setting of Discipleship in the Gospel of Mark*; Suzanne Watts Henderson's *Christology and Discipleship in the Gospel of Mark*; and Adam Winn's *The Purpose of Mark's Gospel*.

59. Elliott, "Household/Family," 62.
60. Melbourne, *Slow to Understand*, and Best, *Following Jesus*.
61. Donahue, *Theology and Setting*, and Henderson, *Christology and Discipleship*.

Howard Clark Kee

In *Community of the New Age*, Howard Clark Kee argues that the Markan community is an apocalyptic community which views Jesus heralding an eschatological vindication from the corrupt powers of the world.[62] Kee expands the "horizon" of Mark interpretively in order to understand the community of Mark which in turn will aid in understanding the gospel itself. For Kee, it is necessary for biblical interpretation to include elements of social history, that is, sociological models, to understand how the community of Mark emerged.[63] Kee identifies four essential elements required for interpretation of Mark: (1) the literary genre; (2) the oral and written tradition used by Mark; (3) the literary forms included in Mark; and (4) the interrelation of social, literary, and conceptual modes.[64] Kee concludes that Hellenistic models of rhetorical literature would have influenced Mark. In addition, with reference to Jesus' miracles, the closest literary forms are from the eschatological literature of post-exilic Judaism.[65] Within this genre of literature, Mark utilizes smaller pieces of oral and written tradition. Kee provides an analysis of three types of tradition: (1) units of oral tradition; (2) small collections of narratives and/or sayings; and (3) Jewish prophetic-apocalyptic practices of eschatological exegesis.[66] Of course, these analyses are hypothetical and it is difficult to prove definitively what material and traditions Mark utilized to write his gospel. Further, Kee analyzes how these types of tradition are used in the style and structure of Mark. From his literary analysis, Kee concludes,

> Written in biographical style, like other apocalyptical writings, the Gospel of Mark addressed the critical needs of his community in his own time by telling us about the acts and words of a man who stood in a special relationship to God as his agent and spokesman, whose mission was to form about him the obedient covenant people, whose opposition included historical-political powers, demonic and cosmic powers, whose last reported utterances included prophecies of judgment on the wicked and disobedient as well as of deliverance for the persevering faithful, and whose departure from life was shrouded in mystery of a kind that faith alone could penetrate.[67]

62. Kee, *Community of the New Age*, 106.
63. Ibid., 3.
64. Ibid., 9–11.
65. Ibid., 29–30.
66. Ibid., 49.
67. Ibid., 76.

After delineating the literary aspects of Mark, Kee moves onto the more crucial scope of his work: a social-historical analysis of Mark.

In order to complete this social-historical analysis, Kee reviews the social locations (*Sitz im Leben*) of the genres of which he believes Mark to be comprised. Kee provides information about the social dynamics of prophetic movements and the development of Hasidism as a model of a Jewish sect. He then compares these with the disciples in Mark as a model of the Markan community for which the gospel was written. Kee describes the community with five particular aspects: (1) a prophetic-charismatic ministry; John the Baptist and Jesus announce the kingdom of God to which the disciples are called peremptorily also to proclaim.[68] The community experiences (2) the transformation of social and economic structures. There is a radicality to discipleship: one must abandon ordinary human ties to be a disciple. Family is redefined in terms of discipleship. One must abandon possessions to follow Jesus. Children and Gentiles are welcomed into the community.[69] Mark's community maintains (3) an avoidance of political involvement. When Jesus is questioned about honor to Caesar or God in Mark 12:13–16, he refuses to take sides.[70] (4) There are esoteric aspects to the community. God grants special revelation to the community so that it alone understands God's purposes. This is particularly useful for the Messianic secret. The identity of Jesus remains a secret "as a central, pervasive element in the community's understanding of itself and of Jesus as those to whom it has been revealed that the kingdom of God is given–not to those who seize power–but to those who are faithful, suffering obedience, receive it as a gift."[71] Finally, (5) there is an inclusive aspect of the community. Akin to the second aspect, the community of Mark "was open across social, economic, sexual, and ethnic barriers."[72]

The intersection of Christology and discipleship occurs most significantly in Kee's fifth chapter. Mark portrays the community as citizens in the kingdom of God, an eschatological family, a new covenant people participating in a new exodus. Jesus then functions as the agent who establishes the new community, though Christology is of secondary importance to the primary issue of the community's identity.[73] For Kee, the definition of agency goes beyond christological titles and requires a review of the revelatory

68. Ibid., 87.
69. Ibid., 89–92.
70. Ibid., 93.
71. Ibid., 96.
72. Ibid., 97.
73. Ibid., 107.

and redemptive roles Jesus has in Mark.[74] Although these analyses appear to be linked, there is no correlation between who Jesus is as convener of the new covenant community and the identity of the new covenant community. Even in his lengthy descriptions of Jesus as Son of God, Son of David, and Son of Man, there is no concrete reference to the eschatological family to which these might bear some relationship. He does conclude that Jesus is the initiating agent and paradigm, thus following Jesus requires certain responsibilities and sacrifices.

Kee concludes his book with a chapter on eschatology and the Markan community. For Kee, apocalypticism is a significant component for Mark's gospel. Essentially, now that the community is identified as an eschatological covenant people, it must live into that identity. This identification creates a certain ethic which hearkens back to the expectations of the disciples within the gospel itself: community roles, severing family ties, giving up of possessions, and love for neighbor. For Kee, the intersection of Christology and discipleship points to the reality of the Markan community living "in a proleptic way the life of the kingdom of God, and through its message, its witness or life, and its charismatic powers, it is calling the world to join it in obedient, joyful anticipation of the kingdom's consummation."[75]

Although Kee has made a significant contribution in the utilization of multiple methodologies and the endeavor to understand that the literary components of Mark must be understood within the social-historical context of Mark, Kee maintains an historical-critical approach to the world behind Mark. The conclusions Kee draws serve only to highlight who the community of Mark is and why its members would need the Gospel of Mark, rather than to highlight what discipleship is and how it relates to Christology within the Markan narrative for its own sake. Any formulation of the intersection of Christology and discipleship falls short because of Kee's methodological limitation to remain in the historical-critical realm. The categories of disciple (community) and Jesus remain separately approached categories. The intersection of Christology and discipleship is nominal and becomes subject to the identity of the Markan community outside of the gospel text.

John R. Donahue

John R. Donahue primarily addresses the role and theology of discipleship in his short volume, *The Theology and Setting of Discipleship in the Gospel of*

74. Ibid., 116.
75. Ibid., 174–75.

Mark. The intersection with Christology is not intentional but by no means insignificant. Donahue spends a large part of his essay determining the identification and role of the twelve. He challenges the view that the role of discipleship belongs solely to the twelve named disciples in Mark. "Not only does Mark not single out the twelve or distinguish them clearly from other groups, but there are a large number of other places where people, who are called explicitly neither the twelve nor disciples, do those very things the latter are called to do, to teach and do mighty works."[76] Donahue concludes that the stories specifically regarding the twelve belong to a larger umbrella of discipleship that is not limited to the twelve.

Donahue addresses several issues in the discipleship debate. Firstly, he describes the nature of the call to discipleship. It is important not only to focus on the role of the twelve, but also to focus upon what it means to heed the call into that role. Donahue surveys several Markan texts (Mark 1:16–20; 3:13–19; 6:6b–13). As he surveys Mark 6:6b–13, the mission of the twelve, Donahue observes that "the twelve who will respond immediately to Jesus' command function as models of faith and at the same time form a new family around Jesus which is a substitute for the natural family."[77] Donahue will pick up on this new family in his discussion of the community of disciples in Mark.

Secondly, Donahue attends to the negative view of the disciples that has been so prevalent in scholarly literature. He would suggest that there is the possibility for "positive significance on the negative picture of the disciples."[78] Akin to the discussion on discipleship above, Donahue summarizes the debate in a discussion of the works of Theodore Weeden and Werner Kelber. He surmises that their theories rely too heavily on a construct of Markan opponents, for which there is no real evidence. Rather, Donahue believes the way to understanding the negative view of the disciples is one which gives them a positive meaning, along the lines of Ernest Best and Robert Tannehill. But, Donahue throws one final wrench into this discussion by suggesting that all of these works on discipleship maintain an individualized view as opposed to a communal view, which dominates the rest of his study. Hence, he sees that a correct understanding of discipleship in Mark requires an awareness of the social-historical setting and comprehension of the dyadic personality where the individual relates to the larger whole.

---

76. Donahue, *Theology and Setting*, 8–9.
77. Ibid., 18.
78. Ibid., 24.

Donahue's brush with Christology occurs in the final section of his book. As he discusses the nature of the community of discipleship, he again turns to the language of family and household that Mark uses to describe them in 3:20–35. As Jesus is rejected by his own family, he creates a new family for disciples. He is the one who calls to discipleship, and those who follow him leave their own family behind and belong to a new family. "Solidarity with Jesus in suffering makes of one a brother, sister or mother to Jesus who himself is truly Son of God when he can address his father in faith and trust before his impending cross."[79]

Donahue identifies a second text which alludes to the community of disciples as a family, namely, Mark 10:29–31. Once the disciples have left their families, the reality of the new family is one of household service (*diakonia*).[80] Donahue suggests the predominant views of family life contemporary with Mark are subverted by the call to discipleship into a new family headed by Jesus. The third text Donahue uses is Mark 10:42–45. This adds to the notion of household service. A disciple of Jesus is a servant, first and foremost. Again, Donahue touches upon Christology with discipleship: "the community is one which has been freed by Jesus, but freed for a deeper level of mutual service done in solidarity with Jesus who by the paradoxical renunciation of power became the source of liberation for others."[81] Lastly, Donahue addresses the community of disciples as a watchful community based on Mark 13:33–36. Household and servant language is used in the parable which suggests the community of Mark is a house church which gathers in mutual service and awaits the return of their master, Jesus.[82]

The most significant contribution in Donahue's work is his recognition of the importance of the household and family language Mark utilizes in describing discipleship. It is unfair to be too critical of Donahue's failure to tie discipleship together with Christology. However, it is regrettable that he was unable to delve deeper into this connection that he observes several times in his book. It is surprising that Donahue only mentions Jesus as a son two times in reference to this language. Jesus is the leader of this new family, and yet Donahue does not seem to indicate the significance of his role particularly as a son in this new family. This study will address that shortfall.

---

79. Ibid., 36–37.
80. Ibid., 39.
81. Ibid., 49–50.
82. Ibid., 51.

Suzanne Watts Henderson

In *Christology and Discipleship in the Gospel of Mark*, Suzanne Watts Henderson is responding to three issues in previous scholarship. She claims that Markan interpretation has been dismissive of the first half of the Gospel of Mark, that there has been an overemphasis on the identity of Jesus, and that there has been a tendency to see a striking division between Jesus and the disciples.[83] To combat these three concerns, Henderson proposes a new way to look at discipleship in a close, exegetical reading of six episodes in the first half of Mark that reveal discipleship in its intended form. Her work quickly becomes a study on discipleship, but she continually claims that the connection between discipleship and Christology is found in *presence* and *practice*. "By combining the followers' call to be in Jesus' *presence* and with the expectation that they will *practice* the demonstration of God's coming kingdom, the evangelist sets the terms for understanding the gospel's account of the disciples' mounting incomprehension."[84]

Henderson divides her study into two major sections. In the first section she examines the relationship of Jesus and those who follow him. She provides a close reading and exegesis of the calling of the first disciples in Mark 1:16–20 and of the mountaintop commissioning of the twelve in Mark 3:13–19. She demonstrates the direct interaction between Jesus and the disciples. This section elucidates what it means to be a disciple or follower of Jesus: to be called by Jesus, to be with Jesus, and to be sent out by Jesus, all within an apocalyptic setting.

In the second section, Henderson explores the practice of discipleship. Mark 4:1–34 further reveals what it means to be a disciple. "Through the parabolic discourse, Mark's Jesus conveys to his disciples the hope that, even in the face of prevalent obstacles, God's kingdom will take root and yield fruit."[85] Henderson briefly mentions the redefinition of family ties for the followers of Jesus. She sees this reference to family making two claims in Mark: the family, or the crowd, seated around Jesus may be open to the news of God's reign and they will actively do the will of God.[86] However, she maintains the disciples are drawn together through the presence of Jesus and the practice of the will of God.

Henderson also exegetes the commissioning of the twelve in Mark 6:7–13 in terms of discipleship as practice; the feeding of the five thousand

---

83. Henderson, *Christology and Discipleship*, 13.
84. Ibid., 24.
85. Ibid., 25.
86. Ibid., 100–101.

in Mark 6:30–44 in terms of discipleship as presence; and the incomprehension of the disciples in Mark 6:45–52 in terms of discipleship as (foiled) presence. It becomes clear that Henderson's work is predominantly about discipleship. She is addressing the negative portrayal of the disciples that has dominated so much of recent scholarship under the guise of Christology. Christology is necessary because it gives definition to the identity and work of the disciples, but she does not delve into the definition of Christology in Mark and how this relates to discipleship. For Henderson, correct (or incorrect) Christology by the disciples determines their practice. Henderson wants Christology to function as a tool for understanding discipleship. "The interpretive results of this study expand the horizon of Mark's Christology so that it encompasses both Jesus' particular messianic role and his followers' intended function in the messianic age that he inaugurates."[87]

Henderson's study is significant in that, akin to John R. Donahue, she endeavors to break open the negative view of the disciples that has been so predominant. Christology plays a part in this; the identity of Jesus and the comprehension of this identity determine discipleship. "Mark's Christology drives his portrait of discipleship in just this respect: true discipleship entails *both* full-fledged trust in the reality of God's coming rule, as evinced in and through Jesus, and active stewardship of the messianic power conferred by Jesus upon the disciples."[88] But, the fact remains that Henderson's study is a study in discipleship with a precursory glance at Christology to aid in her efforts.

Adam Winn

Very briefly, and in segue to the discussion of Mark and its Roman imperial context, it is necessary to mention *The Purpose of Mark's Gospel* by Adam Winn. Winn proposes a historical context for Mark that departs from the view Mark was written before the fall of Jerusalem. Winn suggests a Roman context during the reign of Emperor Vespasian (69–79 CE) as part of his outline to determine the purpose and origin of the Gospel of Mark.[89] Utilizing this date and provenance, Winn surveys major themes in the Gospel of Mark: the incipit, Christology, discipleship, and eschatology. Although addressed as separate categories, Winn intertwines Christology and discipleship by stating that correct discipleship recognizes the true, suffering, identity of Jesus. He suggests that Mark is responding to historical

---

87. Ibid., 246.
88. Ibid., 248.
89. Winn, *Purpose of Mark's Gospel*, 43–91.

persecution and a christological crisis in which Jesus' true identity was being challenged.[90]

Winn concludes that "Mark's primary purpose was to respond to Flavian propaganda that had created a christological crisis for his community in Rome."[91] Regardless of Winn's conclusions, he makes an important contribution in the dating of Mark. He puts the gospel in an imperial transitional period that significantly impacts its Christology and discipleship. The characterization of Jesus in Mark may be seen over and against the presentation of Vespasian in the Roman Empire. Winn is restricted, though, by his historical-critical methodology, and he does not push the issue of empire, both in resistance and mimicry for Mark's community. Consequently the intersections of Christology and discipleship remain largely undeveloped.

Attempts at intersections of Christology and discipleship are either, in the case of Donahue and Winn, implicit and unintentional, or in the case of Kee and Henderson, in name only. Each author suggests that, for Mark, who Jesus is determines who the disciples are and how they shall live. Yet, they fall short in that Kee and Winn focus on the historical context and lose sight of the narrative context of Mark; and Henderson's work is clearly a study in discipleship. Donahue provides a way forward by recognizing the family and household language at work in the Gospel of Mark and the role of discipleship and how Jesus relates to this new family of disciples. Yet his discussion remains limited and his insight is not elaborated.

ROMAN IMPERIAL CONTEXT AND THE INTERSECTION OF MARKAN CHRISTOLOGY AND DISCIPLESHIP

As this book will focus on the intersection of Christology and discipleship in the Gospel of Mark within a Roman imperial context, it is necessary to review previous work that has engaged the gospel in an imperial context. I will address three contributions that consider Mark in its relation to its Roman imperial context: *Binding the Strong Man: A Political Reading of Mark's Story of Jesus* by Ched Myers, *Hearing the Whole Story: The Politics of Plot in Mark's Gospel* by Richard Horsley, and *The Son of God in the Roman World: Divine Sonship in its Social and Political Context* by Michael Peppard.

---

90. Ibid., 150.
91. Ibid., 203.

Ched Myers

Ched Myers provides a significant contribution to the discussion of the Roman imperial context and the Gospel of Mark.[92] Methodologically, Myers recognizes the limitations that historical-critical and literary methods have had in Markan scholarship in that the former utilizes the gospel as a window to get to the historical situation while the latter often ignores the historical situation all together. Myers argues for a socioliterary reading of the Gospel of Mark. Mark is "an ideological narrative, the manifesto of an early Christian discipleship community in its war of myths with the dominant social order and its political adversaries."[93]

Myers places the Gospel of Mark at the height of the Jewish War, around 69 CE in Galilee. He is quite specific regarding date and place, suggesting that the story of Jesus both reflects its own historical events as well as speaks to the situation of the Markan community. The Gospel of Mark "is a synchronic portrait, describing the function of institutions and social dynamics, rather than a diachronic one, which would be concerned with the chronological shifting of person and events."[94] In that case, Myers provides a thoroughgoing analysis of the historical situation of the Jewish War and the time leading up to the destruction of the Jerusalem temple by the Romans in 70 CE. Myers relies heavily on the writings of Josephus to understand the popular resistance movements, and at the same time criticizes the social-historical location of Josephus as a Jew who has given his loyalty to the Romans.

His analysis draws out important aspects of the Jesus/Markan communities' social-historical location: not only were they up against the Roman Empire, but they also had to resist the work of the Pharisees, Herodians, and the Sanhedrin. These three groups were ethnically and religiously tied to Jesus and the early Markan community, and yet they often prevailed against and ruled over the rural, poor Galileans. Mark's gospel is one way of confronting and resisting these powers and principalities.

According to Myers, there are four ways in which people responded to the Roman Empire and its colonization efforts.[95] The first was to succumb to colonialism and to collaborate with the Romans. In Palestine, this occurred through the imperial cult and the ruling classes such as the

---

92. Myers, *Binding the Strong Man* is a pioneering work engaging imperial realities a decade before such questions started to gain much more attention in gospel studies.

93. Ibid., 31.

94. Ibid., 42.

95. Ibid., 80–87. Myers bases these categories on the work of Holzner, *Reality Construction*.

Herodians who practiced "cooperative nationalism." They were Jewish, yet they honored (and worked for) Rome. The second response includes the reform movements of the Essenes and the Pharisees. The Essenes were a Jewish movement that chose to withdraw from society as a way to protest and resist the Roman colonizers. The Pharisees, on the other hand, were a reform movement that challenged "the elitist clerical classes that made attempts to be populist"[96] in an attempt to build an alternative political base. Thirdly, the Zealots' and other popular resistance movements' responses to Roman imperialism was one of loyalistic radicalism. They sought "structural change for the purpose of restoring or purifying traditional values."[97] The final means of responding to the Romans was to be alienated, confrontative, or nonaligned. An alienated group "is portrayed as resolving social tensions through 'introjected' or 'symbolically transferred' aggression, and summarily dismissed as incidental to political culture."[98] Myers contends that this final means of response is a legitimate strategy and the very one that the Gospel of Mark employs.

Myers begins his commentary with the understanding that the community of Mark was being challenged by rebel recruiters, "who were trying to drum up support for the resistance around Palestine, and no doubt demanding that Mark's community 'choose sides.'"[99] In the end, however, Mark (and Jesus) demonstrates that radical discipleship as subversive resistance is the only way, not the way of the rebels, to revolt in Jerusalem. Myers follows this path through his commentary, dividing the Gospel of Mark into two distinct halves or books with parallel elements: prologue/call to discipleship, campaign of direct action, construction of new order, extended sermon, "passion" tradition, and symbolic epilogue.[100] And although Myers contends this path is subversive resistance, the language he utilizes is that of revolution and revolt, suggesting that Mark, in Myers's interpretation, "assumes, clarifies, and intentionally subverts his semantic field"[101] as part of his ideological strategy.

By way of conclusion, Myers summarizes Mark's gospel as a criticism of Mark's own historical and political location. Mark becomes a sociopolitical critic of the Jewish ruling elite, Roman imperialism, the reform movements, and the rebels. Mark also becomes a socioeconomic critic of the

96. Ibid., 83.
97. Ibid., 83–84.
98. Ibid., 85.
99. Ibid., 86.
100. Ibid., 112.
101. Ibid., 97.

symbolic order and the political economy. As an alternative and subversive political practice, Mark demonstrates in his gospel one that uses "leadership accountable to the 'least' in the community," a politics of servanthood.[102] In addition, Myers contends that Mark's Jesus advocated civil disobedience. For example, the disciples break the law as their first public action. Jesus also practiced revolutionary nonviolence, most notably in his crucifixion. As an alternative and subversive socioeconomic practice, Jesus practices solidarity with the poor and the Gentiles in the feeding stories. So, in the end, "at the heart of Mark's political, social, and economic alternatives to the dominant order lies a radical new symbolic system based upon the primacy of human need."[103]

Myers has made an incredible contribution to Markan scholarship and has paved a way for a multi-disciplinary approach to the context and the narrative of the Gospel of Mark. He limits his work to the text of the gospel without offering a systemic analysis of the person of Jesus, Christology. He notes this in his conclusion, suggesting that he strongly believes that to "read Mark is to read Jesus."[104] But he does provide some concluding christological comments, suggesting that the categories of prophet, priest, and king are the best way to understand Jesus. These categories remain strongly within the Jewish context.

My critique of Myers is twofold: (1) Myers becomes so entrenched in the history of the Jewish war, that the Gospel of Mark becomes only one way among others to respond to the Roman Empire and the Jewish elite leaders. In a way, Myers limits the role of the gospel to the false alternative of the Jewish war rather than the larger social-historical context of Roman-occupied Palestine. (2) Myers is convinced that the Gospel of Mark is only for the sake of resistance and subversion, as we will also see in Horsley. His analysis is too monolithic in its presentation of imperial negotiation. Myers does not suggest that the mimicry of and the desire to overtake the dominant forces exist in the Gospel of Mark. Still, Myers's work will be important to this study for his perception of the ruling powers and his analysis of the social, political, and economic context of Mark and Jesus.

Richard Horsley

In *Hearing the Whole Story: The Politics of Plot in Mark's Gospel*, Richard Horsley attempts "to cut through many unwarranted interrelated

102. Ibid., 434.
103. Ibid., 443.
104. Ibid., 444.

assumptions and concepts to arrive at more appropriate literary and historical approaches, analyses, and constructions"[105] in the Gospel of Mark. Horsley outlines his argument in ten steps, or chapters (pp. xii-xv). (1) It is necessary to read the whole story of Mark. (2) One must relocate the story in the context of ancient Palestine under Roman imperial rule and hear it as a story about subjected people, perhaps even giving voice to such people. (3) It is necessary to hear Mark's story as an oral performance. (4) The gospel is about more than just discipleship. (5) The dominant plot of Mark's gospel focuses on Jesus. (6) It is necessary to reexamine the standard view of Mark as "apocalyptic." (7) Once the reader recognizes the dominant plot of Mark's story, Jesus' renewal of Israel in Galilean villages in opposition to the Jerusalem rulers, then the subplot of Jesus' controversies with the scribes and Pharisees falls more clearly into place. (8) If Mark's Jesus is actually defending Israelite covenantal law, there is opportunity for a more complete review of the relationship of Mark's story to Israelite cultural tradition. (9) The women in Mark's gospel emerge as the paradigms of following and serving in the movement of renewal of Israel. (10) The story is "in-formed" by particular (oral) "scripts" operative in the Galilean and Judean villages in which the Jesus movement represented by Mark emerged. "Discerning the presence of these patterns in popular Galilean and Judean culture enables us to understand how Mark's story emerged and resonated with its historical context."[106]

Throughout his work, Horsley tends to combat the current interpretations and methodological approaches to Mark. Although his is a narrative approach addressing the oft-cited oral nature of Mark and Mark's use of "sandwich stories," he limits the plot outline of Mark to conflict, specifically conflict with authorities. Horsley also states that there is no room for a christological interpretation of the Gospel of Mark. "The double meanings woven into the fabric of Mark's narrative lead us to recognize that, much to the dismay of those who would mine Mark as a vein of unambiguous christological statements, what have been taken as 'titles' of Jesus may be, in effect, metaphors. In Mark 'son of man' appears only as a self-reference by Jesus or as a future figure 'coming with the clouds of heaven,' and never as a 'christological title' of or for Jesus."[107] Rather than utilizing a christological approach, Horsley contends that Jesus is a political agent sent to do the work of manifesting God's kingdom in the world among the people of Galilee.

---

105. Horsley, *Hearing the Whole Story*, xii.
106. Ibid., xv.
107. Ibid., 20.

Perhaps it is for the sake of argument for context, history, and politics, but Horsley significantly downplays a theological or christological understanding of the Gospel of Mark. He makes an artificial distinction when he sees the Gospel of Mark "as a story about a movement among imperially subjected people" rather than a "scriptural story of salvation."[108] Horsley provides a thorough analysis of the community Mark addresses, including its political, social, and historical situation. In his narrative approach, he compares Mark with apocalyptic literature. Horsley addresses the presence of the Roman Empire in Galilee and how this reveals itself as a political struggle in the Gospel of Mark.

Akin to Myers, Horsley also addresses the role of the Pharisees and the Jewish leaders in the Gospel of Mark. For Horsley, Jesus' primary role is a leader of a resistance movement, a movement that is specifically meant to renew popular Israelite tradition. "Mark's story, focused on events of Jesus' heading a movement of Israel's renewal in Galilean villages, must be understood squarely in the interaction between Galilean popular Israelite tradition and the great tradition of Jerusalem that had been imposed roughly a century and a half before."[109] Mark's story is a renewal movement of the Mosaic covenant and a new exodus. In this story, the disciples, the ones who would appear to follow Jesus and continue this renewal movement, fail. In a significant observation, Horsley points out that it is the women in the Gospel of Mark who are the true followers and harbingers of the renewal movement.

In the end, Horsley sees Mark's story as a renewal movement, specifically a cultural and political renewal movement, which denies the religiosity that was an integral part of the historical context. Horsley is intent on Jesus being a leader of a resistance movement that fights against the Roman occupation and any that would collaborate with that occupation. As Mark's Jesus is a leader of resistance, Horsley too is a leader of a resistance movement against a too-narrow theological and christological interpretation of Mark. He wants to maintain the gospel and Jesus rooted in an Israelite tradition resisting the Jerusalem elite and the Roman Empire. Unfortunately, Horsley's approach then becomes so narrowly focused on resistance that he misses the nuances of how communities negotiated the powers and principalities they encountered. Resistance is central and important, but there were other ways that Jesus and Mark's gospel dealt with oppression and empire. "Most of the political life of subordinate groups is to be found neither in overt collective defiance of powerholders nor in complete hegemonic compliance,

---

108. Ibid., 29.
109. Ibid., 161.

but in the vast territory between these two polar opposites."[110] Horsley refuses to acknowledge this.[111] His work, however, is significant to the topic of Mark and the Roman Empire and he provides some helpful analysis of understanding the historical and political context of Mark's gospel. As noted previously, Horsley's discussion fails to note the significance of Christology and discipleship that does exist in Mark and diminishes interaction between the presentation of Jesus and any relationship to the presentation of the disciples.

Michael Peppard

In a more recent contribution, Michael Peppard has written *The Son of God in the Roman World: Divine Sonship in Its Social and Political Context*. Peppard's intent is "(1) to critique the conceptual framework within which the term 'son of God' has usually been construed in biblical scholarship and (2) to reinterpret divine sonship in the sociopolitical context of early Christianity."[112] In the first three chapters, Peppard points out that the concept of divine sonship within Christianity has been limited to a post-Nicene understanding where "begotten not made" becomes a central defining factor. Instead, Peppard focuses upon the social and political ideology of the first century and the figure of the Roman emperor who was designated as a "Son of God." He also critiques the notion that sonship by adoption was somehow a lesser kinship relationship than sonship by birth and demonstrates the significance and centrality of adoption in the perpetuation of imperial dynasties. Peppard suggests that "the adoption of adult males helped to stabilize ruling families and formed a key part of imperial ideology."[113] Peppard's purpose is to relocate the metaphor of divine sonship in its original context of Roman imperial ideology in association with the Roman emperor as this will provide a more accurate understanding of divine sonship as associated with Jesus in early Christianity (pre-Nicea).

After his critique and analysis of divine sonship in the first century, especially in association with the Roman emperor, Peppard offers a reading of the Gospel of Mark. Key for Peppard's interpretation is the notion of

110. Scott, *Domination and the Arts of Resistance*, 136.

111. Though Horsley has supported and utilized the work of James C. Scott and its contribution to the study of the New Testament, he maintains the emphasis on resistance, without the nuance of any imperial or elite imitation as a part of the hidden transcript of resistance. See Carter, "James C. Scott and New Testament Studies," 85.

112. Peppard, *Son of God in Roman World*, 3.

113. Ibid., 4.

adoption and the baptismal scene in Mark 1:9–11. Peppard states that the divine designation of Jesus as God's Son and the descent of the Spirit as a dove can be directly connected to the Roman ideology of divine sonship and the Roman emperor. "The dove will be interpreted as an omen and countersymbol to the Roman eagle, which was a public portent of divine favor and ascension to imperial power."[114] Peppard establishes a Roman provenance composed by a Judean-Syrian-Roman for the Gospel of Mark in the limited internal evidence as well as the patristic evidence and tradition. Drawing on the work of others,[115] Peppard notes the prevalence of Roman imperial ideology throughout the territories and provinces by means of coinage, portraits, propaganda, and emperor worship which become central to the characterization of Jesus as a divine son in the empire of God who is also worshipped in Palestine.[116]

Central to Peppard's argument is the concept of adoption. He makes clear in both chapters 3 and 5 that adoption in the first century was equally binding as conventional kinship and that adopted sons, especially those adopted by the Roman emperor, had equal status and honor as children born into the family. Peppard provides a summary of the conventional scholarly interpretation of Jesus' baptism in Mark in light of Jewish practice and ideology, especially Ps 2:7 and Isa 42:1. Moreover, Peppard points out that Jewish adoption was not a widespread practice based on biblical and rabbinic materials, though there are some key biblical instances (Moses, Joseph, Ruth, David) in which adoption or fosterage was practiced. Rather, adoption is better understood in its metaphorical role for the relationship between God and God's children, Israel, in the Hebrew Bible. Based on the Hebrew metaphor and the Roman practice of adoption, Peppard suggests that the language of adoption is clearly present in Jesus' baptism when God says, ἐν σοὶ εὐδόκησα, which is better translated, "I am pleased to choose you."[117]

Alongside the language of adoption is the role of the Spirit and its description as a dove in Mark 1:11. Peppard again considers the Roman context and interprets the role of the Spirit in terms of the Roman concepts of *genius* and *numen* where the Spirit guards as a tutelary *genius* and expresses the will of God by the *numen*.[118] Peppard indicates that there is

---

114. Ibid., 87.

115. Especially, Deissmann, *Licht vom Osten*; Crossan and Reed, *In Search of Paul*; Crossan and Reed, *Excavating Jesus*; Collins, "Mark and his Readers." See, Peppard, *Son of God*, 27.

116. Peppard, *Son of God in Roman World*, 93.

117. Ibid., 107–12.

118. Ibid., 114.

imperial imitation in Mark, "The Spirit is concentrated in the '*paterfamilias*' (God) and his chosen son (Jesus)—just like in the imperial family—while it watches over the other members of the family and empowers them to do the will of the *pater*."[119] Finally, he provides a summary of the ancient literature on augury and the significance of the eagle and the dove, concluding that the dove is an omen which signifies the divine election of Jesus in contrast with the symbol of the eagle in Roman imperial ideology.

Peppard briefly surveys the significance of Jesus' divine sonship at his baptism for the rest of the gospel. He notes the absence of any earthly father throughout the gospel and concludes that the divine father, God, establishes the legitimate father-son relationship with Jesus which has continuing effect for the new kinship group that Jesus creates. Peppard also notes the significance of Jesus' identity as a son of God at the transfiguration and crucifixion. "In the end, Mark's view of divine sonship, which had been refracted throughout the gospel in the light of the Roman emperor, now shines through unmediated. It is Jesus who is the Roman world's 'son of God'– sorrowful as a Roman criminal, and powerful as a Roman emperor."[120] His concluding chapter synthesizes literature from the first three centuries prior to the council of Nicea to demonstrate the shift in the metaphor of adoption of one equal to a biological relationship to one that is lesser than a biological relationship.

Because Peppard's work is focused primarily on divine sonship and the father-son relationship, it is primarily christological in scope. He does suggest that the kinship relationship established between God and Jesus at the baptism through the descent of the dove is extended to Jesus' disciples and followers through the Spirit. In his focus on divine sonship in Roman imperial ideology as compared with Jesus, Peppard fails to acknowledge other aspects of kinship that are present both in the characterization of Jesus and the roles of the disciples and those who follow Jesus including immediate agency, advocacy, and the restoration of kinship relationship through the benefit of healing. Due to spatial constraints, he only surveys the gospel content that directly addresses kinship relationships in association with discipleship. His work is an important contribution to the role of kinship in the Gospel of Mark in the context of the Roman imperial world. Peppard brings to the fore the central kinship relationship and identifying marker of Jesus as the adopted Son of God and demonstrates the impact this has for discipleship.

119. Ibid.
120. Ibid., 131.

CONCLUSION

This chapter has covered a vast array of Markan scholarship within the categories of Christology, discipleship, and the context of the Roman Empire in order to locate the argument of this study. While the significance of the various contributions to each category within Markan studies should not be lost, however, one conclusion emerges very readily. It is clear that a separate, categorical approach to Christology and discipleship has divided the two so much that they seem to be distinct disciplines. In the works that have claimed to engage Christology and discipleship, they remain, largely, separate discussions. The Gospel of Mark has clear titles for Jesus, and it is important to recognize the significance of these titles, especially designations of "Son" within the narrative and sociohistorical contexts of Mark. In relation to the presentation of disciples, without the discussion of the failure or incomprehension of the disciples in a narrative and historical context, we would not have a full, multifaceted understanding of the followers of Jesus in Mark. Discipleship rests for much scholarship largely on role and function as opposed to identity in relation to Jesus. In the brief mentions of discipleship and kinship, the possibility opens up to approach discipleship and Christology as connected or integrated categories in the Gospel of Mark, where they are interdependent and mutually define one another. For example, it is only after Jesus is proclaimed God's Son that he inaugurates his ministry which begins with the calling of the disciples out of their own kinship networks to follow Jesus (1:9–20). Also, Jesus defines discipleship within the context of abandoning his kinship of origin and creating a new kinship group of those who do the will of God (3:20–35). I will argue that kinship language and structures draw Christology and discipleship together in the Gospel of Mark. This argument will be further strengthened through a narrative approach with the understanding that Mark was written in the context of the Roman Empire as literature of resistance, imitation, and negotiation.

In the next chapter, I will outline my methodology in terms of narrative, kinship, and imperial negotiation. Within this multi-disciplinary approach Christology and discipleship will find their nexus that unfolds in the narrative of the Gospel of Mark in language of kinship and the concept of sonship.

2

Methodology

IN CHAPTER 1, I surveyed previous scholarship on Christology and discipleship in Mark, indicated a failure to hold the two together, and proposed the possibility of understanding Christology and discipleship as connected or integrated categories centered on the notion of kinship, especially sonship. In this chapter, I will construct a multidisciplinary approach to Christology and discipleship in the Gospel of Mark through the methods of narrative criticism; social-science criticism, especially studies of kinship; and imperial critical approaches. In outlining these methods, I will highlight the initial contribution of each method in showing the importance of kinship, especially sonship, as the nexus between Christology and discipleship.

NARRATIVE CRITICISM

"Narrative criticism has come to be understood as the analysis of the story-world of a narrative along with the analysis of its implied rhetorical impact on readers."[1] Narrative approaches in biblical studies have contributed significantly to the study and interpretation of the Gospel of Mark.[2] Mary Ann Tolbert summarizes some aspects of this approach to Mark in its narrative form in her 1996 work, *Sowing the Gospel*. Primarily, it is necessary to remember that Mark "is a self-consciously crafted narrative, a fiction, resulting

---

1. Rhoads, *Reading Mark*, 24.
2. In addition to the work of Rhoads, see also: Kingsbury, *Christology of Mark's Gospel*; Iersel, *Reading Mark*; Wegener, *Cruciformed*; and Smith, *Lion with Wings*. For a general introduction to narrative criticism see Powell, *What is Narrative Criticism?* For an exhaustive and comprehensive bibliography on various methodological approaches to Mark's gospel, see Telford, *Writing on the Gospel of Mark*.

from literary imagination, not photographic recall."[3] Second, narrative approaches address the gospel in its extant form and as a coherent narrative. Finally, it is important to read Mark within its context. "Writing, like any form of communication, is a deeply social activity, and exploring the matrix of ideas, conventions, social, educational, and political dynamics in which every text is rooted is also part of employing a literary perspective."[4] For this study, a narrative approach to Mark will help to maintain its integrity as a unified story while I analyze the social and political dynamics that are present within the narrative.

Plot

The study of narrative has its roots in the work of the ancient philosopher Aristotle and his analysis of tragedy in *Poetics*.[5] Aristotle divides tragedy into six component parts with plot and character being the most significant elements. Simply put, plot is the chain of events that occur in a narrative. Tragedy is to be a representation (*mimesis*) of life, which is action, and thus plot becomes the central aspect of tragedy. Aristotle provides several other criteria for successful plot in *Poetics*. A plot has a beginning, middle, and an end. The length of a plot must be neither too short nor too long, but a length that remains easily in one's memory. The actions and events of the plot are carefully and purposefully constructed; to leave one part out would ruin the whole plot. These carefully constructed actions and events create a unity which is largely based on causality. "Events are the consequences of previous events and the cause of subsequent events."[6] Reversal (a change of state) and recognition (a change from not-knowing to knowing) are important components of plot. Finally, a successful plot will arouse feelings of pity and tragedy.

Aristotle provides the most basic definition of plot as the arrangement of events in a narrative. Seymour Chatman furthers this definition by insisting that there is a hierarchy to this chain of events. Chatman divides plot into *kernels* and *satellites*. Kernels are the central plot events from which the rest of the plot is derived. "They are nodes or hinges in the structure, branching points which force a movement into one or two (or more) possible paths."[7] Satellites are the minor plot events which give flesh to the ker-

3. Tolbert, *Sowing the Gospel*, 30.
4. Ibid., 33.
5. Aristotle, *Poetics*, 54–63.
6. Carter, *Matthew: Storyteller*, 134.
7. Chatman, *Story and Discourse*, 53.

nels' skeleton. They are not as crucial to the narrative; that is, the narrative logic is not destroyed but the narrative would be lacking by their absence.

In discussions on the narrative of Mark's gospel, theoretical analyses of plot are notably missing.[8] Scholars have spent the majority of time focused upon the structure of the narrative and how it is divided (geographically, theologically).[9] Structure and plot, however, are not the same thing. Chiefly, structure refers to how the narrative is told (discourse) more than how the story is arranged (plot). The primary definition of plot in Markan scholarship lies with David Rhoads in *Mark as Story*. Plot revolves around conflict.[10] David Rhoads approaches plot through its conflicts and suggests that conflicts in Mark are central to the plot and ought to be analyzed. In Mark, Jesus, as the protagonist, is in conflict with nature, supernatural forces, with other people and authorities, and even with himself. "In the Gospel, all these conflicts occur within the larger context of God establishing his rule over (against) all other powers and claims to authorities, and the conflicts come to focus on the protagonist Jesus, the agent of God's rule."[11] In effect, it is Jesus' identity as a Son that causes, escalates, and ultimately resolves the conflicts in Mark. Again, this has more to do with discourse than story. Before discourse can be properly analyzed and interpreted, the plot and its arrangement must be discerned. At its most basic form, the plot of Mark will reveal significant meaning and purpose for this study. Kevin Larsen grants that "we must recognize and/or remember that the arrangement of the material is the most important clue to the gospel's theological"–I would add, christological–"core."[12]

As noted above, theoretical discussions of plot and the Gospel of Mark are not prevalent but studies that have addressed Markan plot will

---

8. There are a few contributions that provide theoretical discussions of plot and the Gospel of Mark which will be addressed below.

9. For a helpful summary of scholarship on the approach to Mark's structure see, Larsen, "Structure of Mark's Gospel," 141. For an example of the geographical approach see Kelber, *Mark's Story*.

10. Rhoads, Michie and Dewey, *Mark as Story*, 73–96. Rhoads acknowledges that he follows the theoretical work of Chatman in his own *Reading Mark*, 6, but he provides no analysis of Mark's plot in terms of Chatman's definition of plot. Kingsbury, *Christology of Mark's Gospel*; Horsley, *Hearing the Whole Story*; Tolbert, *Sowing the Gospel*, and Malbon, in her chapter "Narrative Criticism," in *In the Company of Jesus*, 1–40 also regard plot in terms of conflict. Smith in *Lion with Wings* analyzes the plot of Mark following the work of R. Alan Culpepper on the Gospel of John. His analysis is Aristotelian in approach regarding causation; however, it still revolves around conflict.

11. Rhoads, *Reading Mark*, 7.

12. Larsen, "Structure of Mark's Gospel," 141.

be addressed here. Ernest Van Eck provides the first discussion of Markan plot.[13] Van Eck begins his study with a brief survey of the term plot originating with Aristotle. He addresses the work of Seymour Chatman but dismisses it in favor of his teacher's work, that of Andries G. Van Aarde, on point of view, narrator, and implied reader/author which demonstrates a collapse of Chatman's theory of story *and* discourse. Van Eck concludes that a plot analysis must study the narrated characters, time, space, the role of the reader in the narrative, and the causality that exists among these narrative elements.[14] Van Eck takes each one of these narrative aspects and develops a plot analysis of Mark. For example, in terms of time, Van Eck divides the gospel into two lines of action that Van Aarde has designated as "the sequential level of the Jesus-mission and the sequential level of the disciple-mission."[15] He then provides a plot based on the Jesus-mission and a plot based on the disciple-mission. After four plausible plots, Van Eck formulates the plot of Mark: "Jesus Christ as Son of God, in accordance with the will of God, but with the aid of the Jewish leaders, had to suffer. Jesus, however, announces at his resurrection that true life follows suffering which culminated at the cross."[16] Van Eck then tacks on the parable of the vineyard in Mark 12:1–12; he summarizes its place within the plot of Mark and then analyzes the plot of the parable itself. He disjointedly concludes that this pericope functions as the plot of the entire gospel in a nutshell because its plot content lines up with the gospel's plot content. Although methodologically confusing, Van Eck puts forth a theoretical approach to plot in the Gospel of Mark which is not based on conflict.

In a structuralist approach to the Gospel of Mark, Paul L. Danove provides a thoroughgoing theory on plot and a plot analysis of the gospel.[17] The first part of his book is a theoretical analysis of plot beginning with Aristotle's *Poetics*. He summarizes Aristotelian plot as "the structure of order (formal cause) and the proper sequencing of the order (efficient cause) of the tragedy's organization."[18] That is to say, the simple alignment of events does not create a tragedy, but particular order is necessary. Danove then makes his way through several contemporary approaches to Aristotelian plot in order

---

13. Van Eck and Van Aarde, "Narratological Analysis of Mark 12:1–12," 778–800.
14. Ibid., 782.
15. Ibid., 783.
16. Ibid., 792.
17. Danove, *End of Mark's Gospel*. Structuralism is the critical approach that attempts to reveal the deep thought structures that are embedded in a narrative text.
18. Ibid., 10.

to highlight his own theory comprised of several definitions and premises. Chief among them are the first definition and the first premise:

> [D1] Plot is the principle of causal completion in narrative directed to a particular emotional response which structures events into beginnings, in which anything is possible through middles in which some things become probable to ends in which everything is necessary or certain.
>
> [P1] Plot is the efficient cause of narrative ("the principle of causal completion in narrative").[19]

Other definitions and premises of plot concern author intentionality and the parameters of the method of plot analysis itself. With a brief reference to Chatman's work on real author and implied author, Danove moves on to a structuralist method of plot analysis.

Due to the structuralist nature of Danove's method, his actual analysis of Mark's plot is too complex to go into detail here. His main contribution is providing an actual theory of plot to the Gospel of Mark even if he applies it in conjunction with other methodologies. His basic approach to Mark is to organize the plot into "six candidates for first tier constituents: 1:1; 1:2–15; 1:16–8:26; 8:27–10:52; 11:1–15:41; and 15:42–16:8."[20] These six candidates appear to correspond to six major narrative blocks akin to Chatman (or five plus the incipit), but because he understands plot as an abstract principle "deducible from the intentionality (final cause), structure (formal cause), and structured events (material cause) of a narrative," structure surpasses causality.[21] Danove also becomes the catalyst for the work of Jacob Naluparayil and his approach to Markan plot.

Jacob Naluparayil offers a chapter in his published dissertation on the plot of the Gospel of Mark with a brief reference to the theory of plot.[22] He also addresses the work of Chatman, but like Van Eck, he moves away from it in order to focus on efficient cause in the narrative as delineated by Danove. For Naluparayil, cause in the Gospel of Mark can be found in the conflicting points of view.[23] Thinking the things of God becomes the correct point of view according to Naluparayil's analysis of Mark which is revealed through the person and identity of Jesus. He concludes, "Markan plot is *the*

---

19. Ibid., 15.
20. Ibid., 134.
21. Ibid., 17.
22. Naluparayil, *Identity of Jesus*, 291–430.
23. Ibid., 295.

good news of Jesus Christ, Son of God (1:1), i.e., it is the narrative communication that Jesus of Nazareth is Christ and the Son of God."[24]

Point of view, however, trumps the arrangement of the plot in Naluparayil's approach. Rather than the plot as the chief sequence of events out of which other literary devices and narrative techniques flow, plot is used as a device for the divine point of view to be portrayed.[25] The reversal of the priority of point of view over plot is subtle, but significant. Chatman distinguishes between content, which includes plot, and expression, which includes point of view. Plot is a part of the content of a narrative, a basic building block, without which there would be no possibility of expression, of voice, or of point of view. Content must have priority, even if the point of view is to reveal the identity and purpose of Jesus in order that the reader may think the things of God.

Just the same, Naluparayil's structural analysis of Markan plot will prove useful to my own. He looks at the work of Danove and modifies his outline slightly:

> Mark 1:1–Good news of Jesus Christ, Son of God
>
> Mark 1:2–13–God's sending of a divine person as the Lord and His "beloved Son" in Jesus of Nazareth
>
> Mark 1:14–8:26–The reign of God has disembarked through the person and ministry of Jesus the Son of Man
>
> Mark 8:27–10:52–The divine destiny of suffering and death–"the way" of the Son of Man and discipleship
>
> Mark 11:1–15:41–The Son claiming his heritage and identity is brought to death
>
> Mark 15:42–16:8–The ultimate failure of the discipleship and the hope of the resurrected Jesus.[26]

What Naluparayil demonstrates is the prevalence of the work and the role of Jesus as a Son within the action and events of the plot. The arrangement of events in the Gospel of Mark displays the identity, role, and work of Jesus as a Son. Naluparayil, however, maintains a christological predominance in his structural analysis by only briefly mentioning the impact Jesus' role as a Son has on the disciples and discipleship.

---

24. Ibid., 301.
25. Ibid., 302.
26. Ibid., 304.

Robert Longacre provides another plot analysis of Mark.[27] Longacre also defines plot as the succession of happenings which are recounted, but he bases his theory on that of Paul Ricoeur, which centers on conflict. Although plot revolves around conflict, he utilizes a series of narrative components that break Mark down into a series of narrative blocks, or episodes, which correspond nicely to Chatman's satellites and kernels. The schema he follows includes: "1) *stage*, 2) *inciting incident*, 3) *mounting tension*, 4) *climax*, 5) *denouement*, 6) *closure*."[28] The stage lays the foundation and provides the time, place, setting, and participants that comprise the story world. The inciting incident is that which the story hangs on, the event which is unexpected and routine-breaking. The mounting tension is a series of events or episodes that give depth to the plot. The climax and the denouement are further episodes that resolve the conflict. Finally, closure brings an end to the narrative. Within this template, Longacre concedes that narrators cannot tell all that there is to tell of a story, and therefore, choose certain events to highlight, known as action peaks. In addition, there are didactic peaks, or lengthy segments of reported speech where thematic material is developed.[29] Other aspects of a narrative include a title or aperture and a finis. Longacre points out that there may also be plots and sub-plots, or stories within a story.[30] He also notes that narrators may construct events in such a way as to highlight certain parallelisms or in a chiastic manner with a pivotal centerpiece. "At all events the narrator is likely to echo at beginning and end–and maybe also in the center–certain themes."[31]

As Longacre applies his theory to Mark, he notes that each of the ninety-one pericopes, or episodes, identified by Nestle-Aland contains certain introductory elements that may be temporal, locative, circumstantial, or participant-presentative.[32] These pericopes form the basis of the plot structure; as episodes, they are at "the lowest level of discourse embedding."[33] From these episodes, Longacre constructs Mark's plot, first into a larger plot of six major episodes which contain within them several other layers of discourse, or sub-plots. Longacre's general overview of Mark's plot is as follows. He includes the subplot of Episode 6 because it contains within it the climax and denouement for the whole gospel:

27. Longacre, "Top-Down," 140–68.
28. Ibid., 141.
29. Ibid., 144.
30. Ibid., 141.
31. Ibid., 142.
32. Ibid., 145.
33. Ibid.

TITLE/APERTURE of whole 1:1	
STAGE	The ministry of John the Baptist: 1:2–8
EPISODE 1	(INCITING INCIDENT): 1:9–13 The Spirit comes on Jesus and confirms his Sonship, the heavens are 'split' 1:9–11 The Spirit 'drives' him out to be tempted by the Devil 1:12–13
EPISODE 2	The rise to prominence 1:14–5:43
EPISODE 3	At full tide, Jesus a power figure and nurturer 6:1–8:26
EPISODE 4	(PIVOTAL): 'Who is he?' 8:27–9:50
EPISODE 5	The last journey to Jerusalem 10:1–52
EPISODE 6	(PEAK): 11:1–16:8
Episode 1	(Inciting Incident): The Triumphal Entry 11:1–11
Episode 2	(The DIDACTIC PEAK of the whole book): Teaching amid controversy 11:12–13:37
Episode 3	(The ACTION PEAK of the whole book): Events which culminate in the crucifixion (CLIMAX) and resurrection (DENOUMENT) 14:1–16:8[A]

A. Ibid., 147.

Rather than a prologue, the narrative of Mark is set by the stage which contains the brief story about John the Baptist. The plot of Mark truly begins with the inciting incident of Jesus' baptism by John in the Jordan (1:9–13). Longacre maintains that the baptism and the temptation should be held together as one episode due to the presence of the Spirit, the identification of Jesus as the Son of God, and the presence of Satan which point to the larger themes of the gospel: the transfiguration (Pivotal Episode) and the identity of Jesus further highlighted at the crucifixion (Climax); and the emphasis on exorcism which highlights Jesus' conflict with the establishment of the day.

Longacre bases his theory of plot on conflict, but his analysis of the events as they occur in Mark serves to highlight the work and identity of Jesus as a Son. "The putting together of 8:27–9:50 as central and pivotal to the whole work, connecting plausibly with the baptism and temptation in the Inciting Incident and with the trial scene at the end, foregrounds the question of the identity of Jesus."³⁴ His analysis also emphasizes Jesus' sonship in connection with discipleship, though minimally, as Longacre also maintains a christological focus in his plot analysis. The central aspects of Longacre's plot include the identity of Jesus at the beginning, middle, and end, but they also include Jesus' action and teaching. Jesus' identity as a Son and his teaching of disciples as the Son lead to his death, and ultimately, resurrection.

Each of the above-mentioned approaches to Markan plot provides an actual discussion on the theory of plot and some sort of plot analysis. However, Van Eck and Van Aarde abandon plot to focus on other aspects of narrative, especially point of view, to analyze the gospel. Danove and Naluparayil maintain a structuralist approach to the gospel, and so the structure of the narrative supersedes the arrangement of events in terms of plot. Finally, Longacre offers an analysis that ties more closely to his theoretical approach to plot. The plot structures or analyses offered assert a christological focus rather than a balance of Christology and discipleship.

In my own analysis of the narrative, the Gospel of Mark leads the reader/audience through a series of events that focus on the ministry of Jesus in Galilee and encounters with other characters. The gospel's ordering provides the implied reader with certain knowledge about the plot, characters, and setting of the gospel. Chief of these is the knowledge in Mark 1:1, that Jesus Christ is the Son of God.³⁵ Before the reader meets any characters, even before the reader finds out where the story takes place, the narrator identifies Jesus as the Son of God. This immediately gives rise to the significance of the sonship of Jesus and its centrality to the unfolding of the plot of the gospel. The phrase evokes images from the traditions of kingship and sonship in the Hebrew Bible which establish agency as a key element of what sonship connotes,³⁶ but it also echoes the imperial context of Mark and

34. Ibid., 163.

35. For a recent and comprehensive analysis of the textual controversy of Mark 1:1, see Wasserman, "The 'Son of God,'" 20–50. Wasserman argues that the longer reading of Mark 1:1 should stand. The majority of ancient manuscripts, the church fathers, and early versions of the New Testament support the longer reading. He divides the controversy into two main readings: (1) Ἀρχὴ τοῦ εὐαγγελίου Ἰησοῦ Χριστοῦ (τοῦ) υἱοῦ (τοῦ) θεοῦ (ℵ¹ A B D L W Δ ƒ1.13 33 579 582ᶜ 820ᶜ 1555ᶜ 𝔐 a aur b c d f ff² l q r¹ VL9A vg syᵖ·ᵖʰ·ʰ got saᵐˢˢ bo geo² aeth arabᵐˢˢ slav Irˡᵃᵗ Sever Cyr Ps-Ath Ps-Vic; Ambr Chrom Hierᵖᵗ Aug) (2) Ἀρχὴ τοῦ εὐαγγελίου Ἰησοῦ Χριστοῦ (ℵ* Θ 28ᶜ 530 582* 820* 1021 1436 1555* 1692 2430 2533 l2211 syᵖᵃˡ saᵐˢ arm geo¹ arabᵐˢ Orᵍʳ·ˡᵃᵗ Serap Bas CyrJ AstI Hes; Vic Hierᵖᵗ). Wasserman likewise insists that internal evidence within Mark also indicates the longer reading based on ancient practices of titling works including υἱός language and the thematic purposes of Mark. If the title to the gospel is rejected, the first appearance of the reference of Jesus as God's Son occurs at his baptism in 1:9–13.

36. See Collins and Collins, *King and Messiah*, 1–38.

the status of the Roman emperor as a *divi filius*, or son of god. It will be only in the turn of events, actions, and encounters of the characters that what it means for Mark to declare Jesus as the Son of God in 1:1 will be revealed.

Although a large part of this study will approach the narrative and the plot episodically, it is important to remember these episodes occur within a larger, cohesive narrative. Within this cohesive narrative is an overarching structure that is central to this interpretation. Seeing the plot as an elaboration of 1:1, I divide the gospel into four distinct narrative blocks that are marked by three events (kernels) experienced by Jesus.[37] Chatman notes that kernels function as hinges or branching points in the narrative. They further the plot by raising and answering questions. Later kernels act as consequences of earlier kernels. Minor plot events, or satellites, function to elaborate and complete the kernel.[38] In my interpretation, the central events that drive the plot of Mark include Jesus' baptism (1:9–13), the first passion prediction and the transfiguration (8:31—9:10), and the crucifixion (15:21–41). The rest of the plot derives itself from, leads from, or leads to these main events. The baptism identifies Jesus in similar terms to the incipit and inaugurates his ministry. There is then a series of scenes that comprise calling disciples, teaching disciples, healings, miracles, and conflicts with local leaders that leads up to the first passion prediction and the transfiguration that anticipates his future vindication in the resurrection and return. At this point, there is a shift. Jesus' identity as God's Son is defined further by predictions of his suffering, death, resurrection, and return. Jesus performs only one more healing as he and the disciples leave Galilee and head to Jerusalem where Jesus will be crucified. There is still a series of teachings and conflicts with the Jerusalem leaders; however, these events drive the characters toward Jesus' arrest and crucifixion, where Jesus is identified once more as God's Son at his death. The narrative concludes with the proclamation of Jesus' resurrection which provides a step toward the vindication anticipated at the transfiguration and fulfills the prophecies about Jesus' crucifixion.

---

37. See Myers's discussion dividing Mark's narrative into two distinct books (with caveats) in *Binding the Strong Man*, 109–21. Tolbert, *Sowing the Gospel*, 107, provides a summary of a division of Mark into two parts weighing heavily on the geography of the narrative: the first part of Mark happens in and around Galilee, while the second heads toward and takes place in Jerusalem, 113–14. The moment of division occurs around the confession of Peter in Mark 8:27–30. This moment is immediately followed by the first passion prediction and thereafter by the transfiguration.

38. Chatman, *Story and Discourse*, 53–54.

The First Kernel: Baptism (1:9-13)

The first kernel begins at Jesus' baptism in Mark 1:9-13.[39] Jesus comes up out of the water, "καὶ φωνὴ ἐγένετο ἐκ τῶν οὐρανῶν· σὺ εἶ ὁ υἱός μου ὁ ἀγαπητός, ἐν σοὶ εὐδόκησα." "And a voice came from the heavens, 'You are my son, the beloved one, in you I am well pleased.'"[40] A voice (of God) comes out of the sky and declares Jesus as God's Son, reiterating the claim in 1:1 and designating him as an agent of God's purposes, chiefly to establish God's empire (βασιλεία τοῦ θεοῦ) (1:14-15).[41] The baptism functions as a point of departure, moving the action away from the work of John the Baptist and launching the work of Jesus. This kernel inaugurates the ministry of Jesus and the reader enters into the miracles and healings, the calling of the disciples, and the teaching of crowds in the region of Galilee. It also raises the question of what it means to be God's beloved Son which will be elaborated in satellites and subsequent kernels. The minor plot events, or satellites, that find their anchor in the baptism of Jesus are a result of and elaboration of the inauguration of his ministry by the revelation of his identity as God's Son. As Robert Longacre has demonstrated, these events are aligned in such a way that Jesus' identity continues to unfold through his actions and encounters with others.[42]

The unfolding of Jesus' ministry as the Son of God begins as he enters Galilee preaching the gospel and claiming that the empire of God has come near (1:14-15). In a series of satellites, Jesus works as God's agent to secure God's purposes, including bringing God's realm, or empire (βασιλεία), into the world. As the agent of God's purposes, Jesus procures disciples in 1:16-20 and begins teaching in the local synagogue in 1:21-22. He demonstrates authority as God's agent over unclean spirits and illness. In Capernaum, Jesus heals a man in the synagogue (1:21-28); he heals Simon Peter's mother-in-law (1:29-31); and he heals a leper in a neighboring town (1:40-45). Back in Capernaum, crowds gather for healing, but the final story recounted is the healing of the paralytic (2:1-12).

The next satellites demonstrate Jesus' authority as God's Son over traditional expectations and the law. Jesus is seen eating with his disciple Levi and other tax collectors (2:13-17); people notice that Jesus and his disciples

---

39. The first narrative block, 1:2-8 functions as a prologue and satellite to the first kernel giving rise to the circumstances of Jesus' baptism in the Jordan by John the Baptist.

40. All translations are my own unless otherwise indicated.

41. I will translate βασιλεία as "empire" rather than "kingdom" to emphasize the juxtaposition of God's empire with that of Rome's.

42. Longacre, "Narrative Analysis," 149-53.

do not fast (2:18–22); Jesus and his disciples do not follow the standard Sabbath traditions (2:23–28). In each of these scenes, Jesus responds with an element of teaching that further demonstrates his authority as God's Son over the law and tradition. Next, Jesus heals the man with the withered hand in the synagogue on the Sabbath as a culmination of these first two demonstrations of authority (3:1–6). The series of satellites concludes with a summary of Jesus' healing, his popularity, and his identification as the Son of God (3:7–12). Just as these satellites began with the call of disciples, so it is now followed by the call of the twelve, with a further assertion of Jesus' claim on people's lives in the calling of disciples (3:13–19).

It is important to note at this point one rhetorical device that highlights the ordering of events in the Gospel of Mark: his use of "sandwich stories" or chiasm.[43] Gordon Lathrop refers to these structures as circles. "It becomes clear that the use of this circular mode, this A-B-A structure of narrative, does not only convey a passage of time. It intends to convey important meaning by its juxtapositions."[44] In the instance of the healing and teaching stories, they are "sandwiched" by the calling of disciples. Jesus' identity as a Son and his authority over evil spirits, illness, law, and tradition are intricately bound with his relationship to his disciples. It is within the context of calling disciples that Jesus demonstrates his authority as a Son by demonstrating his power over spiritual and physical realities. Teaching and healing will become two elements of discipleship.

The next sequence of events in Mark 3:20–35 is another sandwich story that further highlights Jesus' mission as God's Son, especially in relationship to the role of the new family of disciples Jesus has called over and against Jesus' original kin (3:13–19) and functions as a satellite by elaborating the new identity of recipients of Jesus' ministry. After the call of the twelve disciples, Jesus returns home. He is immediately sought out by the crowds, but this time, his family (οἱ παρ' αὐτοῦ) hears of it and they seek to restrain him. Before his family interacts with Jesus, the scribes from Jerusalem come and accuse Jesus of being ruled by Beelzebul and casting out demons by

---

43. Edwards argues that "Mark sandwiches one passage into the middle of another with an intentional and discernible *theological purpose*. The technique is, to be sure, a literary technique, but its purpose is theological; that is, the sandwiches emphasize the major motifs of the Gospel, especially the meaning of faith, discipleship, bearing witness, and the dangers of apostasy" (Edwards, "Markan Sandwiches," 196). In addition, Edwards suggests that the middle of the story provides the definition to the theological purpose of the interpolation. Edwards does not identify Mark 1:16–3:19 as a sandwich story, but he does identify the pericope immediately following as one. See also Shepherd, *Markan Sandwich Stories* for a detailed analysis of intercalations throughout the Gospel of Mark.

44. Lathrop, *Four Gospels on Sunday*, 75.

the power of Satan. Jesus responds by claiming that an empire divided and a house divided cannot stand. "How can Satan cast out Satan?" The scene ends with the arrival of Jesus' mother and brothers. But, Jesus does not acknowledge them as family. Instead, he declares that whoever follows the will of God will be his brother, mother, and sister. It is not Satan who establishes the household and empire of God; rather it is Jesus the Son and those who do the will of the Father that create the new household of disciples.

Mark 4 comprises the next satellite elaborating the kernel of Jesus' baptism and identity as the Son or agent of God's reign. Jesus begins teaching the disciples and the crowds in parables. Although the disciples respond with incomprehension, Jesus insists that he is teaching them the secrets of the empire of God; part of the proclamation of the empire of God is the revelation of that empire by its agent, by the Son himself. The primary message of the empire of God is the proclamation and reception of the word of God. This empire seems small and insignificant, like a small seed, and yet it will grow great through proper understanding and reception.

Immediately following the teaching in parables, Jesus demonstrates his authority as God's Son over nature and again over demons. In Mark 4:35–41, Jesus and the disciples plan to cross the Sea of Galilee. In the middle of the night a great storm arises and the disciples fear for their lives. Jesus is powerful enough that he stops the storm. The disciples' response demonstrates both the extent of Jesus' authority as the Son ("Who then is this that even the wind and the seas obey him?" 4:41) as well as their lack of comprehension. On the other side of the lake, Jesus and the disciples encounter the Gerasene demoniac. This demon identifies Jesus as υἱὲ τοῦ θεοῦ τοῦ ὑψίστου (Son of the Most High God, 5:7) agreeing with and contextualizing the divine disclosure at Jesus' baptism. Jesus heals the man of the demon named Legion and sends it into a herd of pigs that then drown themselves in the sea. The shift in geographical location suggests Jesus' authority as God's Son over demons (Legion) also extends beyond his own cultural and geographical setting.

Jesus and the disciples return to the other side of the sea and there is another sandwich story in Mark 5:22–43 which elaborates Jesus' identity as God's Son in further healings. This is the story of the woman with the flow of blood surrounded by the healing of Jairus's daughter. The satellite begins as Jesus reenters Galilee and is immediately approached by Jairus, a synagogue leader who asks healing for his little girl. On the way to Jairus's home, he encounters the woman with the flow of blood who is healed upon touching his garment. Again, as the Son of God, Jesus exercises his authority to heal. In dismissing the woman he addresses her with a kinship term, "daughter" (θυγάτηρ) in 5:34. While Jesus is still talking to the woman, people came from Jairus's house to tell him, "ἡ θυγάτηρ σου ἀπέθανεν" ("Your daughter has died.") Jesus tells Jairus not to fear, but simply to believe. Jesus raises the daughter of Jairus, again not only exercising his authority as God's agent and Son to heal, but displaying his authority over death itself.

Elements in each story serve to emphasize one another and connect the stories together. In the instance of the woman with the flow of blood and the healing of Jarius's daughter, the evident connection is that Jesus provides healing to two female characters. Moreover, he provides healing through touch: the woman with the flow of blood touches the hem of Jesus' garment, while he takes the little girl by the hand and tells her to wake up. Perhaps less noticeable but equally significant is the use of the term ἡ θυγάτηρ, daughter. Jairus, a community leader and a man with social and religious status, tells Jesus that his daughter is ill (5:22–23). When Jesus heals her, he takes with him Peter, James, John, and Jairus and his wife. The little girl has the protection and advocacy of her father and subsequently Jesus. The woman with the flow of blood, however, has no name and no status, and because of her illness, she is ritually impure.[45] The disciples do not even recognize she is present due to the crowd. When she comes forward and confesses to Jesus, he draws her into relationship and calls her "daughter" (5:34). The woman with the flow of blood comes under the protection and care of Jesus just as Jairus has provided for his daughter. Mary Ann Tolbert suggests the unlikely circumstance that the woman was excluded from her community and family due to her illness; however, she does note, "The woman is now under the protection of a new 'father,' Jesus, who has the power to heal her and to intercede for her in the public realm."[46] In calling the woman "daughter," Jesus as the Son recognizes their common kinship.

In juxtaposition to restoring kinship to the woman with the flow of blood and the little girl, Jesus returns to Nazareth and his own kinship group in Mark 6:1–6. But he is not welcome and they are offended at his claim to authority since the people of Nazareth know Jesus' family. In Nazareth, Jesus is identified as the son of Mary and the brother of James, Joses, Judas, Simon, and some unnamed sisters. The lack of reference to Jesus' father could be considered an insult to Jesus by the residents of Nazareth inferring that Jesus' father is unknown or Jesus is illegitimate.[47] Ironically,

---

45. She is not necessarily separated from her family or community; in Mark she is in the midst of a big crowd. For a discussion on the woman with the flow of blood in Matt 9:18–26 (with implication for Mark) and the state of her "impurity" and its Jewish background see Levine, "Discharging Responsibility," 379–97.

46. Tolbert, "Mark," 355–56.

47. Collins, *Mark: A Commentary*, 291. There is some textual variance in 6:3. "The earliest surviving MS (fragmentary) of Mark, $\mathfrak{P}^{45vid}$, a number of miniscules (f^{13} et al.),

the reader knows the divine disclosure of Jesus' identity as God's Son established in 1:11.

The next three satellites comprise another intercalation which associates suffering and sacrifice with following Jesus the Son. In 6:7-13, Jesus has again left his original kinship group and he calls his disciples in order to send them out two by two to begin doing the work that he started: casting out demons and healing the sick. This discipleship is interrupted by a story about Herod and John the Baptist in 6:14-29 that shows opposition to the mission alliance of John, Jesus, and disciples. When Herod hears about Jesus, he believes that John the Baptist has been raised from the dead. Mark then proceeds to relate the beheading of John due to Herodias's grudge against him. John the Baptist proclaims the truth about the couple's improper kinship, and he is arrested and subsequently killed for his actions. His disciples come and take his body away for burial. The scene ends and the narrative shifts back to the return of Jesus' disciples in 6:30-32. They tell Jesus all they did, and he invites them to come away and rest awhile.

Instead of resting, Jesus and the disciples are followed by a large crowd in 6:33-44. This and the subsequent scenes demonstrate Jesus' sonship in terms of power, authority, and compassion. Jesus has compassion for the crowd and he begins teaching them. Out in the wilderness, there is no easy access to food. From the little bread and fish that they have, Jesus feeds five thousand men, not including women and children, thus displaying his authority over food access and supply. After the meal, Jesus sends the disciples in a boat to Bethsaida while he goes to pray. In the middle of the night he appears to walk on the water toward the disciples in the boat. Again, Jesus demonstrates his power over the sea and yet the disciples still do not understand. The chapter ends with people bringing their sick to Jesus for healing, echoing 1:34.

Mark 7:1-23 portrays another meeting with the Pharisees previously encountered in 2:16-28. They see Jesus and the disciples eating without washing their hands. This provides another opportunity for Jesus to demonstrate his authority as God's Son over the law, and in this instance within the context of kinship and the fourth commandment of honoring mother and father. Jesus suggests that the Pharisees' effort to follow God has resulted in their failure to follow God and his command for right relationship with family. The scene ends with instruction for the disciples where Jesus explains that evil comes from within a person.

---

and some early versions (it vg^{mss} bo^{mss}) read τοῦ τέκτονος υἱὸς καί '(Is not this the) son of the carpenter and (of Mary),'" Collins, *Mark: A Commentary,* 287-88nd. She suggests that there could have been assimilation of Mark to the parallel in Matt 13:55 or to correct the derogatory nature of referring to Jesus' mother rather than his father.

In chapters 7 and 8, there is a series of healing and feeding scenes that echo and continue to emphasize both Jesus' authority as God's Son and to demonstrate power over demons, illness, and nature and their conjunction with discipleship. He encounters a Syrophoenician woman who seeks healing for her demon-possessed daughter. In verbal repartee, the woman challenges Jesus' initial rejection and wins healing for her daughter. On his way back to Galilee, Jesus enters the Decapolis where he heals a deaf and mute man and again astounds the people with his power in healing. He again demonstrates his authority as God's Son over food access in the feeding of the multitudes where Jesus feeds four thousand with seven loaves of bread and a few fish. In Dalmanutha, Jesus and the disciples encounter the Pharisees, who, ironically, ask for a sign from heaven. This begins a period of instruction for the disciples who still do not understand Jesus' power and authority. This scene takes place while they are traveling by boat on the Sea of Galilee immediately after Jesus has fed the multitudes. And yet, the disciples fail to understand Jesus' power over the sea, his authority over the law, and his ability to provide for many.

The healing of the deaf mute in the Decapolis in chapter 7 may also be viewed as the beginning of another sandwich story which surrounds the feeding of the four thousand and ends with the healing of the blind man in Bethsaida in 8:22–26. In both stories, Jesus uses the laying on of hands and his saliva to provide healing. The power demonstrated in the healing of the deaf and blind is juxtaposed with the feeding of the multitude and the instruction to the disciples and their failure to understand his power and authority.

Verse 8:27 begins the transition to the next kernel in the Gospel of Mark. Jesus is with the disciples on their way to Caesarea Philippi and he asks them about his identity. Peter identifies Jesus as the Messiah which echoes 1:1 in part, but not completely. Peter fails to acknowledge Jesus as God's Son and so is not aligned with God's declaration in 1:9–13 of Jesus as God's Son. Perhaps it is due to Peter's partial confession, but Jesus commands the disciples not to tell anyone about him. Nevertheless, the scene has posed the crucial question of Jesus' identity; Jesus will provide crucial information regarding his sonship in the second kernel of the gospel.

The Second Kernel: Passion Prediction and Transfiguration (8:31– 9:10)

The second kernel of Mark comprises 8:31–9:10. Jesus provides the first prediction of his crucifixion immediately followed by his transfiguration.

Chatman indicates that kernels function as hinges and branching points in a narrative. Kernels act as points of departure to move the action forward. Kernels further the plot by raising and answering questions. Later kernels are often consequences of previous kernels. Satellites further elaborate and complete kernels.[48] The passion prediction and transfiguration become a branching point in the plot of Mark and move the plot events toward Jerusalem and the crucifixion. Up to this point, the first kernel has declared Jesus' identity and the satellites have elaborated what his sonship looks like in specific scenes. Jesus has been exercising his authority as God's Son, demonstrating his command over nature, the law and tradition, unclean spirits, and illnesses. Jesus has gained in popularity and prestige (4:1; 6:54–56). Jesus has also gained enemies who view him as a blasphemer and lawbreaker (2:7, 24) and who seek to accuse and destroy him (3:2, 6). The passion prediction alongside the transfiguration affirms Jesus' role as God's agent as he was identified at the baptism in 1:9–13, but it provides a further answer to the question of Jesus' identity. Thus it reveals that Jesus comes to give up his own life and to call disciples to do the same. Jesus makes it clear that as disciples, they must understand that their Messiah is one who will suffer and be put to death. And furthermore, as disciples of Jesus, they must be prepared to give up their own lives for the sake of the gospel, for that is how they will save their lives. Although Peter refers to Jesus as the Messiah, Jesus refers to himself as the Son of Man. As the Son, Jesus will undergo suffering and be put to death, but he will also return in glory with the Father and his shame and suffering will be vindicated. Just the same, as Jesus foretells the (apparent) shameful death of the Son, he also claims the honorable glory that the Son will receive.

Therefore, this second kernel embraces both the first passion prediction and the transfiguration. In Mark 9:2–10, Jesus leads three of his disciples up a mountain and undergoes transfiguration before them. This event echoes the baptism with similar characteristics. καὶ ἐγένετο νεφέλη ἐπισκιάζουσα αὐτοῖς, καί ἐγένετο φωνὴ ἐκ τῆς νεφέλης· οὗτός ἐστιν ὁ υἱός μου ὁ ἀγαπητός, ἀκούετε αὐτοῦ. (And a cloud came and covered them, and a voice came from the cloud, "This is my son, the beloved one, listen to him," 9:7). There is a voice (of God) from the sky declaring Jesus as his Son. Again, Mark provides christological revelation with Son of God language which serves to echo the claims made at the baptism (1:11).

The passion prediction and transfiguration serve as a hinge in Mark's plot to force the action of the plot toward a particular end: even as the question of Jesus' identity as God's Son is answered in the transfiguration, the

48. Chatman, *Story and Discourse*, 53.

passion prediction indicates his identity as a Son will lead him to the crucifixion (15:21–41), the final kernel. In the first kernel of Jesus' baptism, the knowledge of his sonship was limited; in the second kernel the knowledge of Jesus' sonship is revealed to three disciples of Jesus who witness the transfiguration. At the baptism, only the reader and Jesus are aware of Jesus' identity as God's Son or agent. At the transfiguration, God tells Peter, James, and John that Jesus is his Son and instructs the disciples to listen to Jesus. This instruction grants further authority to Jesus as God's chosen agent, as well as underscores what Jesus has just revealed about his identity in relation to his crucifixion and resurrection (8:31–38). Now, three disciples receive fully the identity of Jesus as God's Son, yet this reception occurs alongside instruction regarding Jesus' arrest, suffering, and death, which the disciples, represented by Peter, had rejected. In addition, Jesus appears to Peter, James, and John in a blazingly white form accompanied by Moses and Elijah (9:3–4). Not only does the transfiguration echo the baptism, but it also stands at the center of the gospel as an anticipatory vision of the resurrected Jesus, signaled in 8:31, and of his triumphant return after his crucifixion, the third kernel. The kernel of passion prediction and transfiguration also raises further questions about Jesus: Are Jesus' predictions reliable? How will the crucifixion occur? Will he die at the hands of the Jerusalem authorities? Will the anticipatory vision of Jesus as triumphant Son of God be fulfilled? The third kernel, the crucifixion, addresses these questions.

In the immediate satellite following the second kernel when Jesus, Peter, James, and John descend from the mountain, Jesus instructs them to tell no one about what they saw. The Son and his disciples arrive upon a scene involving another son who is suffering from spirit possession. The father of the boy is his advocate who seeks healing. The disciples are unable to heal the boy, but upon the confession of faith from the father, Jesus commands the spirit to come out of the boy and the boy is restored to health. As a satellite, this scene corroborates the knowledge of Jesus' authority and sonship just revealed in the transfiguration by displaying his power over the spirit and ability to restore the son to his father. Jesus and the disciples depart for Capernaum. On the way, but privately, Jesus gives his second passion prediction to the disciples. This second passion prediction is also a satellite of the transfiguration; in juxtaposition with christological identification and glorification, it elaborates the means to glory and vindication. The agent of God must suffer and be killed and then be glorified. Again, the passion prediction, which functions as a summary of the gospel's plot in the second half, is accompanied by instruction to the disciples to sacrifice and serve others to the point of welcoming a child (παιδίον) with little or no social status as equivalent to welcoming Jesus the Son and God the Father. After further instruction to the disciples, Jesus encounters the Pharisees in 10:1–12. They ask him about marriage and divorce. Again, Jesus demonstrates his authority over Jewish law and tradition, indicating even stricter guidelines regarding marriage and divorce. Again, Jesus instructs the disciples, as in 9:37, to let the children come, for they are the true heirs to the empire of God. He adds that in order to inherit the empire and eternal life one must sell one's possessions and give the money to the poor. Although the disciples have left their original kinship systems for Jesus' sake, he promises that they will receive kinship abundantly both now and in the age to come. The emphasis on status and sacrifice arises out of the gospel's second kernel, namely the first passion prediction and the transfiguration (8:31–9:10). The Son of God, and the disciples, will not receive glory without suffering and sacrifice, including a loss of honor and even life.

After this instruction on discipleship and kinship, Jesus predicts his death and resurrection for the third time in 10:32–34, again emphasizing the second kernel's link between glory as witnessed at the transfiguration but achieved through suffering and sacrifice. Jesus' passion prediction is accompanied by instruction on discipleship. It is important to note that another rhetorical device Mark utilizes in the plot of the gospel is the repetition of similar episodes in series of three. The three passion predictions (8:31; 9:30–31; 10:32–34) are quite similar in that Jesus is instructing his disciples about what is to happen to him, resulting in their misunderstanding. In the first two instances, he also tells them he will rise again after three days thus underscoring the anticipatory vision of resurrection in the transfiguration. These series emphasize and bring a focus onto their subject matter; in the case of the passion predictions, the emphasis of instruction about the Son and suffering indicate that kinship and discipleship will lead to death. The latter two predictions serve as satellites leading up to and away from the first passion prediction and the transfiguration, the second kernel in Mark, by tempering the glorified identity of God's agent. The question posed by the first kernel–what does Jesus' sonship involve?–is here answered in terms not just of service (healing, feeding, forming disciples) but also in terms of suffering and death to establish God's empire. In the instances of the passion predictions, the passion itself; the instruction to the disciples; the process of arrest, trial, and crucifixion; and his self-reference as the Son of Man are all emphasized and focus the audiences' attention on those elements leading to a clearer understanding of Jesus' role as God's agent and his call to the family of disciples. The plot itself, the arrangement of events, in this case in a series of three, highlights the significance of kinship and its affiliation with discipleship.

After the third passion prediction (10:32-34), the disciples again fail to understand the nature of discipleship with Jesus, and they seek to gain power and honor for themselves in 10:35-45. Jesus instructs them that discipleship requires slavery to others. Here again, Jesus refers to himself as the Son of Man who came to serve which tempers the glory seen at the transfiguration. Jesus is God's Son who will be glorified, and yet glory assumes the face of slavery. After this, Jesus and the disciples arrive in Jericho on their way to Jerusalem. Bartimaeus, the blind beggar, seeks Jesus for healing, calling him "Son of David" in 10:46-52. With a title of honor, Bartimaeus echoes the honor Jesus received at the transfiguration and also foreshadows Jesus' triumphant entry into Jerusalem. As soon as he receives healing, Jesus instructs him to depart, but instead, Bartimaeus follows him on the way.

Mark 11 comprises the arrival of Jesus into Jerusalem and functions as another satellite of the passion prediction and transfiguration kernel. Jesus enters the city like his ancestor David did, upon a colt in a triumphal manner (11:7-10). On the next day, in triumph and glory as God's agent, Jesus enters the temple, and when he sees the people selling items, he drives them out claiming, οὐ γέγραπται ὅτι ὁ οἶκος μου οἶκος προσευχῆς κληθήσεται πᾶσιν τοῖς ἔθνεσιν; ὑμεῖς δὲ πεποιήκατε αὐτὸν σπήλαιον λῃστῶν. (Is it not written, "My house will be called a house of prayer for all the nations?" But you have made it a den of thieves.) This scene elaborates the second kernel by demonstrating Jesus' violent stance as God's agent, who interprets the scripture and exercises authority over the cultic practices of the Jerusalem temple by allowing no one to sell or buy any more goods to offer sacrifice. Jesus' violent actions also represent a challenge and threat to the Jerusalem authorities, elaborate the second kernel of Jesus' prediction of his arrest, and further the plot toward the crucifixion and final kernel of Mark.

On their way into Jerusalem on the next morning, Jesus offers his disciples instruction on prayer. He encourages them to have faith but also to offer forgiveness in prayer, so that the Father in heaven may offer forgiveness to them. This is immediately followed by Jesus' encounter with the priests, the scribes, and the elders in the temple. They want to know by whose authority Jesus teaches. But by a challenge-riposte, he does not answer them.[49] Instead, chapter 12 begins with Jesus telling the parable of the tenants and

---

49. Malina and Rohrbaugh, *Social-Science Commentary*, 334-35. In the competition for honor challenge-riposte was a central and public game. "The game consists of (1) a challenge (almost any word, gesture, action) that might undermine the honor of another person and (2) a response that answers in equal measure or ups the ante (and thereby challenges in return). Both positive (gifts, compliments) and negative (insults, dares, public questioning) challenges must be answered to avoid a serious loss of face" (*Social-Science Commentary*, 334).

the vineyard that condemns the Jerusalem authorities. The implication is that Jesus is the heir, the Jerusalem authorities are the wicked tenants, and the temple is the vineyard, and the master will come and destroy the tenants. In further elaboration of the second kernel, Jesus as the Son has come to claim his inheritance, but as his previous passion predictions have indicated and as the Jerusalem authorities have plotted, Jesus will be arrested and killed. Jesus stands as the heir in the parable, the heir who should receive glory and honor as he received it at the transfiguration. Yet, the Jerusalem authorities refuse to ally themselves with God's perspective (as the gospel presents it). The heir receives suffering and death as the passion predictions indicate; his vindication will come in the form of vengeance from the owner (father) upon the tenants.

Alongside Jesus' claim to authority in the Jerusalem temple, he is questioned about his allegiance to the Roman emperor. The Pharisees and the Herodians are trying to trap him in another challenge-riposte exchange. They are unsuccessful and are astounded when he answers their query by apparently honoring God *and* the emperor. This satellite reflects the second kernel by continuing to demonstrate Jesus' honor and authority as God's agent as it was designated at the transfiguration. This is followed by a conversation with the Sadducees on marriage and the resurrection in 12:18–27. Then, a scribe comes and asks what the greatest commandment is. The chapter ends with teaching about the Son of David, warning against the scribes, and observation of the widow's mite. These satellites of conversation and teaching in the shadow of the Jerusalem temple magnify Jesus' authority as the Son sent to inaugurate the empire of God and also challenge and anger the Jerusalem authorities so that the plot moves ever closer to the crucifixion, the third kernel of Mark's plot.

Jesus continues his instruction to the disciples, specifically Peter, James, John, and Andrew, in the "Little Apocalypse" in Mark 13. Jesus reveals to the three that were present at the transfiguration what is to come. This is the culmination of teaching on discipleship before the events of the passion and crucifixion occur. In addition to the prophecy regarding the fall of the Jerusalem temple, Jesus also foretells the consequences of following him. Discipleship will lead to suffering and arrest. Families will break apart and Judea will be destroyed. But Jesus also promises a victorious return which elaborates the appearance of Jesus at the transfiguration, the second kernel. Mark 13:26 says, "Then they will see the Son of Man coming in the clouds with great power and glory." This image is reminiscent of and an extension of Jesus at the transfiguration where he appears in glory in blazing white alongside Moses and Elijah and then covered in a cloud. The Little Apocalypse reminds the reader of the power and authority granted to Jesus by

God but also looks forward to the resurrection and the triumphant return of Jesus, this time with a stern warning to be ready and to keep awake for no one knows when these events will occur except the Father.

Mark 14 opens with the announcement of the preparation for the Passover and the plot on Jesus' life. This designates the beginning of the end, a movement toward the final kernel of the crucifixion, the fruition of Jesus' predictions, and the culmination of his sonship and call to discipleship. Still, it connects to the second kernel because it echoes the prophecies of arrest and death of the victorious, transfigured Son. The next scene portrays the woman with the alabaster jar who anoints Jesus. Jesus interprets her actions as preparation for his burial, giving her prophetic status. Jesus and the disciples then celebrate the Passover together and share the last supper in 14:12–26. During the meal, Jesus predicts the betrayal that Judas has initiated. When they go out to the Mount of Olives, Jesus tells the disciples that they will all desert him. In a final desperate action, Jesus takes Peter, James, and John and asks them to keep vigil with him three times; and three times, they fail. In fulfillment of Jesus' predictions, Judas returns with a crowd from the chief priests, the scribes, and the elders in order to arrest Jesus.

Throughout his arrest and trial, Jesus maintains his identity as a Son doing God's will. His prediction of abandonment by the disciples culminates in Peter's denial which sandwiches Jesus' exchange with the high priest. As Jesus acknowledges who he is and agrees that he is the Messiah, the Son of the Blessed One,[50] and as he claims that the Son of Man will return in glory and power, Peter denies Jesus three times. The next morning, the Jerusalem leaders bring Jesus to Pilate, the Roman prefect of Judea. Jesus gives no testimony to Pilate, who offers Jesus' release, but the people call for Barabbas's release and Jesus' execution. In an ironic gesture, the soldiers take Jesus, dress him in a purple cloak, crown him with a crown of thorns, and mockingly pay him homage as King of the Jews.

The Third Kernel: Crucifixion (15:21–41)

Jesus is not able to save himself from crucifixion. That is, the crucifixion scene answers several questions raised by the second kernel and moves the action ahead.[51] The second kernel's declaration about Jesus' crucifixion and

---

50 Juel, *Messiah and Temple*, 77–79, contains a discussion on the circumlocution of "the Blessed One" for God. He designates it as a "pseudo-Jewish expression" akin to the common designation of God as "the Holy One, Blessed be He." Matt 26:63 alters the High Priest's words from ὁ υἱὸς τοῦ εὐλογητοῦ to ὁ υἱὸς τοῦ θεοῦ. See also Hahn, *Titles of Jesus*, 284, and Marcus, *Mark 8–16*, 1004.

51. Chatman, *Story and Discourse*, 53.

resurrection raised questions: Are Jesus' predictions reliable? How will the crucifixion occur? Will he die at the hands of the Jerusalem authorities? As the Son, he does not use the authority and power that he displayed throughout his ministry in Galilee. Jesus' predictions are reliable; he is handed over to the Jerusalem authorities, who in turn, hand him over to the Roman authorities for execution. Jesus dies alone, derided by others, and abandoned by his disciples. At the moment of his death there is one final theophany that echoes the baptism and transfiguration and stands as the final kernel in Mark. "Καὶ τὸ καταπέτασμα τοῦ ναοῦ ἐσχίσθη εἰς δύο ἀπ' ἄνωθεν ἕως κάτω. Ἰδὼν δὲ ὁ κεντυρίων ὁ παρεστηκὼς ἐξ ἐναντίας αὐτοῦ ὅτι οὕτως ἐξέπνευσεν εἶπεν· ἀληθῶς οὗτος ὁ ἄνθρωπος υἱὸς θεοῦ ἦν." (And the curtain of the temple was torn in two from top to bottom. And a centurion standing opposite him seeing how he breathed his last said, "Truly this man was the Son of God," 15:38-39). If the temple curtain can be understood cosmically,[52] then the sky opens up and a voice declares that Jesus is God's Son. These elements were also present at the baptism and crucifixion. The kernel of the crucifixion is the final branching point of the plot of Mark, the glorified Son is killed as he prophesied. The major plot action ends for the main character, Jesus, at his death, and the plot moves towards its conclusion. The crucifixion satisfies the question posed by the transfiguration: How will Jesus be glorified? Jesus' death is required for his vindication. The crucifixion also stands as a consequence of the previous kernels and their satellites: God's agent who acts with power and authority is killed by those whom he threatened and who plotted against him.

The resurrection stands as a satellite to the crucifixion and as a conclusion to the gospel, fulfilling the prophecy that Jesus would be killed and raised on the third day. Thus, the resurrection is a step toward the

---

52. Ulansey, "Heavenly Veil Torn," 123-25. In his comparison of the baptism and crucifixion scenes in the Gospel of Mark, Ulansey suggests that the outer curtain of the temple was torn in two. The connection is strengthened when he considered Josephus's description of the outer veil in *War* 5:212, 214: "πρὸ δὲ τούτων ἰσόμηκες καταπέτασμα πέπλος ἦν Βαβυλώνιος ποικιλτὸς ἐξ ὑακίνθου καὶ βύσσου κόκκου τε καὶ πορφύρας θαυμαστῶς μὲν εἰργασμένος οὐκ ἀθεώρητον δὲ τῆς ὕλης τὴν κρᾶσιν ἔχων ἀλλ' ὥσπερ εἰκόνα τῶν ὅλων." (And before these (doors) was a Babylonian woven curtain equal in length, embroidered with blue, and fine linen, both scarlet and purple. On the one hand marvelously made but not without having observed the mixture of material yet as an image of the whole.) "κατεγέγραπτο δ' ὁ πέπλος ἅπασαν τὴν οὐράνιον θεωρίαν πλὴν ζῳδίων" (And the curtain had traced on it all the heavenly sights, except the zodiac). Ulansey concludes, "Thus, upon encountering Mark's statement that 'the veil of the temple was torn in two from top to bottom,' any of his readers who had ever seen the temple or heard it described would instantly have seen in their mind's eye an image of the heavens being torn, and would immediately have been reminded of Mark's earlier description of the heavens being torn at the baptism" ("Heavenly Veil Torn," 125).

vindication and triumph of the Son who was crucified. On the third day, Mary Magdalene, Mary, and Salome go to the tomb to anoint Jesus' body. However, the body is not there and an angel announces that Jesus has been raised from the dead. The angel also instructs them to inform the disciples Jesus has gone on to Galilee where he will meet them. In an odd concluding statement, the women flee without telling anyone anything for they were afraid.[53] The gospel concludes with the knowledge that the Son, although he suffered and was crucified, has been raised from the dead and honor and glory have been restored to him.

In this survey of Mark's plot, the recognition of the three kernels of the baptism, passion prediction and transfiguration, and crucifixion frames the two narrative blocks which revolve as satellites and serve to inform and elaborate the information provided in the kernels. Jesus is the Son of God and the actions and events portrayed as satellites in the gospel serve to highlight that fact. The satellites point to his authority as God's Son and agent over illness, demons, nature, law, and tradition. But, the satellites also indicate the purpose of the Son and his new family of disciples: service leads to suffering and death. And moreover, as in the identification of Jesus as God's honored Son and agent in the three kernels of Mark, the promise of vindication will come with the return of the Son and honor, glory, and family will be restored. The plot is the arrangement of events which, in this case, highlights the life and ministry of the gospel's main character: Jesus and his relation to, and calling of, his disciples. It is to characterization that I now turn.

Character

Seymour Chatman defines character as a paradigm of traits. "The paradigmatic view of character sees the set of traits, metaphorically, as a vertical assemblage intersecting the syntagmatic chain of events that comprise the plot."[54] A character is a composite of his or her traits which a reader notices and assembles from actions, words, relationships, and settings.[55] Elizabeth Struthers Malbon bases her analysis of characters on "what they say and by

---

53. I follow the short ending of Mark that ends at 16:8. Collins states, "The earliest recoverable ending of the Gospel of Mark is ἐφοβοῦντο γάρ ('for they were afraid'). ℵ B et al. attest this ending, which is the shortest... Although some scholars think that the author did not intend to end the Gospel at this point, most agree that this is the earliest ending that can be reconstructed on the basis of the available evidence." Collins, *Mark*, 780–81ng.

54. Chatman, *Story and Discourse*, 127.

55. Carter, *Matthew: Storyteller*, 167.

what they do and by what others (the narrator and other characters) say and do to, about, or in relation to them."[56] As narrative progresses, certain traits are revealed about a character through description and action. The audience utilizes this knowledge of traits to build a character and to account for actions that may occur in the narrative. If an action does not fit into a character's collected traits, then the audience adds another trait.

The main character of the gospel is Jesus and he is introduced, as I have already noted, in Mark 1:1. It will be necessary to pay particular attention to the way the character of Jesus develops through Mark's narrative and how he interacts with his disciples and others he meets along the way. This early characterization is significant in that it is the first description the reader hears about Jesus and it shapes how the audience perceives Jesus throughout the gospel. The sequence in a narrative matters. "In classical narratives, events occur in distributions; they are linked to each other as cause to effect, effects in turn causing other effects, until the final effect."[57] This applies to characterization as well. Jesus is initially defined as a Son; traits of sonship are linked to other traits, and the full extent of Jesus as a Son is revealed through the rest of the gospel; that is, kinship leads to suffering and death for Jesus and, as he teaches, for disciples. A primary function of a son is to be an agent of his father, one who represents and does the work of the father. "The relationships between fathers and sons were the primary connections governing the systems of politics and kinship, which were the two dominant and overlapping 'social spheres' of Roman society."[58] Halvor Moxnes notes that the primary family relationship illustrated in several New Testament texts is the relationship between father and son. "The right of the son to inherit not only the property of his father, but also his role and authority upon his death, emphasises the special character of this relationship."[59] In each kernel of Mark: 1:9–13; 8:31–9:10; 15:21–41, Jesus is identified as God's Son thereby highlighting the role of agency to build God's empire in the establishment of a family of disciples, even in the midst of suffering and death.

In my discussion of Mark's plot, I indicated several times where Jesus' actions designate his authority and agency as a Son. The entire ministry in Galilee serves as satellites to the kernel of God's revelation of Jesus' sonship in 1:9–13 at his baptism, providing the audience with traits of Jesus' sonship. As the Son, Jesus is able to heal people with illness (1:29–31); likewise

---

56. Malbon, *Mark's Jesus*, 14.
57. Chatman, *Story and Discourse*, 46.
58. Peppard, *Son of God in Roman World*, 52.
59. Moxnes, "What is Family?," 34.

he is able to heal people who are possessed by demons or unclean spirits (1:23–26).

As a Son, Jesus also calls for disciples to follow him and to create a new kinship group that announces the empire of God and provides healing and forgiveness (3:16–35). "'Kin' are those who are 'kind' in the sense of 'being of the same sort as oneself, being like oneself.'"[60] In utilizing kinship terms, Mark's Jesus provides a certain characterization to those who follow him. A new kinship group, a new family, is created that sets parameters for the role and function of discipleship and followers of Jesus. DeSilva concludes, "The emerging community of disciples becomes this hundredfold family, a body of people united by a common devotion to Jesus and his teaching, committed to love, support and help one another as completely as any natural family."[61]

In an earlier article on "Reflected Christology," Elizabeth Struthers Malbon highlights a critical point: "The disciples are only disciples in relation to Jesus. A disciple is to be a reflection of his teacher. Thus Jesus' discipleship instruction also implies a 'christology,' a 'christology' that can be reflected in the actions of his followers—the disciples, other followers, and even the implied audience."[62] In her work, Malbon has provided a fuller portrait of discipleship, defining the notion of discipleship as "fallible followers."[63] She regards the major characters (the twelve) and the minor characters (women, exemplary characters) within the characterization of discipleship. If characterization is partly defined by how characters interact with one another, then it makes sense that each character who interacts with Jesus by following him or seeking him out ought to be considered within the category of discipleship. Malbon further illuminates this notion,

> "Reflected christology" suggests that how other characters relate to Jesus may in fact mirror how Jesus relates to God. The mirror the opponents of Jesus hold up is distorted; sensing that Jesus is involved in a conflict of cosmic proportions involving God, they link Jesus with the wrong pole (3:22–30). The mirror the disciples hold up is dim, but good enough to see Jesus–and themselves!; in shock they drop the mirror. The mirror the exemplars hold up is small, but polished; in their brief and specific actions

---

60. DeSilva, *Honor*, 164.
61. Ibid., 197.
62. Malbon, "Reflected 'Christology,'" 133.
63. See Malbon, "Fallible Followers," 29–48.

they mirror how Jesus relates to God and thus to others–or perhaps how Jesus relates to others and thus to God.[64]

Based upon the work of E. M. Forster, Malbon defines characters as flat or round. Flat characters "are simple and consistent."[65] They may appear one time or multiple times in a narrative but always with predictable actions or words. Round characters, on the other hand, "are dynamic and complex. They may reveal new aspects of themselves or even change."[66] Rather than categorize the characters as flat or round, I will be analyzing discipleship in terms of kinship and interaction with Jesus in the following chapters. As Mark's Jesus claims in 3:35, "Whoever does the will of God; this one is my brother and my sister and my mother." Discipleship is characterized within the bounds of kinship as it relates to Christology. Jesus as the Son and designated agent of God teaches, heals, exhorts, and serves those in his kin group. Following Jesus necessitates entry into the family of disciples, even if that means being a fallible follower or an exemplary follower.

Point of View

Not only does the Gospel of Mark emphasize the role of Jesus as the Son by means of the plot and characterization, but the author's point of view also accentuates sonship and kinship. Seymour Chatman defines point of view as "the physical place or ideological situation or practical life-orientation to which narrative events stand in relation."[67] He very clearly states that point of view is a perspective and not an expression. Point of view is expressed by means of voice. Chatman divides point of view into three categories: *perceptual, conceptual,* and *interest*. A perceptual point of view is a literal point of view, i.e., through someone's eyes. A conceptual point of view is a figurative point of view, i.e., through someone's worldview. An interest point of view is transferred, i.e., from someone's self-interest.[68] Narratives can contain any one of these or a combination thereof. Point of view can be complicated by the fact that it is employed by author, narrator, and character in a narrative. All three points of view are included in the Gospel of Mark. Although some characters' views may not see Jesus as the Son, the author, narrator, and character of Jesus do exhibit this point of view. And primarily,

---

64. Malbon, "Reflected 'Christology,'" 137.
65. Malbon, "Narrative Criticism," 10.
66. Ibid., 11.
67. Chatman, *Story and Discourse*, 153.
68. Ibid., 151–52.

"the point of view from which the implied author tells the story is central to evaluating the actions, words, relationships, and values of the gospel's plot and characters."[69]

The initial verses of Mark's gospel provide the perspective, the point of view, about Jesus. In Mark 1:1, the verse that stands over the entire gospel, Jesus is introduced as the messiah, the Son of God. Mark 1:2–3 reinforce the perspective by quoting prophetic scripture: "See, I am sending my messenger to prepare the way of the Lord." Mark 1:4–8 provide the testimony of John who bears witness to Jesus, the Son. At the baptism of Jesus in 1:9–11, as Jesus rises up out the Jordan River, he hears a voice coming out of the heavens declaring him to be a Son. Now, God the Father reinforces the perspective of Jesus' sonship. The chief relationship marker between Jesus and God is Jesus as God's Son. Mark makes this clear in a literal point of view of the audience, Jesus, and God; in the audience's eyes, in Jesus' eyes, and in God's eyes, Jesus is the Son.

Point of view is significant for kinship as it relates to discipleship as well. Initially, Jesus calls his first disciples in Mark 1:16–20. The significance for kinship as it relates to discipleship is that Peter, James, John, and Andrew abandon their original kinship groups and begin to follow Jesus. Original kinship is deserted for a new kinship group who recognize the sonship and agency of Jesus. In Mark 2:13–14, Jesus calls Levi, the son of Alphaeus, away from his duties as a tax collector. Jesus' disciples consist of a group of folks with relatively low status, such as fishermen, or those with a bad reputation, such as tax collectors.[70] In Mark 3:13–19, Jesus calls the twelve. Their purpose is to accompany Jesus but also to be sent out to preach and cast out demons. Jesus the Son extends the agency of his Father to the disciples so that they also have authority to proclaim God's message and to heal. A further reference of discipleship connected with kinship occurs in Mark 3:31–35. Jesus' mother and brothers come to find him. In each verse, "mother and brothers" is repeated so that the audience hears "mother and brother(s)" a total of five times. Here, Mark is emphasizing the words ἡ μήτηρ and οἱ ἀδελφοί in an effort to demonstrate that Jesus is redefining these terms. Mothers and brothers (and sisters) of Jesus are no longer defined by their original kinship relationships but by those who do the will of God. The emphasis on these words and the repetition help the reader to understand

---

69. Carter, *Matthew: Storyteller*, 105.

70. Malina and Rohrbaugh note, "The Greek term *telones* refers to toll collectors employed by those contracting directly with local elites to collect fees on the movement of goods. Many, if not the majority, of toll collectors remained poor. Those who did not were universally presumed to be dishonest" (Malina and Rohrbaugh, *Social-Science Commentary*, 154). For a more detailed treatment of tax collectors, see pp. 415–16.

Jesus' point of view toward discipleship and kinship. Kinship is termed by means of discipleship, and discipleship becomes a new means of kinship.

Setting

The final aspect of narrative theory that is noteworthy for this study on kinship and discipleship in Mark is setting. "The setting 'sets the character off' in the usual figurative sense of the expression; it is the place and collection of objects 'against which' his [sic] actions and passions appropriately emerge."[71] In effect, the setting contributes to the plot and the characters by providing a context, and one that may very well influence how the plot and the characters are perceived by the audience. Context has many dimensions including social, political, geographical, and religious which will affect the plot and characters.

The first half of Mark, which comprises the first narrative block, takes place largely in the geographical region of the Galilee. Within this larger geographical setting, there are more particular settings in which the characters move, act, and encounter one another. Jesus is often seen teaching in the synagogues or by the sea (1:21, 39; 2:13; 3:1, 9). Many healing and teaching events also occur within the setting of the household or a similar kinship setting.[72] As soon as Jesus begins his ministry, the calling of disciples takes place in 1:14–20. Jesus encounters James and John within their kinship setting. They are with their father and his hired workers when Jesus calls them to follow. In this instance, the disciples are abandoning their original kinship network to become followers of Jesus. The first healing that Jesus provides is that of Simon Peter's mother-in-law in the house of Simon and Andrew in 1:29–31. Jesus heals the kinswoman of his disciple in the setting of his own household.[73] In addition, they brought more folks requiring healing to the house in 1:32, "and the whole city gathered at the door." Shortly thereafter in 2:1–12, Jesus provides healing for the paralytic, also ἐν οἴκῳ. Jesus addresses the paralytic as τέκνον, child, adding another layer of kinship to the kinship setting of the household. Jesus defines true kinship over and against original

---

71. Chatman, *Story and Discourse*, 138–39.

72. As noted in chapter 1, Elliott, "Household/Family," 36–63, provides a significant study on the household and family language in the Gospel of Mark. Though a social-science approach, Elliott highlights the significance of the household language in the gospel.

73. It is possible that Jesus lived with Peter in his house in Capernaum or that he established residency elsewhere in the city. See MacAdam, "Domus Domini," 46–76 for a helpful discussion on the archaeological and biblical research about Jesus and Capernaum.

kinship while he is εἰς οἶκον in 3:20–35. Jesus raises the daughter of Jairus in the synaogogue leader's home in the presence of Jesus' closest disciples, Peter, James, and John and the little girl's mother and father in 5:35–43.

Within the second narrative block of Mark, there are three episodes that occur within the setting of the household and are important to kinship and discipleship. In 9:33–37, Jesus and the disciples are in Capernaum, ἐν τῇ οἰκίᾳ and he asks the disciples what they had been arguing about on the way. They were arguing for honor among themselves, but Jesus corrects their desires for greatness in another "marriage" of kinship and discipleship: εἴ τις θέλει πρῶτος εἶναι, ἔσται πάντων ἔσχατος καὶ πάντων διάκονος (If anyone desires to be first, he will be last of all and servant of all). Utilizing an image of the basic structure of the Roman Empire, true discipleship means utter slavery (10:44), as a slave within the household does the menial tasks.[74] However, in the case of discipleship with Jesus, this slavery will lead to honor and greatness. In 10:10, the disciples and Jesus are εἰς τὴν οἰκίαν when they ask Jesus about marriage. In addition to the discussion on marriage, the disciples also complain about children being brought to Jesus. Jesus rebukes them and tells them ἄφετε τὰ παιδία ἔρχεσθαι πρός με, μὴ κωλύετε αὐτά, τῶν γὰρ τοιούτων ἐστὶν ἡ βασιλεία τοῦ θεοῦ (Let the children come to me, do not forbid them, for such is the empire of God). Again, Jesus provides instruction on discipleship within the setting of the household and using the language of kinship. Finally, before Jesus is arrested, tried, and crucified in Jerusalem, he holds the last supper with his disciples in 14:17–26. The last supper is the final scene in which Jesus instills his message and imparts his final teaching to his disciples. Jesus and the disciples share their final meal together in the guest room of a house. Mark 14:14 indicates that the disciples prepare the meal in a guest room. Jesus instructs them to speak to the τῷ οἰκοδεσπότῃ (the master of the house). The final scene of the disciples together with Jesus, with the exception of the garden of Gethsemane, occurs within the setting of the household.

In addition to the immediate setting of the household throughout the gospel, it is also important to lift up the larger setting of the Roman imperial context in which Mark takes place as this will also affect the understanding of Christology and discipleship in the context of kinship. The Gospel of Mark is set in the regions of Galilee and Judea, both of which were under

---

74. As Mark ties slavery (δοῦλος) and servanthood (διάκονος) together in 10:43–44, I view the two terms, if not as synonyms, in very close proximity to one another. Household slaves often lived in close proximity to their owners and served in all aspects of the household's function. See Glancy, *Slavery in Early Christianity*, 45. Moreover, slaves received their social status and social identity from the households who employed them. See Martin, "Slave Families," 207–30.

Roman rule in the first century CE.[75] Not only is the Roman imperial setting of Mark implicit from the external historical reality of the gospel, but there are also several scenes in Mark that explicitly display the Roman imperial setting.[76] Chiefly, Jesus inaugurates and establishes ἡ βασιλεία τοῦ θεοῦ (the empire of God) as his primary purpose (1:15) which is the same designation (ἡ βασιλεία) for the Roman Empire that is present through occupation and rule in Galilee and Judea. The Gerasene demoniac designates himself "Legion" in 5:1–20. When Jesus exorcises the demons, they ask to possess a herd of pigs and subsequently kill themselves in the Sea of Galilee. Legion is also the designation of a group of Roman soldiers and cavalry. Interestingly, "Caesar's tenth legion (Legio X *Fretensis*) had, among other things, the image of a boar on its standards and seals . . . it took part in the first Jewish war and was subsequently stationed in Jerusalem."[77] Mark explicitly acknowledges the setting of the Roman Empire within the scene of Herod's birthday party in 6:14–29. King Herod Antipas inherited the tetrarchy of Galilee from his father, Herod the Great, but it was only with the approval of Caesar Augustus, the emperor of Rome. Mark holds the ruling family responsible for the death of John the Baptist. Another reference to the setting of the Roman Empire made explicit in Mark is the conversation Jesus has with Pharisees and Herodians regarding taxes in 12:13–17. Jesus takes a Roman imperial coin and uses it to make a point about the reign of God (ἡ βασιλεία τοῦ θεοῦ) over and against the reign of the emperor (ἡ βασιλεία τοῦ Καίσαρος). Those listening acknowledge that the face on the coin is that of the emperor. One final reference to Rome is in the trial and crucifixion of Jesus in 15:1–39. Not only must Jesus stand before the Jewish authorities, but because they do not have the power to execute him, he is brought before the governor, the leader of the Roman province of Judea, Pontius Pilate, to be tried and ultimately condemned. Finally, the death of Jesus is witnessed by a Roman soldier, a centurion. The Roman Empire would have influenced the culture and form of society, even in its territories. As a foreground to the Gospel of Mark, the work of Jesus, his relationships with disciples and followers in terms of kinship and his identity as a son stand in stark contrast to the reign of Rome and its claim on discipleship, kinship, and sonship concerning their subjects. The influence of imperial Rome will be addressed further below in the discussion of imperial critical approaches to Mark.

75. Myers, *Binding the Strong Man*, 39–90 provides a detailed overview of the social-historical setting of Mark.

76. Moore, "'My Name Is Legion,'" 24–44 provides a very helpful summary on the imperial references that occur within the Gospel of Mark.

77. Collins, *Mark: A Commentary*, 269.

Plot, character, point of view, and setting are all crucial aspects of studying narrative. By focusing upon these aspects of narrative and the Gospel of Mark, the notion of sonship is clearly a prevalent part of the events that shape the narrative, the identity of the main character, Jesus, and that this sonship is the perspective of the narrator and characters within the gospel. This perspective on Jesus' identity as a son further highlights the definition of discipleship in terms of kinship, especially as it relates to the settings of the household and the larger setting of the Roman Empire.

KINSHIP AND HONOR: SOCIAL-SCIENTIFIC CRITICISM

Social-scientific critical approaches to the New Testament utilize the methodologies present in cultural anthropology in order to interpret and understand scripture, especially the social and cultural structures that may be present within the text.[78] These studies often utilize anthropological models of social relationships to analyze and organize the social structures that are exhibited in the Bible. By doing this, modern readers have a clearer picture of the institutions and social dynamics that were present in first-century Palestine and the Mediterranean region since most often, their institutions and values will differ greatly from those conveyed in the New Testament.[79] Anthropological models may be applied to all aspects of culture and society including politics, religion, economics, and kinship.

Kinship

According to anthropology all human societies utilize kinship as an organizational structure. "That is, they all impose some privileged cultural order over the biological universals of sexual relations and continuous human reproduction through birth."[80] However, kinship structures and relationships have also been extended to others outside blood and marriage relationships. "These include blood, feeding and eating together, nurturance, working together, cooking from the same oven, living together, sharing a code for conduct."[81] This notion of the expansiveness of kinship relationships is evi-

---

78. The seminal work for a social-scientific approach to the New Testament is Malina, *New Testament World*.
79. Hanson and Oakman, *Palestine*, 2.
80. Parkin, *Kinship*, 3.
81. Poetker, "'My Mother,'" 65.

dent in the practice of adoption in Roman society. The legal adoption of one by another made the relationship of father and son legal and binding to the point that kinship based on blood or marriage was irrelevant. Kinship by adoption became equal to conventional kinship within Roman society.[82] "The adopted son was really to become the son and agent of the adoptive father; he was not a substitute son, nor some kind of second-class son. The adopted son also exchanged his own [status] and took over the status of the adoptive father."[83]

Because first-century Roman and Palestinian life revolved largely around kinship, Mark utilizes kinship language to define the primary relationships of both Jesus and the disciples as a means to designate them as honorable characters worthy of status and attention. K. C. Hanson helpfully and concisely describes kinship in connection to sonship: "At the most general level, kinship has two basic social functions: group formation and inheritance."[84] Kinship provides group formation and identity along with the possibility of handing down the family's possessions which include status and honor. Hanson and Oakman utilize the model of Emmanuel Todd to understand kinship in the first-century Mediterranean.[85] Within his seven family types, the endogamous community family is the model that provides the best description of ancient Mediterranean families. Its characteristics include "1) equality between brothers established by inheritance rules; 2) cohabitation of married sons with their parents; and 3) frequent marriage between the children of brothers."[86] Kinship relations were of central significance in the first-century world of Jesus. "In the Mediterranean world of antiquity the extended family meant everything. It was not only the source of one's status in the community, but also functioned as the primary economic, religious, educational, and social network."[87]

Central to this model of kinship is the notion of patrilineal descent. In its most basic definition, "Patrilineal ideology traces a lineage through a line of male descendants. Sons inherit property from their fathers and typically

---

82. A most noteworthy example is the adoption by Julius Caesar of Octavian, his great nephew. For a summary of adoption in Roman society see Peppard, *Son of God in Roman World*, 54–55.

83. Kunst, *Römische Adoption*, 294, quoted by Peppard, *Son of God in Roman World*, 54.

84. Hanson, "Kinship," 66.

85. Hanson and Oakman, *Palestine*, 22–23.

86. Todd, *Explanation of Ideology*, 133, as quoted by Hanson and Oakman, *Palestine*, 23.

87. Malina and Rohrbaugh, *Social-Science Commentary*, 414.

incorporate wives into their own line."[88] Caroline Johnson Hodge notes that there are several normative traits among kinship groups who organize themselves according to patrilineal descent. "(1) Members descend from a common male ancestor; (2) they have inherited the characteristics of that ancestor; (3) they understand themselves as a corporate group linked by some organic connection."[89] Kinship structures based on patrilineal descent ensures that "name, goods, privileges, political, religious and economic duties are passed from father to son."[90] The father-son relationship becomes the primary kinship relationship and the means of establishing and maintaining the kinship group.

The designation "son" occurs within the broader framework of kinship systems. David A. deSilva further develops kinship as it relates to sonship: "A person's family of origin is the primary source for his or her status and location in the world and an essential reference point for the person's identity."[91] In addition to Jesus being identified as the Son of God in the Gospel of Mark, several other characters are identified as "sons" (James and John, 1:19, 3:17, 10:35; Levi, son of Alphaeus, 2:14: James, son of Alphaeus, 3:18; Bartimaeus, 10:46; and Alexander and Rufus, 15:21). "The father's reputation becomes the starting place for the reputation of the children."[92] As a son, Jesus derives his identity, reputation, purpose, authority, and actions from his father, God. His character, his actions, and his interactions with other characters are based in this primary kinship relationship to the Father. In addition, God is presented primarily in terms of his relationship with Jesus. Jesus is the Son of *God* or God is *Father*.[93] God is a father who provides for his children; he gives healing, nourishment, and forgiveness through the work of his Son. God is a listening father (11:25) and will grant vindication to his faithful children (13:26–27). God is also presented as the leader or ruler of the empire (ἡ βασιλεία) that Jesus inaugurates in 1:14–15.[94] God is Ruler and Father made known through the agency of his Son, Jesus.

Not only is Jesus identified in terms of kinship with the Father, but throughout the Gospel of Mark he also designates disciples and those who follow him in terms of kinship. Jesus establishes a new family of mothers,

88. Hodge, *If Sons, then Heirs*, 22.
89. Ibid., 23.
90. Poetker, "'My Mothers,'" 77.
91. DeSilva, *Honor*, 158.
92. Ibid., 163.
93. For ὁ υἱὸς τοῦ θεοῦ see 1:1, 11, 23; 3:11; 5:7; 9:7; 14:61; 15:39. For God as ὁ πατήρ see 8:38; 11:25; 13:21; 14:36.
94. For ἡ βασιλεία τοῦ θεοῦ see 1:15; 4:11, 26, 30; 9:1, 47; 10:14–15, 24–25; 12:34; 14:25; 15:43.

brothers, sisters, daughters, children, and slaves when he calls them to follow and provides benefactions of exorcism, healing, hospitality, and teaching. In utilizing kinship terms, Mark's Jesus provides a certain characterization to those who follow him. Chiefly, those who do the will of God characterize Jesus' kinship group (3:35). A new kinship group, a new family, is created that sets parameters for the role and function of discipleship and followers of Jesus.

Kinship must also be understood as it relates to other aspects of social and economic structures, including that of the household. Although kinship and household are categorized separately in anthropological studies, they often overlap and are interrelated. Where kinship is based primarily on human relationships and their organization, the household often includes kinship structures, but also buildings, other human beings, land, animals, and products produced, consumed, and disbursed.[95] Within the category of household, kinship members may hold specific functions and roles. For example, the head of the household of the Roman *domus* is referred to as the *paterfamilias*, literally, "the father of the family." Aristotle defined the basic social unit as the household containing the most fundamental relationships of master and slave, husband and wife, father and children.[96] "In this description, the terms *master*, *husband* and *father* describe the same individual, who is thus placed at the hub of the family unit, the 'head' in relation to whom the other members of the family take their bearings."[97] Moreover, the Roman imperial state was also based upon the *domus* where the emperor stood as the *paterfamilias* of the entire empire.[98] Within the Gospel of Mark, not only are Jesus and the disciples defined and identified according to kinship relationships, but they also have functions and roles that are determined by the household. Not only is Jesus identified as the Son and relates to the disciples as a brother, but he also establishes a household where he functions as the head of that household, as the *paterfamilias* (1:29–31). Simultaneously, Jesus is able to be both the Son of God and also the head of the family, the *paterfamilias* of the disciples and followers.

Honor

In ancient Palestinian and Roman society, honor was a (the?) central value. "Honor is the status one claimed in the community, together with

---

95. Pomeroy, "Some Greek Families," 155.
96. Aristotle, *Politics*, 13.
97. DeSilva, *Honor*, 173.
98. Hodge, *If Sons, then Heirs*, 27.

the all-important public recognition of that claim ... It meant access to power and privilege that could be gained no other way."[99] The gospel writers, including Mark, present Jesus in such a way that he becomes the most honorable, even in his suffering and crucifixion. Mark does this through ascribed and acquired honor, the honor that Jesus is given through his relationship with God as in the baptismal scene and the honor he achieves in interactions with others, such as calling disciples. In order to be legitimate and valued, Jesus must be the most honorable. In turn, Jesus' honor may be bestowed upon those with whom he associates, i.e., his disciples and those who follow him.

In ancient Mediterranean society one's honor could be challenged and taken away or acquired through the public game of challenge-riposte. Challenge-riposte consists of "1) a challenge (almost any word, gesture, action) that might undermine the honor of another person and 2) a response that answers in equal measure or ups the ante (and thereby challenges in return)."[100] The challenge-riposte game occurred among social equals, and both positive and negative challenges required a response. Jesus is constantly being challenged in the Gospel of Mark, especially by the Pharisees, the priests, and the scribes.[101] For example, the very first challenge-riposte scenario occurs in Capernaum while Jesus is at home in 2:1–12. Jesus heals the paralytic boy who is lowered through the roof because there is no room to bring him to the door. Jesus initially tells the boy, τέκνον, ἀφίενταί σου αἱ ἁμαρτίαι (Child, your sins are forgiven). In the setting of his home and utilizing a kinship term, Jesus forgives the paralytic. There were some scribes nearby who offer a challenge (Jesus' honor is magnified because the challenge occurs in their hearts, but Jesus hears them anyway.), τί οὗτος οὕτως λαλεῖ; βλασφημεῖ· τίς δύναται ἀφιέναι ἁμαρτίας εἰ μὴ εἷς ὁ θεός; (Why is this one speaking like this? He blasphemes; who is able to forgive sins except God alone?) Jesus responds to the challenge by upping the ante. Not only does he prove that he has the authority to forgive sins, he heals the boy of his paralysis. Those who witness the encounter grant Jesus more honor: ὥστε ἐξίστασθαι πάντας καὶ δοξάζειν τὸν θεὸν λέγοντας ὅτι οὕτως οὐδέποτε εἴδομεν (Therefore all were amazed and they glorified God saying that they had never seen anything like this). Jesus as the Son, as the agent of God, has used his authority to give forgiveness and healing to the boy and the witnesses around him recognize this.

---

99. Rohrbaugh, "Honor," 111.

100. Malina and Rohrbaugh, *Social-Science Commentary*, 334.

101 Ibid., 335, indicates the challenge-riposte scenarios: 2:1–12; 2:15–17; 2:18–22; 2:23–28; 3:1–6; 3:20–34; 7:1–8; 10:1–12; 11:27–33; 12:13–17; and 12:18–27.

Defining Jesus and the disciples in terms of kinship is a means of granting them ascribed honor. Richard Rohrbaugh notes that "ascribed honor comes primarily from one's family, one's ancestry. Those born into great families share an indelible mark of honor. . .Honor status is thus given or ascribed at birth, which meant that all members of the family, both male and female, were at roughly the same honor level."[102] One way to grant honor to Jesus and those who follow him is to grant them ascribed honor through kinship with God. "Being the son of a village artisan family, Jesus' legitimacy as a public figure was nil. If he is the Son of God, however, his legitimacy is beyond question."[103] Hence with the double declaration in 1:1 and 1:11 of Jesus as God's Son and the declaration in 3:34–35 of disciples as brothers, sisters, and mothers to Jesus, kinship and honor become the means of understanding Christology and discipleship in Mark. They also become the means of understanding the intersection of these two central aspects of the gospel. Who Jesus is as a Son defines and ascribes honor to those who become his followers, who become a part of his kinship network.

IMPERIAL CRITICAL APPROACHES

By way of understanding Mark in its context, I will utilize the methodological approach of empire studies. Mark was written in a particular time and place; it was written shortly after the fall of Jerusalem (70 CE) in the larger context of the Roman Empire.[104] It will be necessary to address the notion of sonship as it was understood in an imperial context and to note the possible intersections of sonship within Mark and within the Roman Empire. Are sonship and discipleship a means of negotiating and perhaps, resisting, the imperial forces that may have subjugated those who heard Mark's gospel?

Significant for this study will be the theoretical view that Rome established itself as a centralized historical bureaucratic empire. As Dennis Duling notes, "Most important, the emperor attempts to establish the political sphere as discrete and autonomous. To do so he must weaken political ties to, and ideologies of, traditional 'ascriptive' groups based on kinship, clan, territory and religion."[105] He must also strengthen an alternative kinship system. One way he accomplishes this is by the use of the title *pater patriae*, father of the fatherland. Not only was it a political title to grant honor to the

---

102. Rohrbaugh, "Honor," 118.
103. Malina and Rohrbaugh, *Social-Science Commentary*, 409.
104. See the discussions on the work of Adam Winn and imperial critical approaches to Mark in chapter 1.
105. Duling, "Empire," 52.

emperor, but also it redefined his relationship with his subjects. "It presented his 'unlimited political power' not in terms of tyranny but in terms of *patria potestas*, binding his fellow citizens to him like sons to a father in *pietas*, the loyalty or allegiance of appropriate duties and obligations."[106] In effect, the emperor is the father of the kinship network of the Roman Empire. In this kind of empire Rome may have political power but, at the same time "ascriptive" groups persist and resist the centralized power. The persisting and resisting groups will be seen in the kinship networks established by Jesus' sonship and discipleship in the Gospel of Mark.

As noted in chapter 1, Adam Winn suggests that the historical context for Mark is within the Roman Empire during the rule of Emperor Vespasian (69–79 CE).[107] Through a survey of the internal and external evidence for Mark's date and provenance and primarily through an analysis of Mark 13 as a *post factum* prophecy,[108] Winn argues convincingly that Mark wrote his gospel after the destruction of the Jerusalem temple. In addition, he places the composition of Mark in Rome, written for a group of Christians who would have witnessed the spoils of the destruction of Jerusalem in Titus and Vespasian's Triumph and who may be experiencing some sort of crisis.[109] He places the gospel in an imperial transitional period that significantly impacts its Christology and discipleship.[110] The characterization of Jesus in Mark may be seen in relation to the imperial self-presentation of Vespasian in the Roman Empire with elements of mimicry, competition, and antithesis.

If the Gospel of Mark were written shortly after the destruction of Jerusalem in 71 or 72 CE, there are several events in the reign of Vespasian and in his relationship with his son Titus that will impact the perception of the Gospel of Mark. Among these include the prophecies surrounding the reigns of Vespasian and Titus, the inscriptions and images on imperial coins that establish the new Flavian reign and Titus as *Caesar Augusti filius*, the beginnings of a hereditary dynasty, the triumph of Titus and Vespasian, and the propaganda to champion Emperor Vespasian's reign.

---

106. Carter, *John and Empire*, 237.
107. Winn, *Purpose of Mark's Gospel*, 43–91.
108. Ibid., 64–68.
109. Ibid., 173–78.

110. Winn is not the only one to provide a post-70 dating for the composition of Mark. See also, Nineham, *Gospel of St. Mark*, 41–42; Hooker, *Gospel according to Saint Mark*, 8; Schnelle, *History and Theology of the New Testament*, 201–202; Donahue and Harrington, *Mark*, 41–47; Marcus, *Mark 1–8*, 37–39 who has a post-70 dating but sets the composition of Mark in Syria; and especially Incigneri, *Gospel to the Romans*, 116–55.

The biographer Suetonius (ca. 69–ca. 130 CE) provides an account of the lives of the emperors including Vespasian and his son, Titus. At the very beginning of his account of Vespasian, Suetonius remarks that Vespasian's rule was preceded by a chaotic and tumultuous time of civil war from the reign of Nero to Galba to Otho to Vitellius. There were four rulers within one year (68–69 CE). But now, at last, peace and prosperity for a few were restored through Vespasian. Although he ascended the throne primarily through his military prowess and with the support of the legions, there were some prophecies and other portents legitimating his reign that surrounded his ascension. Suetonius makes note of this:

> There had spread over all the Orient an old and established belief, that it was fated at that time for men coming from Judaea to rule the world. This prediction, referring to the emperor of Rome, as afterwards appeared from the event, the people of Judaea took to themselves; accordingly they revolted and after killing their governor, they routed the consular ruler of Syria as well, when he came to the rescue and took one of his eagles. Since to put down this rebellion required a considerable army with a leader of no little enterprise, yet one to whom so great power could be entrusted without risk, Vespasian was chosen for the task, both as a man of tried energy and as one in no wise to be feared because of the obscurity of his family and name. Therefore there were added to the forces in Judaea two legions with eight divisions of cavalry and ten cohorts. He took his elder son as one of his lieutenants, and as soon as he reached his province he attracted the attention of the neighbouring provinces also; for he at once reformed the discipline of the army and fought one or two battles with such daring, that in the storming of a fortress he was wounded in the knee with a stone and received several arrows in his shield.[111]

This prophecy was also pronounced by the Roman historian Tacitus and the Jewish historian Josephus.[112] Tacitus includes both Vespasian and his son, Titus, as subjects of the prophecy. Josephus himself offers the prophecy to Vespasian, designating Vespasian and Titus as emperors.

Emperor Vespasian took the throne in 69 CE. As he reigned from Rome, his son Titus led the siege on Jerusalem. Titus returned to Rome

---

111. Suet. *Vesp.* 4.

112. Tacitus, *Histories*, 5.8.3; Josephus, *War*, 3.399–404, 4.623. Winn, *Purpose of Mark's Gospel*, 160, 178, 180, 183, 199, strangely states that Vespasian himself claimed to be the Messiah for which there is no evidence. The prophecy is attested by the historians, but Vespasian is not the source of the prophecy about himself.

in 71 CE when he celebrated his triumph along with his father, Vespasian. Although the Senate decreed that they should each have their own triumph, when Titus is reunited with his father, Josephus recounts that they decided to have one big triumph together to celebrate the victory over Jerusalem.[113] Adam Winn provides a succinct summary of Josephus's lengthy description and notes that while the triumph was primarily to celebrate the victory over the Jews, it was also a means of propaganda for Vespasian to establish power and authority over Rome as emperor.[114] Josephus "reports that the entire military, arranged in companies and divisions, came out to the site of the triumph while it was still night. At day break, Vespasian and Titus came out from the temple of Isis wearing purple imperial robes and laurel crowns. As they took their seats on ivory thrones, loud acclamations came from the soldiers and continued until Vespasian signaled for silence."[115] The triumph continued with the procession of all the spoils of the war, including the contents of the Jerusalem temple. Vespasian was followed by his son Titus and was also accompanied by his younger son, Domitian. The triumphal procession concluded at the temple of Jupiter Capitolinus where a Jewish captive was brought to be killed. A shout of victory went up at the announcement of his death and the day ended in feasting, "for this was a festival day to the city of Rome, as celebrated for the victory obtained by their army over their enemies, for the end that was now put to their civil miseries, and for the commencement of their hopes of future prosperity and happiness."[116] All of this has occurred in thanks to Emperor Vespasian and his son Titus.

Suetonius states that Titus enjoyed a close relationship with his father and assisted him in the running of the empire. In fact, Titus was so beloved, that even before Vespasian became emperor, Emperor Galba considered adopting Titus as a son to be his heir to the throne.[117] After the fall of Jerusalem, Suetonius notes that all the soldiers under Titus' command knelt down and proclaimed him emperor.[118] Titus did not rebel against his father, but returned peacefully to Rome. "From that time he constantly acted as colleague with his father, and, indeed, as regent of the empire. He triumphed with his father, bore jointly with him the office of censor; and was, besides, his colleague not only in the tribunitian authority, but in seven

---

113. Josephus's account of the triumph: *War*, 7.117–59.

114. Winn, *Purpose of Mark's Gospel*, 164. See also Beard, *Roman Triumph*, especially 93–101.

115. Winn, *Purpose of Mark's Gospel*, 164–65.

116. Josephus, *War*, 7.154.

117. Suet.*Tit*.5.

118. Ibid.

consulships."[119] Titus acted in behalf of his father. Although initially he had a bad reputation for licentiousness due to his affair with Berenice, Herod's daughter, Suetonious suggests that Titus became very virtuous and benevolent.[120] Titus inherited the throne when his father died in 79 CE; he reigned for two years until he died, after which his brother, Domitian, ascended to the throne.

In addition to Vespasian's military exploits, there is also a story told about him where he acts as a healer of a blind man and a lame man in 69–70 CE. The healings occurred while Vespasian was in Alexandria on his way back to Rome after he was in Judea putting down the Jewish revolt. The Roman historians Tacitus, Suetonius, and Cassius Dio each recount this healing story.[121] Tacitus begins his retelling, "During the months while Vespasian was waiting at Alexandria for the regular season of the summer winds and a settled sea, many marvels occurred to mark the favour of heaven and a certain partiality of the gods toward him."[122] Apparently, the god Serapis compelled a blind man to throw himself at the mercy of Vespasian and seek healing. The blind man asked Vespasian to touch his eyes with spittle. Also a lame man approached Vespasian to touch his foot and heal him. Vespasian refused at first, but in the end he healed both men. Tacitus concludes, "The hand was instantly restored to use, and the day again shone for the blind man. Both facts are told by eye-witnesses even now when falsehood brings no reward."[123] The final statement of Tacitus is compelling in that it suggests that these stories were told for Vespasian's gain. Eric Eve suggests that these healings served a three-fold purpose to support Vespasian in garnering the role of emperor for Rome. First and foremost, the healings "seem designed to demonstrate the close association between the new emperor and the god."[124] Eve goes further to suggest that not only did these healings indicate a close relationship with the god Serapis, but also Vespasian was to be identified with the god.[125] Secondly, Vespasian needed the support of the locals as he was preparing to return to Rome; thus the stories may have been told to garner the support of Alexandrians. Finally, "if Vespasian (or his supporters) felt the need to legitimate his accession in this way, it is surely towards the beginning of his reign that such propaganda would have been most

---

119. Suet.*Tit*.6.
120. Tacitus, *Histories*, 2.2; Dio Cassius, *Roman History*, 65.15.
121. Tacitus, *Histories* 4.81; Suet.*Vesp*. 7.2; and Dio Cassius, *Roman History* 65.8.
122. Tacitus, *Histories*, 4.81.
123. Ibid.
124. Eve, "Spit in Your Eye," 6.
125. Ibid.

useful."[126] Vespasian was not of noble birth and was not necessarily so well known that he was the first choice for emperor.[127] It was therefore necessary that stories and propaganda be spread in order to help build his reputation and legitimize his accession to the throne. Eve concludes: "The accounts of Vespasian's healings at Alexandria were circulated in the context of portents and prophecies purporting to show that Vespasian enjoyed divine favour."[128]

In addition to the stories, prophecies, and omens told about Vespasian and his sons, the coinage produced by imperial mints at the beginning of Vespasian's reign also provides important information about the establishment of the Flavian dynasty and the beginnings of a hereditary monarchy. Vespasian was not deified until his son, Titus honored him ca. 79 CE. It is only after which his sons use the title *divi filius*.[129] But Vespasian modeled his reign after Caesar Augustus and allowed for the emperor cult, especially in the eastern part of the empire. Vespasian would have been granted divine status and was viewed as savior (σωτήρ), benefactor (εὐεργέτης), and master (κύριος and δεσπότης).[130] Like Augustus, Vespasian sought to secure for dynastic succession of his sons and this is evidenced in the earliest coinage from his reign. Some of the most common denarii that were minted from 69–70 CE and circulated throughout the empire include images of Emperor Vespasian on the face and on the obverse images of his sons Titus and Domitian.[131] Ian Carradice indicates that coins with images of Vespasian on the face with images of Titus and Domitian on the obverse would have been in heavy circulation in 69–71 CE in order to establish the hereditary dynasty.[132] On one such coin, the images of Titus and Domitian are accompanied by a legend that describes them both as *Caesar Augusti filius*, son of Augustus Caesar.[133] Not only does Vespasian establish his hereditary dynasty, but he also connects his dynasty with the deified Caesar Augustus, in effect declar-

---

126. Ibid., 7.

127. See Levick, *Vespasian*, 67–70, on the propaganda campaign for Vespasian, with special attention given to the prophecies surrounding his accession.

128. Eve, "Spit in Your Eye," 11.

129. Scott, *Imperial Cult*, 40, argues for a 79 CE consecration of Vespasian as *divus* based on an inscription on the arch of the Aqua Marcia at Rome from 79 CE that claims Titus as *Divi f(ilius)* and other inscriptions from the same year.

130. Ibid., 20–22.

131. For a recent summary of the cataloguing and circulation of Flavian imperial coins, see Carradice, "Flavian Coinage," 93–117. Carradice analyzes the frequency that the coins occur in found hoards to get a better understanding of their frequency in circulation.

132. Carradice, "Flavian Coinage," 112.

133. Scott, *Imperial Cult*, 23.

ing his own sons to be sons of (a) God, thus ensuring an heir and peaceful transition of power.

Suetonius, Tacitus, Dio Cassius, and Josephus have all provided detailed accounts of the lives and relationships of Emperor Vespasian and his son Titus. In order to form a basis for assessing interaction with or interference with the Gospel of Mark, it will be necessary to demonstrate how the reign of Emperor Vespasian and his relationship with his son points to a model of empire to which Mark and his community may be responding in his gospel. In order to perpetuate legitimacy for the throne, Vespasian and his supporters would have promoted him through propaganda that spread throughout the empire. In addition, Vespasian is the head of the new Flavian dynasty; that is, his reign implements a new inherited line of rulers. Not only is Vespasian himself central to the success of the Roman Empire, but his first born son, Titus, plays a pivotal role in that he is the anticipated ruler who will follow his father and continue the success and prosperity that Vespasian has achieved.

In a discussion on models of empire, Dennis Duling notes that, "Ramsay MacMullen once said that the key to Roman social relations was 'verticality.'"[134] Not only does verticality apply to social relations, but it also applies to kinship relations as well. Peter Garnsey and Richard Saller define family within the Roman Empire as all those who were under the father's power.[135] As the father stands at the head of the household with all his family members below him, so too, does the emperor stand at the head of the empire as the *pater patriae*. This is doubly reinforced when the father-son relationship of Vespasian and Titus is highlighted. An often-used model to highlight the vertical stratification of the Roman Empire which will also prove helpful to this study is the work of Gerhard Lenski.[136] As agrarian societies advanced, so did the possibility of gaining more and more control and power over these societies through exploitation and bureaucratic and military institutions. "This model implies that those who successfully compete for control of this growing agricultural surplus gradually grow in political and economic power, privilege and prestige."[137] Lenski divided his model into three social strata: (1) rulers, (2) other governing rulers and their servers, and (3) merchants, peasants, and artisans. At the very bottom

---

134. Duling, "Empire," 57.
135. Garnsey and Saller, *Roman Empire*, 127.
136. Lenski, *Power and Privilege*.
137. Duling, "Empire," 54.

of the lowest strata are those termed "expendables," which includes bandits and prostitutes.[138]

At the top of this model sat the rulers, in the case of the Roman Empire the emperor and his household. In addition to the social and political stratification that this implies, it is also important to note the stratification within the kinship system. The emperor was known throughout the empire as *Patria patriae*, Father of the Fatherland.[139] "*Pater*, Dio claims, acknowledges that the emperor has the same authority (ἐξουσία) over his subjects as the father once had over children (παῖδας—the term may include slaves and other subjects) —that of *patria potestas*."[140] Not only did this language of fatherhood provide definition to the structure of empire, but it also served as propaganda to publicize and legitimize the role of the emperor within the larger empire. Father of the Fatherland served to define and idealize the relationship between emperor and subject. "The ruled depend on the ruler. Duties and obligations, not tyranny and submission, shape the relationship."[141]

Within this model of empire, with the Roman elite at the top with the emperor and his household, the community of Mark and the characters in his gospel, including Jesus and the disciples, would find themselves at the very bottom among the peasantry, artisans, prostitutes, and bandits. One other social model that will prove helpful is the scale for measuring poverty in cities of the Roman Empire developed by Steven Friesen in an effort to provide differentiation among the 90 percent of the population that were labeled "poor."[142] This scale consists of seven categories: (PS1) Imperial elites; (PS2) Regional or provincial elites; (PS3) Municipal elites; (PS4) Moderate surplus resources; (PS5) Stable near subsistence level; (PS6) At subsistence level; and (PS7) Below subsistence level.[143] Friesen states, "The overwhelming majority of the population under Roman imperialism lived near the subsistence level, that is, categories PS5–7. 'Subsistence level' is here defined as the resources needed to procure enough calories in food to maintain the human body."[144] A family living at the subsistence level (PS5–6) would need 1,000 denarii annual income to live in a city or 300 denarii to live in rural areas. On the other hand, elite members of equestrian order (PS2) needed

---

138. As summarized by Duling, ibid.

139. This title was first given to Augustus in 2 BCE. But, as D'Angelo, "Abba and 'Father,'" 623, notes, *pater* and *patriae* were already in use for Julius Caesar.

140. Ibid., 623. Dio Cassius, *Roman History*, 53.18.3.

141. Carter, *John and Empire*, 238.

142. Friesen, "Poverty in Pauline Studies," 323–61.

143. Ibid., 341.

144. Ibid., 343.

to have property holdings valued at 400,000 sesterces (100,000 denarii).[145] The subsistence level poor would be far removed from the elite ruling class, and they would not have received the benevolent, paternal care that the title *pater patriae* assumes. Instead, *pater patriae* served as propaganda to the lowest members of the "family" of Rome. It was a "program designed to veil the brutality of Roman military rule and the hatred directed against it by its subjects, on the one hand, and, on the other, to legitimate its demand for ultimate allegiance and its incursions into the private lives and families of its subjects."[146]

The most blatant and apparent response to the kind of oppression and exploitation that the lowest-stratified "children" received from the "fatherland" was the very armed resistance and rebellion that some Jews fought and was put down by Vespasian and ended with the destruction of Jerusalem by his son Titus. It has been argued that there have been other responses and ways of negotiating the Roman Empire besides armed rebellion and uprisings that are exhibited by Jesus and the gospel writers, including Mark. The primary resource for this model of empire negotiation is the political scientist, James C. Scott. Scott resists the common view of an either/or response, that is, either armed resistance against dominating forces or submission to those forces. Scott argues that the middle ground reflects much ambiguity and disguise.[147]

If the predominant model for the Roman Empire is a vertical hierarchy where the elite ruling power of the emperor and his family maintain most of the resources, power, and control and the peasants, artisans, prostitutes, and bandits experience exploitation and subjugation, then Scott provides a model of resistance and negotiation for the lowest strata of the empire. One way to subvert and resist the public displays of power by the elite of the Roman Empire is through hidden transcripts of resistance. Richard Horsley notes that two things were necessary for the creation of hidden transcripts: a social space which is protected from control and surveillance from the powers above and active people who foster the alternative discourse.[148] In addition to the hidden transcripts of resistance present among those who are subordinated by oppressors, it is also important to acknowledge that simultaneously there are matters at work that solidify the public, dominant discourses. These then interact and affect those hidden transcripts. In his work about prestige as a larger part of the dominant discourse, Scott

---

145. Ibid., 345.
146. Elliott, "Household/Family," 63.
147. Scott, *Domination and Resistance*, 136.
148. As summarized by Horsley, "Introduction," 10.

suggests that any references to social order, be it positive or negative, "are a symbolic gesture of domination which serves to manifest and reinforce a hierarchical order."[149] All social expectations and configuration reflect the larger dominant structure and its power over both classes: oppressor and oppressed, rich and poor, elite and peasant. One who does not follow social mores would be considered to be insubordinate. Unlike the possession of actual skills or talents, prestige is something that is bestowed on someone in a role of power. It is necessary for subordinates to believe in the prestige of the dominant in order for the social structure to be maintained. The more prestige that is bestowed on the dominant party, the stronger the hierarchical structures. The hierarchical structure is preserved because the dominant classes control the public discourse; they possess the prestige.

The dominant, public discourse remains, but behind it often lies a subversive discourse, one that would seek to upend the dominant discourse even as it plays into it. Unfortunately the subversive discourse is not usually made public. Scott notes that one "consequence of a 'regulated' public transcript is that dissonance will normally be expressed in subtle, veiled, and muted forms. There is every reason for the dominant to make certain resistance stops well short of direct challenges in public."[150] There is no question that resistance exists; however, the dominant discourse is usually powerful enough to withstand it or to shut it down. Resistance and negotiation remain in spite of the Roman Empire's effort to squelch it; I understand the Gospel of Mark to be concrete evidence of that fact. And as much as a subordinate group would react against a dominant discourse, they are also affected and directly influenced by that dominant discourse. So much so that the hidden transcript and subversive discourse might be a mirror reflection or direct inversion of the dominating structure.[151] Mark utilizes the designation of Jesus as Son, his inauguration of the empire of God, and the creation of a new kinship group of disciples and followers as a means of resisting, imitating, competing with, and negotiating the Flavian hereditary dynasty and reign of the Roman Empire.

It is from this point of view that I will examine the kinship language and relationships of Jesus and the disciples in the Gospel of Mark. Within the narrative context of the gospel, Mark characterizes Jesus, the disciples, and those who follow as members of a kin group. Jesus, as the Son and designated agent, does the work of the Father (God) to inaugurate his empire in the world. Jesus then teaches, heals, exhorts, and fellowships with those who

---

149. Scott, "Prestige as the Public Discourse," 147.
150. Ibid., 164.
151. Scott, *Domination and Resistance*, 102–3.

follow him, those who become brothers and sisters in this new family. This story of Jesus and those who follow him occurs in the larger setting of the Roman Empire, written during the Flavian dynasty following the fall of Jerusalem. James Scott refers to this alternative discourse within the setting of domination as using the language of dominant ideology. "We may consider the dominant discourse as a plastic idiom or dialect that is capable of carrying an enormous variety of meanings, including those that are subversive of their use as intended by the dominant."[152] Jack Elliott concludes,

> Use of this household management tradition served the aim not of assimilating to Greco-Roman patterns of domination, but of resisting pressures to conform under the assurance that one's place of belonging was in the *oikos tou theou*, not the emperor's *patria*, that one's father was not the Roman emperor claiming to be *pater patriae*, but the merciful heavenly father/progenitor who raised Jesus from the dead.[153]

One might modify Elliott a little to say belonging not only in the emperor's patria, but also in the οἰκός τοῦ θεοῦ. The new family inaugurated by Jesus in the new empire of God stands as a means of negotiating and resisting the Roman Empire that subjugates and robs them of any kinship identity except that as exploited subjects of the emperor.

In this chapter, I have presented the methodology that I will use to analyze kinship and discipleship in the Gospel of Mark. In an analysis of the plot, setting, character, and point of view, the identity and role of Jesus as a Son stands in the foreground, along with the call and characterization of disciples and those who follow Jesus as members of a new kinship group. The concepts of kinship and honor were presented in terms of a social-science approach so that their function may be understood and interpreted within the larger Roman imperial context in which the narrative occurs. In the next chapter, I will focus more closely on the kinship language, Jesus' sonship, and discipleship in the first narrative block of the Gospel of Mark.

---

152. Ibid.
153. Elliott, "Jesus Movement," 198–99.

3

Mark 1:1—8:30

MY ARGUMENT IS THAT kinship provides the nexus between Christology and discipleship in the Gospel of Mark. In the gospel narrative, Mark utilizes the kinship between Jesus and God and the kinship between Jesus and the emerging community of disciples as a means of realigning conventional roles of kinship to negotiate its Roman imperial context.

Mark establishes Jesus as God's Son from the outset of the gospel. This primary kinship relationship of father and son defines Jesus' identity and primary purpose in the Gospel of Mark: to establish God's empire by proliferation of its message (1:14–15) and recruitment of a new family of disciples (1:16–20). The sonship of Jesus also serves to present Jesus as the most honorable, providing him with authority, power, and social status to teach, to provide healing, and to provide access to social situations and to food that might otherwise be denied. Jesus' sonship and authority to act as God's agent are challenged by others, notably the scribes and the Pharisees, in competition for honor. In reflection of the first kernel where Jesus is acclaimed as God's Son at his baptism (1:9–11), he maintains his honorable status throughout the first two narrative blocks (1:1–8; 1:9–8:30), building up his reputation and gaining a large following which he designates, using kinship terms, as his "children" (2:19) and "brothers and sisters" (3:33–35). Moreover, the primary relationship of father and son is reiterated in several satellites throughout the second narrative block when Jesus is identified as a Son by demons and by himself (Son of Man).

In addition to Jesus' sonship with God, kinship is a defining relationship marker between Jesus and the disciples. Once Jesus embarks upon his ministry, he immediately calls a core kinship group of disciples. These disciples leave their original kinship networks (in whole or in part) to follow, accompany, and do the ministry of Jesus (1:16–20). Moreover, this kinship relationship becomes explicit at Mark 2:19 and again at 3:35 when Jesus defines discipleship in terms of kinship. Jesus first refers to his disciples as his "sons" (οἱ υἱοί, 2:19). Then Jesus denies his original kinship network and proclaims that his mother, brothers, and sisters are those who do the will of God (3:35). Jesus extends his honor and authority to the disciples as his family, enabling them to participate in the ministry of Jesus and establishment of God's empire. In addition to the twelve, Jesus also invites into kinship relationship those who follow him and seek him for healing; he provides hospitality, welcomes them into the household, and addresses them in kinship terms. This new kinship system established by God's Son for the new family of disciples functions over and against the current kinship systems maintained by the Roman imperial world and those who collaborate with it (Jewish leaders) that deny access not only to social standing, but also even to basic necessities of food and health. Categories of kinship thus provide the nexus between the gospel's presentation of Jesus (Christology) and the presentation of the disciples (discipleship). The kinship between Jesus and God and between Jesus and the disciples are imitative and contestive means to negotiate Mark's Roman imperial context.

In chapters 3 and 4, I will present a commentary on the Gospel of Mark that will demonstrate how kinship categories provide the nexus between Christology (Jesus' kinship with God) and discipleship (Jesus' kinship with the disciples).[1] Chapter 3 will discuss the first two narrative blocks (1:1–8:30) divided into their component kernel and satellites. In each section, I will address any kinship terms that arise including son (υἱός), father (πατήρ), child (τέκνον), bridegroom (νυμφίος), mother (μήτηρ), mother-in-law (πενθερά), brother (ἀδελφός), sister (ἀδελφή), daughter (θυγάτηρ), wife (γυνή), slave (δοῦλος), servant (διάκονος), family (οἱ παρ' αὐτοῦ), and household (οἶκος, οἰκία). I will then demonstrate kinship as the nexus between Christology and discipleship in each pericope in terms of Jesus' sonship and/or in terms of discipleship. Even pericopes that do not contain explicit kinship language still have implications for kinship as the nexus between

---

1. In this commentary, I approach the Gospel of Mark in its narrative context, viewing the plot events and character development centrally. The gospel is also situated in an historical context. While Mark addresses, interprets, and refers to historical events, I do not view Mark as an historical report. Mark has particular viewpoints that are not necessarily historically accurate or ones that I condone, but they are present in the narrative and will be addressed in terms of my thesis. I will also address Mark's narrative episodically in order to follow the plot events and character development in terms of the nexus between Christology and discipleship. There will be repetition of my thesis statement and key points that will remind the reader that the characterization of Jesus as a Son and the designation of disciples and followers as family are developed through the entire narrative.

Christology and discipleship in Mark as I will demonstrate. I will account for scriptural echoes that elaborate the kinship implications for Christology and discipleship. Finally, I will demonstrate how kinship in terms of sonship and discipleship imitate and contest Mark's Roman imperial context.

1. 1:1 JESUS CHRIST, SON OF GOD

Before the narrative of Mark begins, the gospel opens with an incipit, or a title in 1:1: Ἀρχὴ τοῦ εὐαγγελίου Ἰησοῦ Χριστοῦ υἱοῦ θεοῦ (The beginning of the gospel of Jesus Christ, Son of God). As I noted in chapter 2,[2] Mark 1:1 is the first characterization that Mark gives about Jesus, and that Jesus is presented in kinship terms as the Son of God. This is also the most prominent, yet also textually the most controversial, identification of Jesus as the Son of God because not all of the manuscripts include this kinship designation for Jesus.[3] I conclude that the designation of Jesus as the Son of God in 1:1 is part of the original text because the majority of ancient manuscripts, the church fathers, and early versions of the New Testament support the longer reading. It is crucial to the unfolding of the plot of Mark where Jesus' kinship with God will be elaborated in his ministry and in the extension of kinship to his disciples.

In his article about the structure and purpose of Mark's gospel, M. Eugene Boring claims that Mark's purpose was primarily a christological purpose. "The structuring principle of Mark's narrative is not something to do with the *life* of *Jesus* as a 'great man,' but the *role* of Jesus in the plan of *God*."[4] That is, from the outset of the gospel, Jesus' role and identity are framed in kinship language as Son of God. Thus, I divide the plot of Mark into four narrative blocks based on this kinship Christology which begins with a title and introduction in the gospel's opening verse. The title includes the identification of Jesus as the Son of God which, according to Boring, is a theme for the entirety of Mark's gospel.

The significance of identifying Jesus in kinship terms as Son of God will be further developed by Mark in the actual narrative of the gospel. It is developed immediately in 1:1 by juxtaposing "Son of God" with "Christ."

---

2. See chapter 2.

3. For a recent and comprehensive analysis of the textual controversy of Mark 1:1, see Wasserman, "The 'Son of God,'" 20–50. Wasserman argues that the longer reading of Mark 1:1 should stand. Wasserman also insists that internal evidence within Mark also indicates the longer reading based on ancient practices of titling works including υἱός language and the thematic purposes of Mark.

4. Boring, "Mark 1:1–15," 46.

Christ becomes a subset of the primary kinship designation of Jesus as Son of God. Joel Marcus suggests that there is restrictive apposition at work between the two titles, "so that the second *qualifies* the first."[5] Son of God defines what type of Christ Jesus is. This has implications in the interpretation of Christ from its Jewish roots. Moreover, the use of the Son of God in apposition with Christ expands the notion of messiahship and marries the Jewish and Roman traditions that the Gospel of Mark engages.

The assertion of Jesus' identity as "Christ" or "Son of God" in 1:1 evokes some intertextual echoes that provide the reader with some important initial understandings. Both concepts have a strong background and tradition in the Hebrew Bible.[6] "Christ" translates the Hebrew root משח which denotes "anointing." Priests and prophets were anointed or commissioned for their priestly or prophetic work (Lev 4; 1 Kgs 19:16). The tradition of anointing for kingship goes back to the role of Samuel who anointed the first three kings of Israel (1 Sam 2:10, 35). In the course of a corrupt monarchy and eventual destruction of the kingdoms of Israel and Judah, "the concept of messiah became attached to the idealized figure of a 'King to Come' (Jer 23:5–6; Ezek 34:23–4)" who is also identified in kinship terms as a Son of God (2 Sam 7:13; Pss 2, 45, 89, 110, 132; Isa 9; Zech 12:8) "even though he is not identified with the deity in a full sense."[7] In addition, the concept of messiah has a minor role in apocryphal literature and the Dead Sea Scrolls where it is understood that the messiah will return variously as an eschatological priest and king (*Pss Sol* 17; *4 Ezra* 13). Adela Yarbro Collins concludes that the Qumran community "expected an eschatological leader who would lead the faithful in battle against their enemies, especially the Romans, reestablish an autonomous kingdom of Israel, and rule as king

---

5. Marcus, "Mark 14:61," 130. Marcus is trying to connect the question of the High Priest with the charge of blasphemy brought upon Jesus in the trial scene. He is also highlighting the connection with other Messiah-types in first-century Judaism. Thus, the Messiah-Son-of-God becomes a messiah-type over and against the others. Marcus concludes, "'Son of God' (14:61) is understood in terms of participation in God's cosmic lordship (14:62; cf. Ps 110:1), and that it is this participatory understanding of sonship that gives rise to the charge of blasphemy (14:63–64). The Markan Jesus implies in 14:62 that he will sit at God's right hand and come with the clouds of heaven, and that this description of a transcendent future indicates part of his understanding of the title he has just accepted, 'Son of God.' An approach to equality with God, then, is suggested, and this approach leads naturally to a charge of blasphemy on the part of his opponents" (139).

6. For a christological analysis of the use of the Hebrew Bible in the Gospel of Mark, see Marcus, *Way of the Lord*.

7. Samuel, "Beginning of Mark," 413–14.

with wisdom and justice."[8] In identifying Jesus as Christ the gospel marks him as one anointed or commissioned by God to an as yet undefined role.

The anointed king of Israel is also depicted in kinship terms as "Son of God" in the Hebrew Bible. In Pss 2:7, 89:26-27, and 2 Sam 7:13-14, King David is referred to as "Son of God." The kinship language denotes, in context, that he will receive divine favor and sanction to rule over Israel. In addition, other heavenly beings are referred to as "son(s) of God" in Gen 6:2; Ps 29:1; Dan 3:25. Here the kinship language denotes a special relationship with God with attributes of power and authority. Son of God designations are also present in apocryphal literature (Sir 4:10b; Wis 2:18) as a depiction of a just man and in the Qumran community (4Q174; 4Q246) where Son of God functions as an attribute and honorific for a messianic king.[9] The kinship language of sonship represents one who is chosen, who has the ability to exercise agency on behalf of God, and who is a recipient of God's authority.

Pervasive throughout the Roman Empire, both in the East where the Gospel of Mark is set and in the West, where the Gospel of Mark may have been written, was the use of the imperial cult as a means of promoting the reputation and legitimacy of the Roman emperor. Kinship language is pervasive. "As *imperator* and *princeps* Augustus promoted myths and stories to propagate a belief that he was the son of a god and that Julius Caesar was a god himself."[10] Adela Yarbro Collins notes that "from 27 BCE until 3 CE, Augustus' official name in Greek documents was Αὐτοκράτωρ Καῖσαρ θεοῦ υἱὸς Σεβαστός ('Emperor Caesar Augustus Son of God')."[11] Emperors Tiberius, Nero, and Domitian also appropriated the title *divi filius*.[12] Vespasian and Titus, while they did not utilize *divi filius* were referred to as *divi augusto vespasiano* and *Tito divi vespasiani filio vespasiano* respectively.[13] The kinship language designates the legitimacy of the emperors and their right to assume the throne as honored heirs and members of the divine dynasty that is established in terms of sonship with Julius Caesar by Caesar Augustus.

Craig Evans compares the beginning of the Gospel of Mark with the Priene Calendar inscription which was written in honor of Caesar Augustus

8. Collins, *Mark: A Commentary*, 55.
9. Collins and Collins, *Son of God*, 72-73.
10. Samuel, "Beginning of Mark," 410.
11. Collins, "Worship of Jesus," 254.
12. For a summary of inscriptional evidence of *divi filius* for Emperors Augustus through Vespasian, see Kim, "Anarthrous υἱὸς θεοῦ," 232-36. See also Mowery, "Son of God," 100-110, for a more careful analysis and a critique of Kim.
13. Stevenson, Smith, and Madden, *Dictionary of Roman Coins*, 336.

ca. 9 BCE. The most relevant portion reads ἤρξεν δέ τῶι κόσμωι δι' αὐτὸν εὐαγγελί[ων ἡ γενέθλιος] τοῦ θεοῦ, "And since the birthday of the god Augustus was the beginning of the good tidings for the world."[14] Evans provides an analysis of the language in the inscription, language which Mark echoes. The inscription indicates that Caesar Augustus precipitated a new era for Rome and his rule inaugurated the principate. The Roman Republic was over and the emperor alone now ruled. Caesar Augustus was lauded for bringing peace, prosperity, and stability to Rome as a son of god.[15]

In 68–69, the year of the four emperors, Rome was thrown into turmoil until the relative stability brought about by Vespasian, right around the time the Gospel of Mark was written. Both the reign of Augustus and the reign of Vespasian were greeted as "good news" throughout the empire. "According to Josephus, 'every city celebrated the good news [εὐαγγέλια] and offered sacrifices on his behalf.'"[16] In imitation of the "good news" brought by the reigns of Augustus and Vespasian, Mark establishes Jesus, the Son, and primary agent, of God by virtue of his kinship relationship with God, as a new beginning of good news for the world. As Augustus and Vespasian ruled over their households and empire, Jesus, the Son of God builds God's empire by forming a core kinship group of disciples (1:16–20; 2:13; 3:13–19) and an extended family of followers (3:31–35).

The incipit of Mark 1:1 could very well be a means for Mark and his community of negotiating the power and influence of the Roman Empire. Mark establishes Jesus as the Son of God competing with, while also imitating, the deified Vespasian and his son, Titus. There is a clear parallel between naming Jesus as a Son of God and the inauguration of his gospel and the emperor as *divi filius* and the proclamation of his reign as gospel for his subjects. Simon Samuel notes, "The use of 'son of God' appropriates and, at the same time, abrogates the son of God status of the Roman emperors."[17]

The kinship language attributed to Jesus in his designation as Son of God in Mark 1:1 points to his chosenness, agency, and authority which will be further elaborated in the narrative of Mark when Jesus will act as the Son of God with God's authority in his teaching, exorcising, and healing. Moreover, the nexus of Christology and discipleship in terms of kinship

---

14. Evans, "Mark's Incipit," 69. The connection between Jesus and the Priene Calendar Inscription was made previously by Koester, "Jesus the Victim," 12–13, whose work Evans notes. See Evans, "Mark's Incipit," 68n6.

15. Evans, "Mark's Incipit," 69–70.

16. Evans, "Beginning of the Good News," 94, compares the Priene Calendar Inscription about Caesar Augustus and descriptions of Vespasian's accession by Josephus. See Josephus, *War*, 4.614–19.

17. Samuel, "Beginning of Mark," 416.

is anticipated by Jesus' designation as Son of God when it is juxtaposed to the role and actions of the Roman emperors. Just as the emperor extends his kinship as *pater patriae* to his household and empire, Jesus will extend his kinship with God to a core kinship group of disciples and an extended family of followers in order to establish the empire of God. Kinship is the nexus of Christology and discipleship whereby Jesus as the Son of God will establish his empire by the creation of a kinship group of disciples.

2. 1:2-13 THE BAPTISM OF THE SON OF GOD

After the incipit, the first narrative block elaborates Jesus' kinship with God as Son and Christ through biblical prophecy and through the ministry of John the Baptist and his prophecy about Jesus. Mark elaborates Jesus' kinship with God as a Son in a melding of Isaiah 40 and Malachi 3 providing Jesus with the scriptural authority for his work and ministry.[18] This elaboration establishes that as God's Son, Jesus is God's messenger and the one who prepares the way for God's presence in the world. Jesus' kinship with God is now supported by biblical witness which provides further legitimacy for Jesus' sonship and anticipates that he is the one who will establish God's empire by means of a core kinship group of disciples and an extended family of followers.

Jesus, primarily presented in kinship terms as the Son of God, makes his entry into the world through the ministry of John the Baptist. Mark indicates that John was also in the wilderness baptizing. He was popular and had garnered a following from Judea and Jerusalem (1:5), cementing his honor and authority as a prophet. Following the identification of Jesus by his kinship relationship as God's Son (1:1) and the prophecy that elaborates Jesus' sonship as a Son who brings God's message (1:2-3), John's further prophecy underscores the exalted significance of Jesus' kinship with God. John's prophecy designates Jesus as a most honorable and worthy Son of God. Even with John's own honorable status as a prophet, he will not be worthy to do the work of a household slave (1:7), further emphasizing the honor Jesus holds.[19] John has been offering a baptism of repentance for the forgiveness of sins, a means of restoring one's relationship with God. John states that he baptizes with water, but Jesus will baptize with the Holy Spirit

---

18. Tolbert, *Sowing the Gospel*, 239-48, provides a discussion on 1:1-3 and whether it refers to Jesus or John. Tolbert argues that the only possible referent to 1:2-3 is Jesus because he is the only character presented thus far in the narrative. It is only after this that John is introduced.

19. Marcus, *Mark 1-8*, 152.

(πνεύματι ἁγίῳ). The reference to the Holy Spirit intimately connects Jesus' work with God and God's eschatological salvation just as he is connected in terms of kinship as God's Son, continuing to establish Jesus' worth and honor.[20]

The second narrative block of Mark begins with the first kernel: Jesus' baptism (1:9-11). This scene repeats the kinship language of 1:1 as God now designates Jesus as God's Son, providing the launching point for his ministry as God's chosen agent (1:11). While John was baptizing in the wilderness at the Jordan River, Jesus comes and he is baptized by John. As Jesus comes up out of the water, the heavens are torn open, the Spirit descends upon him like a dove, and a voice claims, σὺ εἶ ὁ υἱός μου ὁ ἀγαπητός, ἐν σοὶ εὐδόκησα (You are my son, the beloved, in you I am pleased). The first textually uncontested claim of Jesus' kinship is directly from the mouth of God (metaphorically speaking). Jesus' identity is fixed at his baptism which precedes and leads directly to his ministry.

Jesus' baptism is the first kernel of the Markan plot that leads to the latter two kernels of the first passion prediction and transfiguration (8:31-9:10) and the crucifixion (15:21-41) as argued in chapter 2.[21] Several elements, including a reference to the heavens, a voice coming from the heavens, and Jesus designated in the kinship language of "son," echo throughout these passages (1:9-11; 9:2-9; 15:33-39). The baptism of Jesus confirms Jesus' identity as God's Son and inaugurates his ministry with God's direct declaration of Jesus' sonship and anointing with the Holy Spirit. Having employed kinship language, the first kernel raises the questions of how Jesus will act as God's Son and agent and how his identity will be revealed. At the baptism, it is only Jesus himself and the reader/audience who are aware of Jesus' identity as God's Son. These questions will be answered in the satellites that revolve around the baptism and the later kernels of the first passion prediction and transfiguration and the crucifixion.

In an analysis of the beginning of Mark, Santiago Guijarro compares the Gospel of Mark to several accounts of Hellenistic "lives."[22] Guijarro is

---

20. A more extensive discussion of the Holy Spirit follows below. Marcus notes the significance of the Holy Spirit for the Hebrew Bible and Qumran: God gives the spirit to the anointed one (2 Sam 23:1-2; Isa 11:1-2; 61:1; *Pss. Sol.* 17:37; *1 Enoch* 49:3; 62:2). Marcus, *Mark 1-8*, 152. Kingsbury suggests a connection with Joel 3:1-2 and Num 11:29. "In this view, therefore, Mark would have understood the expression 'baptizing with the Holy Spirit' to refer in a broad sense to the eschatological salvation that God achieves through the agency of Jesus, the Mightier One" (Kingsbury, "Spirit and the Son of God," 197).

21. See Ulansey, "The Heavenly Veil Torn," 123-25, for the inclusio regarding the baptism and crucifixion.

22. Guijarro, "Why Does?," 28-38.

concerned that the beginning of Mark does not include a birth narrative or a genealogy of Jesus. Instead, Mark begins with the work of John the Baptist and the baptism of Jesus. Guijarro concludes that Mark's prologue does not begin like the Hellenistic "lives" and include information on ancestry and education, because Mark is quite aware of Jesus' humble origins as a carpenter or artisan from Nazareth and son of Mary with no mention of a father (6:3). Instead, since "lives" were to praise their subjects and highlight their character, Mark focuses on Jesus' divine kinship and ascribed honor in the event of his baptism. The most common and important way to acquire honor was by virtue of the family into which one was born.[23] Mark makes clear at the very beginning of his gospel that Jesus has a particular origin. "The key moment is the vision after his baptism, where Jesus' ascribed honor is finally revealed . . . God himself has declared him his Son."[24] With this kinship language, Jesus is connected intimately with God as his Son and by virtue of that kinship relationship, Jesus is ascribed the highest honor.

In his work on Roman imperial ideology and the Gospel of Mark, Michael Peppard analyzes Jesus' baptism in light of first-century Roman culture, especially in terms of ideology of the emperor.[25] Kinship relationships provide a central resource, notably adoption as a son and the concepts of *numen* and *genius*. In part, Peppard argues for a Roman provenance for Mark and reads this baptismal scene in relation to the important kinship practice of adoption. Peppard explains the significance of adoption in securing succession and granting prestige, especially among the Roman imperial elite. The Roman emperor during the life of Jesus was himself an adopted son of Julius Caesar. "If readers of Mark consider the resonance of the concept of adoption in the Roman ideology of Mark's era, it does not appear to be a 'low' Christology at all. To the contrary, adoption is how the most powerful man in the world gained his power."[26] The baptism scene in the Gospel of Mark is the moment that God selects and adopts Jesus as his Son (1:10–11) with the effect that with this kinship relationship as God's Son, Jesus will exhibit more power and authority than the Roman emperor.

Peppard further illuminates the significance of kinship and of this adoption motif by reading the Spirit in terms of the Roman concepts of *genius* and *numen*, as they were combined in the emperor. He defines *genius* as a life-force that ensures the continuation of a family (passed on by both

---

23. Ibid., 32.

24. Ibid., 33. Guijarro acknowledges that υἱός τοῦ θεοῦ may be a later addition to 1:1 and so does not include it as part of his analysis.

25. Peppard, *Son of God*, 86–131.

26. Ibid., 95.

procreation and adoption) and also a tutelary spirit that protects its members during their lifetimes. *Numen* can be understood as the expressed will of a divine being.[27] Peppard makes it clear that he is drawing on a functional relationship between the Spirit and *genius* and *numen*, and not a linguistic connection. "Like the *genius*, the Spirit is the unifying life force of a family, the divine family inaugurated by God's election of Jesus as Son. The Spirit is possessed by Father, Son, and all the new members of the family."[28] The *numen*, or the Spirit, "expresses the will of God in the world. It has endowed Jesus with God's power, and others who possess it also do God's will (Mark 3:35)."[29] Kinship is the nexus of Christology and discipleship in the work of the spirit that compels Jesus and the disciples to do the will of God and unites them as a family.

Mark also depicts the unifying life force of the spirit as a dove descending upon Jesus (1:10). Peppard interprets the dove imagery in comparison with the practice of augury and omens with bird imagery surrounding the accession of various Roman emperors including Augustus, Tiberius, Domitian, and Vespasian.[30] Rome and its emperors are often associated with the eagle, a symbol of military might and victory. "The eagle leads every Roman legion; it is the 'king' (βασιλεύς) and 'most warlike' (ἀλκιμώτατος) of all birds, a 'sure sign of empire' (τῆς ἡγεμονίας τεκμήριον), and an 'omen' of victory (κληδών)."[31] Moreover, the eagle represents the *genius*, the unifying life force, of the Roman imperial dynasty often defined in terms of sonship from Augustus to Tiberius all the way to Vespasian. In contrast, the dove has served as a representative of Syria-Palestine and often symbolizes nonviolence and peace.[32] Peppard notes that the dove is often portrayed as a contrasting symbol to the eagle. As the eagles are present at the election of Roman emperors, Mark depicts the Spirit as a dove at the election of Jesus as the Son of God as a means of imitation and contest. "The bird omen of the dove instead portends the accession of a different son of God, whose rise to

27. Ibid., 113.
28. Ibid., 114.
29. Ibid.
30. Ibid., 116–18.
31. Ibid., 120.
32. Ibid., 118–21. Peppard cites both Tibullus (*Elegiae* 1.7.18) and Lucian (*De Dea Syria*, 14, 33, 54) who associate the dove with the region of Syria-Palestine. See Catullus and Tibullus, *Catullus, Tibullus*, 228–29; and Lucian, *Anacharsis or Athletics*, 356–57, 388–89, 404–405. Peppard juxtaposes this dove imagery with contrasting imagery between the eagle and the dove, citing Judg 11:7 which compares Israel to a dove acting peacefully and with forgiveness and *The Letter of Aristeas* which describe doves as gentle and clean, the attributes of which people should emulate.

power, though it would be mocked and suspended by the colonial authority, would ultimately be vindicated by his adoptive father."[33] The Spirit in the form of a dove confirms Jesus' kinship relationship as God's Son and stands as the representative of the transmission of God's power and authority to the Son, Jesus. It also defines that kinship not in terms of the military eagle-like power of Rome's emperors but as a more dove-like sonship marked by nonviolence and peace.

In addition, it is the Spirit–the unifying lifeforce of a family inaugurated by God's election of Jesus as Son–that drives (ἐκβάλλει) Jesus into the wilderness and into temptation by Satan for forty days (1:12–13). The ability of the Spirit to "drive" Jesus into the wilderness demonstrates the power it possesses as *genius*, asserting authority over the Son of God to do the will of God. Mark does not spend a lot of time on the temptation of Jesus, but it is not without significance. Jeffrey B. Gibson notes that the very use of the word πειραζόμενος brings with it connotations that would evoke certain assumptions from the implied audience about Jesus' time in the wilderness and his identity expressed in kinship terms. A person described in this way was "being probed and proved, often through hardship and diversity, in order to determine the extent of one's worthiness to be entrusted with, or the degree of one's loyalty or devotion to, a given commission and its constraints."[34] In effect, Jesus' honor and loyalty as a Son are examined and tested.

The testing of Jesus as a Son occurs εἰς τὴν ἔρημον (1:12). The wilderness evokes other tests of honor and loyalty such as that of the Israelites as "sons of God" (Exod 4:22; Hos 11:1) after their exodus from Egypt. God's covenant faithfulness endures the Israelites' trial and God continues to provide for his children just as the angels wait upon (διηκόνουν) God's Son Jesus (1:13). Moreover, Jesus, as God's Son, will provide and care for his own children (2:19), his core kinship group of disciples and extended family of followers, who find themselves in need in the wilderness (6:30–44; 8:1–10).[35] Kinship provides the nexus for the gospel's presentation of Christology and discipleship.

The Spirit driving Jesus into the wilderness also echoes the story of creation in Gen 1:1—2:3. It is the Spirit of God (πνεῦμα θεοῦ) that hovers over the waters at creation (Gen 1:2) and it is Adam (אדם or ἄνθρωπον)

33. Ibid., 124.

34. Gibson, "Jesus' Wilderness Temptation," 12.

35. Jesus is primarily identified as a son (of God), but within the context of the family and household of disciples, Jesus' role is that of the *paterfamilias*. While not the disciples' "father" per se, Jesus functions as the head of the household with father-like attributes. Jesus acquires these attributes because of his sonship. See chapter 2.

who is with the wild beasts and has dominion over them (Gen 1:26). In the second creation story, Adam fails in his worthiness and loyalty to God as he is tested by the serpent (Gen 3:6–7). Adam is cast out of the garden and he becomes alienated from creation and the wild beasts. Jesus placed in the wilderness with the beasts hints at a reversal and restoration of God's created order.

Finally, the angels wait upon Jesus as God's Son (1:13). Again, Jesus' time in the wilderness evokes images of the Exodus where angels assist the people as children or "the sons" of God (Exod 3:10; 14:19; 23:20, 23; 32:34; 33:2) and images of the prophet Elijah who is served by angels (1 Kgs 19:5–7).[36] Each echo strengthens the tie that Jesus has with God expressed in kinship language (son) and the purpose of his ministry to act as a faithful Son, as God's agent in the world as confirmed by the Spirit, the unifying life force of the divine family inaugurated by God's election of Jesus as a Son.

At the very beginning of Mark's gospel, not only does Mark employ kinship language to define Jesus as the Son of God (1:1) but also presents God using kinship language to designate and choose Jesus as his Son (1:11). The added imagery of the Spirit descending upon Jesus at his baptism adds another component of identity and purpose in kinship terms to Jesus. Like the Roman *genius* and *numen*, the Spirit works in and through Jesus to do the work of God in the world, to give rise to the empire of God in the world, and to empower and bring together the core kinship group of disciples and the extended family of followers who do God's will. Just as the emperor's *genius* commanded obedience, adoration, and worship, so too, does the Spirit as the unifying life force of the divine family inaugurated by God's election of Jesus as a Son. The Spirit not only empowers Jesus' identity and actions as Son of God, but as is evidenced throughout Mark, the Spirit also compels and directs the disciples and those who follow Jesus (13:11).

The sonship of Jesus and his kinship with God is designated and affirmed in the biblical witness about Jesus (1:2–3), in the ministry of John the Baptist and his prophecy about Jesus (1:4–8), in the baptism of Jesus (1:9–11), and in his testing in the wilderness (1:12–13). As the spirit descends upon Jesus, the unifying life force of the divine family inaugurated by God's election of Jesus as a Son, it drives him into the wilderness and subsequently into his ministry which inaugurates the empire of God. Moreover, the driving force of the Spirit compels Jesus to do the will of God. These events anticipate the nexus of Christology and discipleship by means of kinship when Jesus, as the Son of God, will call a core kinship group of disciples to accompany him and assist in his ministry and in the establishment of

---

36. This is summarized by Moloney, *Mark: Storyteller*, 61–62.

God's empire (1:16-20; 3:13-18) as well as an extended family of disciples who are designated brothers and sisters of the Son because they do the will of God (3:31-35).

3. 1:14-15 THE SON INAUGURATES THE EMPIRE OF GOD

Jesus begins his ministry with his entry into Galilee and his proclamation of the good news of the empire of God. That is, the first satellite that elaborates the role of Jesus as God's Son, as the agent of God's purposes, does so by presenting him proclaiming the good news of God's empire. This proclamation also leads the way to the narrative block which comprises the preaching, ministry, and healing in and around the Galilee. This satellite echoes the language of 1:1. The Gospel of Mark begins with the Ἀρχὴ τοῦ εὐαγγελίου Ἰησοῦ Χριστοῦ υἱοῦ θεοῦ (The beginning of the good news of Jesus Christ, Son of God) and the ministry of Jesus begins with Jesus κηρύσσων τὸ εὐαγγέλιον [τῆς βασιλείας] τοῦ θεοῦ (preaching the good news of the empire of God) corroborating the prophecy about God's Son who will be his messenger (1:2-3).[37] The scene provides important definition for the kinship term "Son of God" in that a primary role for the Son of God is to establish the empire of God by telling everyone about it and by forming a new community or kinship group of disciples.

Βασιλεία τοῦ θεοῦ evokes certain images which draw on both the Hebrew Bible and the Roman imperial context in which Mark was written.[38] There is no direct reference to "the kingdom of God" in the Hebrew Bible with the exception of Wis 10:10 where Wisdom guides a righteous man and

---

37. A D W 𝔐 lat sy^p bo^{pt} contain this reading. Collins notes "This reading is no doubt an assimilation of the phrase τὸ εὐαγγέλιον τοῦ θεοῦ ('the good news of God'), which is unusual in the Gospels (but see 1 Thess 2:2, 8, 9; Rom 1:1; 15:16; 2 Cor 11:7), to the more common notion of the βασιλεία τοῦ θεοῦ ('kingdom of God')." Collins, *Mark*, 134nk. Keck notes that the definition of εὐαγγέλιον as evoking military or political victory suggests that Jesus was victorious in a power struggle with Satan in the wilderness. "This interpretation of the passage supports what was said about Jesus as the Stronger One: Mark's Jesus is the victorious Son of God who returns from the testing-ground with the εὐαγγέλιον" (Keck, "Introduction to Mark's Gospel," 361-62).

38. There is a vast amount of scholarship on the subject of "the kingdom of God" both in the Synoptic Gospels and the New Testament. Most of these studies focus on the definition and distinct nature of "kingdom" as it occurs in the text (spatial, time, metaphor, etc.). See Maloney, *Jesus' Urgent Message*, 45-74; and Beavis, *Jesus and Utopia*, 71-83, for discussions and the history of scholarship on the Kingdom of God in Mark. In reference to the Kingdom of God and Mark 1:15, the focus is largely on "gospel" and "time." See Collins, *Mark*, 153-55; or Gutierrez, "Mark 1:14-15," 427-31, as examples.

shows him the kingdom of God (βασιλείαν θεοῦ). However, the idea that God is king and notions of God's rule are prevalent in the Bible.[39] Eugene Boring interprets the first-century Jewish understanding of "the kingdom of God" from a three-fold perspective: (1) God's rule is eternal and God is the creator and ruler of the universe (Ps 103:19). (2) God's rule is present to and in the lives of those who are obedient (Deut 6:4). (3) There is a future rule of God where God's reign will be reestablished and creation will be restored to God's sovereignty (*As. Mos.* 10.1–3a).[40] Boring concludes that Mark's depiction of the kingdom corresponds to this Jewish understanding: "The kingdom dawns and becomes real in the ministry of Jesus, is presently hidden in this worldly reality, and will be revealed in power when Jesus appears as the apocalyptic Son of Man (9:1)."[41] This explanation, however, does not pay attention to the reality of the Roman Empire that serves as a foreground to Mark, neither does it incorporate the fact that Mark presents Jesus' proclamation and enactment of God's empire as a central elaboration of his kinship to God as God's Son.

Βασιλεία evokes the Roman Empire, the reigning power in the Mediterranean region.[42] "In any Roman province, the primary referent of *basileia* would have been the *imperium Romanum*."[43] The Roman Empire was the political, social, military, and religious sovereign power and would have provided, or denied, access to property, goods, food, and status. The phrase would also evoke images of the local Galilean ruler "King" Herod Antipas who was aligned with Rome. Herod Antipas is responsible for the arrest of John the Baptist (1:14; 6:17), an event mentioned immediately prior to

39. See 1 Sam 12:12; Pss 5:2; 10:16; 44:4; 47:7–8; 68:24; 93:1; 96:10; 99:1; 146:10; Isa 6:5; 33:22; 44:6; 52:7; Zeph 3:15; Zech 14:9, 16; Mal 1:14. In addition there are references to the "Kingdom of the Lord" in 1 Chr 28:5; 2 Chr 13:8; Ps 103:19.

40. Boring, *Mark: A Commentary*, 52.

41. Ibid., 53.

42. Carter notes, "The noun βασιλεία can indicate both 'royal power' and 'territory' (BAGD, 134–35). A survey of the usage in Josephus and the LXX confirms these dimensions. Sometimes the term refers to quite limited power and territory, but the term also refers to extensive empires: Babylonian, Median, Persian, and Alexander's in Dan 2:37–45, to Alexander's in 1 Macc 1:6, to Antiochus Epiphanes' and the Seleucids' in 1 Macc 1:16, 41, 51; Josephus, *War* 1.40; 7.40, and to Rome's empire in Josephus, *War* 5.409 (Vespasian)" (Carter, *Matthew and the Margins*, 571–72n8). Carter also notes the numerous references to Rome's power and territory to certain rulers, especially in Judea and Galilee. See Josephus, *War*, 1.392, 396, 398, 457–58, 2.93–94, 215, 220 among others.

43. Moore, *Empire and Apocalypse*, 38. Moore suggests that Mark's use of ἡ βασιλεία τοῦ θεοῦ is an example of *catachresis*, a term utilized by Gayatri Spivak that "denotes the process by which the colonized strategically appropriate and redeploy specific elements of colonial or imperial culture or ideology" (Moore, *Empire and Apocalypse*, 37).

Jesus' pronouncement of God's empire. Once John the Baptist has been arrested by ὁ βασιλεὺς Ἡρῴδης, Jesus announces the arrival of ἡ βασιλεία τοῦ θεοῦ. Jesus, as God's Son and agent establishes an empire that is in direct opposition to, but also in distinct mimicry of, the Roman Empire.[44] Mark utilizes the language of the Roman Empire; the terms εὐαγγέλιον and βασιλεία would have evoked the reign and power of the Roman emperor (Vespasian), his son (Titus), and those leaders aligned with him.[45] Simultaneously, Jesus, affiliated in terms of kinship as the Son, inaugurates the empire of *God*, who is not only the sovereign of the land, but the creator of the heavens and the earth (Ps 93:1).

Jesus' kinship as Son involves, then, establishing God's empire. The content of his message requires his hearers and recipients, his core kinship group of disciples and his extended family of followers, to repent and believe in the good news (μετανοεῖτε καὶ πιστεύετε ἐν τῷ εὐαγγελίῳ) in 1:15 exhibiting the nexus of Christology and discipleship in terms of kinship. The concept of repentance has already been evident in the work of John the Baptist, but Jesus now requires faith (*fides*, πίστις). In the first-century Mediterranean world, faith and belief were not conceptual notions that indicated a person thought something existed or trusted that a person or idea was sound and true. Rather, faith and belief "point to the social, externally manifested, emotional behavior of loyalty, commitment, and solidarity."[46] Warren Carter notes the use of *fides* and πίστις in the imperial and political aspects of the Roman world. "*Fides* is not a static or internal quality, but one that is displayed in actions and lived out in relationships and through societal structures in the context of patron-client obligatory relationships."[47] A most notable patron-client relationship in the Roman first century would have been that between the emperor and his subjects. In imitation and contest, Jesus' proclamation and command required followers to turn toward him in commitment and fidelity and to give their trust and loyalty to God's Son and to God's empire rather than to the Roman emperor and his imperial dynasty. Faith, and the lack thereof, will continue to play a central role throughout the Gospel of Mark in Jesus' ministry, his authority, and his

---

44. Even as subordinate groups oppose and contest those who subjugate them, the dynamic of imitation and mimicry also exists. Carter notes oppressed people "resent the power that is being exerted over them, yet they recognize that being able to wield power is desirable. They long for what they resist. They resemble what they oppose. Imitation coexists with protest, accommodation, and survival" (Carter, *The Roman Empire*, 24).

45. Evans, "Mark's Incipit," 69.

46. Malina and Rohrbaugh, *Social- Science Commentary*, 359.

47. Carter, *John and Empire*, 267.

establishment of God's empire and God's family. Through this call to repent and believe in the good news, Jesus calls people to experience kinship with God as "sons" (2:19) and brothers and sisters (3:35), thereby participating in his kinship as Son of God. Kinship thus provides the nexus for the gospel's presentation of Christology and discipleship.

4. 1:16–20 THE SON CALLS HIS NEW BROTHERS AND FIRST DISCIPLES

This nexus becomes evident in one of Jesus' initial acts as God's Son and agent, namely to call a core kinship group of disciples for the new empire in 1:16–20. As he is walking alongside the Sea of Galilee, he sees Simon and his brother Andrew, fishermen, and Jesus commands them to follow him. Jesus claims he will make them ἁλιεῖς ἀνθρώπων (fishermen of people). Walking a little further, Jesus comes upon James, the son of Zebedee, and his brother, John. He also commands them to follow. James and John leave their father in the boat with the hired help and they also follow Jesus.

This satellite elaborates the first kernel of Jesus' baptism by demonstrating that Jesus' role as Son and agent extends beyond him to others; Jesus' kinship with God extends to his disciples who are also depicted in terms of kinship in following scenes (2:19; 3:33–35).[48] As the βασιλεία comes among humans, its agent, God's Son, requires faith and fidelity to Jesus and God and membership in a new kinship community. The Son's first encounter with other people after his baptism is when he calls them to discipleship. Jesus' sonship correlates directly with the establishment of his family of disciples.

The empire of God immediately disrupts existing kinship networks and calls disciples to enter God's empire through faith in and kinship with the Son, Jesus. Jesus establishes his new family by commanding Simon, Andrew, James, and John to accompany him. The word "disciple" (μαθητής) is not used by Mark at this point, but discipleship is implicit; Jesus asks the fishermen to δεῦτε ὀπίσω μου (Follow me) and ἠκολούθησαν αὐτῷ (they followed him).[49] Following Jesus requires these men to leave their original kinship groups, their occupations, and their cultural and social statuses. Malina and Rohrbaugh observe that Simon, Andrew, James, and John act abnormally

---

48. Kozar, "Forsaking Your Mother-in-law," 37.

49. Malina and Rohrbaugh suggest that although discipleship language is not directly used, it is implied. "In philosophical writings in antiquity the term 'follow' often describes the relationship of teacher and disciples" (Malina and Rohrbaugh, *Social-Science Commentary*, 149).

by leaving their occupations and their families to follow Jesus because they would have cut themselves off from their livelihood. The implication is that, like Jesus before them in the wilderness (1:9–11), they depart from their kinship networks to follow him.⁵⁰ Moreover, Andrew and James are both initially identified in terms of their kinship relationships as τὸν ἀδελφὸν (brother) in 1:16 and 19. Not only do Peter, Andrew, James, and John leave their original kinship groups, but they also reconstitute their "brotherhood" as they follow Jesus the Son and enter into his kinship network (3:31–35) in reflection of the nexus of Christology and discipleship in terms of kinship.⁵¹ In addition, when James and John abandon their father, they not only cut themselves off from their family and livelihood, but their departure would negatively affect their father's honor and authority.⁵² By following Jesus, James and John transfer the authority and honor they previously gave to their father to Jesus. They establish a new kinship group in the empire of God (βασιλεία τοῦ θεοῦ) one that is made up of a family of disciples who follow Jesus and do his father's will (3:31–35).

The call to follow Jesus is in direct opposition to the social and cultural expectation to maintain close-knit family (birth) ties in order to maintain social and economic standing in the first century Mediterranean region.⁵³ Jesus, the Son of God who proclaims the good news of the empire of God, effectively commands his followers to abandon their position in the Roman Empire as lower-class fishermen living in a distant, Roman province⁵⁴ for a new position in the empire of God. In the ancient Mediterranean, fishing was an embedded part of the Roman imperial economy. Although fishermen maintained a lower social status, elites and tax collectors relied on fishing families and hired hands to contribute goods and services in fish, nets, and fish products.⁵⁵ The fishing families and hired hands were indebted to the local brokers and tax collectors from whom they received fishing rights and

---

50. Ibid., 146, 149.

51. Ahearne-Kroll, "'Who Are My?,'" 11, observes that the original kinship ties are not completely abandoned since Peter and Andrew and James and John follow Jesus as brothers and Jesus heals Peter's mother-in-law. I argue that Jesus does not dismiss kinship ties since his community of disciples is structured in terms of kinship, but that these ties are reoriented so that kinship with Jesus as his disciple and doing God's will becomes central.

52. Moxnes, *Putting Jesus in His Place*, 56.

53. Malina, *New Testament World*, 82–83.

54. See Myers, *Binding the Strong Man*, 135–36 for a brief discussion on the social location of the disciples as lower-class-family fishermen, but not at the very bottom of the social scale.

55. See Hanson, "Galilean Fishing Economy," 99–111.

capitalization.⁵⁶ Although the empire will not be destroyed by the disciples' departure from their work as fisherman, the economy will be disrupted. The new disciples will instead serve as fishermen of people in the place where the empire is established, status yet to be determined. Jesus' kinship as God's Son inaugurates his ministry and requires the extension of that kinship to a new family of disciples who will participate in God's empire as fisherman to increase the kinship network of God and Jesus.

Although kinship language is not used explicitly for the initial call of Jesus' disciples, there are implications in the scene that anticipate the construction of the community of disciples identified in terms of kinship (3:31–35). Chief of these is that the four "brothers" are called out of their original kinship networks so that they can follow Jesus, thereby creating a new "band of brothers" that is based on their accompaniment of Jesus, the Son of God. Furthermore, by following Jesus and creating an alternative kinship network, the disciples transfer their kinship identities, their fidelity, and their honor from their original kinship ties to Jesus. The disciples' "new allegiance to Jesus takes precedence over the traditional societal ties to household, possessions, and occupation and thus subordinates and relativizes them,"⁵⁷ but does not abandon them completely (1:29–31).The disciples anticipate the kinship network that Jesus will explicitly designate in 3:31–35, already demonstrating the nexus of Christology and discipleship in terms of kinship.

5. 1:21–28 JESUS THE SON IS THE HOLY ONE OF GOD

In an illustration of the nexus of Christology and discipleship in terms of kinship, the new band of brothers then witness Jesus demonstrate authority and power as God's Son in his first act of healing after teaching in the Capernaum synagogue ὡς ἐξουσίαν ἔχων (as one having authority) in 1:21–28.⁵⁸ A man with an unclean spirit is present in the synagogue; he identifies and addresses Jesus as ὁ ἅγιος τοῦ θεοῦ (the Holy One of God). Jesus commands the spirit to be silent and to come out of the man. The spirit obeys Jesus and the man is healed. Those who witness the exorcism marvel at Jesus' authority in both his teaching and his power over unclean spirits. Though

---

56. Hanson and Oakman, *Palestine*, 99.

57. Carter, "Matthew 4:18–22," 68.

58. Although 1:21 might suggest that it is only Jesus who enters the synagogue, 1:29 makes clear that Peter, Andrew, James and John were with him (Καὶ εὐθὺς ἐκ τῆς συναγωγῆς ἐξελθόντες ἦλθον εἰς τὴν οἰκίαν Σίμωνος καὶ Ἀνδρέου μετὰ Ἰακώβου καὶ Ἰωάννου.).

the unclean spirit recognizes Ἰησοῦ Ναζαρηνέ, ὁ ἅγιος τοῦ θεοῦ (Jesus of Nazareth, the Holy One of God) and obeys his command, the witnesses raise the question of Jesus' teaching and authority, τί ἐστιν τοῦτο; (What is this?) In effect, the witnesses raise questions about Jesus' identity as the Son of God by questioning who it is who gives a new teaching with authority. Up to this point, only Jesus and the reader are aware of Jesus' identity from the initial kinship language that designates him Son of God in 1:1 and 1:11. The crowd, however, fails to recognize Jesus as God's Son or grant him any particular identity due to their different point of view; they focus upon his actions and designate his teaching and healing as a new teaching (διδαχὴ καινή) that fits within their own frame of reference. Now, an unclean spirit identifies Jesus in intimate relationship with God as one set apart for divine service and makes a public pronouncement of Jesus' power and authority as the Holy One of God, even if it is largely ignored by the crowd. The term "holy" (ἅγιος, קדש) defined in a cultic sense suggests someone, something, or some place which is set apart for particular use by God without moral implications.[59] Holiness denotes a function of use for or in service of the divine. Although the demon's identification of Jesus is not ὁ υἱός τοῦ θεοῦ, it is an echo of Jesus' sonship in that it suggests a close relationship with God and points toward Jesus' agency as God's Son.[60] To be the Son of God is to be an agent of the divine will and purposes; to be a holy one of God is to be recognized as set apart for divine service. Moreover, "Holy One of God" is a subset of "Son of God" because other demons (3:11 and 5:7) will identify Jesus as "Son of God."[61]

In an attempt to gain control over Jesus, the demon names him and identifies his status.[62] This identification as the "Holy One of God" evokes the prophetic tradition and aligns Jesus' status as a prophet along with the likes of Elisha (2 Kgs 4:9).[63] It also echoes the attribute of the priest Aaron as the "holy one of the Lord" (Ααρων τὸν ἅγιον κυρίου; Ps 106:16).[64] Each of these references grants Jesus a status that aligns him closely with God though not explicitly in kinship terms. Although Jesus is not directly identified by the spirit as ὁ υἱός τοῦ θεοῦ, the nature of the genitive construction

---

59. Bromiley, *Theological Dictionary*, 14.

60. Hurtado, *Lord Jesus Christ*, 287. Hurtado ties in the other references to demons and their identification of Jesus as "Son of God" in 3:11 and 5:7.

61. Brower, "Holy One and His Disciples," 58.

62. Myers, *Binding the Strong Man*, 142.

63. Ibid.

64. Marcus, *Mark 1–8*, 188.

of ὁ ἅγιος τοῦ θεοῦ suggests that the father-son relationship is implied.⁶⁵ The unclean spirit recognizes the special relationship Jesus has with God, which is designated in terms of sonship and accompanied by the decent of the Spirit (of God) at 1:10–11. The identification of Jesus as ὁ ἅγιος τοῦ θεοῦ by the spirit also serves to highlight Jesus' identity as one set apart for divine service by God, designated at his baptism and signified by the descent of the Spirit as a dove, in this case to establish God's empire through preaching, teaching, and now exorcism. As the Holy One of God and as the Son of God, Jesus acts as an agent of God set apart for divine service and purpose, exercising God's power and authority in behalf of his disciples and extended family of followers. Furthermore, the spirit's fearful response to Jesus indicates his power and authority have implication beyond what the reader has experienced: the spirit fears for its very existence because Jesus is ὁ ἅγιος τοῦ θεοῦ.⁶⁶ Moreover, Jesus is bestowed with the Spirit from God, a unifying life force of the divine family of God and Jesus which stands in direct contrast to the "unclean spirits" who are dividing and destructive forces.⁶⁷ Jesus' command to the spirit to be silent may be due to the first-century tradition of naming to gain power over someone or to the fact that Jesus' identity as God's Son is not yet public knowledge.⁶⁸ Nevertheless, the unclean spirit obeys Jesus' authority and the man is healed.

This is Jesus' first act of healing in the Gospel of Mark. Although onlookers observe his teaching and healing as "new" and marvel at it, Jesus has yet to create any conflict or threat by his work in the synagogue. The exorcism serves to highlight Jesus' authority and power over unclean spirits as he acts as God's Son and agent of power over unclean spirits and begins to establish the empire of God. Teaching and acting with authority (1:22), and not in the manner of the recognized scribal authorities (1:22), may be viewed as a subversive act because Jesus acts outside the bounds of kinship. Furthermore, the demon possession serves to emphasize Jesus' identity as God's agent publicly, in a way that indicates agency and intimacy of relationship, but not overt kinship which would result in charges of blasphemy.⁶⁹

---

65. Brower, "Holy One and His Disciples," 58.

66. Chilton, "Exorcism of History, 223.

67. In this first instance, the man with the unclean spirit does not have control over his own body. The depiction of Legion in 5:1–20 demonstrates the destructive and divisive power of the unclean spirits when the possessed man is not able to live with his family or in his community.

68. It is only Jesus (and the reader) who hears him identified as God's Son when he comes up out of the water at his baptism (1:9–11).

69. One of the charges brought against Jesus in 14:61–64 is blasphemy due to his identification as the Son of the Blessed (ὁ υἱὸς τοῦ εὐλογητοῦ).

James C. Scott notes that spirit possession "represents a quasi-covert form of social protest for women and for marginal, oppressed groups of men for whom any open protest would be exceptionally dangerous."[70] Therefore, the demon is able to identify Jesus as the Holy One of God publicly without putting Jesus or the possessed man at risk.[71]

Although Jesus is not directly identified in kinship terms as the Son of God when the unclean spirit speaks to him in the synagogue, the address of "Holy One of God" does identify Jesus in terms of a close relationship with God. Jesus the Son is addressed as one who has been set apart for divine service. Moreover, this Son and Holy one of God acts with authority and power that he received from God in his teaching and his exorcism. Kinship then serves as the nexus of Christology and discipleship when his new band of brothers witness Jesus acting with God's authority as the Son and Holy One of God. Jesus demonstrates his agency as the Son of God by exorcising the unclean spirit, agency that he will then hand on to his core kinship network and band of brothers, the disciples (3:15).

6. 1:29–31 ESTABLISHING A HOUSEHOLD: THE SON HEALS SIMON PETER'S MOTHER-IN-LAW

The nexus occurs again in the second satellite of healing when Jesus the Son and his new band of brothers, Simon, Andrew, James, and John depart the synagogue and go to the house of Simon and Andrew. Upon entering the house, Jesus and the disciples learn that Simon's mother-in-law is ill. In Jesus' second act of healing, he approaches Simon's mother-in-law and helps her to stand by taking her by the hand. At that moment, she is healed of her fever and she begins to serve them.

Not only does Jesus display his authority as God's Son for healing in the public place of the synagogue, but he also brings his power and authority into the household. In his act of healing, Jesus restores Simon's mother-in-law to her place of service within the household structure; she is able to provide hospitality.[72] The household of Simon and Andrew becomes the

---

70. Scott, *Domination and Resistance*, 141.

71. Moore, *Empire and Apocalypse*, 27, proposes that each exorcism in the Gospel of Mark should have some anti-colonial significance because of the blatant anticolonial significance in the exorcism of the Gerasene demoniac (5:1–20).

72. Trainor, *Quest for Home*, 91–95, provides an interesting, but highly speculative, discussion about Simon's mother-in-law, her healing, and the role of the household in the Gospel of Mark. He construes that Jesus establishes a new household of disciples over and against the traditional Roman *domus*. Trainor suggests that the mother-in-law's service is representative of the diaconal service provided by disciples. Certainly,

household of Jesus and those who are following him, his kinship group of disciples. Within the household, Jesus, as God's Son, extends his healing powers to those who are now a part of his extended family. Daniel Harrington notes, "This healing account not only has a christological function, but also stresses discipleship. Those first called to be disciples are mentioned explicitly as witnesses."[73] Harrington does not observe, however, that kinship provides the nexus between Christology and discipleship. Simon, Andrew, James, and John, as Jesus' new brothers, have followed Jesus into the house and now witness his healing power as the Son of God (or at least as the Holy One of God as he is publicly identified in 1:24).

Although Simon, Andrew, James, and John appear to have departed from their original kinship networks in 1:16–20, they do not completely give up their family ties. Andrew and Simon have a house in Capernaum and they extend hospitality to Jesus, James, and John. Simon and Andrew's household stands at the center of a new household and a new kinship group which is being formed by Jesus, defined by his kinship relationship as God's Son. In addition to the brothers, Simon and Andrew, Mark informs the reader that Simon's mother-in-law also resides in the house and now welcomes Jesus, the Son of God, and the brothers James and John. John Elliott notes the significance of the house/household in the first century:

> Historically and geographically, *oikos/oikia* designated one's place of origin and ethnic roots, one of the bases of one's social identity. Socially, it designated the kin group to which one belonged and the lineage that also determined one's identity. Economically, the *oikos/oikia* constituted the production base and chief locale of a family's income and livelihood. Psychologically, one's *oikos/oikia* was one's place of belonging, the primary source of one's emotional support, and the chief object of one's commitment and loyalties. Culturally, the expectations, values, and norms associated with family life and relations informed most of the scripts of everyday conduct.[74]

The household will continue to be a central part of Jesus' ministry and a place where he exercises his power and authority for healing as God's Son throughout the Gospel of Mark. This locale is first established here as the

---

there are women who followed and served Jesus throughout his ministry, but it is not clear that the mother-in-law's role was a move toward some egalitarian idea of household where she acts as a deacon or a host in a house church. She is simply healed and her place within the household is restored to her.

73. Donahue and Harrington, *Gospel of Mark*, 85.
74. Elliott, "Household/Family," 41.

place of hospitality to Jesus and his new family of followers and the place of healing offered to his follower's family members.

As noted above, the household and kinship group is a central building block in the first-century world of the Mediterranean. Moreover, the Roman Empire itself was modeled after the basic household unit where the emperor, also known as the *pater patriae*, stood as the *paterfamilias* of the household of Rome.[75] Michael Trainor observes the absence of a *paterfamilias* in this scene at Simon's home.[76] The implication is that either Simon has begun to fill the role as *paterfamilias* for the household, or even more, upon Jesus' entrance into the house or in his act of healing for Simon's mother-in-law, Jesus the Son assumes the role of *paterfamilias*, thus establishing a new household for the empire of God.[77] As the *paterfamilias*, Jesus functions as the patron of the household, providing the benefaction of healing to his client. In patron-client relationships a social superior (patron) would grant some sort of need in the form of favor or benefaction to a lower-status person (client). In return, the client would offer honor and loyalty to the patron. Moreover, patron-client relationships are understood in terms of kinship. "By entering a patron-client arrangement, the client relates to his patron as to a superior and more powerful kinsman, while the patron sees to his clients as his dependents."[78] Once Jesus, as the Son of God, has offered healing to Simon Peter's mother-in-law, she offers him loyalty by waiting upon him and serving him. Moreover, Jesus as *paterfamilias* stands as the head of a new household comprised of a family of disciples which provides an opportunity for alternative loyalty rather than the loyalty required by the emperor and his household of Rome.

Kinship is the nexus of Christology and discipleship where Jesus the Son of God establishes a household of disciples and provides benefits of healing for his family members. In turn, those who receive healing and a place in the household (either as core kin members or extended family) demonstrate faith, fidelity, and service to God's Son.

7. 1:32–34 THE SON EXTENDS HIS KINSHIP TO AND HEALS THOSE WHO ARE ILL

After multiple demonstrations of the nexus of Christology and discipleship in terms of kinship such as the inauguration of God's empire by Jesus'

---

75. See the discussion of the emperor as *pater patriae* in chapter 2.
76. Trainor, *Quest for Home*, 92–93.
77. See chapter 2.
78. Malina and Rohrbaugh, *Social-Science Commentary*, 388.

establishment of a core kinship group of disciples, teaching with authority in the synagogue, and extension of kinship in the benefit of healing to the man with an unclean spirit and Simon's mother-in-law, the Son's reputation has grown so that many come to seek healing and exorcism: καὶ ἦν ὅλη ἡ πόλις ἐπισυνηγμένη πρὸς τὴν θύραν (And the whole city was gathered at the door, 1:33). In the household of Simon, Jesus continues the work he began as God's Son by healing and casting out demons. Jesus does not allow the demons to speak for they know him (1:34). This serves as an echo to 1:24 where the unclean spirit in the synagogue identifies Jesus as the Holy One of God (ὁ ἅγιος τοῦ θεοῦ) and reminds the reader of Jesus' primary kinship relationship and identity as God's agent, and therefore, Son.

This summary immediately follows the healing of Simon's mother-in-law and the setting is still Simon's house in Capernaum. Jesus continues to demonstrate his authority over illness and demons. And as God's Son, Jesus achieves these healings within the household. Trainor suggests that the crowd has gathered within the house; to receive healing from Jesus, it is necessary to enter into his household. "Mark is indicating the growing attraction of Jesus' household in which the disciples are gathered, healed, called to ministry, and into which the socially rejected gather. The popularity of this house is emphasized."[79] Again, Jesus acts as the host, assuming the role of the *paterfamilias*, offering hospitality, and more importantly, healing and exorcism to those who seek it, to those who are a part of his core kinship group of disciples and to those who enter into his extended kinship network. Jesus continues to offer healing as a form of benefaction; Jesus is the patron and superior kinsman, who offers the gift of healing to his clients, his family. Kinship binds Jesus' identity as God's Son with discipleship where the Son provides the benefits of healing and hospitality to those who are and will become his family of followers. In return, these clients, followers and disciples, give loyalty and honor to Jesus, increasing his reputation. Not only does Jesus act with authority and power as God's Son in 1:32–34, but the summary also demonstrates the extent of Jesus' popularity so early in his ministry. God's Son has the power to teach, to heal, to exorcize, and now, by welcoming them into his household, to garner a large following which Jesus will designate, using kinship terms, as his "children" (2:19) and "brothers and sisters" (3:33–35). Kinship is the nexus of Christology and discipleship: Jesus, as the *paterfamilias*, provides hospitality and healing to an extended kinship group of disciples and followers who seek him in his household.

---

79. Trainor, *Quest for Home*, 95.

8. 1:35-45 THE SON EXERCISES PRIESTLY AUTHORITY: JESUS HEALS THE LEPER

On the next day, Jesus, the Son of God, travels with the brothers Simon, Andrew, James, and John beyond Capernaum preaching and casting out demons in the synagogues after spending time in prayer (1:35-39). Kinship is the nexus of Christology and discipleship where Jesus the Son gives his message of God's empire and extends benefactions of exorcism in the presence of his band of brothers and in behalf of an extended kinship network. In reiteration of 1:14-15, Jesus embarks as the Son of God to proclaim the message (κηρύξω) of the empire of God (1:38-39). The scene underscores important content for the kinship language identifying him as Son of God.

Jesus is approached by a leper who seeks healing. Moreover, this leper appears to know that Jesus has the power to heal him by the nature of his request, "If you desire, you can make me clean," (ἐὰν θέλῃς δύνασαί με καθαρίσαι, 1:40). This leper grants Jesus honor and respect by kneeling before him (γονυπετῶν). Once Jesus heals him, the leper further honors and glorifies Jesus and his healing power by going out and proclaiming (κηρύσσειν) what had happened to him, so much so that Jesus' popularity increases even more.[80]

The healing of the leper not only demonstrates Jesus' continued healing power but it also demonstrates his authority over issues normally reserved for priestly authorities. Jesus' authority, even in his priestly action, arises out of his identity as God's Son, expressed in terms of kinship. Jesus' act of healing (καθαρίζω) is the same as the declaration of cleanliness made by a priest (Lev 13:17).[81] The healing of the leper demonstrates the extension of Jesus' authority to the priestly realm and scriptural interpretation. Jesus then tells the leper to go to the priest to show his healing in further reference to Lev

---

80. Malina and Rohrbaugh, *Social-Science Commentary*, 151; Edwards, *Gospel According to Mark*, 72; and Myers, *Binding the Strong Man*, 154, all suggest that 1:45 indicates that Jesus has assumed an unclean status due to touching the leper and so he cannot go into a town. However, this does not account for the latter part of 1:45 where Jesus' popularity is such that "they came to him from everywhere," (καὶ ἤρχοντο πρὸς αὐτὸν πάντοθεν). This verse demonstrates the snowball effect of his popularity and reputation for healing from 1:28, 1:32-34, 1:37, 1:45, to 2:2, not his impurity. Furthermore, Mark does not indicate that Jesus considered himself impure before returning to Capernaum in 2:1. Jesus returned to Capernaum after a few days (δι' ἡμερῶν). Perhaps he was waiting for the period for purification to pass, which according to Lev 22:7 is only until sundown. It is more likely that he spent those days ministering to the people who sought him in 1:45. Neither Malina and Rohrbaugh, Edwards, nor Myers address the time Jesus is away or his return to Capernaum in terms of his connection with the leper.

81. Malina and Rohrbaugh, *Social-Science Commentary*, 151.

13:17 and in demonstration that although Jesus has authority over the law, he does not necessarily dismiss it. In additional support of Jesus' cultic authority, the leper ignores the call to go to the local priest, and instead goes out and tells what Jesus has done for him. As a recipient of Jesus' healing, the leper enters into Jesus' extended kinship network and acts as a disciple by displaying loyalty to the Son in the leper's dissemination of his message of Jesus' act. Though kinship language is not used, this healing act provides the nexus of Christology and discipleship in that in an act of discipleship, kinship members brought into the family by Jesus' benefit of healing now go forth to tell what God has done for them through God's Son, Jesus.

In return for the benefaction of healing granted to him by Jesus as patron and more powerful kinsman, the leper's proclamation helps to spread the reputation of Jesus so that his popularity continues to grow. Now, not only is a whole town gathered about Jesus' door (1:33), but his reputation for healing, casting out demons, and now ritual purification has spread regionally so that people enter his household from everywhere (πάντοθεν, 1:45). Jesus the Son continues to demonstrate the authority and power that he has received from God (1:10–11), acting as a patron for the benefit of his family, welcoming others into his household, healing, preaching, and teaching his new family of followers to establish God's empire. In the nexus of Christology and discipleship in terms of kinship, the message of the empire of God, first manifested by the Son, Jesus (1:14–15), is now proclaimed by his kinship network of disciples and followers (recipients of healing).

9. 2:1–12 THE SON HEALS THE PARALYTIC, HIS CHILD

The nexus is further illuminated as Jesus the Son provides benefactions and extends kinship to followers. After healing many who gathered at Simon's door and a journey to neighboring towns to preach in the synagogues, perform exorcisms, and to provide healing to a leper, Jesus returns to Capernaum where he is ἐν οἴκῳ (at home, 2:1).[82] Whether Jesus has returned to Simon's house and established it as his household, or that he has established residency elsewhere in Capernaum, Jesus is in a household with his core kinship group of disciples and his extended family of followers who have sought him for healing when so many come to see him that there is no room at the door to enter.[83] Jesus again acts as the *paterfamilias* welcoming

---

82. Painter, "When Is a House Not Home?," 498–500, provides a brief discussion on the definition of house and home and its use in the Gospel of Mark. He suggests that Jesus established his own house in Capernaum.

83. Trainor, *Quest for Home*, 95, notes that the only house mentioned at this point

people into his home and granting healing through his power and authority as God's Son and agent.

When four men carry a paralytic to see Jesus, there is no room for them to enter and so they climb up to the roof and lower the young man so that he can gain access to Jesus (2:3–4). In response to their τὴν πίστιν (faith), Jesus grants forgiveness to the paralytic. This is the first explicitly named demonstration of the faith Jesus commands in 1:15. It exhibits the paralytic's and his friends' loyalty and trust in Jesus and his authority as the Son and agent of God's empire. "The concept of *fides* (Latin) or *pistis* (Greek for 'faith/belief'; the verb is *pisteuō*) was an integral part of Roman elite and imperial self-understanding and actions that centered on faithfulness or fidelity in honoring the commitments into which Rome and another people or community entered."[84] The paralytic and his friends seek out healing, a benefaction from Jesus, in the same way people would seek benefaction or favors from patrons. In return, clients would give honor and loyalty to their patrons; clients would place their faith in their patrons. Moreover, relationships between patron and clients are understood as kinship relationships. "The relationships and roles, obligations and responsibilities between the patron and his or her clients is shaped into what social-scientists call 'fictive kinship' or 'pseudo-kinship.'"[85] Jesus as patron will provide for his clients as a father provides for his children; in return, Jesus, the Son, demands honor and fidelity both for himself, and his father, God. Jesus is the Son of God and yet functions as God's agent and representative and thus, patron and *paterfamilias* of the family of disciples and followers. Thus, kinship provides the nexus of Christology and discipleship in terms of patronage. Jesus' sonship with God provides benefit and care for his family of disciples. In turn, Jesus' family of disciples gives honor, faith, and fidelity to their patron and superior kinsman, Jesus.

This nexus is further illustrated when Jesus addresses the paralytic in kinship terms as τέκνον (child or son). Adela Yarbro Collins states that Jesus addresses the paralytic along the lines of a wise man or teacher addressing his pupil (Prov 31:2; Sir 2:1; 3:1).[86] I argue that within the setting of the household, the use of τέκνον is a kinship term. Also, in Proverbs and in Sirach, the recipients of wisdom are the actual children, belonging to the father (Prov 1:8; Sir 3:1). The derivation of τέκνον is τίκτω (I bear) and means "that

---

in Capernaum is the house of Simon and Andrew; thus it is logical to assume that this is the house where Jesus is residing. See also Edwards, *Mark*, 74.

84. Carter, *John and Empire*, 266.
85. Hanson and Oakman, *Palestine*, 75.
86. Collins, *Mark*, 185. See Liddell and Scott, *Intermediate Greek-English Lexicon*, 797.

which is born" thus, "child" or "descendant." It is an explicit kinship term. Jesus the Son, functioning as the *paterfamilias*, designates the paralytic as a member of his household by calling him "child" within the setting of Jesus' house. Although Jesus does not initially grant physical healing to the paralytic, the act of forgiveness by the Son of God restores the paralytic to his community (and/or now to Jesus' household).[87] The term of address also places Jesus in the superior role as "father," or at least as agent of his father, God.[88] Jesus' authority to heal and to establish a new household is granted to him by means of his kinship identity as God's Son. Kinship serves as the nexus of Christology and discipleship as the Son of God grants a place in the household and extends healing to the paralytic, whose act of faith in Jesus marks him as a disciple, and extended family member, of Jesus.

Jesus' gift of forgiveness launches the first of a series of challenge-riposte scenes in the Gospel of Mark, and the first public test for Jesus' honor.[89] Jesus' teaching, exorcisms, and acts of healing have gained him fame and popularity in Galilee. In addition, he has also attracted the attention of the local legal experts: the scribes (2:6). Before Jesus physically heals the paralytic, he forgives him of his sins; that is, Jesus as the Son acts as God's agent or broker and grant's God's forgiveness to the paralytic (2:5). The scribes question Jesus' authority to forgive, for only God is able to grant forgiveness. The scribes do not challenge Jesus directly; he perceives it τῷ πνεύματι αὐτοῦ (in his spirit, 2:8) which further demonstrates Jesus' power and authority as it was given to him by God and signified by the Spirit at the baptism (1:10). As if he were addressed directly, Jesus responds to the challenge to both his honor (reputation) and his authority to forgive sins by physically healing the boy and telling him to get up and walk (2:11).[90] Jesus also demonstrates that the scribes are his opponents: they do not align themselves with Jesus, and therefore with God. "The visible benefit proves the unobservable one, demonstrating that his declaring forgiveness is not blasphemy but the real

---

87. Malina and Rohrbaugh, *Social-Science Commentary*, 152.

88. Martin, "It's My Prerogative," 71.

89. Malina defines challenge-riposte as "a sort of constant social tug of war, a game of social push and shove ... The channels are always public, and the publicity of the message guarantees that the receiving individual will react in some way, since even his nonaction is publicly interpreted as a response" (Malina, *New Testament World*, 33). Challenge-riposte contains three phases: (1) the challenge; (2) the perception of the message by the individual and the public; (3) the reaction of the challenged one.

90. Malina and Rohrbaugh note: "The action of restoring the man to a state of functioning normally (the priority in our society) would have been viewed easier in that society than restoring him to a state of significance and stature in the community" (Malina and Rohrbaugh, *Social-Science Commentary*, 154).

conferral of God's gift."[91] As God's Son and agent, Jesus is authorized and able to grant forgiveness to the paralytic in behalf of God. As a new member of Jesus' kinship network, and in an act of following Jesus, the paralytic obeys the command of his new and more superior kinsman and gets up and walks. This further demonstrates the Son's power to heal those who have entered into his extended kinship network. Those who witness the forgiveness and the healing of the paralytic ἐξίστασθαι (were amazed) and δοξάζειν τὸν θεὸν λέγοντας ὅτι οὕτως οὐδέποτε εἴδομεν (glorified God saying, "We have seen nothing like this." 2:12). The public's reaction sustains Jesus' honor and authority, first ascribed to him in kinship terms as God's Son, and designates him as the winner of the challenge.

As Jesus responds to the challenge of his authority to act as God's Son and agent and to confer God's forgiveness on the paralytic, he uses the self-referential designation, in kinship terms, of ὁ υἱὸς τοῦ ἀνθρώπου (the Son of Man) in 2:10. This is the first instance of this kinship designation and it is used within the context of Jesus' defending his authority to grant forgiveness. Jesus identifies himself as a Son, as an agent of God, by his words. He acknowledges the claim of the scribes that God alone can forgive sins, but then demonstrates and designates his agency as the Son who is able to confer God's forgiveness. Jesus' use of ὁ υἱὸς τοῦ ἀνθρώπου primarily evokes the kinship relationship Jesus already has with God. "In effect, [Mark] uses Son of man to interpret and to give content to the conception of Jesus as Son of God."[92] It may also remind readers of its Hebrew Bible use as a descriptor in Dan 7: one who comes ὡς υἱὸς ἀνθρώπου from the heavens and is given authority over all empires (Dan 7:13-14).[93] Furthermore, the title is used ninety-three times by God to address the prophet Ezekiel (Ezek 2:1, 3, 6). The address designates the prophet as a human being, in stark contrast to God.[94] Marcus states that the title in conjunction with Ezekiel emphasizes "his human status in solidarity with those to whom he is sent and in contrast to the divine word with which he is commissioned."[95] Since it is an address from God to God's prophet, it also evokes a sense of prophetic authority

---

91. DeSilva, *Honor*, 134.

92. Perrin, "Son of Man Traditions," 358. Perrin notes instances in the Gospel of Mark that tie "Son of Man" and "Son of God" closely together, including 3:11 that illustrates Jesus' authority as the Son of God, which relates to the authority of the Son of Man in 2:10 and 2:28.

93. See the discussion on Son of Man in chapter 1.

94. Moore also notes "while the book of Ezekiel has regularly done duty as 'background' for this enigmatic Markan expression, it is not the main scriptural text that has been so adduced" (Moore, "Why There Are No Humans or Animals," 87).

95. Marcus, *Mark 1-8*, 528.

bestowed on Jesus.[96] Regardless of the evocation, the concept of agency in sonship is most prevalent in Jesus' use of ὁ υἱὸς τοῦ ἀνθρώπου.[97] In this case, Jesus designates himself as a Son in relationship to human beings. Jesus utilizes his role as a son "of man," as an agent of human beings to act with authority and power to heal and to grant God's forgiveness to those who believe. In the nexus of Christology and discipleship in terms of kinship, Jesus has the power to forgive as God's Son. As the Son of Man, this forgiveness is granted to his family of disciples and followers, in behalf of whom the Son of Man works.

In addition to establishing his honor and authority as one who grants healing and forgiveness in behalf of God the Father over and against the traditional, scribal authority, Jesus continues to establish his household as an alternative to, but in imitation of, the ruling household of Rome. Jesus acts as the agent of the Father, building an alternative kinship group, providing benefaction, hospitality, access to healing, and restoration to community in the same way the emperor and his household would provide for the Roman Empire. Unlike the emperor, who "distributed his benefits individually to those who had access to him and, more broadly, to favoured groups, notably the Roman plebs and the army,"[98] access to Jesus the Son seems relatively unlimited. Even with a crowd at the door of the house, the paralytic and his friends are able to gain access to Jesus through the roof. Jesus heals as many as seek him out, and like the emperor's reputation for benefaction, Jesus' reputation for benefaction for his family and clients spreads throughout the region (1:45; 2:1–2).

The nexus of Christology and discipleship in terms of kinship is prevalent in the healing of the paralytic. While Jesus the Son is at home, he offers benefactions by means of healing to those who come into his house, thereby offering them a place in his kinship group. Moreover, the paralytic and his friends demonstrate discipleship to the Son in their faith in Jesus' authority and power. Jesus then uses his authority as God's Son to grant forgiveness to the paralytic, whom he calls "child," further emphasizing discipleship in terms of kinship. When Jesus' authority is challenged, he refers to himself as "Son of Man," defending his authority by aligning himself and indicating his agency of human beings. In one more display of the nexus of Christology and discipleship in terms of kinship, the Son of Man provides another benefaction and heals the paralytic by commanding him to get up and walk. In

---

96. Donahue and Harrington, *Gospel of Mark*, 26.

97. Edwards, *Mark*, 80, also notes the connection between Son of Man and Son of God.

98. Garnsey and Saller, *Roman Empire*, 149.

an act of discipleship and following Jesus, the paralytic obeys Jesus and gets up and walks. Jesus, the Son not only has the power and authority to extend forgiveness of sins, but he also gives physical healing to those who enter into his family of disciples. Kinship is the nexus of Christology and discipleship.

10. 2:13-17 THE SON EXPANDS THE CORE KINSHIP GROUP OF DISCIPLES AND CALLS LEVI

The nexus continues in the call of Levi which echoes the calls of Simon, Andrew, James, and John in 1:16-20. Just as Jesus walked along the sea and saw the fishermen, he also sees Levi son of Alphaeus (Λευεὶν τὸν τοῦ Ἀλφαίου) sitting in the tax booth and commands him, as he did the others, "Follow me," (ἀκολούθει μοι). Demonstrating kinship as the nexus of Christology and discipleship, Jesus as the Son of God, calls Levi to follow him and to be a part of his new family of disciples. In a further echo of the first call of disciples where Jesus enters into the house with Peter, Andrew, James, and John (1:29), Jesus is at home with this newest disciple.[99] Instead of offering a healing, Jesus shares a meal and then faces a challenge by the Pharisees who accuse him of eating with tax collectors and sinners, which would be socially dishonorable (2:16).[100] Jesus responds to this verbal challenge with a bit of wisdom that those who are well require no doctor, but those that are sick do (2:17). Jesus suggests that illness is an analogy for sin; that is, both illness and sin separate one from his or her family or community.[101] By providing hospitality to his disciples, tax collectors, and sinners, Jesus grants them a place in the community, specifically as a part of his family that forgives their sin and restores their social status. The nexus of Christology and discipleship is exhibited in the Son's extension of kinship to those who need a place in the community and forgiveness of sins. As a disciple of Jesus,

---

99. NRSV translates 2:15 as "Levi's house," though the Greek simply states "his house," (ἐν τῇ οἰκίᾳ αὐτοῦ). The fact remains Jesus is in a home with his family of disciples, akin to 1:29-31.

100. Malina and Rohrbaugh note: "The Greek term *telones* refers to toll collectors employed by those contracting directly with local elites to collect fees on the movement of goods. Many, if not the majority, of toll collectors remained poor. Those who did not were universally presumed to be dishonest" (*Social-Science Commentary*, 154). Toll collectors and any other "sinner" who did not observe Torah would have caused a scandal in dining with Jesus. Malina and Rohrbaugh state: "Meals were times at which purity rules were taken very seriously by those of the house of Israel concerned with distancing themselves from nonobservant out-groups" (155).

101. Ibid., 155.

Levi participates in table fellowship and hospitality with his new brothers, the core kinship group of disciples.

As in the previous challenge to Jesus (2:8), his honor is at stake in the challenge of his meal practices by the scribes and the Pharisees (2:16). The popular reputation Jesus has achieved appears to be at stake in the eyes of the Pharisees due to the social status of those with whom Jesus dines. Jesus' response is in line with the ministry that he has provided: healing, exorcism, preaching, teaching, and hospitality. Each of these acts results in the fact that people are restored to, maintain, or are provided a place in the community, or even more, a place in the household and family of Jesus. A physician heals those who are sick so that they may be well and do their daily work and live their daily lives in their communal place or household. Jesus heals those who have demons (1:21–27), who cannot walk (2:1–12), who have been separated by their community by leprosy (1:40–45), or who are not able to fulfill their roles in the household (1:29–31). In 2:15, Jesus also provides hospitality by dining with, being at home with, and offering a place within his kinship group to those who may otherwise be excluded from this type of event. His kinship with God expressed in his identity as Son of God means actions of healing, exorcism, hospitality, and establishing a community of followers identified in the next scene also in kinship terms as "children" (2:19).

11. 2:18–22 CHILDREN OF THE BRIDAL CHAMBER

In another challenge to Jesus, to his identity as God's Son and to his authority over his family of disciples, people observe that John's disciples and the Pharisees practice fasting, but Jesus' disciples do not. As in the challenges given to Jesus in the healing of the paralytic (2:1–12) and the call of Levi (2:13–17), this question disputes both Jesus' authority over traditional practices and his authority to lead a group of disciples. The question arises from the traditional, required practice of fasting initiated by the Day of Atonement (Lev 16:29, 31) but continued in a regular manner to indicate devotion and piety (2 Sam 12:16; Ps 35:13).[102] The question assumes a nexus between Christology and discipleship by means of Jesus' instruction and the disciples' practice. Jesus responds by claiming that the time Jesus has with his disciples is not a time for fasting, rather it is a time of celebration like a wedding feast where Jesus is the bridegroom. His response in verse

---

102. In the first century, the Pharisees fasted twice a week (Mondays and Thursdays). This may be the root of the people's question toward Jesus. See *Did.* 8:1; *b. Ta'an.* 12*a*; Luke 18:12.

19 transposes the nexus into terms of his identity (bridegroom as kinship metaphor) and their identity (children/sons of the bridal chamber), thus kinship is the nexus of Christology and discipleship.[103] "If the disciples of John and the Pharisees grasp the significance of his person," Jesus' identity as the Son of God, "they will understand why they should celebrate rather than fast."[104] The term bridegroom (νθμφίος) conjures up the sense of two kinship groups uniting into one family; Jesus the bridegroom celebrates the feast with his new family that he has established. Jesus, the Son of God, comes to bring good news to those whom he encounters and those who follow him; it is a time of hospitality and meal fellowship, a family celebration. Jesus, the Son of God and bridegroom, produces, or "sires" the sons of the bridal chamber, his disciples demonstrating kinship as the nexus of Christology and discipleship.

Jesus refers to the wedding guests as the sons of the bridal chamber (οἱ υἱοὶ τοῦ νυμφῶνος) in 2:19. Not only does Jesus identify himself in terms of kinship as the bridegroom, but he also identifies his disciples in familial terms as his children. Again, kinship is the nexus of Christology and discipleship because Jesus' identity as Son and bridegroom is in direct correlation with his disciples as sons of the bridal chamber in terms of kinship. As the bridegroom, Jesus gathers and celebrates with his sons of the bridal chamber, his disciples whom he has "fathered" in their call to discipleship. In turn, the disciples, as sons of the bridal chamber, will observe his practices of hospitality and meal fellowship and they will not fast. Jesus indicates that his time with his children is limited and that he will be taken away from them. This is the first reference to Jesus' arrest and passion. Jesus then provides the parameters for the disciples' fasting: not according to traditional practices, but according to the absence of the bridegroom when his children, the disciples, will be grieving for him.

In the latter two parables of the patch and the wineskins, Jesus also indicates that he is doing a new thing. "Traditional rituals are suitable for traditional situations, but new situations require new responses. Custom, law, and ritual are not condemned, but they are subordinated to the changing requirements of people in ever-new situations."[105] Jesus and his family of disciples do not hold to the former traditions because they do not correspond to the work and ministry of Jesus. Moreover, Jesus exercises his

---

103. Tait, *Jesus, The Divine Bridegroom*, 297–98, notes that the phrase implies an intimate (kinship) relationship between the bridegroom and "children of the bridal chamber." The phrase comes from the Hebrew בני החופה and is also found in Matt 9:15 and Luke 5:34.

104. Edwards, *Mark*, 90.

105. Tolbert, *Sowing the Gospel*, 134.

authority as God's Son over and against traditional expectation. Therefore, a new community, a new family of disciples must be formed akin to a new garment that could be made (1:21) and the new wine in fresh wineskins (1:22). The Son of God acts with authority and power over law and tradition; he does not dismiss law and tradition, but his relationship to them requires those who follow him, his family of disciples, to hold the same stance.

The disciples are children (οἱ υἱοὶ) of the Son of God; their kinship relationship requires obedience and loyalty to Jesus' authority as the Son of God. While the bridegroom Jesus is present, discipleship requires the sons of the bridal chamber to feast rather to fast. Kinship serves as the nexus of Christology and discipleship as the Son of God establishes a new family of disciples.

12. 2:23–28 JESUS IS THE SON OF MAN

The nexus of Christology and discipleship in kinship terms is evident in this scene centering on the authority of the Son of Man. Jesus' authority subsequently has implication for the disciples' Sabbath practice. In the satellites up to this point, Jesus demonstrates his authority as God's Son in providing hospitality for his disciples, tax collectors, and sinners at Levi's house (2:13–17). Jesus' authority as the Son and the bridegroom affect the practice of fasting for the disciples, who are the sons of the bridal chamber (οἱ υἱοὶ; 2:18–22). When the disciples are observed plucking grain from a field on the Sabbath (2:23–28), Jesus utilizes his authority as the Son of Man to defend this Sabbath practice of his core kinship group of disciples. The nexus of Christology and discipleship is represented in terms of kinship when Jesus the Son extends his authority to his family of disciples and defends their actions and practices.

It is the Pharisees who encounter the disciples plucking grain on the Sabbath (2:24). The Pharisees offer a challenge and claim that what the disciples are doing is not lawful. They imply that the disciples are reaping the grain from the fields which is not allowed on the Sabbath (Exod 34:21). However, Mark states that the disciples are τίλλοντες, "plucking" the grain, which is legal on the Sabbath (Deut 23:25). "The discrepancy between what the disciples are described as doing and the objection of the Pharisees puts the latter in a bad light . . . The Pharisees thus are portrayed as excessively strict in their observance and as attempting to impose their view on others."[106] Jesus, as head of his family of disciples and their representative, offers another interpretation of the law citing David and his companions in

---

106. Collins, *Mark*, 201–2.

1 Sam 21. That is, kinship as the nexus of Christology and discipleship is evident in his defense of his household because Jesus the Son provides the authority and permission for his family of disciples to pluck grain on the Sabbath. Although they ate the bread of the Presence, which was designated for the high priests, their actions were acceptable because of their need for food. Jesus implies that basic needs, such as hunger, may be met on the Sabbath, even if that means performing labor. The reference to David may also be a means of invoking his power and authority as king over and against the legal tradition of the Pharisees. "Just as David had authority to override conventional interpretations of the will of God because he was God's chosen one, so also Jesus," as God's Son, "has authority to interpret and proclaim the will of God"[107] and to defend his household of disciples and to extend his authority over conventional Sabbath tradition to his family of disciples. The nexus of Christology and discipleship is exhibited through Jesus' authority about and defense of his disciples' Sabbath practice of plucking grain.

Not only does Jesus as the Son have the authority to grant forgiveness on behalf of God (2:5), but he also demonstrates authority over Sabbath practice and his disciples' actions. Jesus emphasizes his authority over the Sabbath by the final saying regarding the matter in 2:27–28. In a reference to the creation story and the establishment of the Sabbath (Gen 2:1–3), Jesus states τὸ σάββατον διὰ τὸν ἄνθρωπον ἐγένετο (the Sabbath was made on account of a human being). He then adds the inverse: καὶ οὐχ ὁ ἄνθρωπος διὰ τὸ σάββατον (and not a human being on account of the Sabbath). Jesus does not hesitate to note that he himself, the Son of God, as the Son of Man and agent of humanity is Lord over the Sabbath. In his interpretation all people have authority over the Sabbath since it was created by God for them, but also because they are Jesus' kin, he gives them agency and authority. The nexus of Christology and discipleship is demonstrated in the Son of Man's authority to provide authority over the Sabbath for his family of disciples. Jesus' sonship, and the disciples' authority as members of Jesus' household, is further highlighted and elaborated in this satellite. Moreover, Jesus, as the Son of Man, is κύριός (Lord) of the Sabbath. Jesus stands as God's representative, as God's agent, and therefore has authority and power over the Sabbath, but he also stands as an agent of humanity, as father to his disciples (2:19), providing them with authority over the Sabbath.

This satellite and the two before it (2:13–22) also demonstrate Jesus' authority over food and food practices (washing, fasting). Local societal authorities, in this instance, the Pharisees, and the Roman Empire in general, set the rules for and accessibility to food. In this scene, Jesus proves his

107. Ibid., 205.

authority concerning access to food. "Jesus is not only defending discipleship practice against the alternative holiness code of Pharisaism, he is going on the offensive, challenging the ideological control and the manipulation of the redistributive economy by a minority whose elite status is only aggrandized."[108] Jesus provides his own interpretation of the law over and against the Pharisees so that his family of disciples may eat.[109]

Jesus also defends their access to wheat within the Roman Empire. Wheat was the main staple in the Roman Empire; it was imported, stored, and distributed to its citizens for their subsistence.[110] Access to food and its distribution indicated power. Elite citizens would have access to nutritional foods beyond the basic staple foods wheras non-elites would have struggled for adequate nutrition. The majority (90 percent) of the Roman Empire existed at the subsistence level.[111] Carol Wilson notes that access to food relied on the location of consumers and distribution-acquisition of enough varying food types.[112] In rural areas families depended upon crop production for food and for income to purchase or exchange for food they couldn't produce, seed, and equipment. In urban areas families relied upon employment for income and benefits from the elite to acquire food. Other factors that determine access to adequate food include wealth and status, rent, tax, tithe, financial obligations, and the availability of alternative food sources (foraging and hunting). Most people who were at the subsistence level remained at the subsistence level because the elites would acquire any surplus in the form of rent, tax, or repayment of loan. Due to the obligations placed upon small land owners, tenant farmers, and day laborers by the elites, food scarcity was quite common.[113] Moreover, the high variability in the crops due to weather, volatile wheat prices, and issues of distribution due to administrative inefficiency, corruption, transport breakdown, speculation, and war could all lead to food shortage.[114] For those at the subsistence level, food scarcity resulted in poor nutrition, a near-constant state of indebtedness toward elites, and a lower life expectancy.

By extracting the surplus from those at the subsistent level by means of tribute in the form of taxes and rent and redistributing the food for their

---

108. Myers, *Binding the Strong Man*, 161.

109. Carter, *Matthew and the Margins*, 265.

110. Garnsey and Saller, *Roman Empire*, 83–87.

111. See the discussion of Friesen's social-stratification model of the Roman Empire in chapter 2.

112. Wilson, *For I Was Hungry*, 63–70.

113. Ibid., 81.

114. Garnsey, *Food and Society*, 34–35.

own means, the elite maintained control and power both over food sources and the economy.[115] Jesus, the Son, defends his family's, the disciples', access to basic nutrition in spite of the first-century realities of food scarcity for people who lived at a subsistence level. Unlike the Roman Empire, whose agents would have procured the grain and removed it to Rome, Jesus, the Son, grants access and ensures grain provision for his kinship group of disciples. The nexus of Christology and discipleship occurs in terms of kinship when the Son of God grants authority over and access to food for his household of hungry disciples.

In a challenge to Jesus' authority as the Son of God and to his disciples' Sabbath practice, Jesus defends his family. Jesus utilizes his authority as God's Son and establishes his authority and agency for human beings as the Son of Man. The nexus of Christology and discipleship is in terms of kinship where Jesus exercises his authority over and defends his core kinship group's Sabbath practice and access to food.

13. 3:1-6 THE SON HEALS THE MAN WITH THE WITHERED HAND

The nexus continues in the final pericope in 2:1–3:6 where Jesus establishes his power and authority as God's Son and extends healing and authority to his kinship group of followers which began with the healing of the paralytic in 2:1–12, Jesus is again in the synagogue on the Sabbath. Rather than verbally challenge Jesus, the Pharisees simply observe Jesus' behavior toward a man who has a withered hand. Jesus as the Son of God has already demonstrated to the Pharisees his authority over the Sabbath in the previous scene where the disciples were plucking heads of grain. In knowing what the Pharisees were thinking, another demonstration of his divine sonship, Jesus challenges them in an effort to maintain his authority and the disciples' Sabbath practice: "Is it lawful to do good or to do harm on the Sabbath, to save life or to kill?" (3:4). Jesus is met with silence as he heals the man with the withered hand. The Pharisees' silence indicates that Jesus has triumphed in the challenge-riposte. The Pharisees have no other response except to act in anger and plan for a way to destroy (ἀπολέσωσιν) him. "Note, however, that in a challenge and response situation, those who resort to violence lost. Violence indicates wits have failed and bully tactics have taken over."[116] As God's Son, Jesus is victorious in his honor and in his power to heal over the Pharisees, who squander any remaining honor they had by resorting to

---

115. Hanson and Oakman, *Palestine*, 105.
116. Malina and Rohrbaugh, *Social-Science Commentary*, 156.

violence. Jesus, the Son, defends his authority and the Sabbath practice of his family of disciples. Moreover, eating and healing are means to save life. The Son of God proves his authority and provides sustenance and healing for his family of disciples and followers.

These five scenes of challenge and riposte along with Jesus' demonstration of priestly authority (1:35–45), bestowing God's forgiveness of sins (2:1–12), authority over cultural and religious expectations (2:13–28), and power to heal (3:1–6) illustrate Jesus as the most honorable Son of God and display what his sonship comprises. His ability to best his opponents and to act with authority and power provide substance and definition to Jesus' sonship. This honor, power, and authority also illustrate the popular following Jesus has achieved, along with a family of disciples, so that his reputation and honor continue to grow, and as Mark mentions, becomes a threat to his opponents, so much so that they look for a way to destroy him (ἀπολέσωσιν; 3:6). Kinship serves as the nexus of Christology and discipleship; in the demonstration of authority and power by the Son, Jesus also instructs his family of disciples that they too have authority over traditional Sabbath practice.

Jesus' healing of the man with the withered hand could also evoke a healing story about Vespasian that was told in imperial propaganda supporting his accession to the throne. According to the account by Dio Cassius, while Vespasian was in Alexandria waiting to return to Rome, he was approached by two men for healing. In the accounts of Suetonius and Tacitus, it is a blind man and a lame man who approach Vespasian.[117] One was blind and one had a withered hand. Alongside these healings, Vespasian also visited the temple of Serapis where he received a favorable omen. Vespasian's healing powers helped to convince the imperial world of his worthiness as emperor both in the demonstration of his healing powers and by aligning him closely with the god Serapis, divinely sanctioning his reign.[118] Jesus, the Son of God who also received divine sanction, is also able to heal a man with a withered hand. Moreover, Jesus the Son has authority and power to heal all who seek him out for healing.

The man with the withered hand is just one in a long list of healings that Jesus will provide for those who enter into his kinship group of followers showing him to be the most honorable Son of God and most worthy as an agent of the empire of God. Unlike Vespasian, whose story of miraculous healing is used as divine sanction and propaganda for his reign as emperor

---

117. Dio Cassius, *Roman History*, 65.8.1. See the discussion in chapter 2. See also the sections of the healing of the deaf and mute man and the blind man at Bethsaida below.

118. Eve, "Spit in Your Eye," 4.

of Rome, a central part of the work of Jesus as God's Son is to provide healing to those who are in need. These miraculous healings also demonstrate the divine sanction Jesus has as God's Son in establishing God's empire. In the nexus of Christology and discipleship by means of kinship these healings also extend Jesus' kinship with God to those who become his family of disciples and followers.

14. 3:7-12 DEMONS IDENTIFY JESUS AS THE SON OF GOD

Jesus, the Son of God and head of his family of disciples, departs with the core kinship group of disciples to the sea continuing to reflect kinship as the nexus of Christology and discipleship. A summary of Jesus' popularity in 3:7-12 follows the healing satellite in 3:1-6 where Jesus further displays his authority over the law and tradition concerning the Sabbath and the initial conspiracy for his death is established. In the description of his healings, Mark notes at 3:11 that whenever Jesus healed people with unclean spirits, the spirits identified him as ὁ υἱὸς τοῦ θεοῦ and they fell at his feet. This satellite echoes Jesus' first healing in the synagogue in 1:17-28 where Jesus heals a man with an unclean spirit who identifies him as ὁ ἅγιος τοῦ θεοῦ (the Holy One of God). It also corroborates Jesus' identity as ὁ υἱὸς τοῦ θεοῦ as it was given in the title (1:1) and at his baptism (1:9-11). The kinship language of Jesus as the Son of God appears to encapsulate the first satellites of healing and teaching in the Gospel of Mark (1:16-3:12). Everything Jesus has accomplished up to this point–calling the first disciples, healing in the synagogue, healing at home, teaching, proving authority over Sabbath traditions–has been accomplished as the Son of God for the benefit of the core kinship group of disciples and extended family of followers.[119] Kinship with God is thus shown to comprise the honor and authority to establish a new family of disciples, to provide them with hospitality, and to grant an alternative understanding of the law and tradition. In turn, disciples and those who follow Jesus grant him honor, faith, and fidelity. Jesus' kinship with God is extended to them, demonstrating kinship as the nexus of Christology and discipleship.

This summary also demonstrates the reputation and honor Jesus has acquired both as the Son of God and by his actions of healing and teaching. Large crowds, who come from beyond the region of Galilee, have begun

---

119. Keck, "Mark 3:7-12," 343, makes the same observation. However, Keck categorizes ὁ υἱὸς τοῦ θεοῦ within the θεῖος ἀνήρ concept which is an inadequate category for Jesus in Mark (see chapter 1).

following Jesus (3:8). Jesus' popularity has extended beyond and is not limited to the Galilee. Everyone who is sick desires to have access to Jesus and to touch him (3:10). Jesus' success in healing garners more recipients of his healing power and authority and more members of his extended kinship network. And finally, the unclean spirits bow down to Jesus (3:11). The word for "fall before" (προσπίπτω) occurs three times in the Gospel of Mark (3:11; 5:33; 7:25), each time it is an inferior person prostrating him or herself before Jesus as if Jesus were a superior.[120] Jesus is popular, powerful, and honored as those in need approach him as a patron, as a superior kinsman who will provide for his dependents, his family of clients and disciples. The nexus of Christology and discipleship is demonstrated in the honor bestowed upon Jesus, the Son of God, by his disciples and followers and followers and recipients of healing who enter into his extended kinship network.

In the gospel's narrative world, it is Jesus, not the local authorities of the scribes and the Pharisees, not the Roman Empire or emperor, who is greeted with such honor, who utilizes authority and power as God's Son to provide healing to the many who seek him out. The crowds demonstrate a shift in allegiance from the local societal authorities and the Roman Empire to Jesus Christ, the Son of God. The family of disciples and followers enters into kinship with and gives allegiance to God through Jesus' healing power over them and the benefits he provides as their most powerful and honored kinsman, further emphasizing the nexus of Christology and discipleship in terms of kinship. Mark demonstrates Jesus' accessibility and willingness to assist all those who seek him out, whereas the local authorities stand only to critique and cite the religious and legal traditions, and the Roman Empire stands as a demonic power oppressing those under their control.

The demons identify Jesus in kinship terms as the Son of God. Jesus is able to act with authority and power to exorcise the demons and provide the benefaction of healing to those who seek him. The nexus of Christology and discipleship in terms of kinship is evident in Jesus the Son extending benefits of healing and exorcism to an extended kinship network of followers and disciples.

15. 3:13-19 THE SON COMMISSIONS HIS CORE KINSHIP GROUP OF DISCIPLES

The nexus of Christology and discipleship by means of kinship is solidified following the initial satellites of the Son of God's healing, teaching,

---

120. Edwards, *Mark*, 104.

exorcising, and preaching in and around Galilee where Jesus inaugurates the empire of God (1:14–15), calls his core kinship group of disciples (1:16–20; 2:13–15), and extends his kinship network by offering the benefit of healing and exorcism, and when Jesus formally defines his core kinship group of disciples in 3:13–19. Jesus, the Son of God, summons (προσκαλεῖται) and appoints (ἐποίησεν) twelve men whom he names apostles (ἀποστόλους) to accompany him in his ministry. Christology and discipleship intersect by means of kinship when God's chosen agent and Son, Jesus, also grants his family of disciples authority to preach and to cast out demons (3:14–15). Akin to the previous call stories (1:16–20), some of these men are identified with their original kinship networks: James the son of Zebedee and John, the brother of James, and James son of Alphaeus. Now they are identified as members of Jesus' core kinship group of the twelve disciples. Jesus, the Son, calls the twelve as his children (2:19) to establish the empire of God; kinship defines the relationship between Christology and discipleship. Mark also indicates that Jesus renames Simon as Peter and James and John receive the nickname, "Sons of Thunder," further cementing the kinship ties between Jesus and his disciples by his authority to give them new names. When Judas Iscariot is named, the reader learns that he will betray Jesus (3:19). This prediction of betrayal provides an elaboration to the plot on Jesus' life that was initiated by the Pharisees and Herodians (3:6) and foreshadows Jesus' arrest. After the twelve are named, Jesus returns home (εἰς οἶκον).

The call of the twelve may evoke Exod 24:9–11, where Moses leads the seventy elders up to Mount Sinai to meet God. "The fact that the mountain which Jesus climbs is not named allows it to take on connotations of the mountain of God or the cosmic mountain, the place where heaven and earth meet and where a holy man encounters God and the people receive revelation."[121] Just as Moses is the leader of Israelites called by God to do God's will among the people, so too is Jesus God's chosen agent. Part of Jesus' role as God's agent is to extend the authority and power he has as God's Son to his kinship group of disciples commissioned to preach and exorcise demons (3:14–15). Suzanne Watts Henderson notes the intertextual echoes this satellite has with Exod 19:3–7. Although Jesus (as God's agent) calls the disciples, whereas God calls Moses, Henderson concludes, "Jesus assumes Moses' position as intermediary between God and the people whom God has chosen."[122] Because of Jesus' kinship with God (1:1; 1:11), rather than simply as a called leader chosen by God like Moses, Jesus has even more authority and power to extend God's agency to his kinship group of disciples.

121. Collins, *Mark*, 215.
122. Henderson, *Christology and Discipleship*, 80.

As God's Son, Jesus' extension of his authority and power to the disciples makes them agents of God's empire, full members of the new kinship group Jesus establishes which further emphasizes the nexus of Christology and discipleship in terms of kinship.[123]

The call of the twelve also stands as Jesus' establishment of the new household and family in the empire of God which will be further elaborated in the next satellite (3:20–25). John Donahue notes "more explicit than in the call of the first four disciples is the incorporation of those called into a new social unit or group, 'the twelve,' with a new identity symbolized by the new names given to the first three listed."[124] Jesus, the Son of God, establishes a family of sons (οἱ υἱοί; 2:19) comprised of brothers (and eventually, sisters) to form the nucleus of a new family and household. Each member of the household has specific tasks assigned to them by the Son (from the Father): for these twelve, they accompany Jesus, are sent out, preach, and cast out demons. In the nexus of Christology and discipleship in terms of kinship Jesus, as God's Son, extends his own mission of preaching and exorcising along with God's authority and agency to his core kinship group of disciples. The emphasis on the household is further highlighted when Jesus returns home (εἰς οἶκον) immediately after he calls the core kinship group of disciples.

16. 3:20–35 THE SON OF GOD IDENTIFIES HIS TRUE FAMILY

Mark 3:20–35 comprises a sandwich story or example of intercalation that takes place at the home of Jesus and concerns his family further emphasizing the nexus of Christology and discipleship through kinship. When Jesus returns home, the crowds are so large that there is no room to eat. Instead of participating in an act of healing or teaching, however, Jesus' family (οἱ παρ'

---

123. Henderson indicates an explicit divine revelation in Mark 3:13–19 based on the parallel with Exod 19:3–7 since Jesus serves as both God and Moses. She suggests, "the mountaintop setting hints at both divine disclosure and divine empowerment; and it both recalls God's decisive intervention in Israel's history and anticipates the apocalyptic hope for God's universal sovereignty" (Henderson, *Christology and Discipleship*, 83). Certainly Jesus acts as God's chosen agent establishing a new community of followers to accompany him in the work he has been called to do. But, at this point in the narrative, there is no indication of an apocalyptic hope for God's universal sovereignty either in the work of Jesus and his disciples or those who encounter them. This may well be a conclusion of the gospel in toto, but to make the claim when Jesus calls the twelve in 3:13–19 is extreme.

124. Donahue, *Theology and Setting*, 17.

αὐτοῦ) try to stop him.¹²⁵ Jesus' family returns in 3:31–35 standing outside the house, again with the intent of stopping him and taking him with them.

In the midst of this story is another story of the Jerusalem scribes who accuse Jesus of having a demon and being in league with Beelzebul. In the house with Jesus, they accuse Jesus of casting out demons by the authority of Beelzebul (3:22). Their charge challenges the image of kinship and the Son of God. Jesus responds to their challenge by demonstrating its absurdity. Satan cannot cast himself out (3:23). Furthermore, a house or an empire that is divided cannot stand. Jesus maintains his authority as the Son of God in claiming that it is the scribes who blaspheme against God (3:29). Jesus knows that he casts out demons by God's authority as God's Son and therefore, the challenge of the scribes stands in direct opposition, not only to Jesus, but to God. Subsequently, Jesus cuts them off from the possibility of forgiveness. When Jesus' family returns to ask for Jesus in 3:31, he responds by redefining his family, making explicit the basis of the redefined household that has been emerging since 1:16–20. The kinship network of the Son of God is no longer made up of his mother or brothers and sisters by birth, but rather his mother, brothers, and sisters are those with him in the house, the disciples, who do the will of God. Christology, Jesus' identity as the Son of God, is bound intimately in his relationship with the disciples, described in kinship terms as his brothers and sisters.

There are several aspects of kinship to be addressed in this sandwich story including Jesus' family, household language, and Jesus' new family. Jesus' family of origin comes (from Nazareth) to restrain him. They believe that he has gone crazy (ἐξέστη, 3:21). Quite literally, they believe Jesus is "standing outside" of himself; that is, he has lost the sense of his kinship, social, and cultural identity and is behaving inappropriately. Jesus' behavior and actions directly affect the reputation of his family. If he suffers a loss of honor, so too will his family suffer a loss of honor. "In this case it is most clear that they are hiding what they perceive to be the censurable conduct of a family member not simply in the interest of his reputation but for the sake of the reputation of the whole family (on which so much in village life depends)."¹²⁶ In antiquity, the individual's identity and reputation was dependent upon the group (family) of which he or she was a part; therefore, one was expected to act in accordance with this group (family) identity and reputation. If one did not, then he or she is a deviant and creates a risk to the

---

125. I understand the phrase οἱ παρ' αὐτοῦ to mean "his family." The translation is most obviously supported by 3:31–32. For a discussion on the translation of this phrase for "family," "friends," or "disciples," see Painter, "When Is a House Not Home," 501–3. See also Ahearne-Kroll, "'Who Are My?,'" 12.

126. DeSilva, *Honor*, 172.

honor and reputation of the entire group or family.[127] The fact that Jesus acts with authority, which he did not receive from his family, to cast out demons indicates that he is acting outside of the expected group identity. His family comes to restrain him to protect his reputation and their honor, ignorant of the fact that Jesus receives his authority (and reputation and honor) from God as the Son of God (3:21). Exercising this authority, Jesus binds himself to a new family, his disciples, who do the will of God. The Son's definition and designation of his disciples as his true family demonstrates the nexus of Christology and discipleship in terms of kinship.

The entire satellite takes place outside and inside Jesus' house.[128] Jesus' family is outside of the house trying to seize him while Jesus responds to the challenge of the Jerusalem scribes who are with him inside the house. "With this strong literary play using spatial language of inside and outside, Mark transforms the spatial distance between Jesus and his immediate family into a deeper, metaphorical, and much more permanent distance."[129] In addition, Jesus' response to the scribes also contains household language when he states that a house that is divided cannot stand (3:25). This may point to the reality that Jesus' household allegiances are changing: he rejects his original family for his new family of disciples (3:33–35). Jesus is divided from his original kinship network; therefore that household structure will not survive. Jesus' authority as the Son of God causes a shift and a break in the traditional notions of household and family (and consequently to all aspects of society). It may also point to Jesus' challenge to the household of Rome. Stephen Moore suggests that all of the exorcisms that Jesus performs in Mark should have anticolonial significance.[130] That being the case, "Jesus' boast that his plundering of the property of the 'strong man' portends the end of Satan's empire (3.23–27) could then be read as equally portending the end of Rome's empire, the latter being implicitly construed as but an instrumental extension of the former."[131] In the nexus of Christology and discipleship by means of kinship, Jesus, as the Son of God, creates an

---

127. Malina and Rohrbaugh, *Social-Science Commentary*, 158.

128. Shepherd, *Markan Sandwich Stories*, 111–16 provides a discussion on the setting of this satellite. Of particular interest: "In terms of borders, three features stand out in the intercalation. First is the predominance of spatial borders. There is a repeated reference to *outside*, with the unexpected occurrence of 'insiders' (relatives) being outside (cf. 3:31, 32) and typical 'outsiders' being found inside in close relation to Jesus (cf. 3:20, 32–35 concerning the crowd). The border is the *house*, and it appears to take on symbolic significance, particularly in light of the reference to a 'house divided upon itself' and 'the house of a strong man' in the inner story (3:25, 27)" (ibid., 114).

129. Ahearne-Kroll, "'Who Are My?,'" 14.

130. Moore, *Empire and Apocalypse*, 26–27.

131. Ibid., 27.

alternative household that is comprised of his disciples and followers who are designated in terms of kinship.

When Jesus' family seeks him again in 3:31–32, he rejects his family: his mother, his brothers, and his sisters who are standing outside of the house. Instead he asks those who are seated with him inside the house who his family is. Jesus declares those around him as his family. ὃς γὰρ ἂν ποιήσῃ τὸ θέλημα τοῦ θεοῦ, οὗτος ἀδελφός μου καὶ ἀδελφὴ καὶ μήτηρ ἐστίν (For whoever does the will of God, this one is my brother and my sister and my mother, 3:35). Just as Jesus was declared to be God's Son (1:1; 11), now he defines his mother, brothers, and sisters as he extends his kinship network as the Son to those that follow him (and God), articulating what was being formed since 1:16. Jesus' proclamation of the empire of God, casting out demons, teaching, and healing have created a new household and family for those who receive healing and follow Jesus. Jesus creates an abrupt and overt break from traditional kinship ties. His identity as the Son of God rests in God's declaration (1:11) which is expressed in this newly established kinship network of disciples and followers of God's will. "Jesus redefines discipleship in terms of his family and family in terms of discipleship."[132] In the intersection of Christology and discipleship by means of kinship, Jesus' honor, and the honor of his family, is maintained in this new family of mothers, brothers, and sisters who do the will of God.

In Jesus' new family of mothers, brothers, and sisters, there is a distinct absence of any fathers. There is no reference to Jesus' father listed among those who seek him in 3:31–32 and Jesus makes no reference to a father in the new kinship group he establishes in 3:35.[133] The significance of this is twofold: first, the only legitimate father in the Gospel of Mark is God (1:1). Second, this Father God, who establishes his empire through his Son, Jesus, identified as such at his baptism (1:9–11) stands over and against the other supreme father, *pater patriae*, the emperor of Rome. A new family in Jesus' household is established in the empire of God by the Son; Christology and discipleship are again bound together in kinship.

Kinship provides the nexus between Christology and discipleship. Jesus acts as God's agent and does God's will in the establishment of God's empire; the Son represents the Father as the head of a new household of disciples who also do the will of God. It is an alternative family for those who follow God, but it is also in direct imitation and form of traditional

---

132. Painter, "When Is a House Not Home," 511.

133. Peppard, *Son of God*, 126, notes the absence of an earthly father throughout the Gospel of Mark (from Jesus' baptism). This absence will continue to play a significant role as the plot develops and further encounters with Jesus' family occur.

families (mother, brothers, and sisters).[134] Status, power, security, and family connections are redefined, but are still central to the family Jesus creates. The family of disciples gains their honor, authority, security, and identity from Jesus the Son who represents the will of the Father.

17. 4:1-34 THE SON OF GOD DEFINES THE EMPIRE OF GOD

After Jesus the Son defines who is in his family of disciples, in another demonstration of kinship as the nexus of Christology and discipleship, he defines the realm of the new family, the empire of God in a series of parables in Mark 4. The first parables of the sower and the lamp have to do with the message of the empire, the word. Just as Jesus, as God's Son, was commissioned to preach the good news of the empire of God, the Son provides understanding of God's empire for his kinship group of disciples to preach this message. Although Jesus teaches parables to the largest crowd yet (4:1) who are a part of his extended kinship network by virtue of following Jesus, the message of the parables is meant for those who belong to the core kinship group of disciples who will help establish the empire (4:11).[135] Jesus tells the disciples about the receipt of the word, the reality that it will go out to many places where it may root and grow (4:20), or it may wither and die (4:15-19). Where it does take root, it will be extremely fruitful: thirty,

---

134. Contra Trainor who claims, "In this new household status, power, security and family connections are no longer the values that will determine its membership or structure its lines of authority. It is a renewed Roman *domus* in which the typical *paterfamilias* is absent. The authority of Jesus acting through the household's leadership replaces him. Because Mark presents this household as an alternative religious, economic, and political system that will challenge the status quo of the Roman Empire, it will become the center of a conflict from which neither the household nor its members will be immune" (Trainor, *Quest for Home*, 105).

135. As I have noted above in the discussion on 3:13-19, the disciples function as the core kinship group of disciples who will be the primary enactors of God's empire after Jesus since they receive the extension of God's authority and power through their close kinship with Jesus (3:14-15). However, other characters in Mark who receive healing, exorcism, hospitality, or teaching from Jesus and follow him are also within his extended kinship network. Malbon notes in her thesis regarding Markan characters, "(1) the disciples of Jesus are portrayed in the Gospel of Mark with both strong points and weak points in order to serve as realistic and encouraging models for hearers/readers who experience both strength and weakness in their Christian discipleship; (2) the crowd is also portrayed in the Gospel of Mark in both positive and negative ways in relation to Jesus and serves to complement the disciples in a composite portrait of followers of Jesus; (3) both separately and together, the disciples and the crowd serve to open the story of Jesus and the narrative of Mark outward to a larger group–whoever hears or reads the Gospel of Mark" (Malbon, "Disciples/Crowds/Whoever," 104).

sixty, and even a hundredfold (4:20). For those who are in the empire, for those who hear Jesus' message and become a part of his family, their harvest will be greater than they have ever known. Ched Myers notes that this type of harvest would forever alter the relationship between the farmer and his landlord. "With such surplus, the farmer could not only eat and pay his rent, tithes, and debts, but indeed even purchase the land, and thus end his servitude forever . . . [the parable] envisions the abolition of the oppressive relationships of production that determined the horizons of the Palestinian farmer's social world."[136] Christology and discipleship still have their nexus in kinship because the message of the empire of God proclaimed by the Son for his children will be more fruitful and given to more people (Jesus' disciples as family and extended kinship network) than anyone would expect, even in the light of apparent failure (4:15–19).

Furthermore, Jesus demonstrates that the word must go out, that it cannot be hidden; the message of the empire is necessary to be revealed (4:22). This parable speaks to the continued success of the empire of God. Jesus announces the empire of God through his proclamation, the word. The word is then transmitted to the family of disciples who continue to manifest God's empire. Any story of healing or encounter where Jesus commands secrecy can be interpreted in this parable; the secrets are meant to be revealed and the identity of Jesus as the Son of God and the message of God's empire should be made known. "All the apparent secrets in the Gospel–Jesus' identity" as God's Son, "his healing miracles, his control over evil spirits–have as their goal the revelation of the kingdom, but only those with the ears to hear it will hear it."[137] This is followed by a maxim to heed what is heard, akin to the harvest of the seed sown on good soil: the measure you give will be what you get and more. Those who have will receive more and those who do not will have it all taken away. Malina and Rohrbaugh suggest these verses have to do with making judgments which does not have to do with the message of the empire of God.[138] If they are taken in the context of the other parables, they are about the fruitfulness of the empire. The social reality is that the rich get richer and the poor get poorer. "It is precisely *against* such misanthropic 'realism' that Jesus strenuously warns. As if saying, 'Instead, listen again to the miracle of the seed and the harvest.'"[139] Jesus claims that the empire of God reshapes and reinterprets the social and political experiences of those who are disciples and enter into the family and empire of God. Kin-

---

136. Myers, *Binding the Strong Man*, 177.
137. Tolbert, *Sowing the Gospel*, 161.
138. Malina and Rohrbaugh, *Social-Science Commentary*, 162.
139. Myers, *Binding the Strong Man*, 179.

ship serves as the nexus of Christology and discipleship. Just as God's Son will reap the establishment of God's empire in the world and the formation of a new family of disciples, so will the "sons of the bridegroom" (2:19) reap the benefits of the empire of God. These benefits include the good news of the empire's message and an identity in a family that provides an alternative to the disciples' identity in Galilee under Roman rule.

Jesus subsequently teaches about the nature of the empire of God in 4:26–34. In two more agrarian parables, Jesus likens the empire of God to seeds that grow on their own with no help from the farmer and to a mustard seed, which starts out quite small but grows to become a very large plant. These parables indicate that the empire of God will grow, and will be successful, despite anything or anyone's attempts to the contrary. In a discussion on these parables, Morna Hooker observes "that for the evangelist Mark there was a very close connection between the coming of the kingdom and Jesus' identity as Son of God. And like the parables, these crucial references to the kingdom focus our attention on the person of Jesus, who proclaims and embodies its coming."[140] Additionally, the nexus of Christology and discipleship and the further connections with discipleship are evident in the parables that provide a message of hope to his family of disciples that the empire of God will triumph because the Son has inaugurated it and, like a seed, it grows and will bear fruit.

These parables all speak to the agrarian life that would have been familiar to those who were the initial recipients of Jesus' message of the empire of God. Food production and harvest were also central to the power and control the Roman Empire had over its territories and occupied land. Food grown in Galilee, or a portion thereof, would have been "paid" in the form of taxes to the Roman Empire. Ched Myers strongly indicates that these parables would have elicited from their hearers support for the farmer and those struggling for subsistence and a challenge to those who govern and control food production and access. "Against the cynicism of the economic 'determinism' of the system, Jesus pits the revolutionary patience and hope of the kingdom (4:26)."[141] Jesus the Son tells parables of the empire of God in terms that his family of disciples would grasp and relate. Jesus issues the message that regardless of yield or not, the empire of the Son is present among them and will yield a harvest greater than any has ever known. In the nexus of Christology and discipleship by means of kinship, Jesus has initiated the harvest in the establishment of God's empire through his work and the formation of the family of disciples. "Those who hear this gospel

---

140. Hooker, "Mark's Parables," 82.
141. Myers, *Binding the Strong Man*, 179.

and believe it reveal themselves to be part of the kingdom and, further, are transformed by such a disclosure into producing abundant fruit."[142]

The nexus of Christology and discipleship by means of kinship appears as Jesus, the Son, maintains and defines the empire of God for his family of disciples. The family of disciples will continue to reap what has been sowed by their participation in the work Jesus the Son has begun.

18. 4:35-41 THE SON STILLS THE STORM FOR HIS FAMILY OF DISCIPLES

Following the sermon of parables, the Son and his family of disciples (4:35-36) begin to cross the sea in the evening. The flotilla of boats encounters a windstorm strong enough to frighten the disciples and cause them to fear for their lives. Jesus, however, is asleep in the back of the boat, apparently oblivious to the storm (4:38). As his disciples are endangered, Jesus uses his power as the Son of God to rebuke the storm and to tell the wind to be still, thereby protecting his family from harm in a demonstration of the nexus of Christology and disciples in terms of kinship (4:39). The disciples, however, respond with fear and question the identity of Jesus (4:41). This question of Jesus' identity serves as an echo of the kernel of Jesus' baptism. In 1:1 and 1:11, Jesus is identified as God's Son, but what does this mean and who is Jesus? What is the significance of Jesus' sonship and his declaration of the disciples as his family? In the calming of the storm, Jesus' actions give rise to these questions and they are placed upon the disciples' lips. Who is this? This is God's Son who just provided a sermon on the empire he has come to establish and now makes the wind and the seas obey his commands. This is Jesus, the Son of God, who has authority over illness, demons, the law, cultural traditions, and now, nature, who establishes a new family of brothers and sisters who follow him and do the will of God.

This satellite also characterizes the disciples. Thus far the disciples have been actively following Jesus and entered into his community, his family; they have been recipients of his healing and his teaching. The disciples have witnessed the challenges on Jesus' honor and his triumph. The disciples, like Jesus, have been commissioned to proclaim the message of the empire and to cast out demons (3:14-15). They have been given knowledge about the empire, its apparent failure, its ultimate success, and its presence among them (4:1-34). But by a force of nature, the disciples fear for their lives and fail to trust in the Son of God. James Edwards notes that this scene is told from the perspective of the disciples, further emphasizing their role here

---

142. Tolbert, *Sowing the Gospel*, 164.

and in the ministry of Jesus.[143] The fear of the family of disciples and the failure to trust in the Son of God may be a concrete example of the parable of the sower and the seeds (4:1–20). Jesus has equipped his "sons" with knowledge and a place in the community, but they fail to trust and fall into fear and terror. This may foreshadow the disciples' ultimate failure of Jesus at his arrest and crucifixion (14:50), but it may also further demonstrate the latter parables in Mark 4. Despite the disciples' fear and terror for their own lives, Jesus responds and commands the sea to be still. Despite their lack of faith, the Son of God remains faithful and cares for his family of disciples. Just as God has declared Jesus to be his beloved Son (1:11) and provides him with agency, authority, and power as a sign of this filial relationship, so too does Jesus demonstrate his care and his filial relationship with the disciples by delivering them from harm and providing for them even in their fear and lack of trust. Kinship is the nexus of Christology and discipleship.

Jesus asleep in the stern of the boat in the midst of a major windstorm would also elicit images of the endangered boat in which Jonah sleeps through a major storm. The disciples act like the seafarers who awaken Jonah and hold him responsible for the storm. The storm subsides when Jonah is tossed into the sea (Jonah 1:15). The immediate stilling of the storm evokes awe and wonder in the seafarers who subsequently worship God. Rather than being thrown overboard, Jesus, as the Son of God, invokes God's power and authority over creation to calm the storm. The story of Jonah demonstrates the power God has over nature in the same way Jesus, as God's Son, exercises authority over nature. Moreover, Jesus calms the storm in the same manner by which he performs exorcisms (1:25). "The description of the stilling of the storm in the language of exorcism is intended not simply to demonstrate that Jesus possesses power over nature as well as over illness and demon possession. Its ultimate purpose is to show that Jesus does what only God can do."[144] Who is able to make the wind and the seas obey but the Son of God who has the authority to do it? Furthermore, this power of Jesus as the Son of God extends to the family of disciples, which may elicit their fear. In further demonstration of kinship as the nexus of Christology and discipleship, the disciples question to whom they have bound themselves as family and what it means to follow Jesus and be a member of his family.

---

143. Edwards, *Mark*, 151.
144. Ibid., 150.

19. 5:1-20 LEGION IDENTIFIES JESUS AS THE SON OF THE MOST HIGH

Following a series of satellites where Jesus the Son demonstrates his authority through the teaching of parables and discloses secrets of the empire of God to his kinship group of disciples (4:1-34) and a demonstration of authority and power over the natural world when Jesus the Son calms the storm as his family of disciples cross the Sea of Galilee (4:35-41), Jesus and the disciples encounter a man with an unclean spirit living among the tombs in Gerasa. Mark defines the possessed man as one in particularly dire straits: he lived among the tombs separated from his own family because no one could restrain him or subdue him. He spent all his time crying out (κράζων) and bruising himself with stones (κατακόπτων ἑαυτὸν λίθοις, 5:5). Before Jesus approaches him, the man with the unclean spirit sees him, runs to him, and bows down before him. He identifies Jesus in kinship terms as the Son of the Most High God (υἱὲ τοῦ θεοῦ τοῦ ὑψίστου) and begs Jesus not to torment him (5:7). The man with the unclean spirit identifies himself as "Legion" (λεγιών) and begs not to be sent away (5:9-10). Jesus casts the demons into a herd of swine (numbering two thousand) that subsequently drown themselves in the sea (5:11-13). Those who witness the healing fear Jesus. The healed man longs to go with Jesus, to follow him as his family of disciples do, but instead Jesus sends him home to his family (εἰς τὸν οἶκόν σου πρὸς τοὺς σούς, 5:18-19). The man, however, goes to the Decapolis and proclaims (κηρύσσειν) all that Jesus did. The nexus of Christology and discipleship in terms of kinship is exhibited in the Son's extension of kinship in the exorcism of Legion and in the restoration of the man to his own kinship group (though he continues to follow Jesus by preaching).

This satellite further affirms the kernel of Jesus' baptism by confirming Jesus' identity as God's Son, even ironically by the demon (5:7). It also elaborates the kernel by implying that Jesus' authority as God's Son extends beyond his own region of Capernaum and the surrounding villages. Akin to the healing of the man with the unclean spirit in 1:17-28 and the reference to the demons who identify Jesus in 3:11, the Gerasene demoniac recognizes Jesus as the Son of God (5:7). And not only that, but the demoniac bows down before Jesus, physically honoring Jesus' power and authority over the demon (5:6). In other contexts the verb προσεκύνησεν could be translated as "worship."[145] The demon publicly identifies Jesus as the Son of God, in the

---

145. Malina and Rohrbaugh state that it ought to read "bow before." If the action is by the demon however, "then he is thereby recognizing that the holy man, Jesus, is higher in the cosmic hierarchy than demons such as himself" (*Social-Science Commentary*, 166). Based upon the demon's identification of Jesus as the Son of God the Most

presence of Jesus' disciples (5:7). In the nexus of Christology and discipleship in terms of kinship, Jesus does not refute the address, which further affirms his identity as the Son of God and the disciples' knowledge of that identity in which they participate as doers of God's will (3:35) and sons of the bridegroom (2:19). The demon specifically addresses Jesus as "Son of God Most High" (υἱὲ τοῦ θεοῦ τοῦ ὑψίστου). Adela Yarbro Collins indicates that ὁ ὕψιστος is a divine name for the Hellenistic god Zeus.[146] Ironically, the demon identifies Jesus as the son of Zeus, showing the demon to be demonically wrong about Jesus' identity and kinship. Even more, it emphasizes the anti-imperial sentiments expressed in this satellite when the demon tries to align Jesus with Zeus, the king of the gods who was affiliated with Greek kings and Roman emperors.[147]

This satellite offers the most explicit reference to the Roman imperial occupation of the Deacoplis and the surrounding regions thus far in the Gospel of Mark. Primarily, the demon's name is λεγιών "Legion," a Greek transliteration of the Latin word *legio* which would have referred to a division of the Roman army of at least three thousand men.[148] The demon's name alone evokes the large and invasive military presence of Rome throughout the Mediterranean region in the first century. Moreover, the Decapolis was occupied by Vespasian and three legions of troops.[149] Though arguments have been made against this interpretation, suggesting that "Legion" simply means "multitude" based on the demon's explanation in 5:9,[150] Joshua Garroway points out that there is no Greek literary reference prior to Mark that refers to λεγιών in the sense of its numerical value.[151] When Jesus exorcises the demon, they request to be transferred to a herd (ἀγέλη) of swine (5:11). J. Duncan Derrett suggests that pigs don't normally travel in "herds" and notices the military overtones of this word and its connotation as a band of

---

High, the demon/man with the unclean spirit is definitely recognizing Jesus' power, authority, and agency.

146. Collins, *Mark*, 268. In addition, Collins, 268n60 indicates there are Hebrew Bible and Qumranic evocations of "God Most High" from Deut. 32:8 and 1QapGen 21:2 and 4Q246.

147. Of particular note is the affiliation of Zeus with Mount Carmel which will serve as the location of the transfiguration in Mark (9:2–9). Moreover, Vespasian visits the oracle at Mount Carmel to offer sacrifice after his campaign in Galilee (Tacitus, *Histories*, 2.78). See Wilson, *Caesarea Philippi*, 33 and Horsley, *Galilee*, 253.

148. This definition of λεγιών is generally undisputed; see Collins, *Mark*, 269; Myers, *Binding the Strong Man*, 191; and Horsley, *Hearing the Whole Story*, 140.

149. Josephus, *War*, 3.446–47.

150. See Gundry, *Mark*, 260.

151. Garroway, "Invasion of a Mustard Seed," 62.

trainees.¹⁵² Moreover, Jesus dismisses (ἐπέτρεψεν) them, and when Legion enter the pigs, they rush (ὥρμησεν) over the hillside into the sea (5:13). Both of these words have distinct military overtones: Jesus gives a military command of dismissal and the pigs rush as if they were rushing into battle to their demise.¹⁵³

The covert reference to the Roman army and the military overtones suggest that Jesus as the Son of God Most High exerts his authority and power, not only over demons, but by extension over Roman imperial domination and occupation. Richard Horsley notes the connection between the battle between the "spiritual" forces of God and Satan and their earthly counterparts of Jesus and Rome. Jesus, as God's Son, has already been establishing his authority and power over demons. It is only now that a demon explicitly represents the imperial and military force in the land. Horsley suggests that this exorcism demonstrates that the struggle in the entirety of Mark is against Rome. Once Legion is identified for who he is (Rome, not a demon), "it is now evident to Jesus' followers and to the hearers of Mark's story that the struggle is really against the rulers, ultimately the Romans."¹⁵⁴ In an effort to dechristologize and demythologize Mark, Horsley claims it is the story of Jesus leading a renewal movement that is anti-imperial; but this loses the nuances with which Mark tells the gospel. Jesus' battle is very much against "spiritual" demons; the priorities of his ministry include teaching, healing, and exorcism. It is necessary to understand the invisible powers (solar and astral deities) at work in political and social institutions that represent the power behind the throne.¹⁵⁵ Jesus' battle is also against the powers and principalities, including the Roman Empire, that prevent the establishment of the empire of God. The healing of the Gerasene demoniac demonstrates Jesus' authority as God's chosen agent and Son in both respects.¹⁵⁶ Moreover, in the nexus of Christology and discipleship, the kinship group of disciples have also served as witnesses to Jesus' authority and

---

152. Derrett, "Contributions," 5. Myers, *Binding the Strong Man*, 191; Horsley, *Hearing the Whole Story*, 141; Moore, *Empire and Apocalypse*, 25n2; and Garroway, "Invasion of a Mustard Seed," 66, each reference Derrett who highlights the military overtones in the healing of the Gerasene demoniac.

153. Derrett, "Contributions," 5.

154. Horsley, *Hearing the Whole Story*, 147.

155. Carter notes, "Roman imperial theology claims Rome as the revelation of the gods' will and purposes. Thus, the exercise of Roman power and the sort of world created by it are divinely sanctioned. Rome is agent of the gods and benefactor of (submissive) people." Carter, *John and Empire*, 154.

156. As Moore, *Empire and Apocalypse*, 26, suggests. This leads Moore to make the Gerasene demoniac a hermeneutical key to the entire Gospel of Mark in order to open the door to the presence of the Roman Empire.

power as God's Son in the exorcism of the Gerasene demoniac. The disciples bear witness to the work they have been called to do, and as the bridegroom's sons comprising Jesus' family (3:31–35), this battle will continue through their work of exorcism (3:15) in the establishment of the empire of God.

Joshua Garroway notices the anti-imperial sentiments within this satellite, but he also observes the imperial mimicry in the authority and power of Jesus. As God's Son, Jesus can establish God's empire as an alternative to and in the likeness of the current reigning power. "Where Legion is irresistibly powerful, Jesus is more so. Where Legion is destructive, Jesus has the power to turn its destructiveness against it. If the legions represent the power of Rome, then Mark's message is clear: mighty Rome is as naught before the power of Jesus, the preacher of the kingdom of God."[157] Not only is Jesus powerful against a legion of demons (and a Legion of Rome's army), but Legion has also recognized and honored who Jesus is and who he represents as God's Son. Before their destruction, Legion bows down to Jesus as the Son of God Most High. The heir of the new empire, in the presence of his family of disciples, in an act of exorcism which he has also authorized them to do as his sons, defeats the power of thousands of demons (whom no one could assist, let alone cure) and by implication, the ruling power of the earthly empire of Rome.[158]

Jesus' power and authority as God's Son (over demons and Rome) is further emphasized by the people in the Decapolis who hear of the healing. Rather than respond with wonder and awe, they ask him to leave. "Jesus frightened the local residents, perhaps intimating by his act a disruptive threat to the established Roman order that could bring consequences."[159] Nevertheless, Jesus' acts are proclaimed by the healed man himself. The healed man acts as a disciple, desiring to be with Jesus ($\mu\epsilon\tau'$ $\alpha\dot{\upsilon}\tau o\tilde{\upsilon}$ $\tilde{\mathring{\eta}}$) just as Jesus' disciples and new kinship group who are with him (3:14) and do God's will (3:34–35). Just as Jesus' core kinship group of disciples was given authority to be sent out and to preach the message of the empire of God

---

157. Garroway, "Invasion of a Mustard Seed," 69. The purpose of Garroway's article goes further than the Gerasene demoniac. Garroway sees the Gerasene demoniac as an explanation of the parables in Mark 4 where the kingdom of God "invades" with the pervasiveness of a mustard seed in mimicry of but against the Roman Empire (which is effectively destroyed when Legion is destroyed in 5:13).

158. Rome's ruling power in regions such as the Galilee and the Decapolis was in its military. Garnsey and Saller note that "the army, where it existed in substantial numbers, was arguably the main official instrument of rural Romanization, to the extent that it 'recycled' peasants after exposing them to the dominant culture" (*Roman Empire*, 194). Exposure to Roman elite occurs in the cities (Herod in Caesarea Philippi in 6:14–29 and Pilate in Jerusalem in 15:1–20).

159. Malina and Rohrbaugh, *Social-Science Commentary*, 166.

(3:14), so too does the man go and proclaim what Jesus did for him (5:20). The kinship of the Son of God Most High is conveyed, not only in his acts of exorcism, authority, and power, but also in the proclamation of those whom Jesus heals (and who follow).

20. 5:21-43 THE SON HEALS TWO DAUGHTERS

After the healing of the Gerasene demoniac, Jesus again crosses to the other side of the sea. What ensues is another sandwich story: the healing of the little girl is interrupted by the healing of the woman with the flow of blood which further emphasizes Jesus' healing power as God's Son.[160] This demonstrates the nexus of Christology and discipleship in terms of kinship because Jesus the Son extends his healing powers and brings two daughters into his extended family. As Jesus is again surrounded by crowds, Jairus, a synagogue leader, seeks Jesus, falls at his feet (πίπτει πρὸς τοὺς πόδας αὐτοῦ), and asks for Jesus to lay hands on his daughter who is close to death (5:22-23). As Jesus departs to tend to Jairus's daughter, there is a woman who has suffered from a flow of blood for twelve years who also seeks Jesus for healing (5:25-27). She manages to touch Jesus' cloak and is healed of her ailment. In a confrontation with Jesus, the woman falls at his feet (προσέπεσεν) and tells him what happened (5:33). In response, he lets her go, but not before addressing her as "daughter" (θυγάτηρ). While he is still speaking to the woman, people from Jairus's house come and tell him that his daughter has died (5:35). Jesus takes with him Peter, James, John, and the girl's parents and enters the house. He takes the little girl by the hand, tells her to get up, and instructs her parents to give her food since she is very much alive (5:41-43).

As the Son, Jesus also contextualizes these healings in terms of kinship. In the nexus of Christology and discipleship by means of kinship, Jesus, as God's chosen agent, uses his power (5:30) to grant healing and restore life to those whom he draws into his kinship network. The little girl is fortunate to be represented by her own father (5:22), a synagogue leader (τοῦ ἀρχισυναγώγου)[161] who has honor and resources; he seeks healing

---

160. These two stories not only are connected in shared vocabulary and shared time (twelve-year illness, twelve-year old daughter), but also in their differences: public versus private settings, named family with status versus anonymous woman. For a detailed discussion on these elements, see Shepherd, *Markan Sandwich Stories*, 139-72.

161. Horsley, *Galilee*, 229, notes that ἀρχισυναγώγος would be better rendered "synagogue-head" due to the varied leadership entailed in synagogue life based upon the literary evidence. I utilize "synagogue leader" in order to demonstrate the authority and honor Jairus maintained as a leader in general. I am not implying he was the sole

for his daughter (5:23). Jesus enters into the household and heals the little girl (5:38–41). In the healing of the woman with the flow of blood, she approaches Jesus in the midst of a crowd, but she appears anonymous, she has lost all of her resources looking for a cure, and she is not represented by any family member.[162] However, once Jesus has restored her to health and lets her leave, he calls her "daughter," a term of close kinship.[163] Jesus, the Son, extends his kinship to the woman by healing her and addressing her with a term of kinship. Her faith in Jesus, her belief in his authority and power (through the Father), allows Jesus to welcome her into the new family he has established (3:35). Just as Jesus commanded in 1:15, the woman believes in Jesus' proclamation and empire and commits her fidelity to God's Son. As a daughter, she is now under the protection and care of the Father (in the agency of Jesus). Moreover, Jesus utilizes his own honor and reputation to protect the woman and functions as her *paterfamilias*.[164] The woman acts outside of the expected social norms of first-century Mediterranean culture by seeking her own healing by touching a man in public. "With the woman physically at his feet, feeling ashamed of her boldness, Jesus calls her 'Daughter,' protecting her honor by giving to their encounter the safest relationship for her touch."[165] Jesus, as God's Son, names the woman "Daughter" giving her a place in the family, restoring her to health, and bestowing further honor by commending her faith. The nexus of Christology and discipleship is found in the extension of Jesus' kinship as Son of God to the woman in her healing and by calling her "daughter."

Although the healing of the woman takes place in a very public arena, the raising of the little girl occurs within the household. Akin to the healing of Simon Peter's mother-in-law (1:29–31), Jesus enters into the home of Jairus and his family (5:38). The house belongs to Jairus, but upon Jesus' entrance, he assumes the role of the head of the household: Jesus sends everyone else out (5:40); he invites only Jairus, his wife, and Peter, James, and John into the house; Jesus is the one who tends to the daughter (5:41); Jesus tells the parents to feed the little girl (5:43). Michael Trainor suggests another element in reference to the household and the restoration of the

---

leader of a synagogue in or near Capernaum.

162. As I noted in chapter 2, the woman is not necessarily excluded from her community due to her ailment and she may not be in complete dire straits, but she is in need of healing.

163. This address suggests that the woman is part of a household under the care of a *paterfamilias* which was a primary definition of "daughter" (θυγάτηρ) in Greco-Roman society. See Betsworth, *Reign of God*, 28.

164. Betsworth, *Reign of God*, 106.

165. Cotter, "Mark's Hero," 60.

little girl: Jesus' presence in the house restores the traditional kinship roles of father, mother, and daughter. While it may stretch the point of the story to demonstrate Jesus' authority within the household and his power to heal, "No longer is the father identified by an honorific religious title. Jesus' presence brings about a household of warm familiarity and nurturing relationships, the Roman domestic ideal not lost on Mark's readers."[166] In imitation of the Roman household, epitomized and idealized by the imperial household, Jesus establishes an alternative household where he functions as the *paterfamilias*, agent of the Father God, for his family of disciples. The nexus of Christology and discipleship is located in the extension of the Son's kinship to his family of disciples and extended kinship network of recipients of healing.

Aspects of this satellite also highlight the role of Jesus' honor as God's Son when he provides healing and restores life. Both Jairus and the unnamed woman are described as falling at Jesus' feet when they confront him (5:22; 33). "Once more, falling at the feet of someone is a gesture acknowledging social inferiority, a telling gesture for a ruler of the synagogue."[167] The physical demonstration of respect denotes the honor that Jesus has in his reputation for healing. As God's Son and agent, Jesus is able to grant access to healing from God; he is patron and benefactor for these "children." Moreover, both instances of kneeling occur in public where there would be plenty of people to witness the event (5:21, 24), which further supports Jesus' honorable reputation. When the people from Jairus's home come to tell him that his daughter has died, they refer to Jesus as "the teacher" (τὸν διδάσκαλον, 5:35) which is an honorific title. However, the messengers attribute Jesus with only one aspect of his sonship by identifying him as the teacher. The reference could stand as an honor challenge, suggesting that Jesus has wasted his time healing the woman with the flow of blood and is not capable of healing Jairus's daughter.[168] Jesus maintains his honorable reputation and upholds his kinship with God by providing healing for the woman, and even more, by restoring the daughter to life, proving his power and authority over death itself and continuing to demonstrate the nexus of Christology and discipleship through kinship. Although the little girl is brought back to life inside the home, Peter, James, and John stand as witnesses, and members of the household, who respond with amazement to Jesus' act, providing further corroboration of his reputation and honor as God's Son.

---

166. Trainor, *Quest for Home*, 119.
167. Malina and Rohrbaugh, *Social-Science Commentary*, 167.
168. Marcus, *Mark 1–8*, 370.

The restoration of the little girl also evokes the works of the prophets Elijah and Elisha in 1 Kgs 17:17–24 and 2 Kgs 4:18–37. In both of these stories, the prophet intercedes for a mother who has lost her only child. In each instance, through prayer and touch, the prophets bring the children back to life. Furthermore, all of these events occur within the context of the household. Wendy Cotter observes that the Elijah and Elisha stories were probably not meant to be references to the raising of the little girl in Mark due to the lack of internal evidence among the stories and Jesus' superiority over Elijah and Elisha.[169] Jesus' power and authority extends beyond the prophets'. "For unlike Elijah and Elisha, who must explicitly call on God to perform the miracle, Jesus shows that he has received a heavenly empowerment, a heavenly authorization that neither of these prophets were given."[170] Within the household, as God's Son, Jesus acts as host and father to the little girl and her family; they enter into Jesus' kinship community. Moreover, Jesus is able to heal by a simple touch and a command because he is the Son of God and embodies the power and authority of God. The nexus of Christology and discipleship is located in Jesus' extension of kinship as the *paterfamilias* to the little girl and her parents.

In this satellite of two healings, Jesus, as the Son of God, has acted with compassion; people who need help receive help with no expectation for a return favor. Jesus has also served people (an anonymous woman and a little girl) who would not necessarily merit the healing gift they receive based upon their social status. This highlights Jesus' character as God's Son, especially in light of the social mores in the Roman Empire. "The elements of the narration teach the community about the character of the cosmic power of Jesus . . . This *humanitas* [compassion] of Jesus defines his use of power."[171] The household of Rome serves its own family or those who are able to procure what they need. Furthermore, they have power over life, in that they may destroy it. But Rome cannot raise the dead. "These miracles align Jesus with the ordinary person, and particularly forgotten women, as a contrast to the powerful political and spiritual leaders who never show any

---

169. Cotter, "Mark's Hero," 74. Cotter's article focuses on the characterization of Jesus as a hero/healer in light of Mark 5:21–43. In her analysis of the raising of Jairus's daughter, Cotter provides a summary of the "hero" category in ancient Greek literature (such as Asclepius) and the Hebrew Bible (Elijah/Elisha). Cotter states, "The two concluding miracles about these women balance the big cosmic miracles of the Stilling of the Storm and the wild and frightening, fascinating exorcism of the Gerasene demoniac by showing a more 'Asclepian' Jesus in his intense kindness to these women, his sensitivity, and his unfailing benevolence. For Mark, they function to augment the pathos of the Gospel as Jesus goes to his cross" (ibid., 78).

170. Ibid., 74.

171. Ibid., 75.

interest in the ordinary person's troubles."[172] Jesus welcomes any and all who call upon him to enter into his new kinship group, and with the authority as God's Son he is able to restore life from death.[173]

In the establishment of an alternative household in God's empire, Jesus provides a place in the family for daughters, sons, sisters, and brothers who are in the need of the benefits of healing. In turn, the family of disciples functions as witnesses who will further corroborate Jesus' honor and reputation as God's Son and continue his work of ministry and healing in God's empire demonstrating the nexus of Christology and discipleship in terms of kinship.

21. 6:1-6 THE SON IS REJECTED BY HIS ORIGINAL KINSHIP GROUP

Following the marvelous demonstrations of Jesus' power as God's Son and agent over nature (4:35-41), demons (1:21-27; 5:1-20), illness (1:29-31; 1:40-45; 2:1-12; 3:1-6; 5:25-34), and even death (5:35-43), Jesus returns to his hometown and his family of origin accompanied by his new family of disciples. Akin to the beginning of his ministry in Galilee (1:21), Jesus begins teaching in the synagogue (6:2). The hearers are astounded at his teaching and acknowledge that he has wisdom and power, but they quickly become offended because they know Jesus' family (6:3). The townspeople identify Jesus as a part of his original kinship group, as the son of Mary and the brother of James, Joses, Judas, and Simon (6:3). Jesus' authority is ignored and his honorable status as God's Son is not recognized. Subsequently, Jesus has no authority in Nazareth except to cure a few sick people (6:5). In an ironic turn, Jesus marvels at their unbelief rather than witnesses marveling at Jesus' power and authority and believers' faith (6:6).[174]

This satellite echoes the scene in Jesus' home in Capernaum where his family comes to retrieve him because of his behavior and threat to their honor and social status (3:21, 31-35). Jesus teaches with an authority he has not earned from his family and is not culturally acceptable,[175] but with

---

172. Ibid., 78.

173. Betsworth suggests that the raising of Jairus's daughter "functions proleptically in the Gospel of Mark to anticipate the resurrection of Jesus." Betsworth, *Reign of God*, 113. She demonstrates this through shared vocabulary between this story and Jesus' passion predictions. If it is not interpreted proleptically, it certainly demonstrates Jesus' power as God's Son over life and death.

174. See 1:27; 2:12; 3:7-12; 4:41; 5:20; 5:42.

175. DeSilva, *Honor*, 162.

one that he derives from God expressed in kinship language as the Son of God. "Claims to more than one's appointed share of honor determined by birth thus threatened others and would eventually trigger attempts to cut the claimant down to size."[176] The recipients of Jesus' teaching attempt to put Jesus in his social and cultural "place" by identifying him as "the carpenter, Mary's son," (ὁ τέκτων, ὁ υἱὸς τῆς Μαρίας) in 6:3. Jesus is identified in relationship to his profession as an artisan and to his kinship group of mother and siblings. Jesus' identity as a carpenter emphasizes his humble origins.[177] As I noted in chapter 2, there is no mention of Jesus' father which stands as further insult toward Jesus implying his illegitimacy and a challenge to his honor and authority.[178] Jesus' apparent abandonment of his family, his humble profession, and his illegitimacy cause the people of his village to ignore his teaching and not to recognize his ascribed authority as God's Son.

Jesus responds to this rejection with a direct reference to honor, a sort of verbal riposte to the people's challenge to his authority and his ascribed honor. His response insults his hometown and family and further acknowledges the ties cut in Mark 3:31–35. Moreover Jesus' family never appears in the gospel again. "This statement reveals that Jesus now considers himself dishonored, distanced, rejected at all levels of his familial structures: his immediate family, his household, his related ones, his hometown, and his religion. All this results from opposition to and rejection of his mission, which is constituent of his identity as God's chosen one (1:11)."[179] Moreover, the unbelief of not only the townspeople, but also his family, completely sever the original familial ties and point toward the new family of those who do God's will which Jesus, as God's son, established in 3:35.[180] The nexus of Christology and discipleship is demonstrated in the original kinship ties that are abandoned by God's Son to establish a kinship group of disciples and followers who do God's will.

Jesus' reference to the rejection of a prophet in his hometown also matches a proverbial saying that was prevalent in Greco-Roman literature

---

176. Malina and Rohrbaugh, *Social-Science Commentary*, 168.

177. Brown et al., *Mary in the New Testament*, 61. Malina and Rohrbaugh state, "In asking if Jesus is the craftsman's son [sic], the synagogue participants are questioning how such astounding teaching could come from one born to a lowly manual craftsman (one working in stone or wood). By Jesus' time such craftsmen were often itinerants, especially those living in villages or small towns. They could not make a living in one place. Like all itinerants who did not stay home to protect their women and family honor, they were often considered shameless persons (lacking a sense of what the community valued)" (*Social-Science Commentary*, 169).

178. See chapter 2. See also Marcus, *Mark 1–8*, 374–75.

179. Ahearne-Kroll, "'Who Are My?,'" 15.

180. Barton, *Discipleship and Family Ties*, 90–91, 96.

and a sentiment in the Hebrew Bible. Joel Marcus points to Plutarch who wrote in *De Exilio* 604D, "You would find that the most sensible and wisest people are little cared for in their own hometowns."[181] Furthermore, Israelite prophets were often rejected and scorned for their messages and calls to repentance (2 Chron 24:19; 36:15–16; Neh 9:26). Jesus has already proven his wisdom and honor in the challenge-riposte scenes throughout chapters 2 and 3. Of course, at the end of these scenes, his challengers reacted with anger and planned to find a way to destroy him (3:6). Jesus is again rejected by his family and fellow townspeople, but this time, he marvels at their lack of faith, which prevents him from really using his authority and power as God's Son. Unlike the disciples' apparent disbelief during the storm on the Sea of Galilee (4:40), who are still very much in relationship with and dependent upon Jesus' power and authority as God's Son, Jesus' former kinsfolk have given no loyalty or commitment to him or his ministry. Their unbelief (ἀπιστίαν) is an unwillingness to accept and trust Jesus as anyone except for who they knew him to be: a fatherless artisan from their small village. The denial of the Son's original kinship in favor of an alterative kinship group of disciples and followers who do God's will demonstrates the nexus of Christology and discipleship.

Jesus was compelled by the Spirit to bring his ministry and teaching to surrounding villages (1:14–15) including his hometown of Nazareth. As God's Son he preaches with authority and amazes the townspeople until they recognize Jesus within his family ties but not in terms of his kinship with God. The nexus of Christology and discipleship in terms of kinship is emphasized in this scene by Jesus' rejection and severing of original kinship ties. Without an original kinship network, the Son's family consists of his core kinship group of disciples and extended family of followers who do God's will (3:31–35).

22. 6:7–13 MISSION OF THE CORE KINSHIP GROUP OF DISCIPLES

In an echo of the first commissioning of the twelve disciples in 3:13–19, Jesus calls the twelve to him again and gives them a further mission in the first part of a sandwich story that frames the death of John the Baptist.[182] In

---

181. Marcus, *Mark 1–8*, 376. Edwards, *Mark*, 174n69 also notes the gospel parallels of Matt 13:57; Luke 4:24; 13:33; and John 4:44. In addition, he also cites *Gos. Thom.* 31; *P.Oxy.* 31:1; Philostratus, *Life Apoll.* 1.354.12; and Dio Chrysostum, *Discourses* 47.6 to demonstrate the widespread sentiment.

182. See Marcus, *Mark 1–8*, 385, and Moloney, "Mark 6:6b–30," 648–50.

the nexus of Christology and discipleship in terms of kinship, Jesus, as God's Son, gives the disciples the same authority he has over demons and the same proclamation to deliver (1:15). He provides the disciples with instructions for their travel supplies and their work. The disciples travel two by two with minimal essentials. In addition to safety, traveling companions would have provided support. The nexus of Christology and discipleship occurs in terms of kinship as Jesus the Son of God supported, taught, and cared for his family of disciples, and now the disciples care for one another; brother travels with brother. Two by two may also evoke the Hebrew Bible "stipulation that two witnesses are required to establish legal testimony (Deut 17:6; 19:15)."[183] And as Jesus had success in his ministry, in his proclamation, and healing (3:7–12), so too, do the family of disciples have success in the ministry that Jesus has commissioned them to do (6:13). Kinship serves as the nexus of Christology and discipleship.

Jesus instructs the twelve to travel with minimal provision, specifically with one staff, no bread, no bag, no money, sandals, and one tunic. These provisions, or lack thereof, are the same as the provisions the Israelites travelled with in the exodus from Egypt (Exod 12:11 and Deut 29:5); other sustenance was provided by God in the wilderness.[184] As the Israelites travelled to establish the new kingdom in the Promised Land, so now do the disciples of Jesus travel under the Son's authority and power to establish God's empire. Just as Jesus, as God's Son, has provided for his family of disciples thus far (2:23–28; 4:35–41), God will provide for them on the journey. In the nexus of Christology and discipleship by means of kinship, Jesus' kinship with God extends to his family of disciples.

As the twelve prepare to depart from the "household" of Jesus to go out to preach and provide ministry, Jesus instructs them on their entrance into other households (6:10–11). Jesus tells the disciples, "Wherever you enter in a house, stay there until you leave that place," (6:10). Mark 6:11 implies that the house they enter offers hospitality and is open to the disciples' (and Jesus') proclamation and ministry. If a household is unwelcoming, then the disciples are to leave, and moreover, shake the dust off their feet to indicate the disciples' (and Jesus') rejection of and severing of any ties to that place (much like the rejection at Nazareth immediately preceding this scene). "Shaking off dust from one's feet comes from the belief that Israel was God's 'holy land'; travelers returning from the impure lands that surrounded Israel would shake the dust from their feet [to indicate] . . . the impurity and godlessness of the land they had just left and the holiness of the land they

---

183. Marcus, *Mark 1–8*, 383.
184. Ibid., 389.

were entering."[185] Furthermore, this shaking off of the dust stood as a witness to anyone else of their rejection of the gospel and the disciples' (Jesus') rejection of them. The sandwich story concludes in 6:30, when the disciples return from their missionary work and tell Jesus all that they had done and taught. The twelve are sent out to preach and teach and heal, but they return to the Son as his family of disciples who are also called to be with him (3:14). The nexus of Christology and discipleship consists of a core kinship group of disciples who do the work and ministry of the Son of God, but who also accompany him as members of his family.

23. 6:14-29 KINSHIP GONE AWRY

Within the framework of the mission of the twelve disciples, Mark tells the story of Herod and the death of John the Baptist in an example of kinship gone awry. As Jesus' fame increases, as he establishes an honorable kinship group that does the will of God, Herod hears about Jesus and concludes that he is John the Baptist raised from the dead. John has played a small but significant role in the Gospel of Mark: he served as Jesus' predecessor (1:4), prophesied about (1:7-8) and baptized (1:9) Jesus which revealed the identification of Jesus as God's Son and inaugurated his ministry. According to 1:14, John was arrested and has been imprisoned for most, if not all of Jesus' ministry. John is not mentioned again with the exception of a reference to his disciples in 2:18 when they question Jesus about fasting. Now the reader learns he has died and Mark relates the story.

John preached a message of repentance for the forgiveness of sins and he also spoke out against Herodias, Herod's wife, because of her divorce from her first husband and her adulterous and incestuous marriage to Herod Antipas (6:17-18). Herod Antipas was tetrarch (referred to as ὁ βασιλεὺς, "king," in Mark 6:14) of Galilee and Perea from 4 BCE to 39 CE. He was a Jewish ruler, but served, and was a client to, the Roman imperial elites, following in the footsteps of his father, Herod the Great, and grandfather, Antipater. Herod Antipas was named as heir to Herod's kingdom at one point, but upon Herod's death, and according to the most recent will, the kingdom went to his brother Archelaus. In a kinship and inheritance dispute, Archelaus was in turn challenged by his family. Caesar Augustus decreed that Archelaus could have the title ethnarch, but Herod's kingdom was divided among the three sons, Antipas, Philip, and Archelaus.[186] Within

---

185. Moloney, "Mark 6:6b-30," 654.

186. Josephus, *Ant.* 17.311-17. Archelaus was later removed from his position and replaced by a prefect (17.344; 354).

this circle of imperial elites, client-kings, and regional rulers, politics, honor, kinship, and allegiance played a large part. Herodias was originally married to Herod's half-brother, Philip, but she is now married to Herod Antipas.[187] "Herodias's motivation for pursuing the relationship may well have been increased honor and prestige: Herod the Great had disinherited her first husband, and her new husband was the ruling tetrarch over Galilee and Perea."[188] Although Herodias would have increased her honor and reputation by her marriage to Herod, John accuses them of adultery and incest, matters of kinship (Lev 18:16; 20:21), and presents them with a verbal challenge (6:18). Rather than accept the honor challenge, Herod uses his power and authority to arrest John, and Herodias now desires to kill him. Mark indicates that Herod struggled with what to do with John because he feared John (ὁ γὰρ Ἡρῴδης ἐφοβεῖτο τὸν Ἰωάννην, 6:20). Herod knew John was honorable and listened to him (αὐτὸν ἄνδρα δίκαιον καὶ ἅγιον, 6:20).[189]

Mark portrays the marriage of Herod and Herodias as kinship gone awry and their apparent honor and prestige as not true honor. The couple aspires to political power and closeness with the Roman imperial elites as indicated by the banquet Herod gives for his birthday, a celebration specifically for the *paterfamilias* of the household in Roman culture.[190] Herod's birthday banquet would have been a means to throw a lavish affair to demonstrate his power, prestige, honor, and his Herodian lineage among his circle of elites.[191] Mark states that Herod entertained his courtiers, officers, and the leaders of Galilee (τοῖς μεγιστᾶσιν αὐτοῦ καὶ τοῖς χιλιάρχοις καὶ τοῖς πρώτοις τῆς Γαλιλαίας, 6:21).

Herod's birthday banquet included entertainment which becomes part of Herodias's plot to procure John's death. Herod's daughter[192] dances for the

187. This is according to Mark. Historically, Herodias was married to Antipas' half-brother, Herod. See Josephus, *Ant.* 18:110; 136.

188. Hanson and Oakman, *Palestine*, 79.

189. Cummins insists that Herod was not manipulated by his wife and is innocent in John's death. "That Herod 'feared' John as a righteous and holy man indicates at best a grudging awe and at worst a realization that his own faithless character and conduct paled by comparison. That he 'protected him' carries considerable irony inasmuch as this consisted of the prophet's incarceration and ever-present threat of execution on a ruler's whim. That he 'liked to listen' to John yet was 'greatly perplexed' by what he heard only anticipates his later incapacity to differentiate Jesus from John and to understand their combined message about an emerging kingdom of God which stood over and against his own" (Cummins, "Integrated Scripture," 39).

190. Hanson and Oakman, *Palestine*, 78.

191. Ibid., note that birthday celebrations were reserved for elites in the Roman world demonstrating the influence of the Roman Empire among the Herodians.

192. There are textual variances regarding the paternity of Herod to his daughter.

guests in another demonstration of kinship and honor gone awry (6:22). The daughter's dance would have been sexually provocative as indicated by Herod's and his guests' response, "She pleased Herod and his guests" (ἤρεσεν τῷ Ἡρῴδῃ καὶ τοῖς συνανακειμένοις, 6:22).[193] An unmarried daughter dancing for anyone but her family was dishonorable. "In nonelite eyes, honorable males would not allow a female family member to perform such a display; their failure to prevent her from doing so pegs them as shameless. It is also shameful for any man to be bewitched by the proverbial sensuality of a woman in public."[194] Moreover, Herod publicly offers to give up half of his kingdom to his daughter which he is then honor-bound to maintain (6:22–23). His gesture goes against the custom of inheritance which would designate a male relative as heir of at least the largest portion of his estate.[195] It also goes against Herod's own political aspirations to be "king."[196] The division of the kingdom would also divide, and subsequently lessen, Herod's power, influence, and legacy. This offer to Herod's daughter further affirms John's criticism of Herod and his inability to maintain proper kinship boundaries.[197]

This satellite of honor and dishonor also echoes the story of Esther and King Ahasuerus. Esther is pleasing to the King (Esth 2:9) and he offers her up to half of his kingdom (Esth 5:3). Herod's and his daughter's parallel to King Ahasuerus and Esther is ironic. Esther and the King are portrayed as positive characters but Herod and his daughter are negative characters. "Whereas Esther saved God's people through her ability to please men, Herodias' daughter uses the same talent to bring about the death of God's prophet."[198] Herod's daughter does not seek half of his kingdom, but rather,

---

See Marcus, *Mark 1–8*, 396 for a discussion. "The reading chosen, which makes the performer of the dance that titillates Herod and his guests into Herod's own daughter, accords with the story's general atmosphere of wild abandon" (ibid.).

193. Marcus notes, "In the Septuagint this verb [αἰτέω] often has connotations of arousing or satisfying sexual interest (see e.g. Gen 19:8; Judg 14:1A, 14:3A, 14:7A; Esth 2:4, 9; Job 31:10 and cf. 1 Cor 7:33–34)" (ibid.).

194. Malina and Rohrbaugh, *Social-Science Commentary*, 171.

195. Hanson and Oakman, *Palestine*, 45.

196. Both as the heir of Herod the Great's title (Josephus, *Ant.* 17.146) and at the suggestion by his wife after his brother Philip receives the title king (Josephus, *Ant.* 18.240–41).

197. Mark further highlights this kinship gone awry in the name of all the principle family members in the corrupt kinship system: Herod or Herodias, the feminine form of Herod. Mark 6:22 suggests the name of the daughter is also Herodias (καὶ εἰσελθούσης τῆς θυγατρὸς αὐτοῦ Ἡρῳδιάδος). See Theissen, *Gospels in Context*, 89–97 regarding the role of the Herodian women in Mark as well as among the Herodian dynasty.

198. Marcus, *Mark 1–8*, 402. Cummins also notes the death of Haman and compares

in consultation with her mother, asks for John's head on a platter (6:24). In a final dishonorable display of violence in response to John's challenge, Herod has John beheaded and his head is brought to his daughter who presents it to her mother (6:27-28).

The dishonorable kinship and actions of the Jewish "king" Herod and his family who conspire to be among the Roman imperial elite circles stand against the backdrop of the story of the most honorable Son and (future) king, Jesus. Jesus' fame has reached Herod; the telling of the story of John's beheading at this point illustrates the lengths Herod would go to maintain his apparent honor and reputation and also foreshadows the eventual end of John's successor, Jesus. Just as John challenged the reputation and honor of political leaders, just as he called for repentance and forgiveness of sins, so too, has Jesus started challenging the local Galilean leaders. And like Herodias, they have not stepped up to his challenge; rather they have resorted to violence and conspire to kill him (3:6). After John's beheading, his family of disciples remains faithful and retrieves his body for burial (6:29). Just like John, the Son of God will also be laid in a tomb (15:46; though by this point Jesus' family of disciples will have abandoned him). The nexus of Christology and discipleship is in terms of kinship where, unlike Herod and his family, Jesus the Son demonstrates honorable and appropriate kinship with his family of disciples and followers.

24. 6:30-44 THE SON AND HIS DISCIPLES PROVIDE FOR FIVE THOUSAND

In the feeding of the five thousand, Jesus has withdrawn to a deserted place with the family of disciples after they have returned from their missionary work (6:31-32). The nexus of Christology and discipleship in terms of kinship is evident when Jesus, the Son, and the core kinship group of disciples are unable to escape their fame and popularity and are subsequently followed. A large crowd gathers and Jesus cares for them and teaches them since they are like sheep without a shepherd (ὡς πρόβατα μὴ ἔχοντα ποιμένα, 6:34). When it gets late, the disciples urge Jesus to disperse the crowd so that all may get something to eat (6:35-36). Jesus does not disperse the crowd but instead tells the disciples to take care of them and feed them (6:37).

---

it with the death of John. "The most dramatic and darkest moment in Esther arrives in yet another banquet scene which brings about the downfall and ignominious death of the offensive and wicked Haman who is hanged on the gallows meant for Mordecai (Esth 6:14-7:10). The climactic end to Herod's banquet comes with the gruesome execution of the righteous John the Baptist and the arrival of his head on a platter (Mk 6:27-28)" (Cummins, "Integrated Scripture," 46).

After the disciples respond incredulously to Jesus' request, Jesus successfully feeds the crowd gathered with five loaves and two fish in a demonstration of his power as God's Son to care for his family of followers (6:38-42).

This satellite of Jesus providing a meal (banquet) for five thousand men (not including women and children) is juxtaposed to the story of Herod's birthday banquet. In an appropriate and honorable display of kinship and hospitality, Jesus and his disciples contrast the kinship gone awry. Mark purposely displays the hospitality and access to food that Jesus, the Son of God, is able to provide next to the exclusive banquet for the elite of Galilee that ends, not with twelve baskets of leftovers, but with John's head on a platter. Jesus is portrayed as a compassionate and caring leader who, like Moses who shepherded the people of Israel, organizes, cares for, and provides abundant sustenance for those who have followed him (Exod 16). There are also Hebrew Bible echoes in this feeding story where a prophet is able to miraculously provide food (Elijah and Elisha in 1 Kgs 17:8-16 and 2 Kgs 4:1-7; 42-44). Moreover, Isa 25:6-10 provides a vision of an abundant feast of sumptuous food and wine for the people of God on the eschatological day of the Lord. Visions and demonstrations of abundance give light to the reality that the majority of people lived with inadequate nutrition on a regular basis.[199] Joel Marcus notes, "In all of these stories, as in ours, the miracle is a spontaneous act of generosity, not a response to a request from a person in need, and the mechanism by which it transpires is left obscure, only the subsequent abundance demonstrating its occurrence."[200] The Son of God provides graciously and generously to those who are in need, as though he were providing for his family. The nexus of Christology and discipleship in terms of kinship appears in a meal provided by God's Son and his core kinship group of disciples for the extended family of followers.

In a deserted place where there would be no access to food or merchants, Jesus organizes the crowd into groups and orders them to recline (ἀνακλῖναι), essentially inviting them to a banquet.[201] Although they are not inside a house, Jesus serves as the host of the meal. He takes the five loaves and the two fish that the disciples have given to him, looks to heaven, blesses the meal, and gives the food to the disciples to disperse (6:41). From the provisions, everyone has enough to eat and there are twelve baskets of

---

199. Not only were people hungry, but inadequate nutrition also resulted in deficiency diseases and contagious disease due to a compromised immune system. See Garnsey, *Food and Society*, 43-61. See also the discussion above on food access in Mark 2:23-28.

200. Marcus, *Mark 1-8*, 415.

201. Smith, *From Symposium to Eucharist*, 241, especially when taken in juxtaposition to Herod's banquet in 6:21-22.

leftovers, certainly more than that with which they started (6:42–43). Jesus, the Son, provides a filling meal for people who would make up the population of a larger town. As a demonstration of the nexus of Christology and discipleship by means of kinship, the event emphasizes the ability of Jesus, as God's Son, to provide care and provision for those who follow him, for his family, in abundance. Ched Myers suggests that this event is miraculous only "in the triumph of the economics of sharing within a community of consumption over against the economics of autonomous consumption in the anonymous marketplace."[202] Myers fails to recognize that the Roman economy was not a free market; rather food supply was controlled by and for elites. He also fails to acknowledge the juxtaposition of this feeding story with the banquet of Herod. He does note the reference to Elisha's miracle feeding in 2 Kgs 4:42–44, but again only in reference to its political association with access to food. Myers appears to be refusing the miraculous aspects of these feeding stories in order to emphasize their political and economic aspects. I argue that it is Jesus' ability as God's Son to perform miracles that strengthens his power over and against the reigning political and economic authorities.

In demonstration of kinship as the nexus of Christology and disciples, Jesus and his disciples work together as a family, and so the extension of the Son's authority and role is transmitted to the family of disciples as they help the people orderly to recline and to distribute the food. Unlike Herod who serves up death on a platter, unlike officials of the Roman Empire who take food from those that grow it to serve their own citizens, the Son of God and his core kinship group of disciples provide food in abundance for all of his family who gathered with him: "All ate and were filled," (καὶ ἔφαγον πάντες καὶ ἐχορτάσθησαν).

25. 6:45–52 THE SON WALKS ON WATER

After the meal, Jesus, the Son and the core kinship group of disciples finally have the opportunity for solitude. As he dismisses the crowd, his extended family of followers, he sends the disciples in the boat to go onto Bethsaida while he goes up the mountain to pray (6:45–46). Again, as in 4:35–41, the core kinship group of disciples find themselves in a windy situation, struggling in the boat (6:48).[203] Jesus sees them and so he walks to them on the sea (περιπατῶν ἐπὶ τῆς θαλάσσης), but then Mark states that he intended

---

202. Myers, *Binding the Strong Man*, 206.

203. Ibid., 194–95 connects the two stories about the journeys across the Sea of Galilee.

to walk by them (ἤθελεν παρελθεῖν αὐτούς, 6:48). In like manner to their terror during the storm while Jesus slept (4:35–41), his appearance startles (ἐταράχθησαν) the disciples (6:49–50). Jesus reassures them by identifying himself, "Take courage, it is I [I am]; do not be afraid," (θαρσεῖτε, ἐγώ εἰμι, μὴ φοβεῖσθε, 6:50). Once Jesus enters the boat, the winds die down but the family of disciples are riled up and astounded (καὶ λίαν ἐκπερισσοῦ ἐν ἑαυτοῖς ἐξίσταντο, καὶ ἐθαύμαζον) at Jesus (6:51). Jesus' self-referent (ἐγώ εἰμι) points toward his sonship and kinship with God, which challenges the disciples' faith and comprehension, raising the question of the nexus of Christology and discipleship in terms of kinship. What does it mean for the disciples that Jesus is the Son of God and he declares his disciples as his family?

Jesus the Son has just demonstrated his authority and power over food access and he again shows his power over the natural world. Not only can Jesus tell a storm to be quiet, but the Son of God is capable of walking on the sea, not just the water, but the sea. "The sea is essentially a different entity from water. To walk on the sea is to trample on a being that can engulf people with its waves, swallow them in its deep, and support all sorts of living beings."[204] Moreover, Jesus' power over the sea suggests he is on a par with (or superior to) the Greco-Roman deities of the sea and Roman emperors who were attributed with divine authority over the sea.[205] Power and dominion over the sea were attributed to the Greek god Poseidon who is described as traveling over the sea and the waves in his chariot (βῆ δ'ἐλάαν ἐπὶ κύματ').[206] In this same vein, the emperor Caligula rides across the Bay of Baiae on a bridge of boats in 39 CE in imitation of Alexander the Great.[207] Wendy Cotter notes that one reason for Caligula's ride was to prove his worthiness as emperor. Regarding Caligula's possible succession to the throne, the historian Suetonius cited Thrasyllus the astrologer assuring Tiberius, "Gaius had no more chance of becoming emperor than of riding about over the gulf of Baiae on horseback."[208] If Caligula is able to have power over the sea, he certainly will have power as emperor over Rome. Akin to the Greek deity and the Roman emperor, not only is Jesus able to walk upon the sea, but he exerts the power he has been granted as God's Son to calm the sea and stop the wind as he had done in 4:35–41.

204. Malina and Rohrbaugh, *Social-Science Commentary*, 173.

205. See Collins, *Mark*, 328–33, and her summary of the Greek, Roman, and Jewish traditions of deities, emperors, and divine men and the sea.

206. Homer, *Iliad*, 4–5.

207. Cotter, *Christ of Miracle Stories*, 244–45, connects the significance of this event with Jesus walking on the Sea of Galilee.

208. Ibid., 244. Suet.*Cl.* 19.

In an echo of the calming of the storm in 4:35–41 and in an echo of Jesus using his power as the Son of God to calm the wind and to protect his family of disciples, Jesus answers the question posed in the previous satellite. The disciples ask in 4:41, "Who is this that even the winds and the seas obey him?" Before the question is answered directly, the narrative moves on to the stories of the Gerasene demoniac (5:1–20) and the healing of the woman and the little girl (5:21–43). But, here, when the disciples are again on a stormy sea, Jesus identifies himself (ἐγώ εἰμι). William McInery[209] highlights the epiphany aspects of this story that echo epiphanies in the Hebrew scriptures. Elements include: (1) Jesus' intent to pass by is God's manifestation to people and a means of Jesus revealing himself in his intimate relationship with God as Son.[210] (2) Jesus speaks with the family of disciples just as God speaks with people.[211] (3) The disciples are terrified and Jesus responds calmly with care for his family.[212] (4) Jesus' identity is in terms of his kinship with God (Jesus takes the name of God).[213] Although the Son of God reveals himself fully, invoking the Hebrew name for God, the disciples still do not comprehend. Mark attributes this to a hardening of their hearts (ἀλλ' ἦν αὐτῶν ἡ καρδία πεπωρωμένη), which echoes the sentiment of those gathered in the synagogue in 3:5. Jesus demonstrates his power and authority as God's Son and reveals his identity as such, but the disciples fail to understand. Although the identity of God's Son is evident, faith and fidelity are required for the family of disciples. Even in the disciples' lack of understanding, the nexus of Christology and discipleship occurs in terms of kinship. The disciples' lack of understanding foreshadows their ultimate alienation and abandonment of Jesus (though the Son is still triumphant: Jesus walks on the sea and the winds cease when he enters the boat). Just as Jesus' identity as God's Son will lead to his suffering and death, the family of disciples will also suffer in abandoning Jesus and also abandonment by their own families (13:12). The family of disciples fails to recognize the role and purpose of Jesus' suffering and death in the establishment of God's empire. The fact that these stories have occurred on stormy seas serves to underline the challenges that Jesus the Son and his family of disciples will face in the establishment of God's empire. Christology and discipleship are still bound together by kinship.

---

209. McInery, "An Unresolved Question," 259–61.
210. See Exod 33:19, 22, 34:6; 2 Sam 23:4; 1 Kgs 19:11; Amos 7:8, 8:2; Job 9:11.
211. See Gen 35:13–15; Num 11:17; Judg 6:17; Exod 3:10.
212. See Exod 14:13, 20:20; Zeph 3:16; Gen 15:1; Josh 8:1; Dan 10:12, 19; Tob 12:17.
213. See Exod 3:14; Deut 32:39; Isa 41:4.

The Roman Empire and its military were known for their power and control over land and sea. The Roman army had a fleet of seventy-five to one hundred ships established by Augustus to patrol the Mediterranean and Adriatic Seas.[214] Part of the fleet's responsibility was escorting trade ships and ships carrying grain from the territories to Rome. Although not necessarily as imposing as Rome's land army, Rome's navy was powerful enough to control the seas to protect its interests. Power over the sea is evident in a story related by Josephus during the Jewish War in 67 CE.[215] In the Galilee campaign, and before Vespasian was emperor, he commanded his son Titus and Roman troops in a battle for Taricheae (Magdala) that started and ended on the Sea of Galilee. After an initial attack by Vespasian and naval forces, his son Titus fought the Jewish rebels on land. The Jews fled by boat and were pursued by Vespasian and his forces. Josephus describes a very violent and bloody battle where the Jews had no chance against the Roman military. Vespasian and his naval troops killed 6,500 men in evident triumph over the Galilee and its sea.

In stark contrast, Jesus, in doing the work of his Father, has just provided a meal (nourishment) and hospitality for five thousand men plus women and children and now comes to the aid of his family of disciples who are in peril (or at least making no progress toward their destination) on the sea linking Christology and discipleship through kinship. Vespasian and Titus were lauded for their military might, and their triumph in Rome celebrated the downfall of Jerusalem and the defeat of the Jews, including those who revolted in Galilee.[216] Mark illustrates the establishment of an alternative empire and father-son dynasty in Jesus, the Son of God and his Father for the benefit of the family of disciples in illustration of the nexus of Christology and discipleship in terms of kinship.

The demonstration of Jesus' power over the sea and natural elements and his ability to provide care and sustenance rather than death and destruction both imitates the Flavian dynasty (Vespasian and Titus) and denies the death-wielding power of that father-son duo. Jesus, who manifests the presence of his Father, brings safety and security in his power and authority over the sea, even in the midst of his disciples' incomprehension and hardness of heart. The nexus of Christology and discipleship is in terms of kinship.

---

214. Dunstan, *Ancient Rome*, 235.
215. Josephus, *War*, 3.462–531.
216. Ibid., 7.121–57.

26. 6:53–56 HEALING THE SICK IN GENNESARET

Rather than arriving at Bethsaida, Jesus and the disciples moor at the plain of Gennesaret. This satellite provides another summary of Jesus' ministry and his extensive popularity in the Galilee and the extension of kinship by means of healing in the nexus of Christology and discipleship. As in 1:32–34 and 3:7–12, Jesus' healing power has increased his reputation as God's Son. In Capernaum, they brought the sick and demon-possessed to the Son and he cured many (1:34). Jesus' popularity increases to the point that his reputation precedes him and those who have heard about him come not only from the region of Galilee, but also Judea, Jerusalem, Idumea, beyond the Jordan, Tyre, and Sidon to seek him and press in to touch him (ὥστε ἐπιπίπτειν αὐτῷ ἵνα αὐτοῦ ἅψωνται, 3:10). When Jesus and the disciples arrive in Gennesaret, people recognize (ἐπιγνόντες) Jesus (6:54); the people know Jesus. Again, they bring people for healing from throughout the region (6:55). Moreover, as he continues on his ministry wherever he went, the Son of God is sought out for healing, even if just to touch the fringe of his cloak (6:56) like the woman with the flow of blood (5:28). And like the woman with the flow of blood who is addressed as daughter (5:34), those who touch Jesus enter into his extended family of followers to become his children. The nexus of Christology and discipleship occurs in the benefit of healing that Jesus the Son provides for his extended kinship network.

Jesus was initially quite popular in his ministry garnering a large kinship group of followers (1:32–34), and even after apparent conflict with the local societal leaders (3:6) he maintains his popularity and reputation. Now after the death of his predecessor and some alienation with his own disciples, Jesus' reputation for healing and his popularity continue to grow. "From the moment of Jesus' landing, the same numinous power that he just displayed in walking on the water begins to radiate out and convulse the entire countryside, as people rush about frantically to drag their invalid friends and relatives to spots where, rumor has it, he will pass by (6:55)."[217] The Son of God is welcomed and ushered to the bedsides of all those who are sick and in need of healing. Mark makes very clear the strength of people's faith in Jesus' healing power and in the strength of his healing power as the Son of God. Unlike other healing stories where Jesus lays a hand on a sick person (1:31, 41; 5:41), simply touching the fringe of his cloak is all that is required for healing and for entry into the extended family of followers on the basis of his benefit of healing. Kinship is the nexus of Christology and discipleship in terms of patronage and benefit.

---

217. Marcus, *Mark 1–8*, 438.

27. 7:1–23 THE SON INDICTS THE SCRIBES AND PHARISEES FOR IMPROPER KINSHIP

Juxtaposed with Jesus' popularity and reputation, and extension of the Son's kinship by benefits of healing, is his conflict with the local societal leaders, and now the Pharisees and some scribes from Jerusalem. In this satellite, the Pharisees and scribes challenge Jesus' authority and his disciples' practices concerning food and its consumption.[218] Mark notes that it is not the law with which the Pharisees take issue, but rather the tradition that has grown up around the law that the family of disciples does not follow (7:5). As the Son of God, Jesus is the head of the household of disciples and in turn he is responsible for his family's actions. In another challenge-riposte, Jesus responds to the Pharisees' verbal challenge by offering references to the prophets and pointing out the Pharisees' own hypocrisy in terms of the law and tradition (7:6–8). Jesus then offers his own challenge by claiming that the Pharisees actually violate the law by the very traditions they keep in order to uphold the law in their practice of korban (7:9–13). Contrary to the proper kinship practices and boundaries of Jesus and his family of disciples, those whom Jesus accuses would forsake the care of their parents in order to give their financial and material support as an offering to the temple (7:11–12).[219] Instead of following the commandment, "Honor your father and mother," (Exod 20:12) the Pharisees deny their kinship relationships and responsibilities in order to uphold a tradition. Jesus concludes the challenge-riposte by addressing the crowd with a parable, a word of wisdom, that anything that goes into a person cannot defile (κοινῶσαι), but what comes out of a person defiles (7:15).

Jesus the Son continues to enact his authority and defend the practices of his family of disciples in the nexus of Christology and discipleship in terms of kinship. In this satellite, he demonstrates both his knowledge of scripture and his ability to interpret to defend the actions of his core kinship group of

218. Jesus has previously been challenged by the scribes of the Pharisees regarding with whom he eats (2:16), by John's disciples and the Pharisees regarding the disciples' lack of fasting (2:18), and by the Pharisees again when the disciples pluck grain to eat on the Sabbath (2:24).

219. Marcus, *Mark 1–8*, 452, notes that this accusation may not be historically accurate since there is no other evidence that the Pharisees adhered to this practice and moreover, it is condemned later in the Mishnah (*m. Ned.* 9:1). Marcus concludes that it may be a case where the Pharisees in Jesus' time were much more strict and held to the vows made, even if that meant forsaking the fourth commandment, whereas over time and by the influence of the rabbis, the stringency was relaxed. Furthermore, because Jesus is approached by the Pharisees and the scribes, there may be some priestly influence in the exchange. Marcus notes that "priests would have had a motive for insisting that vows to the Temple be honored" (ibid., 445–46).

disciples (7:6–9). Moreover, Jesus takes the traditions surrounding another law and demonstrates how those traditions have missed the purpose of the law and demonstrate improper kinship practices. Jesus uses the fourth commandment of honoring mother and father to show how the Pharisees fall short of upholding the law, and upholding kinship relationships, in order to follow their traditions. In this exchange, Jesus reveals his ultimate authority over both law and tradition and the ability to establish and maintain a new tradition among his disciples.[220] Jesus utilizes the Mosaic law that deals with kinship: honor your father and mother (Exod 20:12). Although Jesus and his disciples forsake their original kinship groups, the role of kinship and the importance of family relationships are not eliminated, though Jesus' kinship group reorients original kinship relationships. Even as Peter and the other disciples leave everything (10:28) to follow Jesus, they soon return to Peter's home and Jesus cares for his mother-in-law (1:29). Kinship continues to be the social structure upon which Jesus', the Son's, community is established and the community is bound by their kinship relationships to one another (3:35). Not only do the Pharisees and the scribes misinterpret the law, but they corrupt their kinship relationships in a skewed attempt to maintain the law by their tradition.

After Jesus has beaten the challenge of the scribes and Pharisees with his verbal riposte and his parable to those who have gathered, he goes into the house (εἰς οἶκον) with his family of disciples and offers them further instruction (7:17). Inside the house, among his kinship group of disciples, the Son of God offers the interpretation of his parable and demonstrates the locus of impurity, not in unclean hands or food, but in the human heart.[221] The nexus of Christology and discipleship appears in terms of kinship in Jesus' instruction for his family of disciples. No matter what rituals or practices a person may perform according to his or her tradition, evil thoughts (οἱ διαλογισμοὶ οἱ κακοὶ) still come from within and can defile. Furthermore, the evil thoughts are all potential acts that can break down human relationship (kinship) and separate people from one another. The list of vices that Jesus gives falls within the categories of adultery, coveting, killing, bearing false witness, and having false idols first given in the Ten Commandments by Moses (Exod 20:1–17).

220. Salyer, "Rhetoric, Purity, and Play," 163–64.

221. Trainor, *The Quest for Home*, 133–34, claims that this declaration allows for communion between Jews and Gentiles and sets up the next scenes (7:24–37 and 8:1–10) as demonstrations of Jesus' inclusion of the Gentiles. The emphasis is misplaced, for Jesus is not arguing for Gentile inclusion with the Pharisees and the scribes, but rather his own authority (from God) over law and tradition. Gentile inclusion becomes a consequence of this declaration, but is not the inciting force.

Jesus reclaims the law and tradition for the disciples that the Pharisees and the scribes have forsaken. Jesus also redefines the purity boundaries in his kinship group of disciples with markers of vice and mistreatment toward others further demonstrating leadership as the Son over his community, his family, and its tradition and boundaries.[222] Kinship serves as the nexus of Christology and discipleship as Jesus the Son defines the parameters of kinship for his family of disciples.

28. 7:24-30 THE SON HEALS THE SYROPHOENICIAN WOMAN'S DAUGHTER

Jesus appears to depart from Galilee on his own and goes to the region of Tyre. Jesus again enters a house (εἰς οἰκίαν), this time in the hope to maintain anonymity since his popularity has grown so great, even in the borderlands outside of Galilee (7:24). It is not possible, however, and a Gentile, Syrophoenician woman seeks the Son of God for healing for her daughter in further demonstration of kinship as the nexus of Christology and discipleship (7:25).[223] The mother advocates for her daughter, a primary kinship relationship. This satellite echoes that of other healing stories, especially the healing of the little girl (5:21–43), in that the parent seeks help for the daughter. Like the leader of the synagogue, the Syrophoenician woman falls at Jesus' feet and begs for help (προσέπεσεν πρὸς τοὺς πόδας αὐτοῦ, 7:25–26).[224] Unlike the previous story, this satellite occurs within the setting of a household and the woman is not of Jewish origin. Jesus acts as the host as he has before (1:29–34), but he does not initially provide the woman hospitality and refuses to heal her daughter (7:27).[225] Instead he insults her

---

222. Malina and Rohrbaugh, *Social-Science Commentary*, 176, note the significance of purity practices as group boundary markers.

223. The woman's birth information provides information about her social status. Many scholars indicate that the woman held a privileged social status. See Perkinson, "A Canaanitic Word," 68; Ringe, "A Gentile Woman's," 86n13; Theissen, *Gospels in Context*, 72.

224. Glancy, "Jesus," 342–63, provides a case study on the posture of the woman and her characterization, especially in comparison with others who fall at Jesus' feet (Jairus) in the Gospel of Mark.

225. If Jesus and the Syrophoenician had met in the public sphere, such as a marketplace or near a temple or synagogue, it would have been socially unacceptable for Jesus to have responded in such a manner as he does. Although she is a woman, the Syrophoenician is higher in social status, and had they been in Tyre, Jesus would have been the outsider. In the social hierarchy, Jesus, the itinerant, peasant preacher would have been obliged to follow the public transcript and pay honor and respect to one higher in status. One who does not follow social mores would be considered to be

by insinuating that she (like all Gentiles) is a dog who should not be fed along with the children (Israel), thereby challenging her honor and reputation (7:27). The woman accepts the insult as a challenge, and she responds, wins, and achieves healing for her daughter (7:28–29). The power of the Son is so great, however, that he does not even need to see or touch the child. Upon his word, the daughter is healed (ἐξελήλυθεν ἐκ τῆς θυγατρός σου τὸ δαιμόνιον, 7:30).

This is the only challenge-riposte scene thus far that shows Jesus losing, in a manner of speaking. His initial insult stands as a representation of the boundary markers Jesus established in 3:35 and 7:17–23 for his kinship group. The woman is not an insider; she is not a part of the family of disciples and neither is she even a part of the family of Israel. To her credit, the woman demonstrates as much wisdom as Jesus has demonstrated in his own responses to challenges and proves how she and her daughter ought also to be included within the kinship boundaries, even if it is as a dog under the table eating the crumbs (7:28).[226] The woman inserts herself into the extended family of Jesus, the Son, as a demonstration of kinship as the nexus of Christology and discipleship. Throughout the gospel, Jesus has healed as many as have sought him out, regardless of their social standing or their inclusion as disciples or followers. As the demarcations between Jesus and his opponents seem to increase, it appears that others may suffer the consequence. Nevertheless, in a collision of kinship, the mother stands up to the Son of God in behalf of her daughter with a word (διὰ τοῦτον τὸν λόγον) and receives healing by another powerful word of Jesus (7:29). By doing so, Jesus welcomes the woman and her daughter into his kinship group just as his other healings demonstrate entry into Jesus' household (1:29–31; 5:21–43). In effect, there is no loss of honor on either side; this subverts the normal expectations for challenge-riposte and the social reality that honor was a limited good. In the Roman Empire, a society with patron-client relationships at the center, honor was a prized possession. The elite and upper strata of society maintained the most honor, the emperor being the most honorable. Patron-client relationships are unbalanced, that is they occur between people of different statuses. A patron bestows a favor on a client; in return, the client gives his or her patron honor, in effect, losing honor.

---

insubordinate in the public eye. It is significant to note that the parallel version of this story of Jesus and the Canaanite woman in Matthew occurs in the public sphere with the disciples as witnesses (Matt 15:22–28) and Jesus' initial response is that of silence.

226. Setzer states, "We assume that as a Gentile foreigner she does not worry about what goes into her, neither the kashrut nor the ritual purity of the food she ingests. But what comes out of her, her 'logos,' or teaching, identifies her as one who really understands Jesus" (Setzer, "Three Odd Couples," 77).

In the exchange between Jesus and the Syrophoenician woman, the woman maintains her status and achieves healing for her daughter as she enters into Jesus' family as a recipient of his healing power disrupting the expected patron-client exchange of favor and honor. Kinship demonstrates the nexus of Christology and discipleship where Jesus' honor as God's Son continues to increase by adding to the list of his healings and exorcisms and adding to the membership of his family of disciples.

29. 7:31-37 THE SON HEALS A DEAF MAN

Jesus departs from Tyre through Sidon and ends up near the Decapolis where a deaf man is brought to him for healing (7:32). Jesus was in the Decapolis once before where he healed the Gerasene demoniac (5:1-20). In further echo of the healing of the little girl (5:21-43), Jesus heals the man privately (κατ' ἰδίαν) by touching him and speaking to him (Εφφαθά, 7:34). The Son of God demonstrates his power as a healer in his actions typical to traditional healers.[227] Akin to his successful healing stories and where he asks for silence (1:34), the story of this healing is proclaimed with great fervor (7:36). Moreover, in the nexus of Christology and discipleship by means of kinship, the recipient of healing and those who witness the Son's power enter into the family of disciples in their proclamation of the good thing that Jesus has done (3:14-15). The healing powers of the Son of God are underlined, his reputation grows, and his honor increases, so much so that the people are heard alluding to the Genesis creation account and the prophet Isaiah (Isa 35:5-6). The double use of πεποίηκεν/ποιεῖ reminds the reader of God's work of creation in Gen 1:2-2:3 with an explicit reference to Gen 1:31; God surveys what he has done and pronounces them good (καλά).[228] Not only is Jesus connected intimately with God in his creative power by means of his kinship relationship, but Jesus also brings about the new creation prophesied in Isaiah, a sign of which is the healing of the deaf and dumb.[229] The healing power from God is extended through the Son to

---

227. See Collins, *Mark*, 370-74, for a discussion on Jesus' use of saliva and his command, "Be opened," in connection with other ancient healers.

228. Marcus, *Mark 1-8*, 479-80.

229. Marcus notes a twist in Mark's interpretation of Isa 35. "It may not be an accident, then, but a deliberate inversion of a common pattern–one that is perhaps known to Mark from the propaganda of the Jewish revolutionaries–that Mark's own allusion to Isaiah 35 occurs precisely in the context not of the destruction of demonic Gentiles but of Jesus' ridding a Gentile of his demonic impairment and of the Gentile's consequent joyful praise of Jesus–a praise that reverberates in Mark's own predominantly Gentile Christian community" (Marcus, *Mark 1-8*, 481).

recipients of healing who become a part of the extended family of followers in the nexus of Christology and discipleship in terms of kinship.

The Son of God further establishes his empire as Jesus' notoriety and popularity grow beyond the bounds of the Galilee into Gentile territory. Moreover, Mark demonstrates this through a story illustrating Jesus' healing power and popularity in a manner similar to the propaganda spread about Vespasian. As I noted in chapter 2, part of the propaganda campaign surrounding Vespasian and his accession to the throne included stories that heralded his sanction by divine beings, sanction displayed with special power including that of miraculous healings.[230] While Vespasian was in Alexandria, a blind man and a lame man presented themselves for healing.[231] Although the account of Vespasian's healing ties more closely with Jesus' healing of the blind man at Bethsaida (8:22–26), the use of spittle for the blind men and the mute man is a clear connection as is the power of both men to provide healing.[232] Moreover, the successes of the healings were proclaimed to increase the honor and reputation of both men as they endeavor to establish and build their empires. Jesus, the Son of God, demonstrates his kinship with God in his healing power of those who then enter into the empire as extended family members. Kinship provides the nexus of Christology and discipleship.

Jesus extends his kinship as the Son of God to the deaf and mute man by giving him the benefaction of healing. Moreover, in further demonstration of kinship as the nexus of Christology and discipleship, the recipient of healing and witnesses act as disciples proclaiming the good thing Jesus has done. Jesus continues to establish God's empire in his acts of healing, extending God's kinship and increasing his popularity, thereby increasing his extended family of followers.

---

230. See chapter 2.

231. Suet. *Vesp.* 7.2 and Tacitus, *Histories* 4.81 both reference a blind man and a lame man. It should be noted that Dio Cassius, *Roman History* 65.8.1, describes Vespasian healing a man with a withered hand, which echoes Jesus' healing of the man with the withered hand (3:1–6).

232. Collins, *Mark*, 371, notes the connection in the use of spittle. By referencing Suetonius's account (Suet. *Vesp.* 7.2) alone she does not indicate a relationship between the divine powers bestowed on Vespasian that are mentioned in Tacitus, *Histories* 4.81, and Dio Cassius, *Roman History* 65.8.1, and Jesus' divine power as the Son of God.

30. 8:1-10 THE SON AND HIS DISCIPLES FEED FOUR THOUSAND

In the feeding of the four thousand, Jesus and the core kinship group of disciples repeat the feeding of the five thousand with some variation (6:30-44), chief of which is that Jesus and the disciples are in Gentile territory presumably eating with, and welcoming as extended family members, Gentiles.[233] As Jesus was able to provide food administered by his disciples for thousands in the Galilean wilderness, so now Jesus does the same for thousands in the Gentile wilderness in another demonstration of the nexus of Christology and discipleship in terms of kinship.[234] Rather than five loaves and two fish that the disciples provide for Jesus as the host, his family of disciples offer him seven loaves of bread, and almost as an afterthought, they give him a few small fish (ἰχθύδια ὀλίγα). Mark makes no reference to the four thousand being like sheep without a shepherd (6:34), but Jesus has compassion on them (σπλαγχνίζομαι) since they have been with him for several days, some from a great distance, and require sustenance. After blessing the food, Jesus gives it to the disciples to distribute to the crowds as he did in the feeding of the five thousand. After the four thousand have eaten, the disciples gather seven baskets of leftovers.[235]

Just as the Son of God demonstrated that he had access to food and the ability to feed a multitude in the Galilean wilderness, now, in another illustration of the nexus of Christology and discipleship in terms of kinship, Jesus demonstrates that same authority and power in Gentile territory by providing for another group of his extended family of followers.

---

233. Marcus, *Mark 1-8*, 492-93 provides a discussion on the possible redaction of this scene, whether it is simply a repetition of the feeding of the five thousand or a separate story. Marcus argues for two separate stories akin to the feeding stories in the Gospel of John (6:1-14), indicating that the tradition Mark received contained two feeding stories. In a narrative approach, since there are two separate feeding stories in the gospel, they are approached separately, with attention to their similarities and echoes. Marcus also notes that there is no clear change in geography in the narrative so it is possible to assume that Jesus and the disciples are still in the Decapolis.

234. Wefald, "Separate Gentile Mission," 3-26, provides an analysis of Jesus' separate Gentile mission in Mark in a study of the geography presented in the gospel. Wefald discusses the details of the two feeding stories and how the details correspond with their Jewish or Gentile audiences. Whether Jesus has a separate, distinct mission to the Gentiles or not, Wefald establishes with clarity and analysis the ministry Jesus provides to the Gentiles, including the feeding of the four thousand.

235. A concerted effort has been made to understand the numerical significance of the number of people, the number of loaves and fish, and the baskets of leftovers in terms of Jewish or Gentile origins. See ibid., 21-25. The fact remains: Jesus successfully fed a large crowd of people with a small amount of food, two times.

Jesus demonstrates his power concerning access to food over and against the Roman Empire. "Food production, distribution, and consumption were shaped by and expressed the elite-controlled, hierarchical, exploitative political-economic system. Food involved power and hierarchy."[236] Whatever significance the feeding of the four thousand may hold for Jesus' mission to the Gentiles, it shows the expansion and infiltration of Jesus' power as the Son of God. Jesus is able to go beyond the cultural, social, and political boundaries of Galilee and still be able to show power and authority by providing nourishment to a large crowd of people. Moreover, this power is administered by the disciples who distribute the food that Jesus provides; Jesus' power as the Son of God extends to his family of disciples. Although the crowd is too large to fit into a house, Jesus offers hospitality to all who were gathered with them, ordering them to recline as if they were at a banquet (ἀναπεσεῖν). The Son of God and his disciples extend the kinship network to four thousand Gentiles and provide care and food in abundance, in stark contrast to the first-century realities of the distant territories of the Roman Empire.[237] Christology and discipleship are again tied together by means of kinship.

As in the feeding of the five thousand, Jesus and his disciples work as a family to provide for another extended family of followers in need of food. Kinship functions as the nexus of Christology and discipleship as Jesus the Son and the core kinship group of disciples again provide hospitality and benefit through a meal of abundant food. Moreover, Jesus extends this kinship beyond the conventional cultural and kinship boundaries, demonstrating his power as God's Son to establish his empire and provide for a multitude of followers.

31. 8:11–21 THE TESTING OF THE SON

Following the feeding of the second multitude, Jesus and the disciples encounter the Pharisees back in Galilee who offer another honor challenge, testing (πειράζοντες) Jesus and his authority as the Son of God. This time, they ask for a sign from heaven (8:11).[238] Ironically, had they been in attendance

---

236. Carter, *John and Empire*, 221.

237. Garnsey and Saller, *The Roman Empire*, 95–97, note that even if a province did not supply food directly for Rome, provinces supplied food and goods for the Roman Army that occupied the territory. See also discussions on food scarcity and famine: Garnsey, *Famine and Food Supply*, 3–39.

238. Marcus, *Mark 1–8*, 503–6, notes the Pharisees' question and behavior echoes Israel's testing of God in Exod 17:1–7. One notable difference is that God is the one being tested by Israel, not Moses. For Mark to echo this story makes Jesus equivalent

near the Decapolis, they would have seen the sign that Jesus performed in feeding four thousand people. Jesus refuses their challenge, suggesting that he views the Pharisees dishonorably (8:12–13).[239] The reader will remember that the last honor challenge that Jesus won against the Pharisees (3:1–6), the Pharisees conspired with the Herodians and resorted to violence, planning a way to destroy Jesus (αὐτὸν ἀπολέσωσιν). The Pharisees are no longer worthy opponents of the Son of God, and so he ignores them and departs to the other side of the sea. Even in a negative instance, kinship still functions as the nexus of Christology and discipleship. The Pharisees are not a part of Jesus' kinship group and therefore he does not grant them the honor or care that he provides for his family of disciples and extended kinship network as the Son of God.

While in the boat, Jesus has a conversation with the family of disciples. Based on this most recent encounter with the Pharisees, he warns his disciples about the very people who conspire against him, indicating that their threat to Jesus, the Son, is a threat to his family of disciples. In conflict, Christology and discipleship intersect in terms of kinship. Unfortunately, akin to the Pharisees, the disciples do not understand the significance of the feedings of the multitudes. Jesus asks the disciples how many baskets they collected after both feedings. They respond with twelve and seven. Jesus offers no other explanation, suggesting that the significance is self-evident to the disciples. The meaning of the numbers of baskets of leftovers may correspond to a sense of eschatological fullness.[240] The abundant food is a sign of the establishment of God's reign and God's power to provide as it was illustrated in Isaiah's vision of the Day of the Lord (Isa 25:6–10). Twelve corresponds to the twelve tribes of Israel and seven corresponds to the seven days of creation. The nexus of Christology and discipleship occurs in terms of kinship when the fullness of God and his chosen people is (re)established by the Son of God and taken up by his family of disciples. Unlike his treatment of the Pharisees, the disciples' lack of understanding will result in further instruction (8:31). The disciples' response to Jesus also demonstrates the tenuous nature of the family of disciples when there is misunderstanding and incomprehension; this foreshadows the disciples' abandonment of Jesus (14:50). The instruction from Jesus and the care that the Son of God takes to help his core kinship group of disciples understand his purpose and their responsibility in the empire of God, in contrast to his dismissal of the Pharisees, become a focal point as the narrative moves toward the

---

with God since he is the one directly tested by the Pharisees.

239. Malina and Rohrbaugh, *Social-Science Commentary*, 178.
240. Marcus, *Mark 1–8*, 514.

second kernel of Mark, the first passion prediction and the transfiguration (8:31–9:8).

32. 8:22-26 THE SON HEALS A BLIND MAN

Jesus and the disciples arrive in Bethsaida, and like the healing of the mute man (7:32–37), Jesus is presented with a blind man.[241] Again, Jesus demonstrates his healing power as the Son of God and extends kinship in the healing of this blind man. As he used saliva and touched the mute man on the tongue, Jesus uses saliva and touches the blind man's eyes. A slight variation in this satellite is Jesus' apparent inability to heal the man in the first attempt. In the final healing before Jesus' instruction about his passion alongside the reinforcement of Jesus' identity in kinship terms as the Son of God in the transfiguration, Jesus is still able to heal, but appears to falter slightly. The intermediate state of the man's vision "corresponds to the intermediate state of the disciples' spiritual perception at this point and indeed throughout the Gospel; like the disciples in the immediately preceding passage (8:18), the man has eyes but does not yet see clearly, though he will eventually do so."[242] In their incomprehension, the family of disciples fails to grasp the extent of Jesus' kinship as God's Son. In demonstration of kinship as the nexus of Christology and discipleship, Jesus' faithfulness to his father and to his family of disciples will lead to their ultimate success in God's empire.

The healing of the blind man has clear echoes of the healing power of Vespasian in the propaganda spread about him in the leadup to his accession of the Roman throne.[243] While Vespasian was in Alexandria, he was approached by a blind man and a lame man. In order to heal the blind man, Vespasian used spittle upon the man's eyes. As I noted in chapter 2 and in the discussions above of the healings of the man with the withered hand (3:1–6) and the deaf man (7:1–37), these stories were a means of illustrating the ways in which Vespasian was able, prepared, and divinely chosen to become

---

241. There are those who view the healing of the mute man and the blind man as a doublet. See Hooker, *Mark*, 197, 200; Donahue and Harrington, *Gospel of Mark*, 258; and Malina and Rohrbaugh, *Social-Science Commentary*, 179. There are those who view the healing of the blind man in connection with the healing of Bartimaeus (10:46–52). See Taylor, *Gospel According to St. Mark*, 368–69; Marcus, *Mark 8–16*, 597; and Eve, "Spit in Your Eye," 12. In my narrative analysis of Mark, the healing of the blind man at Bethsaida functions in similar fashion to the healing satellites in the first major section of Mark, mostly demonstrating Jesus' healing power as the Son of God. That is not to say that there is no connection with Bartimaeus.

242. Marcus, *Mark 8–16*, 599–600.

243. Tacitus, *Histories* 4.81; Suet. *Vesp.* 7.2; and Dio Cassius, *Roman Histories* 65.8.

the Roman emperor.[244] If Mark is responding to the Flavian propaganda, then Jesus healing the blind man at Bethsaida directly corresponds to Vespasian's healing of the blind man at Alexandria. In addition to the parallel use of spittle in the two stories, Eric Eve concludes the stories' parallel functions:

> This suggestion is reinforced by the parallel functions of the Blind Men of Bethsaida and Alexandria. The story of the Blind Man of Alexandria is part of a propaganda effort designed to legitimate Vespasian as a royal figure favoured by the gods, identified with Sarapis and as son of Ammon [son of a god]. The story of the Blind Man of Bethsaida leads straight into Peter's confession of Jesus as Messiah, followed not long after by the transfiguration at which God declares Jesus to be his son [Son of God]. The similarity between the two stories thus lies not only in the common use of spittle to cure blindness, but also in the ideological contexts of which these stories form a part.[245]

Moreover, this healing story is one in a long line of healing stories about Jesus in the Gospel of Mark. Not only is the comparison between Vespasian and Jesus made in the use of spittle in the healing of a blind man, but the supremacy of the Son of God over and against the Roman Emperor Vespasian (and his son Titus) is demonstrated here and throughout Mark by means of Jesus' powerful acts of healing and providing for any who present themselves in need and enter into his household and family.

Jesus extends his kinship as God's Son to the blind man in the nexus between Christology and discipleship. The failed attempt parallels the disciples' incomprehension. The healing's ultimate success demonstrates Jesus' ultimate success in establishing God's empire and extending kinship to disciples and followers, even if they falter in their faith.

33. 8:27-30 PETER'S PARTIAL CONFESSION OF THE SON

In the final satellite of the second narrative block of the Gospel of Mark, Jesus and the family of disciples are on their way to the villages of Caesarea Philippi. Along the way, Jesus asks the disciples who people think he is (8:27). Akin to Herod's knowledge of Jesus (6:14-16), they identify him as John the Baptist, Elijah, or one of the prophets (8:28). Then Jesus asks the disciples

---

244. Chapter 2.
245. Eve, "Spit in Your Eye," 15.

who they think he is (8:29). Peter identifies Jesus as the Christ (ὁ χριστός, 8:29). Peter identifies Jesus in part: Mark 1:1 identifies Jesus primarily as the Christ, but also as the Son of God, as he is defined in the first kernel, Jesus' baptism (1:11). Peter demonstrates what the disciples have perceived about Jesus in their relationship with him. As his disciples, they have come to know Jesus as the Christ, as the anointed one of God chosen to do God's will and establish his empire (1:14–15). But, as the disciples have already indicated in their misunderstanding and incomprehension (8:14–21), they recognize Jesus only in part; Peter does not indicate Jesus' chief identity marker put forth in Mark as God's Son in the kernel of the baptism (1:9–11). Even with Peter's (and the disciples') lack of understanding, kinship is still the nexus of Christology and discipleship. This satellite of Peter's confession is juxtaposed to the second kernel in Mark, the first passion prediction and the transfiguration which will elaborate Jesus' identity as the Christ, instruct the disciples on the suffering of Jesus, their own suffering as disciples, and reveal Jesus' identity as God's Son to the family of disciples (represented by Peter, James, and John).

Mark places this satellite "on the way" (ἐν τῇ ὁδῷ) to the villages of Caesarea Philippi (8:27). Jesus and the disciples depart from the Galilee and into the tetrarchy of Philip, Herod Antipas's brother (8:27). At the time of Mark's composition, Caesarea Philippi was ruled by Philip's grandnephew, Agrippa II. Caesarea was known for its temple of white marble built by Herod the Great in honor of Augustus.[246] This temple to Augustus would have been a nearby representative of the imperial ruler cult and a bastion of the Roman Empire. Gudrun Guttenberger observes the significance of Caesarea Philippi and its connection with Vespasian.[247] After the uprising at Galilee is put down by Vespasian and Titus in 67 CE, they stayed at the palace of Agrippa II in Caesarea for three weeks which also happened to correspond to the celebration of Augustus's birthday. Josephus also notes that they gave thanks to the god (τῷ θεῷ) for their triumph, suggesting that they worshiped in the temple to Augustus.[248] Father and son, Vespasian and Titus, returned to Caesarea Philippi in 70 CE to celebrate the fall of Jerusalem.[249]

The significance of this location will be further elaborated in the second kernel of the first passion prediction and transfiguration, but for now, Peter's recognition of Jesus as the Christ, and the reader's knowledge that Jesus is also the Son of God, stands in opposition to the ruler cult and the

---

246. Josephus, *Ant.* 15.363–64; and *War*, 1.404–406.
247. Guttenberger, "Why Caesarea Philippi?," 119–31.
248. Josephus, *War*, 3.444.
249. Ibid., 7.121–57.

honoring of the Roman emperor as a deity. "Placing the confession of Peter at Caesarea Philippi makes the point for those aware of the imperial cult practiced there that *Jesus* is the agent of the supreme deity, not the emperor."[250] Moreover, Jesus, the Son of God, stands over against the ruling dynasty of Vespasian and his son Titus. Guttenberger concludes, "Against the background of the temple dedicated to *divi filius* Augustus Mark depicts Jesus as the true emperor arising from Judah, as the king coming from the East in contrast to Vespasian and perhaps in contrast to the hopes linked up to the marriage of Titus and Berenice associated with the hopes for a new Roman-Jewish dynasty."[251] Jesus is the Christ, the Son of God who inaugurates the empire of God in contest with the Roman Empire, but also in imitation, endeavoring to create an alternative father-son reigning dynasty complete with an imperial household of disciples, benefactions, and demonstrations of supreme honor and power, in which kinship provides the nexus between Jesus (Christology) and his disciples (discipleship).

The confession of Peter continues to demonstrate the disciples' lack of understanding of Jesus' identity as God's Son. Though they only recognize Jesus in part, Jesus' honor, authority, and kinship still extend to the family of disciples. The nexus of Christology and discipleship in terms of kinship functions even in the disciples' incomprehension. The twelve will continue in Jesus' ministry, accompanying him "on the way" and witnessing the corroboration of Jesus' sonship (9:7) through the remainder of the gospel.

In the first two narrative blocks of Mark, Jesus is designated as the Son of God to establish the empire of God by administering God's authority and power in Galilee and building up a family of disciples to whom the Son extends God's power and authority to create an alternative imperial dynasty from that of the reigning Roman ruler (at the time of Mark's composition) Vespasian and his son, Titus. Throughout the gospel narrative, Jesus' attributes as God's Son are revealed in his ability to heal, to exorcise, to teach with authority, to provide hospitality, to be a benefactor, to garner a large following, and to lead a family of disciples. Kinship terms and relationships serve as the nexus between Christology and discipleship.

In the course of Jesus' and the disciples' ministry throughout Galilee and the surrounding regions, they encounter some conflict with the local leaders which foreshadows the arrest, betrayal, and crucifixion that is the culmination of the final two narrative blocks of Mark. The family of disciples struggles to comprehend Jesus' identity as God's Son as well as to maintain their faith and fidelity to him. This also foreshadows their ultimate

---

250. Collins, *Mark*, 401.
251. Guttenberger, "Why Caesarea Philippi?," 128.

incomprehension and abandonment of Jesus. As Jesus has demonstrated his most honorable status as God's Son in his ministry in Galilee, he will continue to remain faithful to God and to his family of disciples even as it results in his suffering and death. Even in conflict and apparent failure, kinship serves as the nexus of Christology and discipleship. The Son's kinship with God and his faith and fidelity provide for the family of disciples and ensure their faithfulness and place in the empire of God.

4

Mark 8:31—16:8

THIS CHAPTER WILL CONTINUE the commentary on the Gospel of Mark begun in chapter 3 that demonstrates how kinship categories provide the nexus between Christology (Jesus' kinship with God) and discipleship (Jesus' kinship with the disciples). Following the second kernel of the first passion prediction and transfiguration (8:31–9:10), Jesus' identity as God's Son is confirmed in the presence of Jesus' kinship group of disciples. The latter two narrative blocks (8:31–15:20; 15:21–16:8) and the final kernel of the crucifixion (15:21–41) continue to highlight the intersection of Jesus' kinship as the Son of God and the implications for his family of disciples and extended kinship network. Even in the light of Jesus' death and the disciples' abandonment of Jesus, the Son of God proves to be the most honorable Son who establishes God's empire and gathers a kinship group of disciples which continues to do God's will.

1. 8:31-9:8 THE SON OF GOD PREDICTS HIS OWN DEATH AND IS TRANSFIGURED

The second kernel, which serves as a hinge in the plot of the Gospel of Mark, is Jesus' prediction of his own arrest, death, and resurrection and the transfiguration. After Peter's confession, in the nexus between Christology and discipleship in terms of kinship, Jesus the Son immediately begins to teach his core kinship group of disciples. Just as Jesus will suffer, be rejected by the elders, the chief priests, and the scribes and be killed, but rise up (ἀναστῆναι) after three days (8:31), he also requires his disciples to follow in the path of suffering by taking up their crosses and losing their lives for the sake of the gospel (8:34–35). A new revelation is made about the Son of God: as much as Jesus is honorable and powerful, he will not be treated as such and he will die. Moreover, Jesus himself predicts accurately what will happen to him, and will do so two more times (9:31; 10:33–34).[1] Jesus' prediction of his own suffering and death further demonstrates his authority and power as God's Son. Jesus predicts his own death immediately after Peter's confession in order "(1) to qualify Jesus' messiahship, showing that death and resurrection were in view from the moment that his messiahship was disclosed, and (2) to enhance the portrait of Jesus, by showing that Jesus was fully aware of his fate, long before his decision to go to Jerusalem."[2] Peter confesses Jesus' identity only in part; the passion prediction helps clarify Jesus' identity and purpose more fully which then leads into the affirmation of Jesus' identity as God's Son at the transfiguration (9:7). In addition to preaching the message of and establishing the empire of God by creating a kinship group of disciples and followers, the Son of God is required to undergo suffering and death. The nexus between Christology and discipleship is in terms of kinship because this foreknowledge of the passion of the Son of God is taught to the core kinship group of disciples who will be expected to follow, even to the cross (8:34).

Jesus not only predicts his own suffering and death, but he also predicts his resurrection (8:31), the vindication of his suffering and death over those who rejected and killed him. Jesus' prediction of his resurrection echoes the story of the woman and her seven sons in 2 Maccabees 7. Within an imperial context of suffering and persecution by Antiochus IV Epiphanes, the woman and her sons endure torture and death because they follow God's laws. One son insists that even though they are executed, God will raise them up (ἀναστήσει, 2 Macc 7:9) because of their faithfulness. Another maintains his confidence and faith, even at the point of death, in the hope that God will raise them again. They will receive the justice they deserve in the resurrection, whereas their enemies will not be raised (2 Macc 7:14). The mother herself promises resurrection for her sons because of their suffering and faithfulness (2 Macc 7:23). The mother also speaks about resurrection as a restoration of kinship, urging her last and youngest son to accept his suffering death so that they may all be reunited through God (2 Macc 7:29). "Resurrection of the faithful from the dead emerges in a context of persecution and martyrdom as a means of participating in God's victory over imperial tyrants and death."[3] Just as the mother and sons look forward

---

1. See the discussion on the threefold passion prediction in chapter 2.
2. Evans, "Did Jesus Predict His Death," 91.
3. Carter, *Matthew and the Margins*, 342.

to being reunited, Jesus' prediction of his own resurrection allows for the restoration of kinship relationships that will be severed (14:50).

In the nexus between Christology and discipleship, Jesus' prediction also leads to a new revelation about Jesus' primary kinship group of disciples. After Peter rebukes Jesus, based on Peter's incomplete identification of Jesus as the Christ (8:29), Jesus rebukes Peter (8:33). Jesus accuses Peter of setting his mind on human things rather than divine things. Thinking the things of God means recognizing the nexus between Christology and discipleship in terms of kinship since God has designated Jesus as the Son who will suffer and die and will expect his family of disciples to do the same. Jesus then calls the crowd and the disciples and provides them with further instruction. In order to be a part of the family of Jesus, in order to do the will of God, a disciple must deny him or herself and take up his or her cross (8:34). Just as the Son of God is going to lose his life, so will his family of disciples lose their lives for Jesus' sake and for the sake of the message of the empire of God. The stakes are raised even higher for discipleship. As in first-century Mediterranean families, the boundaries and expectations are clearly demarcated; if one is outside of them there are significant consequences. Jesus makes clear that if there is any sense of shame (ἐπαισχυνθῇ) toward him, the Son of Man, Jesus himself will treat those who regard him shamefully in the same manner at his glorification with the Father (8:38). In further evidence of the nexus between Christology and discipleship in terms of kinship, Jesus the Son predicts the triumph of the empire of God by stating that some members of his family of disciples will live to witness its coming with victorious power.

A week later, Mark provides a glimpse of the glorification of the Son of Man with Jesus' transfiguration (9:2–8). Unlike the first kernel of the baptism (1:9–11) where only Jesus and the readers witness the theophany, Jesus takes his "band of brothers," Peter, James, and John with him up the mountain. They witness Jesus become dazzling white and standing with Moses and Elijah (9:3–4). After the disciples' initial terror at the situation, a cloud envelops Jesus, Moses, and Elijah and a voice (of God) sounds declaring Jesus as his beloved son (ὁ υἱός μου ὁ ἀγαπητός) with the command to listen to him (9:7). Akin to the first kernel of Jesus' baptism (1:9–11), Jesus is identified as God's Son by a voice (of God) emanating from the clouds (νεφέλη). The transfiguration provides more information regarding Jesus' sonship. This time Jesus is presented in conversation with Moses and Elijah. Just as Moses and Elijah encountered God on a mountain (Exod 19–24; 1 Kgs 19), so, too does Jesus, placing him on par with Moses and Elijah. Traditionally,

Moses and Elijah are representatives of the law and the prophets.[4] Jesus has already demonstrated his authority over Jewish law, and there are rumors that he is Elijah or another prophet.[5] Moreover, Elijah and Moses both have prophetic status and both were considered models of the eschatological redeemer.[6] Even more, the traditions surrounding Elijah and Moses suggest that neither one died a traditional death and that both are immortal.[7] Both Elijah and Moses (or one like Moses) were expected to return to earth before the Day of Judgment (Mal 3:22–23, Deut 18:15, 18). "Hence the sudden appearance of 'Elijah with Moses' in the Markan narrative suggests that the transfiguration is an anticipation of the wave of divine glory that is about to flood the earth,"[8] already alluded to in 8:38. Along with the living Elijah and Moses, the transfiguration is also an anticipation of Jesus' resurrection and the final triumph of the Son of God.

This kernel demonstrates the nexus between Christology and discipleship in terms of kinship. First and foremost, the Son reveals that he will suffer and die. Jesus again refers to himself as the Son of Man, both in terms of his suffering and death (8:31), but also his eventual eschatological authority (8:38). The Son of Man reference continues to point to Jesus' sonship in general but in connection with his earthly authority (2:10, 28) and suffering and his eventual eschatological authority.[9] Though this new information about Jesus' death appears to be a tragic turn of events, as the Son, Jesus, already has the foreknowledge and enters into it willingly, further proving his worth and honor as God's Son. Secondly, the suffering and death of the Son is connected to discipleship. Just as it is necessary for the Son to die, so to it is necessary for Jesus' family of disciples to give up their lives, indicating the price of fidelity and loyalty to Jesus and his kinship group.[10] Jesus also indicates the reward of loyalty to him is life and the consequence of loyalty to the world will result in death and dishonor (8:35–38).

---

4. Marcus, *Mark 8-16*, 632.

5. Both Marcus, *Mark 8-16*, and Collins, *Mark*, 422, suggest this interpretation is not appropriate to Mark's understanding of Elijah and Moses. The interpretation should not be limited to Elijah and Moses as representatives of the prophets and the law, respectively, but it should not exclude it. Moses is referenced directly with the law in 7:10.

6. Marcus, *Mark 8-16*, 632.

7. 2 Kgs 2:1–12. The tradition of Elijah as immortal is maintained by Josephus, *Ant.* 9.28. The tradition surrounding Moses' immortality is corroborated by Josephus, *Ant.* 4.325–26.

8. Marcus, *Mark 8-16*, 637.

9. Perrin, "Son of Man Traditions," 362.

10. Malina and Rohrbaugh, *Social-Science Commentary*, 182.

Juxtaposed to the passion prediction is the continued affirmation of Jesus' sonship by God's own voice, this time in the presence of Jesus' disciples and "band of brothers," Peter, James, and John. The transfiguration and declaration of Jesus' beloved sonship assure the disciples of Jesus' identity, authority, and honor, in spite of (because of) Jesus' prediction of his rejection and death. The identification of Jesus as the beloved Son by God also validates Jesus' identity and purpose to the disciples in all that they have witnessed throughout Jesus' ministry thus far. In this declaration, Jesus' authority, healing power, claim to honor, and his mission to establish God's empire as God's son are now confirmed for the kinship group of disciples. Kinship is still at the heart of Christology and discipleship when the family of disciples are commanded by God to listen (ἀκούετε αὐτοῦ, 9:7) to Jesus, God's beloved Son, further tightening the bond of Jesus and the disciples in terms of his sonship. Moreover, the voice's command to "listen to him" secures not only the christological revelation but also what Jesus has said about discipleship. Just as Jesus must suffer so also must the band of brothers and sisters. The first kernel of the Gospel of Mark revealed Jesus as God's Son and inaugurated his ministry where Jesus begins by announcing the empire of God and calling a family of disciples. Likewise, the second kernel of Mark confirms Jesus' identity as God's Son, but augments his ministry by adding the eventual suffering and death of Jesus and Jesus' and God's call to the disciples to listen and bear their crosses.[11]

Just as in the confession of Peter, this kernel takes place in the region of Caesarea Philippi. Moreover, the transfiguration occurs on top of the mountain at the foot of which is the city of Caesarea and the temple to Augustus. God's declaration of Jesus' beloved sonship stands as an alternative to, but in imitation of, the declaration of Caesar Augustus' divine sonship as *divi filius* and any who would follow in his footsteps, namely, Vespasian and Titus.[12] In the place where the emperor was honored as a son of a god, Mark reminds his readers who the true Son of God is, his mission, his eventual fate, and his ultimate triumph along with their responsibilities and destiny in following him. The location of Caesarea Philippi also serves to emphasize the connection between the Herodians and Rome. The temple to Augustus denotes the strong sense of patronage and influence the Roman imperial elite had over the Herodians, a group of Jesus' opponents (3:6; 8:15; 12:13). In no uncertain terms Mark indicates Jesus' superiority as God's Son over and against the legal and prophetic tradition of the Jews and the imperial

---

11. Larsen, "Focused Christological Reading," 44.

12. Wilson, *Caesarea Philippi*, 27–28, notes that the temple to Augustus was not only limited to honoring Augustus but also every succeeding emperor, which would eventually include Vespasian and Titus.

powers of Rome at the transfiguration in the presence of the family of disciples even while the traditions share the same vocabulary and make similar claims for their respective key figures.

The passion prediction and the transfiguration serve as the second kernel of Mark. They corroborate Jesus' sonship in the presence of the family of disciples while at the same time revealing more information about the consequences of Jesus' sonship and the disciples' affiliation with Jesus. In the nexus between Christology and discipleship in terms of kinship, Jesus is still the most honored Son of God who establishes a kinship group of disciples. However, Jesus willingly goes toward death and suffering as God's Son. Moreover, Jesus calls his family of disciples to follow. As the Son goes toward certain death, so too will Jesus' kinship group of disciples suffer and bear their crosses.

2. 9:9–13 ELIJAH

Although the band of brothers, Peter, James, and John has been taught by Jesus about his passion (8:31) and have witnessed the affirmation of Jesus' identity as God's beloved Son in the transfiguration (9:2-8), their comprehension continues to lag, and so Jesus warns them not to tell anyone about what they saw until after the Son of Man rises from the dead (9:9). As they make their way down the mountain, the disciples pose a question that sits squarely in the nexus between Christology and discipleship in terms of kinship. Because of the direct consequences for Jesus' disciples, they question him about Elijah and his return on the "Day of the Lord" (Mal 4:5-6) which they associate with Jesus' resurrection (9:10).[13] "Their confusion is caused by the evidently imminent resurrection of the Son of Man, in spite of the fact that Elijah apparently has not yet come."[14] Ironically, Peter, James, and John just witnessed an appearance of Elijah standing with Jesus at the transfiguration (9:4). Jesus responds first by citing the tradition that the prophet Elijah was expected to return but then provides his own revelation of sorts. Jesus implies that Elijah has already returned, in the form of John the Baptist; now it is time for the Son of Man to enter into his time of suffering.

---

13. I agree with several scholars who suggest that there is a tradition that Elijah is the forerunner of the Messiah. See Cranfield, *Gospel according to St. Mark*, 297–98; Allison, "Elijah Must Come First," 256–58; Marcus, *Mark 8–16*, 649–50. There are others who argue that there is no evidence in the first century CE that this was a widely held view. See Collins, *Mark*, 430; Faierstein, "Why Do the Scribes?," 75–86; Fitzmyer, "More about Elijah," 295–96.

14. Collins, *Mark*, 430.

In two previous satellites (6:14–17; 8:27–31), Elijah has been mentioned in association with John the Baptist and Jesus. Jesus makes clear that he himself is not John the Baptist raised from the dead and neither is he Elijah come back (8:31). "Elijah and Moses belong to the group of God's messengers who are most worthy of honour—yet Jesus is greater than they."[15] However, John the Baptist is clearly Elijah returned. Mark Goodacre notes, "The link between John and Elijah is introduced in 1:6 (clothing), elaborated in 6:14–29 (a new Ahab and Jezebel) and confirmed in 9:11–13 (on the way down from the Transfiguration)."[16] In the connection between Elijah and John the Baptist, Jesus confirms what the disciples have discerned about Jesus' sonship in part: Jesus is the Messiah. For the nexus between Christianity and discipleship in terms of kinship, this designation of John as forerunner and Jesus as Messiah has direct consequence for the disciples. Jesus implies that what happens to Elijah will happen to the Son of Man. And, as Jesus indicated in the second kernel, what happens to the Son will happen to his family of disciples (8:34–38).

As the disciples become aware of Jesus' identity as God's Son, it continues to impact their identity as disciples in a kinship relationship with Jesus (as it did in 4:41). Elijah has returned as John the Baptist and he has suffered at the hands of Herod and Herodias (6:14–29). Jesus confirms his passion prediction by stating that the Son of Man will suffer and be hated. Moreover, alongside this passion prediction is the call to the family of disciples to take up the cross. As the Son of God, Jesus will willingly enter into suffering. The nexus between Christology and discipleship in terms of kinship indicates that as members of Jesus' kinship group, the disciples will also undergo suffering and rejection because of their very kinship identity with Jesus. Just as Elijah acted as the forerunner of the Messiah, so too did John the Baptist act as the forerunner of the suffering Messiah, the Son of God, which in turn will result in the suffering of the family of disciples.

3. 9:14–29 THE SON OF GOD HEALS A SON WITH SEIZURES

As the inner band of brothers descends the mountain with Jesus, the remaining family of disciples has been left to contend with a crowd and a group of scribes (9:14). A man explains to Jesus that he brought his son who

---

15. Hooker, "'What Doest Thou?,'" 63.

16. Goodacre, "Mark, Elijah," 74–75. Goodacre supports this interpretation by suggesting that Matthew's reading of Mark explicitly linking Elijah with John the Baptist (Matt 17:13) is one of the earliest interpretations of Mark that exists.

suffered from a "mute" spirit (πνεῦμα ἄλαλον, 9:17), one that does not speak through the possessed person, but one that causes seizures, to be healed but the disciples were unable (9:18).[17] The nexus between Christology and discipleship in terms of kinship would suggest that the disciples should be able to exorcise the demon because of the authority of God's Son extended to them "to cast out demons" (3:15; also 6:7). "Through their union with Jesus, the disciples possess exorcistic power, which they have demonstrated in action earlier in the Gospel (6:7, 13). Now, however, a second attempt to utilize the power has failed, and at the end of the passage the disciples will return to the question why (9:28–29)."[18] Due to the nature of the spirit, it turns out the disciples do not yet have the knowledge to cast out this demon and it requires Jesus himself to do it (9:29).

This satellite echoes the account of Moses' descent from Mount Sinai and return to the Israelites only to find them worshipping a false idol (Exod 32) in several ways. "In both cases the leader, on his descent, sees a terrible spectacle that is stamped by the continuing presence of sin and hardheartedness in a world that is on the road to redemption."[19] Without their leader, the family of Israel is unable to maintain their faithfulness and fidelity to God. In like manner, without Jesus, the Son of God, the disciples and extended family members who would receive the benefit of healing are not able to maintain their faithfulness to Jesus. Moreover, just as Moses was radiant after his encounter with God in Exod 34:29–30, there are implications that Jesus' transfiguration is still in effect because the people look at him with awe upon his arrival (ἐξεθαμβήθησαν, 9:15).[20]

The exchange between Jesus and the father demonstrates the reality that the family of disciples is not quite ready to act with the authority Jesus the Son has given to them by virtue of their kinship relationship. Akin to Jairus (5:22–23) and the Syrophoenician woman (7:25), a parent again advocates for his or her child. In presenting the child to Jesus, the father believes (9:17) that Jesus has the power to heal his son. Unfortunately, without Jesus present, no one has faith, neither the father nor the disciples, to heal the boy. Jesus identifies them as such, as a faithless generation (γενεὰ ἄπιστος, 9:19),

---

17. Collins, *Mark*, 435–36, provides a brief synopsis of the type of possession, most likely epilepsy (ἐπιλεψία or ἐπιληψίς) in ancient literature including its definition of a divine disease which is refuted by a treatise attributed to Hippocrates. She concludes, "Mark's attribution of the symptoms of the boy to a spirit is similar to the popular or religious view of the sacred disease described in and rejected by this treatise" (Collins, *Mark*, 436).

18. Marcus, *Mark 8–16*, 658.

19. Ibid., 657–58.

20. Ibid., 658.

reminding them and the reader that the kinship relationship with Jesus (and with God) requires faith (1:15). Moreover, the inability of the disciples to exorcise the demon and the doubt of the father puts Jesus' (and the family of disciples) honor at stake. Other people's faith in Jesus provides him (and his family of disciples) with honor and prestige. In the public failure of Jesus' disciples, Jesus' positive reputation for healing and exorcism could falter.[21] Nevertheless, despite the failure of the disciples, Jesus acts with faithfulness as he will care for and heal the boy.

The father's doubt continues through the disciples' inability to heal the boy; the disciples' inability is then extended to Jesus when the father says, "If you can do anything, have compassion on us and help us," (ἀλλ' εἴ τι δύνῃ, βοήθησον ἡμῖν σπλαγχνισθεὶς ἐφ' ἡμᾶς, 9:22). Ironically, this is exactly how Jesus responds to people in need, with compassion and the power to heal or provide for them (1:41; 6:34; 8:2). Reiterating the necessity for faith in the kinship relationship between Jesus and anyone who would follow him or receive a benefit, Jesus proclaims that all things are possible for the one who believes (9:23). Just as Jesus proclaimed as he began his ministry (1:14–15), he reiterates here to the father, to his family of disciples, to the crowd, and even to his adversaries. Jesus, as God's Son, has great power for those who believe in him.[22] It is necessary to place active trust in Jesus, not the local societal rulers and not the imperial elite. Faith and fidelity in Jesus as his kinship group of disciples and followers provide the possibility for great things. In this case, Jesus the Son of God, and no one else, is able to provide healing and restoration of relationship to the demon-possessed boy and his father.

The father confesses his faith in the midst of his doubt (9:24), a concrete example of the dynamic of discipleship that has been portrayed throughout Mark.[23] The disciples believe and follow Jesus, and yet they continue to struggle in their comprehension of Jesus and in their faith toward him. To prove once again his authority and power as God's Son to his disciples and followers, and even to his adversaries who are present (9:14), Jesus commands the spirit to come out of the boy (9:25). Just as in the healing of Jairus's daughter (5:35), the boy appears to be dead. And as he took the

21. Malina and Rohrbaugh note, "That Jesus' disciples could not cast out the demon reflected poorly on Jesus and his movement. 'When Jesus saw that a crowd came running together,' he had to act. Jesus 'rebuked' the unclean spirit (v. 25). Since witnesses were necessary for a grant of honor, the crowd here would be able to reconfirm the honor of Jesus and his movement that was diminished by the inability of the disciples to heal the boy" (*Social-Science Commentary*, 185).

22. See the discussions on faith in chapter 3 in 1:14–15 and 2:1–12.

23. Even as the disciples leave their original kinship networks (in part) to follow and be with Jesus, that is, to have faith in him and give loyalty and fidelity to him, they also display doubt and faltering faith (4:40; 6:51–52; 8:17; 8:32).

little girl's hand, as he took the hand of Simon-Peter's mother-in-law (5: 41; 1:31), Jesus takes the boy's hand and lifts him up, and he stands (9:27). Not only does Jesus establish his own power and authority in the presence of the crowd and the family of his disciples, but in the nexus between Christology and discipleship through kinship, the sonship of Jesus helps to restore a kinship relationship that was disrupted because of the boy's seizures.[24] Jesus has the power to heal, but he also has the power to restore kinship relationships.

In further demonstration of kinship, Jesus and the disciples enter into the house (εἰς οἶκον, 9:28) where he again provides the core kinship group of disciples with further instruction. Although they have been granted the authority to exorcise demons, they have not received all the knowledge that the Son has. It turns out that prayer is the only way that this demon could be exorcised (9:29).[25] Their inability to heal the boy further demonstrates the necessity of faith that Jesus requires. They could not do anything to heal the boy, but in the demonstration of the father's faith in Jesus, the boy was healed. The father's pursuit of healing for his son from Jesus and his faith in him demonstrates the nexus between Christology and discipleship in terms of kinship. Faith stands at the heart of the kinship relationship between Jesus and his disciples and followers.

4. 9:30-32 THE SON PREDICTS HIS DEATH A SECOND TIME

For the second time, in an echo of the second kernel (8:31), Jesus instructs his disciples that he will be arrested, killed, and three days later he will rise (9:31). In the nexus between Christology and discipleship in terms of kinship, it is necessary for the Son to continue to instruct his family about the consequences of his own establishment of God's empire, though this time he does not elaborate the consequences of this action for the disciples. As the disciples continue to demonstrate their misunderstanding of Jesus' identity and actions (4:40; 6:51–52; 8:17; 8:32; 9:18), Jesus continues to teach them just as a faithful kinsman would care for his family.[26] Jesus takes special care

---

24. Malina and Rohrbaugh, *Social-Science Commentary*, 185.

25. The requirement for prayer causes difficulty in reconciling the exorcism story with the instruction for the disciples in that it does not appear that Jesus uses prayer to exorcise the demon. Marcus, *Mark 8–16*, 665, suggests that one possible answer to this conundrum is that the father of the boy does pray as he asks Jesus for help (9:22). In effect, his intercession demonstrates to Jesus his faith in Jesus' ability and subsequently Jesus is able to exorcise the demon.

26. Marcus notes that the imperfect tense "here probably refers to repeated occasions of teaching, since Jesus' desire to instruct his disciples privately explains the

to provide this teaching to the core kinship group of disciples by desiring their presence not be known in Galilee because it would draw a large crowd and distract from his time with the disciples (9:30).

Because Jesus takes such care to teach his disciples, and because this is the second time the passion prediction is recounted in Mark, the content of the teaching is central to Jesus' identity as a Son, the establishment of God's empire, and to discipleship. Jesus emphasizes his kinship relationship (with God and with human beings) in his self-identification of Son of Man. As I noted in the discussion of 2:1–12, Jesus' use of the Son of Man designates him as an agent of human beings who acts with authority and power.[27] In this instance, Jesus demonstrates that the Son of Man has the foreknowledge of his own arrest, death, and resurrection which displays his power, authority, and honor as God's Son.

In the establishment of God's empire, Jesus is questioned and challenged by the local societal rulers (2:7; 2:16; 2:18; 2:24). His ascribed honor from God is not recognized and his teaching and works are considered demonic (Beelzebul, 3:22). Jesus responds to each challenge with a demonstration of his power to heal, to forgive sins, and to speak wisely, which proves his honor and worth as God's Son, but ultimately threatens his adversaries so that they plot his demise (3:6). Jesus will also challenge the Jerusalem societal leaders and the imperial elite rulers when he and the disciples enter Jerusalem (14:32—15:20).[28] Jesus' identification as the Son of God and his establishment of an alternative empire are in direct contest to, but in imitation of, the emperor (who was known as a "son of a god") and the Roman Empire.[29] Ultimately the Son of God will be killed by Roman imperial forces and their Jerusalem allies (15:20).

The nexus between Christology and discipleship in terms of kinship is implicit in this satellite because the teaching of Jesus' identity as the Son and

---

secretiveness of his trip through Galilee, which presumably lasts several days" (Marcus, *Mark 8-16*, 666).

27. See chapter 3.

28. Achtemeier states, "The reference to the journey through Galilee (v. 30) appears to be part of a larger plan designed to show Jesus on the way to the passion in Jerusalem. Beginning with (the passage containing) the confession of Peter (8:27) and carrying through to the arrival in the environs of Jerusalem (10:52; for other references to the journey, see 9:33; 10:1, 17, 32, 46), the way leads to the entry into Jerusalem (11:1–10) and to the cross. Therefore, when Jesus is 'on the way' in this passage, he is, in Mark's understanding, on his way to Jerusalem and to his death on the cross" (Achtemeier, "Exposition," 179).

29. For a discussion on imitation and contest (mimicry and resistance) with the Roman Empire, see chapter 2. See also chapter 3, and chapter 4.

his ultimate death will have direct consequences for the family of disciples.[30] This prediction echoes what Jesus taught them previously (8:31–38), where the nexus between Christology and discipleship was made explicit: to follow Jesus is to take up one's cross. Even as the core kinship group of disciples receives the authority and power to preach the message of the empire of God and to cast out demons, they also receive the consequences of these actions. In kinship with Jesus, the disciples will lose their lives (8:35) as Jesus will, but he also suggests that they will receive glory as Jesus is glorified (8:38).

The core kinship group of disciples responds to Jesus' instruction with incomprehension (9:32). And they do not ask him about it. Thus far the disciples have only been able to identify Jesus partially as the Christ (8:29), and despite his continued instruction, they still do not comprehend. The misunderstanding and miscomprehension leads to their faltering faith and will lead to their ultimate abandonment of Jesus (14:50). However, in the nexus between Christology and discipleship in terms of kinship, Jesus the Son continues to demonstrate his faithfulness toward the disciples in teaching and accompaniment as he will provide in the next satellite (9:33–37). Even as the disciples fail in their fidelity to Jesus and in their kinship relationship with him, the Son continues to act as the superior kinsman providing for his family, even as he goes toward certain death.

5. 9:33-37 THE SON WELCOMES A CHILD

Upon their arrival back in Capernaum and in the house (ἐν τῇ οἰκίᾳ), Jesus asks the disciples what they were discussing on the way. They are silent, though Jesus appears to be aware that they argued about who is the greatest (μείζων, 9:34) and thus provides further instruction to his core group of disciples about discipleship in terms of kinship. After the first passion prediction and Peter's rebuke of Jesus because of his impending death, Jesus instructs the disciples that they must lose their lives for the sake of Jesus and the gospel in order to save them (8:35). The disciples must also take up their crosses (willingness to suffer for him) and follow Jesus (8:34). In response to the question of greatness, Jesus claims that discipleship requires those who

---

30. Robbins, "Summons and Outline in Mark," 97–114, notes the connection between the passion predictions and discipleship in all three passion prediction scenes. He states that Mark purposefully uses series of three throughout the gospel. This series of three is present in both the passion prediction scenes and in the summoning of the disciples. These series of three also present Jesus, "in a role that merges the authority of Yahweh and the prophets with the authority of ethical teachers who embody the system of thought and action they teach to others," thereby making explicit the nexus between Christology and discipleship (ibid., 98).

would be first to be last and servant of all (9:35). In the nexus of Christology and discipleship in terms of kinship, the Son of God utilizes household language of "servant" and the example of children as he instructs his disciples "in the house" on the meaning of discipleship.

Jesus and the disciples are again inside the house (9:33) where Jesus assumes the role of the *paterfamilias* and defines the nature of discipleship in terms of kinship. As Jesus has already predicted, his sonship will require his suffering and death (8:31; 9:31). The most honorable Son knowingly goes forward to a certain death. Those who follow this Son will receive their "honor" and glory by following Jesus and taking up their crosses (8:34). Honor and greatness are not found in the expected, cultural ways of vying for it through patron-client relationships with the more elite members of society. Instead, the most honorable disciple will be the one who is last and the least, such as the servant within the household. Διάκονος refers to the household role of a table server, one who would provide food during a meal,[31] a role that the disciples have already fulfilled (6:30-44; 8:1-10). Jesus makes clear that the greatest honor belongs to those who are a part of his household who provide hospitality to any, especially those who are a part of the lower social strata.[32]

In addition to the example of servanthood, Jesus presents a child (παιδίον) to the disciples (9:36). He instructs them that if they receive a child (9:37), if they provide care for and hospitality to a child, the weakest and most vulnerable of society,[33] then they receive Jesus, and not only Jesus, but the one who sent Jesus, God. The most honorable Son of God who comes to establish God's empire equates himself with a small child. In the Mediterranean world, children had little status in the community or the household. "While a minor, a child was on a par with a slave, and only after reaching maturity was he/she a free person who could inherit the family estate."[34] But here, Jesus places a child in the center (9:36) and suggests that to receive this child is to welcome God. Ched Myers notes that it is remarkable that Jesus

---

31. Marcus notes, "The term is frequently used in Greek literature to indicate a menial worker such as a waiter at table, who is usually a slave (see Xenophon, *Memorabilia* 1.5.2; Josephus, *Ant.* 6.51; etc.)" (*Mark 8-16*, 674-75).

32. See the discussion on social strata categorization by Gerhard Lenski and Stephen Friesen in chapter 2.

33. Children were vulnerable in terms of their mortality rate, poverty, their social standing, and legal rights. See Laes, *Children in the Roman Empire*, especially 22-49; Gundry-Volf, "The Least and the Greatest," 29-60. For a comprehensive overview of children and families in Greco-Roman contexts, see Rawson, *Companion to Families*.

34. Malina and Rohrbaugh, *Social-Science Commentary*, 336. Malina and Rohrbaugh do note that a child's low social status did not mean a child was not loved and cared for.

draws attention to children, and not once, but twice (10:13–16) because they were otherwise considered nonentities.[35] However, Jesus has been providing care and hospitality for children throughout his ministry (5:21–43; 7:24–30; 9:14–29). The significance of this satellite is that he makes their care explicit, he connects them intimately with God in terms of kinship, and he now requires his disciples to follow suit.

With the example of a child, Jesus intimately connects the primary father in the Gospel of Mark, God, with the least and most vulnerable of society. In the nexus of Christology and discipleship in terms of kinship, Jesus' kinship with God is extended to the most vulnerable in this radical provision for hospitality. In Roman elite circles, hospitality was provided not only to provide a benefit to others, but to display one's own honor. Normally, as it is described in Herod's birthday banquet (6:21), only those who can increase and reflect one's honor, not detract from it, would be invited. Jesus has already demonstrated hospitality for the lowest of society (9:36–37) and again demonstrates that the honor he receives from God is extended to those who enter into his kinship network as a means to contest, yet imitate, conventional honor and hospitality codes.

In this satellite, not only does Jesus provide this hospitality, but he now places this responsibility of hospitality directly on the family of disciples. "What is most remarkable about Jesus' teaching here is the connection he draws between divine reordering of power in social relationships (like a child, last and servant of all) and the social practice of welcoming children, a practice directly linked to Jesus and to the God who sent him."[36] The family of disciples will welcome the very presence of God as they welcome children and the most vulnerable into their kinship group. The nexus between Christology and discipleship in terms of kinship is present in the extension of Jesus' kinship with God to the most vulnerable of society and the necessity of the core kinship group of disciples to assume the role of host to the least. Moreover, to receive Jesus is to be childlike (9:37); therefore, the disciples have become children to Jesus and to God and to one another.

6. 9:38–50 THE SON GIVES FURTHER INSTRUCTION ON DISCIPLESHIP

While Jesus continues his instruction of his core kinship group of disciples, John, one of the first of the band of brothers (1:19), tells him they tried to censure someone (τινα) who was exorcising in Jesus' name but was not

35. Myers, *Binding the Strong Man*, 261.
36. Mercer, *Welcoming Children*, 51.

following Jesus and the disciples (ὅτι οὐκ ἠκολούθει ἡμῖν, 9:38). John's report suggests he takes the kinship with Jesus in exorcistic practices (3:15; 6:7) very seriously. He draws a narrow circle. In contrast, Jesus casts a wide circle for the kinship group of disciples, reinforcing what he established in 3:31–35. Jesus' mother, brothers, and sisters are anyone who does the will of God. If someone is working in Jesus' name, then they have entered into his kinship group. They demonstrate their identity as a disciple and give their fidelity and honor to him (no one can speak evil of him, 9:39) in their ability to do mighty works in Jesus' name. The person's ability to exorcise using Jesus' name indicates the power that Jesus has from God and the faith that this person has in Jesus (contra the disciples' inability to help the boy with seizures in 9:18). "Because of this power, even those who start out manipulating Jesus' name for their own purposes may unexpectedly find themselves being drawn into its sphere of influence."[37] The nexus between Christology and discipleship in terms of kinship is evident in the faith and power that draw people, not just into Jesus' "sphere of influence," but into his kinship group (9:40).

The core kinship group of disciples continues to display their misunderstanding and miscomprehension of what Jesus requires of them. The Son makes clear that discipleship will bring suffering and death (8:34–35) and that it requires radical hospitality and servanthood (9:35–37). Their desire to stop someone from utilizing the authority that was directly given them by Jesus (9:38) continues to prove that they do not quite understand and continue to vie for greatness (9:34). To combat this understanding, Jesus provides even more instruction in a group of sayings about the consequences of discipleship and for those, insiders and outsiders,[38] who encounter other believers in 9:41–50. Simply providing a drink of water to one who follows Jesus will grant them a place in the extended kinship group, or at the least they will receive a reward (9:41). This is the third time that Jesus is referred to as the Christ in Mark (1:1; 8:29; 14:61) and the only self-reference for Christ by Jesus. Although the chief identifying marker for Jesus in the narrative of Mark is "Son of God," Jesus is instructing the core kinship group of disciples at this point and identifies himself by means of their understanding based on Peter's confession (8:29).[39] Kinship with Christ requires hospitality for others, but also grants a reward for the work of hospitality by the disciples.

---

37. Marcus, *Mark 8–16*, 686.

38. Collins, *Mark*, 449.

39. Winn, *Purpose of Mark's Gospel*, 100, notes that Christ is not the dominant "title" for Jesus in Mark.

As much as one will receive a reward and enter into the Son's kinship group if he or she provides hospitality to a Christ follower, there are harsh consequences for those who do not provide hospitality and welcome. Even as Jesus casts a wide net to welcome many into his extended kinship network, he establishes boundaries for his kinship group as he did in 7:1–23. Earlier, Jesus provided a list of the vices and mistreatment toward others (7:21–22) that can break down relationship (kinship) in response to the Pharisees' challenge to the disciples' meal practice. Again, as the *paterfamilias*, Jesus protects his family and boundaries from the threat of outsiders. First-century Mediterranean kinship practices were marked by in-groups and out-groups. In this satellite, Jesus is defending his in-group. "In-group members are expected to be loyal to each other and to go to great lengths to help each other."[40] Even as the group boundaries may be fluid and shift, as indicated by Jesus' radical inclusion and hospitality, there are still strict boundaries and requirements to maintain. In the nexus between Christology and discipleship in terms of kinship, Jesus provides means of protection to his family of disciples, especially the least and most vulnerable in this teaching. Because faith and actions of discipleship (9:37, 38–39, 40, 41) are central components to the family of disciples and the establishment of the empire of God, Jesus gives harsh consequences to those who would hurt those inside his kinship group. He does not deny entry into the extended kinship network, but if someone causes another to stumble ($\sigma\kappa\alpha\nu\delta\alpha\lambda\iota\sigma\eta$, 9:42) by hand, foot, or eye, they should acknowledge that sin and be marked themselves by the stumbling they caused others. Otherwise, they will be excluded from Jesus' kinship network and enter into Gehenna (9:43).

The consequences of sin are harsh (the cutting off of limbs and plucking out of eyes). However, as a superior kinsman, Jesus will protect his kinship group at all costs, even if it means harsh exclusion for those who sin against his family of disciples. The hand, the foot, and the eye each evoke the legal passages where the consequences for transgressions against another (or another's spouse) include the removal of the offending body part (Exod 21:23–25; Lev 24:19–20; Deut 19:21). One who sins against another does not have to be removed from the community of the Israelites. However, if one is to remain a part of the community, these are the punishments. The fact that they are visible punishments serves as a warning to others to maintain appropriate boundaries to remain in the extended kinship network. If one does not maintain the appropriate boundaries or does not accept the consequences of his or her transgressions, then they will be cast out of the

---

40. Malina and Rohrbaugh, *Social-Science Commentary*, 373.

community. The ultimate consequence of which is death or entry into Gehenna, a place of eternal punishment (Jer 7:30–34; 19:6–9).

Jesus concludes this teaching with three sayings about salt. "The first two conclude the theme of judgment, and the third wraps the whole section up by returning to the theme of communal discord/concord found at the beginning (9:33–34)."[41] If fire represents the consequences of sin and punishment, then all members of Jesus' kinship network will be "salted," or preserved, in the sin, doubt, and incomprehension that have been pervasive among the disciples (4:40; 6:52; 7:18; 8:17; 8:32; 9:32) which will continue to have effect on the kinship group of disciples and followers in their eventual abandonment of Jesus (14:50). But salt is good (9:50) and fire can have a refining effect (Mal 3:2–3). "Verse 49 supplies an intervening premise, that 'everyone will be salted with fire,' which combines rather nicely with the further implication of vv. 42–48, that one may choose between the fire of gehenna and the fire of self-sacrifice."[42] As Jesus has already claimed (8:34; 9:35), discipleship requires service and sacrifice, to the point that a disciple gives up his or her own life (or portion thereof) for the sake of another, especially one who is more vulnerable (9:42). This type of discipleship contests the conventional cultural expectation that one (or a group) would strive for honor and the protection of one's own interests at the expense of others. In a highly hierarchical society, the upper strata themselves function to make sure that the elite members continue to remain elite at the expense of those below who work to serve them and provide them with more and more honor. Within the context of Jesus' kinship group of disciples, service to the most vulnerable, even at the expense of one's life, becomes a central defining factor. Just as Jesus gives his life in service, so too does his kinship group (10:42–45).

Salt is good; in reality it helps to preserve food which preserves life.[43] The salt of self-sacrifice reminds Jesus' family of disciples that this is the core to their identity within the kinship group and the ethic by which they live their lives and lead the community. A community of those who sacrifice in behalf of one another will live in peace with one another (9:50), as opposed to arguing among themselves about who is the greatest (9:33–34).[44] In the nexus between Christology and discipleship, the Son of God extends the notion of sacrifice to his core kinship group of disciples. Just as Jesus will sacrifice his life for his disciples and extended kinship network, so too does

---

41. Marcus, *Mark 8–16*, 698.
42. Henderson, "'Salted with Fire,'" 52.
43. Cargal, "'If Your Salt,'" 140.
44. Ibid., 136.

he require that disciples sacrifice themselves for the sake of others. Self-sacrifice is a countercultural means of defining the community. It will allow for radical hospitality, inclusion of the most vulnerable, and the possibility of living in peace with one another, not the subjugating, elite-serving Pax Romana of the Roman Empire, but peace with God through his kinship relationship with Jesus.

7. 10:1–12 THE SON ESTABLISHES A HOUSEHOLD CODE

After Jesus offers instruction to the family of disciples one last time in Capernaum, they leave the region and go into the region of Judea and Perea.[45] Jesus' popularity remains (1:33; 2:4, 13; 3:8, 20; 4:1; 5:21, 24; 6:34; 8:1; 9:15, 25), even beyond his home territory, and a crowd gathers to receive teaching (10:1). Jesus' adversaries also gather and present him with an honor challenge in the form of a question on the legality of divorce (10:2). In the nexus between Christology and discipleship, the Son gives further instruction about proper kinship relationships, this time regarding marriage. Moreover, Jesus proves his honor and authority over the law and tradition when he responds to the Pharisees. This honor challenge and teaching begins a larger section on discipleship in terms of the household: marriage, children, slaves, and property.[46]

Household codes existed throughout antiquity as a means to establish a tradition that upheld the ideal household as the foundational and basic unit for society, and even a microcosm of imperial society.[47] The household

---

45. There is a textual variance. I follow Collins's translation, especially since Perea is directly connected with Herod. Collins indicates that the translation is based on ℵ B C* et al., καὶ πέραν τοῦ Ἰορδάνου, "(the region of Judea) and Perea." It most likely means that Jesus travled through Perea to Judea, but could be understood to mean that Jesus traveled to Judea and then to Perea. She concludes, "That the meaning is the former is supported by 11:1, where the place arrived at last is mentioned first. But the ambiguity gave rise to variants. The reading attested by C² D W et al., πέραν τοῦ Ἰορδάνου, '(the region of Judea) beyond the Jordan,' results either from an independent attempt at clarification or an assimilation to the text of the parallel in Matt 19:1. The reading attested by A 𝔐 sy^h, διά τοῦ πέραν, '(the region of Judea) through Perea,' is a more successful attempt at clarification that probably expresses the meaning of the earliest recoverable wording, i.e., the reading attested by ℵ B et al" (Collins, *Mark*, 457na).

46. See Collins, *Mark*, 458. See also Jeremias, *Die Kindertaufe*, 62. Collins and Jeremias argue that Mark used some pre-existing collection of texts in 10:1–31. In the narrative context of Mark it is useful to note that this section divided into household topics comes in the larger context of teaching on discipleship and thus explicitly connects kinship and discipleship.

47. Carter notes the existence of discussions on household management throughout

consisted of four elements: the male's task to earn wealth and three kinship relationships of husband-wife, father-children, and master-slave. "A power dynamic controlled the relationships in which the husband/father/master *ruled over* the wife/children/slaves. The household was hierarchical and patriarchal in that the male held power over the women and children."[48] Each member of the household held specific roles and tasks, often differentiated by gender. While Jesus uses the structure of the household code, his code does not support the societal norm. Jesus establishes an alternative household for his disciples, one where husbands and wives participate in a marriage of "one flesh" (10:8); disciples are children (10:15); following Jesus, not accumulating wealth, grant one a place in the empire/household (10:21); and all disciples are slaves (10:43-44).[49]

Jesus responds to the Pharisees' question about divorce with another question, "What did Moses command you?" At face value, this question evokes the Ten Commandments and the order not to commit adultery (Exod 20:14). However, the Pharisees respond with a reference to divorce proceedings in Deut 24:1-4 where a man might divorce his wife if he finds something unfavorable about her by issuing a certificate of divorce. Jesus then responds by stating that it was their hardness of hearts (σκληροκαρδίαν, 10:5) that required this stipulation for divorce, suggesting that divorce was not acceptable to God. Jesus makes this explicitly clear on his definition of marriage citing Gen 1:27 and 2:24 basically eliminating the possibility for a man to divorce his wife. Jesus defines marriage as a kinship relationship instituted by God which should not be ended by human beings. Moreover, Jesus demonstrates his authority and honor as God's Son by identifying a different locus of authority in Genesis rather than the Mosaic law that the Pharisees cite.

Divorce was a reality in first-century Judaism and in the Roman imperial world. There are several documents which attest the practice of divorce including the Mishnah which provided grounds for divorce (*m. Gittin* 9:10).[50] Josephus affirms the law stipulated in Deut 24:1-4, and stated that only the husband could divorce his wife and the wife may not marry again unless

---

the Greco-Roman world. They "continued after Aristotle (*Pol* 1.2.1-2) in an Aristotelian tradition (the *Oeconomica*; *Magna Moralia*; Philodemus; Arius Didymus, *Epitome*; Hierocles, *On Duties*), in Stoicism (Seneca; Epictetus; Dio Chrysostom), among Neopythagoreans (Okkelos; Callicradtidas; Perictyone; Phintys), and in Hellenistic Judaism (Pseudo-Phocylides, Josephus, Philo)" (Carter, *Matthew and the Margins*, 376).

48. Carter, *Matthew and the Margins*, 376.

49. Ibid., 377.

50. See also the summary in Donahue and Harrington, *Gospel of Mark*, 296-97.

she has her ex-husband's consent.⁵¹ Mary Rose D'Angelo notes the impact that Roman marriage laws and moral propaganda would have had on first-century Christianity and in particular, the Gospel of Mark.⁵² As a means of consolidating power and promoting stability in the Roman Empire, a series of laws on marriage and childrearing were issued by Augustus. "A central effect of the laws and ideology was to make marriage and divorce, adultery and *stuprum*, childbearing and childrearing hot topics of civic and imperial discourse throughout the first and early second centuries."⁵³ D'Angelo concludes that the sixth commandment (Exod 20:14) about adultery is interpreted in terms of the Roman law of adultery. She also notes that by the first century, "Roman moral nostalgia had produced and propagated an ideal of an original, indissoluble marriage comparable to the vision of origins articulated in Mark 10:2–9."⁵⁴ Jesus treats divorce as adultery in this passage, but he is even more stringent than the Roman laws, suggesting that there is no acceptable instance for divorce. Moreover, through the authority he has in his kinship relationship with God, Jesus cites the foundation of creation and human beings by God as the original and indissoluble marriage.

Through contest and imitation, Jesus demonstrates the superiority of the parameters for kinship within God's empire. Within the narrative of Mark, the only other example of marriage is the marriage of "King" Herod and Herodias (6:14–29).⁵⁵ Mark has already made clear that this is a kinship relationship gone awry. He notes that Herodias was originally Herod's brother's wife (6:17) and that John had decreed that their marriage was not legal (6:18). Although there were laws on adultery and moral propaganda that promoted indissoluble marriage, the Jewish and Roman elite example of marriage in Mark suggests that kinship relationships were morally void and did not live up to the Roman ideal.⁵⁶ "The Herodians' use of Roman law for their household arrangements quite simply particularized their acquiescence and complicity in imperial politics, with all its religio-symbolic expropriation of the household as its base unit of power."⁵⁷ Just as John called out Herod and Herodias on their marriage at the risk of his life, so now does Jesus make explicitly clear proper kinship boundaries for his disciples

51. Josephus, *Ant.* 15.259.
52. D'Angelo, "Roman Imperial Family Values," 59–83.
53. Ibid., 67.
54. Ibid., 79.
55. Jeffers, *Greco-Roman World*, 125.
56. It should be noted that marriage and divorce were often used as a means to acquire and consolidate political power, especially among the imperial elite. See Cadwallader, "Markan/Marxist Struggle," 160.
57. Ibid., 159.

in the very region of Perea that was part of Herod's "kingdom" (βασιλεία). Jesus also puts his own life at risk by the assertion of his authority and honor as God's Son before the Pharisees who have already conspired to kill him (3:6). "The author of Mark, and perhaps also the sources of Mark, along with other ancient Jews and the early followers of Jesus, were compelled to make clear (to themselves, as much as to the empire) that they practiced the Roman family values that Romans only talked about, as they worked out for themselves what was good, holy, and pleasing to God."[58] In the nexus between Christology and discipleship in terms of kinship, the Son asserts proper kinship boundaries in terms of marriage as instruction for discipleship in imitation of and contest with the reigning kinship ideology.

8. 10:13-16 THE SON WELCOMES CHILDREN INTO GOD'S EMPIRE

Just as people brought those who were ill and demon-possessed to Jesus for healing (1:32; 2:3; 6:54–56), now people bring children to Jesus in order that he can touch them (ἅψηται, 10:13). The disciples try to rebuke them (either the children themselves or those who bring the children, it is not clear), perhaps because children were vulnerable, dependent, and socially marginal.[59] The disciples again try to act on their own authority, again misinterpreting and misunderstanding the role and purpose of Jesus' sonship and ministry and its recipients (10:13). Jesus, as he has done before (8:32), rebukes the disciples and provides more instruction regarding discipleship. Akin to 9:36-37, Jesus' kinship and blessing extend to all those in need, especially little children, the most vulnerable and the least honored members of society. The nexus between Christology and discipleship in terms of kinship is evident in Jesus' extension of kinship and inheritance of the empire of God to the most vulnerable followers. Moreover, not only does Jesus extend kinship to actual children, but in the metaphor of disciples as children (10:15), Jesus also emphasizes the kinship relationship with those who follow him.

Jesus has already demonstrated his care and welcome to children throughout his ministry in the healing of Jairus's daughter (5:21–43) and the exorcisms of the Syrophoencian's daughter (7:24–30) and the boy with the mute spirit (9:14–29). In this satellite he makes clear to his disciples that as they assume the Son's authority and power granted to them (3:15; 6:7) to provide healing, exorcism, and membership in the kinship group of disciples, they must also know who valid recipients of exorcism and healing

---

58. D'Angelo, "Roman Imperial Family Values," 79.
59. Marcus, *Mark 8–16*, 718.

are. As they have already shown their desire for honor according to imperial standards (9:34), they require continued education that Jesus' hospitality and kinship extends to the most vulnerable and least of all (9:36–37).

The imperial elite example of a child as a member of a "kingdom" (βασιλεία) illustrated in the Gospel of Mark is the daughter of Herodias (6:22–25). Jesus again defines his kinship boundaries in stark contrast to the kinship displayed by Herod and his family. Both Herod and Herodias exploit their daughter for social gain and personal vengeance. Herod allows his daughter to dance provocatively to entertain his banquet guests (6:22). Herodias has her own daughter ask for John's execution as reward for her successful entertainment (6:24). Herodias's daughter is victim and complicit in a death-wielding kingdom, whereas, in the empire of God, children are heirs and recipients of God's blessing through God's Son.[60] Moreover, only the most honored in society and those who would help Herod to acquire more honor and increase his reputation as a member of the imperial elite are welcome at his table (6:21). Jesus welcomes any and all in need (2:3; 6:54–56; 10:14), especially children, and he also instructs the kinship group of disciples to become like a child in order to enter the empire of God (10:15).

Jesus' call to discipleship and membership in the kinship group which constitutes the empire of God requires people to be last and servant of all (9:35); now they are to become like a child, both a literal and metaphorical child, to be the most vulnerable, and most often rejected, members of society.[61] This characterization of discipleship goes against the conventional cultural standard that the most reputable and honored members of the empire are the elite and those closest to the imperial family. Jesus emphasizes his blessing toward this vulnerable group by not only touching them (10:13), but also hugging them and blessing them (ἐναγκαλισάμενος αὐτὰ

---

60. Gundry-Volf notes the connection between Herodias's daughter and Jesus' blessing the children. She acknowledges the exploitation of Herodias; however, she suggests that this story is representative of the contrast between the ministries of Jesus and John the Baptist. "In *Jesus'* ministry children are given life and liberated from evil through a parent's request and its fulfillment. In *John the Baptist's* ministry a child is complicit in the taking away of life through a parent's request and its fulfillment. Thus, Jesus has the power to effect life and liberation for the benefit of children; but John does not: a mere child gets the better of him" (Gundry-Volf, "Children in the Gospel of Mark," 173). I argue that the contrast is between Jesus' kinship and God's empire and Herod's kinship and "kingdom." John the Baptist serves as the forerunner to Jesus, and though he is "less than" Jesus, he is not an enemy. Moreover, John the Baptist is the one who prophesied Jesus' coming and helped to inaugurate his ministry (1:7–9).

61. Even elite children were more vulnerable. Until the *pater* recognized them as legitimate, they could be exposed and die or enter into slavery. See Corbier, "Child Exposure and Abandonment," 52–73; Harris, "Child-Exposure in the Roman Empire," 7.

κατευλόγει, 10:16). This is the first explicit reference to the blessing of a person in the Gospel of Mark.[62] The blessing of children was a Jewish practice of parental blessing of children exhibited in the Hebrew Bible (Gen 9:26–27; 27:1–40; 28:1–4; Sir 3:9). Joel Marcus notes the nature of the blessing that Jacob gives to Joseph's sons, Ephraim and Manasseh in Gen 48 which included an embrace (Gen 48:10) and the laying on of hands (Gen 48:14) which parallels Jesus' blessing in 10:16.[63] Marcus indicates the problem comparing the Hebrew Bible parental blessing with Jesus' blessing of other people's children, primarily that there is no first-century evidence for such a rite. However, with the biblical model, "the parents' request for Jesus to bless their children becomes a plea for him to become a kind of godfather to them, and Jesus goes on to associate these godchildren with his followers."[64] I argue that Jesus becomes the *paterfamilias* (by virtue of his kinship with God) in both his blessing of these children but also in his designation of them, and disciples who are like them (10:15) as heirs of the empire of God (10:14). Judith Gundry concludes, "Jesus' hug, therefore, can be seen as an adoptive embrace, an assumption of a parental role. His subsequent blessing indicates that he has adopted the children in order to pass on an inheritance to them before he dies, and in this way 'save' them."[65] Marcus further connects the disciples and the children as Jesus' kin in the nexus between Christology and discipleship in terms of kinship when he notes Jesus' designation of the disciples as "children" in 10:24 thereby demonstrating that Jesus' kinship with God is extended not only to the disciples but also to all followers of Jesus, including children.[66] This designation of Jesus' disciples as children highlights the requirement that his disciples become like children in order to enter into the empire (10:15).

Not only does Jesus welcome children, bless them, and designate them as heirs of the empire of God, he also indicates that they are a model of discipleship (10:15). The Son declares that the children he has welcomed into his extended kinship network have the attribute (last of all, 9:35) for discipleship in the empire of God. Jesus continues the reversal of the conventional first-century cultural codes of honor by suggesting that sinners (2:17), the sick (2:17), the last (9:35), and now children are the primary

62. Jesus' affirmation of people's faith (2:5; 5:34; 10:52), and his commission to them to depart in peace (5:34) could be interpreted as a blessing. Jesus blesses the bread in the feeding of the five thousand (εὐλόγησεν, 6:41).

63. Marcus, *Mark 8–16*, 717. See also Gundry-Volf, "Children in Mark," 155–56.

64. Marcus, *Mark 8–16*, 717.

65. Gundry-Volf, "Children in Mark," 156.

66. Marcus, *Mark 8–16*, 717.

recipients of his benefactions and honored members of his kinship group.[67] In part, this designation of children as model disciples and recipients of the empire is instruction for the disciples who cause the little ones to stumble by blocking their way to Jesus (10:13). In the nexus between Christology and discipleship in terms of kinship, the Son continues to teach his core kinship group of disciples about their role and purpose, now to embrace and be like the children, the least in their extended kinship network of Jesus followers.

9. 10:17–31 PROPERTY AND WEALTH PREVENT DISCIPLESHIP AND ENTRY INTO THE EMPIRE

As Jesus prepares to depart from the house in Perea (10:10) after demonstrating children as the model for discipleship and designating them as heirs of God's empire in the nexus between Christology and discipleship in terms of kinship, a man comes up to Jesus and kneels before him to ask how he might inherit eternal life. The man addresses Jesus as "Good Teacher," (διδάσκαλε ἀγαθέ, 10:17), perhaps as a means of flattery (akin to 5:35) so that Jesus will bestow the benefaction of instruction on the man. Furthermore, the man's posture suggests he views Jesus with esteem and even a person with higher social status, even though the man has many possessions (10:22).[68] Akin to Peter's partial confession of Jesus in 8:29, the man identifies Jesus only in part. Jesus denies the attribute of "good," claiming that God alone is good (10:18). This statement, along with Jesus' instruction on the commandments, is evocative of the Shema (Deut 6:4) and is similar to Jesus' statement in 2:7, suggesting that Jesus is already trying to instruct the man in the way to eternal life by first acknowledging the central place

---

67. Ibid., 718–19. There is some ambiguity in the translation of 10:15, ὃς ἂν μὴ δέξηται τὴν βασιλείαν τοῦ θεοῦ ὡς παιδίον μὴ εἰσέλθῃ εἰς αὐτήν. It could be rendered, "Whoever does not welcome the empire of God like (he welcomes) a child will not enter into it." Spitaler argues that in the comparison of "welcoming God's kingdom to welcoming a child, the figure motivates social change. The disciples must act like adults, not like children, and demonstrate hospitality toward persons whose status they do not share" (Spitaler, "Welcoming a Child," 425). The empire of God that is being established by Jesus is constituted by his extended kinship network of disciples and followers (3:33–35). For the sake of my thesis, the ambiguity does not make much difference for discipleship since being like a child is equivalent to becoming last (9:35), and welcoming the kingdom as one would welcome a child (like Jesus does) demonstrates the radical hospitality where the first shall be last and the last shall be first (10:15). I am inclined to accept the conventional translation since thematically it is in line with Jesus' instruction to the disciples regarding greatness and honor (10:42–45) in the kinship group of Jesus.

68. See 3:11; 5:22, 33; and 7:25 where those who seek a benefaction from Jesus kneel before him.

God holds.⁶⁹ In response to the man's adulation, "Jesus is simply deflating the man's flattery and repelling his hopes for return ingratiation."⁷⁰ The man has already misconstrued the nature of eternal life and God's empire by suggesting there are stipulations he must follow to secure his inheritance, when Jesus just taught that the empire of God should be received and welcomed as a child (10:15), one who does not have the means to secure an inheritance.⁷¹

Jesus continues to demonstrate his authority as God's Son as a teacher and interpreter of the law as he recites the Ten Commandments that deal with human relationships to the man. Jesus mentions the commandments that regulate proper kinship boundaries. The man indicates that he follows all of these laws. In addition to the instruction Jesus provides as if the man were already a disciple, Jesus also extends kinship to the man by looking at him and loving him (10:21), much like a father loves his child.⁷² The one thing the man lacks parallels the heart of Jesus' instruction to the disciples in these satellites. Jesus instructs the man to sell all of his possessions, to give the money to the poor, and to follow him (10:21). He asks the man to become his disciple, just as he asked Peter, Andrew, James, and John (1:16-20), which now includes becoming last and servant of all (9:35) and like a child (10:15) to enter into eternal life. As the man goes away grieving, demonstrating the challenge of this call, Jesus instructs the disciples yet again (10:23-31). The disciples again demonstrate their misunderstanding and miscomprehension of Jesus. In the nexus between Christology and discipleship in terms of kinship, the Son continues to show care for his core kinship group of disciples, continuing to instruct them in the way of discipleship as a superior kinsman. So much so that when the disciples are perplexed (ἐθαμβοῦντο, 10:24) by his saying, he gives them more information, addressing them as children (τέκνα, 10:24), a kinship term. Jesus continues to demonstrate his role as *paterfamilias*, providing for and trying to protect his kinship group of disciples who will be heirs of the empire of God.

---

69. Ahearne-Kroll connects the verses with the Shema. "In 10:17b the phrase οὐδεὶς ἀγαθὸς εἰ μὴ εἷς ὁ θεός echoes the reference to God in the Septuagint (LXX) of Deut. 6:4, κύριος ὁ θεὸς ἡμῶν κύριος εἷς ἐστιν. In Deut. 6:5-9 the message is clearly that God should be at the center of one's life both interiorly and exteriorly, Jesus seems to assume that if one lived in this way, eternal life would be one's to inherit" (Ahearne-Kroll, "'Who Are My?,'" 16).

70. Barr, "The Eye of the Needle," 34.

71. Ibid.

72. Marcus notes "This verb [ἠγάπησεν] is frequently used for a father's love for his son in Genesis (22:2; 25:28; 37:3; 44:20), and that association fits in with other indications of Jesus' fatherly relation to the rich man in the passage" (Marcus, *Mark 8-16*, 722). Jesus has also referred to the disciples as his children in Mark (2:19 and 10:24).

The nexus between Christology and discipleship in terms of kinship is evident in Jesus' care and concern for a possible new member of his family (3:31–35) and in his instruction to his core kinship group of disciples. Jesus acknowledges the difficulty and challenge of being a disciple of Jesus to enter into the empire of and kinship with God. As Jesus has demonstrated (4:10–20; 8:17–21, 34–38; 9:35–50) when the disciples are unable to understand or follow appropriately, he makes clear that God (through Jesus) continues to extend kinship toward the disciples and all those who seek the empire and eternal life (10:27). Still not convinced, Peter speaks up and claims that they have left everything to follow him, suggesting that they should already be recipients of eternal life (10:28). The nexus between Christology and discipleship in terms of kinship appears yet again in Jesus' reassurance to the disciples. By virtue of Jesus' kinship with God, he extends his kinship to those who have left their original kinship groups (in whole or part) to follow, and he promises that they will receive kinship in abundance now, suggesting that the disciples already have a new, extended kinship group in all those that follow Jesus.[73] Just as in the redefinition of Jesus' kinship group in 3:31–35, Jesus now redefines kinship for the disciples. Jesus provides a promise to those who leave their kinship groups for his sake and the sake of the gospel, even though departing from conventional kinship ties is a marker for discipleship (1:20). And just as there is a conspicuous absence of fathers in Jesus' redefined family (3:34–35), Jesus claims that his followers will leave fathers, but there is no place for fathers in the new, extended kinship group (10:30). The only legitimate father is God and by extension God's Son, Jesus, who functions as the *paterfamilias* for the empire of God on earth. Those who have left their original kinship groups, homes, and fields will also be rewarded with houses and farms (10:30) which will provide the means for hospitality and food access which so many of Jesus' followers have been denied (6:30–44; 8:1–10).[74] Jesus does indicate that it

73. Horsley notes that the disciples do not completely abandon home or family when they follow Jesus. "Even those disciples who left everything to 'follow' Jesus are to be restored to their traditional family/household and village life in a remarkable renewed form (10:28–30)" (Horsley, *Hearing the Whole Story*, 181).

74. May suggests this reward of fields and houses is a means for hyper-compensation in a limited good society to demonstrate the ultimate power and authority God has (with Jesus as his agent and broker) to redistribute land over and against the ruling elites. "Peasants, as the typical followers of Jesus would have been, would have had absolutely no way within their power to increase the available quantities of land. Their only option, if they did own land, would have been to divide and redivide. Only by the unlimited power of the patron, God, could they ever have hoped to increase their holding and social status. They could be guaranteed that the patron was able to deliver because his broker had manifested the patron's 'credit rating' by exorcising demons, healing, and teaching with authority" (May, "Leaving and Receiving," 151).

will not be without struggle and persecution (διωγμῶν, 10:30), which has already been evidenced in the challenges against Jesus (2:18, 24; 3:2, 22; 7:5; 8:11; 10:2), the plot on his life (3:6), and will be seen in desertion of the disciples to protect themselves (14:50). In the age to come, the kinship group of disciples will receive eternal life, the very thing that the man who approached Jesus sought.

As Jesus is departing the region of Perea, the region that belongs to the "kingdom" of Herod Antipas, a Jewish leader in line with the Roman imperial elite, Jesus once more contrasts his establishment of God's empire with that of Herod's "kingdom." Jesus instructs the man and reminds his kinship group of disciples of appropriate and honorable kinship boundaries through the Ten Commandments, which Herod, though a Jew, does not follow as indicated by his adulterous marriage to Herodias (6:17) and exploitation of his daughter for his friends' entertainment (6:22). Moreover, Herod used his wealth and property as a means to accrue honor and to get ever closer to the Roman imperial elite, but often at the expense of those under his jurisdiction, the majority of whom remained at or below a subsistence level of living.[75] Jesus instructs that although one may accrue great wealth and status in the current age, unless they take on the life of discipleship, they will not have a place in the empire of God.

The nexus of Christology and discipleship in terms of kinship is evident in Jesus' restructuring of the kinship group of disciples where Jesus, as God's Son, extends membership and reward to those who follow. In addition to the kinship group, disciples will receive houses and lands; that is, hospitality and food, and ultimately wealth, as a reward for discipleship. Jesus' instruction contests the conventional imperial realities of wealth and status for the elite at the expense of the majority population by redistributing wealth to the kinship group of disciples. It also imitates the conventional structures by establishing an alternative empire and kinship group that maintain kinship structures. However, suffering and service stand at the heart of discipleship and membership in the kinship community of followers of Jesus. The instruction to the disciples and the reminder that the model of discipleship is service is summed up in 10:31 where Jesus reminds the disciples that the first will be last and the last will be first, just as he instructed in 9:35.

---

75. See the summaries on inheritance and economy, especially regarding the Herodians in Hanson and Oakman, *Palestine*, 43–47 and 95–121.

10. 10:32-45 DISCIPLESHIP REQUIRES SERVICE AND SLAVERY

As closure to the extensive instruction on the new household (10:1-45), Jesus predicts his passion and instructs his disciples about it for a third time. In this third and final prediction, Mark makes clear that Jesus and the disciples are on the way to Jerusalem. Furthermore, the core kinship group of disciples continues to demonstrate their miscomprehension of Jesus' identity and purpose (10:32) in their fear and amazement (1:27; 10:24), perhaps responding to Jesus' difficult teaching about discipleship and wealth (10:19-31). In the nexus of Christology and discipleship in terms of kinship, Jesus once more extends his kinship with God to the family of disciples in the form of instruction about his identity and purpose. In the midst of their fear and misunderstanding, Jesus again acts as the superior kinsman and cares for his disciples, trying to help them to understand what it means to follow him and be a part of the extended kinship network of Jesus in the empire of God. In 10:38-40, Jesus will connect his death with the disciples' suffering, just as he demonstrated that discipleship requires his followers to carry their crosses (8:34-35).

This satellite provides more information about the Son of God who has been given glory, but will also suffer by human hands (8:31–9:10). Jesus instructs the core kinship group of disciples that they are going to Jerusalem and it is in that place that the Son of Man will be arrested and be put to death (10:33). Jesus has not only been challenged by the local societal leaders of the Galilee, but he will also face the Jerusalem societal leaders and ultimately, their allies, the Roman leaders (10:33). Jesus makes clear to the disciples who his adversaries are and by whose hands he will die. He also reveals the kind of suffering (mocking, scourging, spitting) he will endure before he dies (10:34). Although it seems as though Jesus will become the most dishonored in his suffering and ultimate death by the humiliation he will undergo at the hands of the alliance of the Jerusalem leaders and the Roman governor,[76] Jesus proves that he is the most honorable Son of God because he knows exactly what will happen to him and he goes forth willingly. Moreover, in addition to his passion, Jesus also predicts his resurrection, demonstrating that he will triumph over the Jerusalem and Roman

---

76. See the discussion on status degradation rituals in Malina and Rohrbaugh, *Social-Science Commentary*, 412–14. They note "The status degradation ritual is a process of publicly recasting, relabeling, humiliating, and thus recategorizing a person as a social deviant. Such rituals express the moral indignation of the denouncers and often mock or denounce a person's former identity in such a way as to destroy it totally" (413).

leaders because they cannot keep him dead or keep him from establishing God's empire.

The theme of suffering that has been present in each of the passion predictions (8:31; 9:31; 10:32-34) evokes the image of the suffering servant in Isa 50 and 53. In an image of salvation for God's people, the suffering servant is present to offer his own life for the sake of the people (Isa 53:4-5). Joel Marcus notes that the image of the suffering servant cannot be separated from the ultimate triumph of God in Isaiah; rather the servant's suffering is the means by which the victory is achieved. "The suffering and death of the Markan Jesus, similarly, is not just a trial to be borne but the means by which God's dominion will be established and the 'many' ransomed from the forces that have held them in bondage."[77] The promise of resurrection also indicates the victory that Jesus will share with the disciples in the restoration of kinship relationships after death has severed them.[78] In the nexus of Christology and discipleship in terms of kinship, the Son of God not only extends kinship to his group of followers, but he gives his own life as a demonstration of the suffering and service that is required in the kinship group of disciples.

This is the first instance in Mark that Jesus directly references the Romans (τοῖς ἔθνεσιν, 10:33) as his adversaries, at least in the sense that the "nations" present in Jerusalem would have been the Romans.[79] There have been numerous other allusions to the Roman Empire, including Jesus' identity as the Son of God (1:1), establishing the empire of God (1:14), the exorcism of Legion (5:1-20), and the story of Herod, a Jewish elite aligned with the Romans (6:14-29). Jesus now predicts that not only were the Jewish societal leaders plotting his death (3:6), who in turn, in their alliance with the Romans, demonstrate Jesus as a threat and adversary to the Roman imperial elite who govern Galilee (indirectly through Herod) and Judea (directly through Pilate). The establishment of God's empire by Jesus, as God's Son, is in contest with and imitation of the Roman Empire. As the Son of God, God's primary agent, and as Son of Man, agent of humanity, Jesus realizes the threat that he poses in providing a new realm for people to find kinship structures, an honorable identity, hospitality, and food access over and against the ruling authorities. In the brief mention of the "Gentiles," Jesus demonstrates his authority and knowledge as God's Son, going toward his suffering and death fully aware. In the nexus of Christology and discipleship

77. Marcus, *Mark 8-16*, 746.

78. See the discussion on kinship and resurrection above.

79. Collins, *Mark*, 485, notes that the act of handing Jesus over to the Gentiles foreshadows the chief priests handing Jesus over to Pilate in 15:1 and the subsequent trial with Pilate in 15:2-15.

in terms of kinship, the Son of God goes before (10:32) his kinship group of disciples, both as a leader in the establishment of God's empire in the face of the Jewish and Roman ruling elite and also as a servant and an example of the discipleship he requires of his kinship followers.

Immediately following the third passion prediction as Jesus and the core kinship group of disciples make their way to Jerusalem, James and John approach Jesus to make a request. The brothers ask Jesus to allow them to sit at his right and left hand in his glory (ἐν τῇ δόξῃ σου, 10:37). As in the healing of the little girl (5:35) and the man who seeks eternal life (10:17), James and John address Jesus as "Teacher" (διδάσκαλε, 10:35), certainly a term of respect, but one that identifies Jesus only in part. Once again the disciples demonstrate their misunderstanding of Jesus' purpose and identity in their partial identification. They continue in their misjudgment when they seek places of honor from Jesus when he is in his glory. In the nexus between Christology and discipleship in terms of kinship, James and John seek a benefaction from their superior kinsman, Jesus. However, they misconstrue the nature of Jesus' benefits and their roles as members of his core kinship group of disciples. "Their outrageous request to be seated in positions of rulership and highest honor at Jesus' right and left hands when he comes into his glory borrow the image of imperial rule, as if that is what Jesus' program of the kingdom is all about."[80] Although Jesus has borrowed structures of honor and kinship from the Roman imperial culture that occupies Galilee and Judea, Jesus is not establishing an empire that utilizes honor and kinship to aspire to greatness at the expense of others. In fact, the state of glory may be construed not only in eschatological terms as the ultimate triumph of Jesus after his death and resurrection, but also at his crucifixion when he loses his life for his disciples and becomes last and servant of all in order to become the greatest (10:43–45).[81]

Rather than give them what they desire or dismiss them as a means to shame them and put them in their place, Jesus again responds as the superior kinsman and provides care and teaching for his family of disciples.[82]

---

80. Horsley, *Hearing the Whole Story*, 193. In the next statement Horsley indicates that Jesus does not even have the power to provide a place of honor or political preeminence for James and John based on 10:40. I would argue that Jesus does have the power and authority to do so by virtue of his kinship with God. It is not his to give because that is not his purpose nor is it the role of discipleship to hold a place of political power or honor.

81. Muddiman, "Glory of Jesus," 57–58, notes that the only other place where right and left are mentioned in Mark is at the crucifixion (15:27).

82. Hutchinson, "Servanthood," 57–58, suggests that their request for a seat of honor was not completely out of line due to the honored place they already had as the inner band of brothers of Jesus (1:19; 5:37; 9:2; 14:33) and the promise of honor by

In 10:38, Jesus responds to their question with another question, "Are you able to drink the cup I drink or to be baptized with the baptism with which I am baptized?" The use of the word cup (τὸ ποτήριον) evokes images from the Hebrew Bible. "The cup is a metaphor for one's portion in life, what one has been given to 'drink,' whether of good or ill."[83] The cup may refer to the cup of salvation (Ps 23:5) or it could refer to the cup of God's wrath (Isa 51:17, 22), which must sometimes be drunk by those who are innocent and not deserving of God's punishment (Jer 49:12). The cup imagery will return when Jesus prays to God in the Garden of Gethsemane for an alternative outcome than the one which will happen (14:36). "Here it is clear that the cup represents the suffering that Jesus is about to endure and that this suffering is part of the divine plan."[84] Jesus elaborates the image of the cup with the reference to his baptism. Jesus' baptism (1:9-11) inaugurated his ministry and the establishment of the empire of God, but it also set in motion the events that would lead to the plot on Jesus' life (3:6) and the suffering and death that he has predicted three times (8:31; 9:31; 10:32-34), which will come to fruition.[85]

Although Jesus' role as God's Son is not to grant places of honor when Jesus comes in glory, he does tell James and John that they will drink the cup and be baptized with the same baptism. In the nexus between Christology and discipleship in terms of kinship, the Son instructs the kinship group of disciples that following him and being a part of his kinship network will lead to suffering and sacrifice (10:39). Once more, Jesus provides the definition of kinship with him in terms of service and suffering (10:42-45). In the midst of this instruction, Mark indicates that the other ten disciples became angry when they hear what James and John asked of Jesus. Perhaps they are envious that Jesus might grant them a special place, but they may also be angry that James and John step outside of the kinship and discipleship boundaries Jesus has in place, from being servant and slave of all to being first and holding the honored position (10:43-44).

Just as Jesus mentioned the Gentiles (10:33) as those who will humiliate and put him to death, he again references the Gentiles here in his instruction on discipleship (10:42). This time Jesus defines the Gentiles as those who have rulers who "lord it over them" (κατακυριεύουσιν αὐτῶν) and

---

following Jesus (10:30).

83. Marcus, *Mark 8-16*, 747.

84. Collins, *Mark*, 496.

85. Contra Collins, *Mark*, 496-97. She claims that the baptism is to be viewed metaphorically to counter the idea that baptism refers to the baptism of John or Christian baptism. I argue that the only other reference to baptism, Jesus' baptism, provides the definition for baptism in 10:38.

are "tyrants over them" (κατεξουσιάζουσιν αὐτῶν). The Romans and those aligned with them (i.e., the Herodians) exercise their power and authority by appropriating as much honor, goods, land, and wealth at the expense of their subjects and those culturally and socially beneath them. Throughout his ministry, Jesus has provided honor, food, hospitality, and healing to those who do not have it. Although Jesus is the most honorable Son of God and has come to establish God's empire, he does not do so by means of appropriation of goods or loss of honor. "The depiction of Jesus' service-unto-death (10:45) somehow grounds the assertion that the way to be exalted is to become the slave of all (10:43–44)."[86] In the nexus between Christology and discipleship in terms of kinship, the Son extends kinship and ultimate honor to those who follow the way of service, much like a slave who is the lowest member of the household, even though it continues to be a challenge for the disciples to perceive and embrace.[87] The Son of Man, agent of humanity, has come to serve and give his life (10:32–34). Jesus extends his kinship in the form of sacrifice to those who follow him and to bring them into the extended kinship network. Just as Jesus calls his disciples to lose their lives to save them (8:35), as the superior kinsman, Jesus will also give his own life for his family of disciples so that he might save theirs.

11. 10:46–52 THE SON HEALS THE SON OF TIMAEUS

Jesus and the core kinship group of disciples continue to make their way to Jerusalem after the third passion prediction (10:32–34) and final instruction to the disciples (10:42–45). In this satellite they stop in Jericho, the location of Jesus' final benefit of healing before his entry into Jerusalem. In the nexus between Christology and discipleship in terms of kinship, the Son extends kinship by means of benefit to a person in need of healing who in turn follows Jesus (10:52), an indication of joining Jesus' family (3:31–35). This healing of a blind person could also stand as a bookend to the healing of the blind man in 8:22–26.[88] These two stories sandwich the passion predictions and instruction on discipleship. Elizabeth Struthers Malbon concludes, "Mark 8:22–10:52 illustrates once again the strong interconnections of the actions of the Markan Jesus: the one who is called 'Christ' and 'Son of God,' the one powerful in healing and teaching, is the very one who insists that he and his followers must serve those with the least power even

---

86. Marcus, *Mark 8–16*, 755.
87. Hutchinson, "Servanthood," 63.
88. Malbon, *Mark's Jesus*, 38.

at the risk of persecution by those with the most power."[89] The healing of blind Bartimaeus is the final act of healing and culmination of the teaching on discipleship before Jesus and the family of disciples enter Jerusalem.

The location of Jesus and the kinship group of disciples in Jericho places them directly on the way from the Galilee to Jerusalem. Jericho was the first city captured by Joshua and the Israelites as they came to possess Canaan (Josh 2; 5:13–6:26). Joshua followed after Moses (Josh 1:1–9), and now Jesus, "the new Joshua, likewise begins his climactic 'invasion' of Judea by passing through Jericho on his way up to Jerusalem."[90] Not only does Jericho evoke images from the Hebrew Bible, but Jericho was also known as the winter resort of the Hasmoneans and Herod the Great.[91] The city became part of the Judean Province governed directly by Rome in 6 CE when Herod Archelaus, Herod Antipas's brother, was deposed as ethnarch.[92] Jesus offers his last benefit of healing in a city once governed by the Herodians, now overseen by the Romans, both of whom he will face as adversaries in Jerusalem (3:6; 12:13; 15:1).

As Jesus and the disciples make their way out of Jericho, a blind beggar on the side of the road calls to Jesus. In the nexus between Christology and discipleship in terms of kinship, the man, identified in kinship terms as Bartimaeus, son of Timaeus, addresses Jesus in kinship terms as the Son of David (10:46–47).[93] Mark identifies Bartimaeus by the Greek translation of his name and then the Aramaic name. Joel Marcus notes that "Timaeus" is "a common Greek name (cf. the title character in one of Plato's dialogues) derived from the word for 'valuable, honored.'"[94] As a blind beggar, Bartimaeus is in the lowest strata of Roman imperial society and would be the least honorable. However, in the instruction on discipleship, Jesus has just

---

89. Ibid., 39.
90. Marcus, *Mark 8–16*, 758.
91. Josephus, *Ant.* 14.410. See Roller, *Building Program of Herod*, 171–74.
92. Josephus, *War*, 2.167.

93. Robbins has observed the connection between Christology and discipleship in this pericope, though not in terms of kinship. "In [this story] the christological image of Jesus and the response in discipleship converge. Throughout the gospel narrative it is implicit that the christological understanding of Jesus' activity is directly related to the kind of activity in which the disciple becomes involved. Christology and discipleship prove to be simply two sides of the same coin in the Gospel of Mark. An erroneous christological perception of Jesus' activity leads to improper expectations and requests, and inept discipleship activity." In the healing of blind Bartimaeus, "a request put to Jesus which reveals a proper understanding of Jesus as he nears the gates of Jerusalem results in true discipleship which produces the willingness to follow Jesus into the city where he meets rejection and death" (Robbins, "Healing of Blind Bartimaeus," 226–27).

94. Marcus, *Mark 8–16*, 759.

informed the disciples that whoever wants to be first will be slave of all (10:44). Within the realm of Jesus' kinship group, the last and least are the most honored members.

Before Bartimaeus enters into Jesus' kinship group, he first addresses Jesus as "Son of David" and asks for mercy (ἐλέησόν με, 10:47). The address references King David, as Marcus notes, the founding king of the Israelite dynasty.[95] Marcus suggests that the only person referred to as the "Son of David" in the Hebrew Bible is David's own son and successor, Solomon (1 Chron 29:22; Prov 1:1; Eccl 1:1; 1 Kgs 1:13; 2:1; 1 Chron 23:1).[96] "In later Jewish literature, partly because of his biblical reputation for wisdom, Solomon becomes known as a great magician, with powers that include miraculous healing and especially exorcism."[97] Dennis Duling, in arguing for the plurisignificance of the "Son of David" in Matthew, defines one aspect of Jesus' Davidic sonship as merciful and therapeutic akin to Solomon.[98] This association with Solomon as a healer also parallels the request for miraculous healing from the Roman emperor Vespasian who also heals a blind man.[99] Marcus concludes that the imagery for David and Solomon may be combined. I argue that "Son of David," like "Christ" and "Teacher," is only a partial identification of Jesus. Jesus is indeed a Son who provides miraculous healing and has come to establish the empire of God, but not in Roman imperial terms and not in some of the Jewish messianic hopes of a military and political leader. He is also a Son who shares healing and exorcism power with his family of followers.

Although Bartimaeus identifies Jesus in part, Jesus responds to his call and asks him what he wants because he is the superior kinsman who provides benefits for those in need. Some try to tell Bartimaeus to be quiet (10:48), in the same way that they tried to prevent children from coming to Jesus (10:13). Bartimaeus tells Jesus he wants to see again and he believes Jesus can heal him (by virtue of his request). In a demonstration of Jesus' authority and power as God's Son, it only takes a word for Jesus to heal Bartimaeus. He simply tells him to go, "Your faith has saved you," (ὕπαγε, ἡ πίστις σου σέσωκέν σε, 10:52) and Bartimaeus can see again. Faith in Jesus demonstrates discipleship and is a marker of loyalty and trust in the empire of God (1:15; 2:5; 5:34). In another act of discipleship, Bartimaeus does not

---

95. Ibid., 762.
96. Ibid., 1120.
97. Ibid.
98. Duling, "Matthew's Plurisignificant," 112–13. See also Duling, "Solomon," 235–52.
99. Tacitus, *Histories* 4.81; Suet.*Vesp.* 7.2.

depart from Jesus but instead begins to follow him (ἠκολούθει, 10:52), entering into the kinship group of disciples. In the nexus between Christology and discipleship, Jesus extends kinship to the least honorable beggar in his final benefit of healing in Mark; in turn, Bartimaeus, who has responded with faithfulness to Jesus, follows him as a disciple.

12. 11:1-11 THE SON ENTERS JERUSALEM

After Jesus' final benefit of healing and extension of kinship to Bartimaeus in Jericho (10:46-52), Jesus and the kinship group of disciples prepare to enter Jerusalem. Before he actually enters the city, Jesus provides a prophecy about his entrance, demonstrating his power and foreknowledge as God's Son. In the nexus between Christology and discipleship in terms of kinship, Jesus extends kinship to the disciples in their participation in the prophecy as the ones who secure the colt (πῶλον) for Jesus' entrance into Jerusalem (11:2). In affirmation of Jesus' sonship and authority, the prophecy occurs just as Jesus predicted (11:4-6). The colt which has never been ridden evokes imagery from Zechariah 9:9 where the king rides into Jerusalem on a young donkey.[100] The Son of God makes his way into Jerusalem as figure of royalty continuing to evoke images of King David and his kinship with the Davidic dynasty (11:7-10).

The core kinship group of disciples and other followers of Jesus spread their cloaks on the colt and on the ground; others lay leafy branches down on the ground for the colt to walk on as Jesus makes his way into Jerusalem. The laying down of cloaks and branches serve as a gesture of honor. "The garments and branches spread on the road form a carpet so that the feet of the colt do not even touch the ground or stones on which ordinary people tread."[101] In addition to the carpet, the people form a procession and pronounced Jesus' entry into the city. Their words, "Hosanna, blessed is the one who comes in the name of the Lord; blessed is the empire of our father David which is coming. Hosanna in the highest," (11:9-10), both honor Jesus and recognize the benefits that he is able to offer with entry into his kinship group. "Hosanna" is the translation of the Aramaic meaning "save us."[102] In addition to images of Israelite kings entering Jerusalem, Jesus' entry is

---

100. Marcus, *Mark 8-16*, 772, notes that πῶλον could be understood as a young horse or a young donkey. He argues for the translation of a young donkey based on Zech 9:9 and the understanding that a donkey or mule is a royal animal.

101. Malina and Rohrbaugh, *Social-Science Commentary*, 195.

102. Marcus, *Mark 8-16*, 779-80, states that "Hosanna" is from Ps 118 and there it is addressed toward God.

similar to that of Simon Maccabaeus (1 Macc 13:51) where Simon enters Jerusalem in triumph accompanied by praise, leafy branches, and hymns, which is later interpreted as his establishment of lordship (14:7).[103] In their blessing, the people recognize the power and authority of Jesus and give him an honorable place, even a royal place, so that he enters Jerusalem as a king.

In addition to Jewish and Israelite triumphal entries into Jerusalem, the portrayal of Jesus entering Jerusalem on a colt in a procession evokes images of the Roman triumphal processions of its emperors after military victories.[104] Hans Leander has provided a reading of Jesus' triumphal entry in terms of Roman triumphs and celebratory welcomes utilizing the work of Homi Bhabha.[105] Descriptions of Roman triumphs have been considered their own literary genre with a shared pattern:

1. The prominent person is greeted and hailed–often as a divine revelation–by the citizenry near the city gates.
2. He (they are all male) is then formally escorted into the city, accompanied by hymns and/or acclimations.
3. The procession typically ends in the temple where some kind of ritual takes place–either a benevolent sacrifice or a hostile expulsion of some kind.[106]

Based on this pattern, the description of Jesus' entry into Jerusalem is very similar to Roman triumphs with the exception of the anticlimactic visit to the Jerusalem temple where no ritual occurs; Jesus simply looked around and then left (11:11).[107] Leander suggests that the use of the colt in 11:3 can be viewed as ἀγγαρεία, or "forced labor," the Roman practice of acquiring beasts of burden from the local population.[108] Jesus imitates the Roman elite by acquiring an animal from the people for his purposes. "He adopts some trappings from Greco-Roman entrance processions and triumphs, but reframes them in a different context (God's empire) and for a different goal (to

---

103. Ibid., 779.

104. Of particular note should be the description of Vespasian and Titus's triumph in Rome after they destroyed Jerusalem. See Josephus, *War*, 7.117–59 and the discussion in chapter 2.

105. Leander, "With Homi Bhabha," 309–35.

106. Ibid., 319.

107. Ibid., 328–29, suggests that the temple event is delayed until the crucifixion and the temple of the curtain is torn in two (15:39) which supports his view of the mimicry occurring that is almost the same, but not quite.

108. Ibid., 324.

serve not dominate, [Matt] 20:25)."[109] In an echo of the prophecy in Zechariah and in parody of the Roman triumph, Jesus enters into Jerusalem as a humble and righteous savior, not a warrior and military leader, on a donkey rather than being pulled by a chariot accompanied by his army (Zech 9:9). In parody and contrast, Jesus enters Jerusalem, not on a warhorse or chariot exerting his political and military might but on a beast of burden used daily by ordinary people.[110]

Alongside the use of the colt, Jesus also refers to himself as "Lord," (ὁ κύριος), an honorific title also used for the emperor, when giving reason for ἀγγαρεία. Jesus processes into the city akin to the emperor as the people shout "Hosanna."[111] It is a cry of exultation and acclamation thereby imitating the Roman triumph, but it is a distinctly Jewish acclamation. The use of "Hosanna" could be seen "as a performative enunciation of a national discourse that both adds to and substitutes its meaning . . . The 'original' anti-colonial Jewish meaning is thereby made unstable and transferred into a more slippery and elusive mimicry of imperial triumphant processions."[112] Jesus is accompanied into the city of Jerusalem and greeted with acclamation like the victorious Vespasian and Titus in Rome, but in contrast, no one from Jerusalem, especially the leaders, comes to greet Jesus or to welcome him as they would have in a Roman triumph.[113] Finally, there is no ritual or sacrifice offered in the triumph. Jesus briefly looks around at the temple (11:11) and then he departs the city. It is only later that he will enter the temple, not to offer sacrifice, but to drive out the buyers and sellers who make possible sacrifice, even in behalf of (περὶ) the Roman emperor.[114]

Jesus is the Son of God who enters into Jerusalem as an emperor akin to those of Rome, continuing to establish the empire of God. And yet, his empire is not based on its military might or the exploitation of people and goods. Rather, the Son of God enters triumphantly and humbly, with acclamation, but without any honor or ritual from the city residents and leaders, illustrating the call to his disciples to be a servant (9:35). In the nexus between Christology and discipleship, Jesus' triumphant entry serves as demonstration of the way of discipleship. He is indeed establishing his empire against the dominating forces of Rome (represented in Jerusalem),

---

109. Carter, *Matthew and the Margins*, 414.

110. Myers, *Binding the Strong Man*, 296.

111. Josephus, *War*, 7.126–27, describes the soldiers offering an acclamation of joy to Vespasian and Titus as they sat down on the tribunal in Rome.

112. Leander, "With Homi Bhabha," 327.

113. Carter, *Matthew and the Margins*, 415.

114. Josephus, *War*, 2.197.

but it is an empire of a kinship network of disciples who serve one another (9:35) and offer their lives for the sake of Jesus and the gospel (8:35).

13. 11:12–25 THE SON ESTABLISHES HIS AUTHORITY IN JERUSALEM

Following the anticlimactic ending of Jesus' "triumphal" entry into Jerusalem and their return to Bethany, Jesus and the core kinship group of disciples (11:14) make their way back to Jerusalem the next day. Along the way, Jesus is hungry and sees a fig tree, but it has no fruit, so Jesus curses the fig tree by his statement, "May no one ever eat fruit from you again," (11:14). On the next day, when Jesus and the disciples return to Jerusalem once again, Peter notices that the fig tree has withered (ἐξηραμμένην, 11:20). Once more, Jesus demonstrates his authority and power as God's Son over creation (4:35–41; 6:45–52) which foreshadows and strengthens his authority he exudes in the Jerusalem temple.[115] In the nexus between Christology and discipleship in terms of kinship, this demonstration of authority becomes a teaching moment for the kinship group of disciples. A defining marker for the extended kinship network of the Son of God is faith (2:5; 5:34; 9:24). Again, Jesus instructs the disciples that the consequences of their faith, their honor and trust in God (and in Jesus as God's Son and agent), will result in powerful acts (11:23), effectively extending Jesus' authority and power to his family of disciples and beyond.

The story of the fig tree is intercalated by Jesus' initial actions in the Jerusalem temple (11:15–19). Upon entering the Jerusalem temple (11:15), Jesus drives out (in the manner of an exorcism)[116] the money changers and

---

115. As noted by Myers, *Binding the Strong Man*, 297–98, Telford connects the symbolism of the fig tree with the Jerusalem temple. "The blossoming of the fig-tree and its *giving of its fruits* is a descriptive element in passages which depict Yahweh's visiting his people with *blessing*, while the *withering of the fig-tree*, the destruction or withholding of its fruit, figures in imagery describing *Yahweh's judgement* upon his people or their enemies" (Telford, *Barren Temple*, 161–62). Telford states that the reason for judgment is due to a corrupt temple and sacrificial system. "In some cases, indeed, the fig or fig-tree . . . can be used expressly as a symbol for *the nation itself* . . . Who could doubt, then, the extraordinary impact that Jesus' cursing of the fig-tree would have produced upon the Markan reader, schooled to recognize symbolism wherever it occurred" (ibid., 162).

116. Marcus states, "'To throw (or cast) out' (*ekballein*) is the term used elsewhere in Mark for exorcism (1:34, 39; 3:15, 22–23; etc.), and its employment here may be a hint that the buyers and sellers who profane the Temple are Satan's tools" (*Mark 8–16*, 782). At the least they "possess" the temple in a way that an unclean spirit possesses a person. Horsley connects the reference to moving the mountain into the sea (11:23), to uprooting the temple and then to Legion being driven into the sea in the herd of pigs

those buying things to offer sacrifice in the temple, effectively putting a halt to the central activity of sacrifice.[117] The temple had three categories of basic operation: administrative, ritual, and economic. Not only did the Jerusalem temple offer the central location for religious sacrifice, purification, liturgy, prayers, and music, but the temple also maintained its own order and purity as well as providing judicial decisions. Furthermore, the temple functioned as a financial institution providing space for money exchange, offering and sacrificial records, and treasury storage.[118] Any halt of sacrificial activity would affect the entire operation of the Jerusalem temple.

Jesus utilizes his authority and power as God's Son and as ruler of God's empire. He then cites the prophets Isaiah (56:7) and Jeremiah (7:11) further demonstrating his ability to interpret the scriptures and defend his authority. The nexus between Christology and discipleship in terms of kinship is evident in Jesus' use of household imagery in his teaching. Jesus becomes the *paterfamilias* of the temple (house of prayer) and those whom he instructs and who receive his teaching, being amazed by it (ἐξεπλήσσετο, 11:18), become his extended kinship network.[119] However, Jesus' authority is challenged once more by the local societal leaders who are plotting to kill him (11:18). As the local societal leaders of Galilee resort to violence when they lose face and their honor challenges with Jesus (3:6), Jesus' authority and teaching threatens the societal leaders of Jerusalem as well. Their honor is further depleted when Mark describes them as being afraid of Jesus (ἐφοβοῦντο γὰρ αὐτόν, 11:18) due to the crowds, which also shows Jesus' own honor and authority over the people. The threat is heightened due to Jesus' brazen act done with such authority in such a public place.[120]

(5:13). Though he concludes, "This certainly does not make the Temple demonstration into another exorcism like that of 'Legion.' And it certainly does not suggest that the Temple and the high-priestly aristocracy are demonic or Satanic (although, in their association with the Romans, they may be implicated as under the influence of demonic forces). But the same struggle that focused on casting out demonic forces in the first half of the story continues in Jerusalem, only now as an explicitly political struggle and focused on concrete human institutions and rulers" (Horsley, *Hearing the Whole Story*, 148).

117. Malina and Rohrbaugh, *Social-Science Commentary*, 197.

118. See Hanson and Oakman, *Palestine*, 127–43.

119. Marcus, *Mark 8–16*, 784. This term, ἐξεπλήσσετο is the same word used in 1:22 when the people in the Capernaum synagogue receive Jesus' teaching and accept him as an authority figure, anticipating the kinship group that he will establish in his teaching, exorcism, healing, and hospitality. It is also used in 6:2 and 7:37, when the people marvel at Jesus' teaching and ability. The term is similar to ἐξίστημι, which also describes the response of the core kinship group of disciples and of Jesus' extended kinship network to Jesus on occasion (2:12; 5:42; 6:51).

120. Hellerman views "the temple incident as Jesus' most overt self-assertion of

Moreover, his act and teaching are honored and received by those who witness them. In the nexus between Christology and discipleship in terms of kinship, those who receive Jesus' teaching enter into his extended kinship network and ignore the local leaders, no longer recognizing their authority and teaching.

As Jesus acts as God's agent in the temple, defining it as his "house" (ὁ οἶκός, 11:17), he also establishes the dynasty of God the Father and Jesus the Son in Jerusalem. Jerusalem was a city occupied and governed by the Roman Empire, ruled by another father-son dynasty of Vespasian and Titus during the composition of Mark. The Roman Empire maintained political and economic control of Jerusalem and even its temple.[121] Like the Romans, as they exercise power and control over the temple by appointing the high priest, Jesus intends to occupy the Jerusalem temple, but he does not seek economic control or look to exploit those who use the temple.[122] Rather, as God's Son, Jesus calls for his house to be a house of prayer for all people. In the nexus between Christology and discipleship in terms of kinship, the Son of God offers hospitality to all (nations) who want to enter and pray in the temple. This notion is expanded in the return to the fig tree and Jesus' reference to faith and prayer to God (11:22–25). It is not through sacrifice in the temple and support of the economic center that supports the Romans,

---

divine authority in the Markan account," even though Jesus' authority as God's Son has been established since the beginning of the gospel (1:1; 1:9–11) and reinforced (9:2–9) as Jesus and the disciples make their way to Jerusalem (Hellerman, "Challenging the Authority of Jesus," 219). Hellerman also notes that Jesus' authority exercised throughout the gospel also contributes to his honorable status.

121. Hanson and Oakman note that in the first century CE, the high priests of the temple "were appointed by Rome or its agents from select families only ... The high priest and the high priestly families, under the oversight and power of the Roman prefect [the Emperor's agent and representative], played a major role in controlling the temple and its operation" (Hanson and Oakman, *Palestine*, 131). Goodman notes in his description of the Jewish temple and its destruction in the first century CE the influence of Rome on the temple leadership, even as it remained a central symbol for Judaism. He suggests that after the Jewish War, the Romans would have re-established the "Temple cult under the leadership of pro-Roman high priests such as had cooperated with the Roman state since direct Roman rule was first imposed in Judaea in 6 CE" (Goodman, *Judaism in Roman World*, 55). Schwartz addresses the role of the emperor and patronage of the Jerusalem temple in the occupations of Persia, Macedonia, and Rome and concludes, "There is no reason to doubt the unanimous claim of the ancient writers that the emperors patronized the temple, supported and were supported by the cult (in that sacrifices were offered on their behalf), favored the priests as a class (and at times other members of the temple staff), and recognized their right to rule the Jews of Palestine 'according to their ancestral laws'" (Schwartz, *Imperialism and Jewish Society*, 56).

122. Herzog recognizes Jesus' action in the temple as a response to the Jewish leaders' (aligned with and controlled by the Romans) "exploitative and oppressive domination of the people through taxation and tribute" (Herzog, "Temple Cleansing," 820).

but it is faith and prayer in God (and in Jesus, God's Son and agent) that will provide authority and power, or at least agency, to those who enter into the extended kinship network of Jesus.

14. 11:27-33 THE SON'S AUTHORITY IS CHALLENGED

On their third day in Jerusalem and second visit to the temple, Jesus is approached by the Jerusalem societal leaders and presented with a verbal challenge that questions Jesus' authority for his actions in the temple. This will begin a series of honor challenges in Jerusalem (11:27-12:34) that are akin to the way that the Galilean leaders challenged Jesus numerous times (2:1-3:6) at the beginning of his ministry. Because Jesus exercises authority without valid political and kinship relationships (as far as the societal leaders see it), then he exercises with an authority that is not legitimate. "The questioners assume that Jesus' own honor did not justify what he was doing so they ask who *gave* him the authority."[123] Jesus meets their challenge with a counterchallenge. Jesus, the extended kinship group of disciples and followers, and the reader, know that Jesus acts with authority from God, as God's agent and Son (1:1, 11), and thus is more honorable than any of the societal leaders who challenge him. So, he asks them about the baptism of John, whether its origin is divine or human. This causes a conundrum for the leaders because John the Baptist had an honorable reputation as a prophet among the people who are witnessing this honor challenge (11:32). Ultimately, in order to save face, the Jerusalem societal leaders are not able to answer the question, which then forces them to lose the challenge and be shamed in public. Again, not only does Jesus have the honor he acquired as God's Son at his baptism (1:9-11) which has been reinforced throughout the gospel narrative (9:2-8), but Jesus again demonstrates his ability to meet every honor challenge that is presented to him.

Just as the threat on Jesus' life is heightened after his initial activity in the temple (11:15-17) due to the very public nature of his act, so now in this subsequent honor challenge are the stakes set high. Joseph Hellerman notes the significance of the setting of this encounter within the temple precincts. Due to the size of the courts within the Herodian temple precinct and the festival of Passover, "It is not unreasonable to assume the presence of several thousand persons in the outer court on the day in question."[124] Moreover, the nature of Jesus' effective counter-challenge forces the Jerusalem societal leaders to try to defend their own honor. Jesus swiftly and deftly takes the

---

123. Malina and Rohrbaugh, *Social-Science Commentary*, 199.
124. Hellerman, "Challenging the Authority of Jesus," 222.

honor challenge against himself and flips it on its head. Moreover, where it takes two questions from the Jerusalem societal leaders to challenge Jesus, he challenges them with one. "His repeated call to his adversaries to respond to his single question also portrays Jesus as taking charge of the encounter."[125] The Jerusalem societal leaders suffer public shaming when they are unable to beat Jesus in his counterchallenge. As the stakes are high, the Jerusalem leaders will seek out further honor challenges to try and trap Jesus (12:13, 18) until they can "win" by witnessing his public humiliation and degradation at the crucifixion.

In the nexus between Christology and discipleship in terms of kinship, the people in Jerusalem who have received Jesus' teaching and accepted his authority have entered into his extended kinship network. They already recognize the authority he has (whether or not they know the origin). The Jerusalem societal leaders do not recognize Jesus' authority which keeps them separate from Jesus and his kinship network. The Jerusalem societal leaders' power over the people has been publically challenged because Jesus, the Son, has given them a different teaching with authority which they have received. Moreover, in Jesus' question to the Jerusalem leaders, he aligns himself with John the Baptist in order to cement the people's respect for him. Although Jesus is the most honorable Son of God who teaches with every authority and power by virtue of his kinship relationship, the Jerusalem religious leaders, like the Galileans before them, never recognize Jesus' honor and authority. The nexus between Christology and discipleship in terms of kinship is evident here. As those who remain outside the household and outside of the bounds of Jesus' kinship network, they do not recognize Jesus' kinship with God. Moreover, the extension of kinship to the crowd in his teaching and authority only serves to threaten the Jerusalem societal leaders and their own place as authoritative leaders and teachers. Jesus' assertion of authority within the temple serves to establish God's empire, to offer a new teaching, one that calls for service and sacrifice (10:43–44), but one also that will lead to Jesus' arrest and apparent loss of honor and authority in the crucifixion.

15. 12:1-12 THE PARABLE OF THE VINEYARD OWNER AND HIS SON

Immediately after Jesus beats the Jerusalem societal leaders at their own honor game, he continues utilizing his authority as God's Son and begins

---

125. Ibid., 224.

to teach them in parables.[126] As Jesus establishes his authority and teaching in the Jerusalem temple, there is a clear, yet heightened, echo of Jesus' establishment of authority at the beginning of his ministry in Galilee. Just as Jesus taught in parables to describe the word and empire of God (4:1-34), once more Jesus speaks in a parable about God's empire.[127] Evoking Isa 5:1-7, Jesus tells the story of a vineyard owner who leases out the vineyard and property to tenants. When it comes time for the harvest, the tenants reject the authority of the owner's slaves and even his son to collect the owner's share. Not only do the tenants reject the son, but they also kill him and throw him out of the vineyard (12:8). Although there is no direct interpretation to the parable, based upon the Jerusalem societal leaders' reaction (12:12), the parable stands as a microcosm of Jesus' ministry and expansion of that ministry into Jerusalem. The vineyard owner is God. The vineyard represents Jerusalem and/or the temple. The tenants are the Jerusalem societal leaders. The slaves are John the Baptist and other prophets. Jesus is the beloved son.[128] Jesus tells this parable in a public place, before the Jerusalem societal leaders who have challenged him, suggesting that they represent the tenants who do not respect the authority of the vineyard owner's son. In the nexus between Christology and discipleship in terms of kinship, Jesus the Son instructs his kinship group of followers about what is going to happen

---

126. The Greek is plural, παραβολαῖς, even though Jesus only teaches one parable to his adversaries.

127. Tolbert ties these two parables together, suggesting that they function as two plot synopses of the Gospel of Mark. "The first emphasizes his task and the second his identity; together they make up the Gospel's basic narrative Christology" (Tolbert, *Sowing the Gospel*, 122). They also function to demonstrate the method of Jesus' teaching in parables and the fact that Jesus remains consistent throughout his ministry in the way he establishes his authority (teaching in the public realm of synagogue and temple). The parables also demonstrate his knowledge about the establishment of the empire of God through the word (it may appear to fail, but ultimately will be successful,) and his own death on account of the empire of God. Jesus remains the most honorable Son because he knowingly goes forth toward his execution.

128. Jeremias, *Parables of Jesus*, 11-13. Jeremias claims that the vineyard is Israel. Marcus also notes that the tenant farmers have broader significance than the Jerusalem leaders, especially as the gospel concludes. "Mark 12:3-5, moreover, speaks allegorically of the murder of the prophets, and in the OT, Jewish traditions, and the NT, these murders are laid at the door not only of Israel's leaders but also of the people as a whole" (Marcus, *Mark 8-16*, 805). He notes the problematic issue of supersessionism and the Christian persecution of Jews, the direction this interpretation takes. Marcus suggests a reading of Isa 5 "to follow the roots of Mark's rented and forfeited vineyard backward into Isaiah's tenderly nurtured vineyard that has sprung Eden-like from God's hand, and to which he remains committed in spite of the wild growth that has sprung up there and that grieves his heart–as he also remains committed to us in spite of all the wildness and murder that have sprung up in ours" (Marcus, *Mark 8-16*, 814).

to him and to the leaders (12:9) over and against those who do not honor the kinship relationships and boundaries Jesus has established.

The parable itself is told in terms of kinship. The setting of the story is an estate (household) and kinship relationships provide the basis for the events that take place.[129] The vineyard owner is the father (12:6), and although he is physically absent from the household, all other characters are connected to him by means of direct kinship or extended kinship.[130] The tenants are in his extended kinship network by virtue of the fact that they work within the household and are to provide the owner with his portion of the harvest. They take care of the household while the owner is away. The slaves are part of the household of the vineyard owner in that they represent his interests and act as his agents. They arrive at the vineyard with the authority of the owner (father) to acquire what is due to the vineyard owner (12:2, 4, 5). When the tenants ignore the authority of the slaves, beat them (killing one of them, 12:5), and send them away, the owner sends the son (12:6). The son acts entirely in the interest of the father and assumes his complete authority when he goes to the vineyard. The tenants recognize his authority, but instead of honoring it, they kill him, thinking that they will then receive the inheritance. Their kinship relationships are askew for they would receive what is rightfully theirs by virtue of working in the vineyard as the owner's tenants. They believe that in killing the son they can insert themselves into that kinship relationship to receive an inheritance.[131]

The household and kinship language is further corroborated by the allusions to God's covenant relationship with Israel, often depicted in kinship language, in this satellite. At the very beginning of the parable, Jesus tells about a man who plants a vineyard. This and some of the other details of the vineyard echo Isaiah 5 where a man has a vineyard, set a watchtower in the midst of it, and dug out a wine press for it (Isa 5:2). In Jesus' parable and in Isaiah, there is much detail to indicate the care that the vineyard

---

129. Although Jesus does not describe a house present on the estate, the household and kinship language is supported by the subsequent kinship relationships of owner (father), tenant, slaves, and son and the Hebrew Bible reference to Isa 5:7 where the vineyard represents the "House of Israel" (οἶκος τοῦ Ἰσραηλ). See below for further discussion of this parable and its allusions to Isaiah.

130. In Matthew's version of this parable, Jesus refers to the vineyard owner οἰκοδεσπότης (master of the house, Matt 21:33), further emphasizing the household language.

131. There is regrettable, retributive violence in this pericope that has led to interpretations of supersessionism and violent persecution of Jews by Christians. Because I am focusing on the kinship relationships exhibited in this pericope and in the Gospel of Mark, I am not addressing the violence in this passage. For a helpful starting place, see Oldenhage, *Parables for Our Time*.

owner goes to in order to establish his vineyard.[132] It becomes clear in Isa 5:7 that the vineyard represents Israel and the vineyard owner is God. With the addition of the tenants, the slaves, and the son, Jesus adds to the Isaiah imagery, bringing in the contemporary players of the societal leaders, John the Baptist (and other prophets), and himself. The societal leaders, in the form of the tenants, have been granted authority to oversee the estate which is represented by Jerusalem and its temple, the economic, political, cultic, and religious center of Israel and surrounding Jewish territories. As has already been indicated throughout the Gospel of Mark, those who come before the Son, such as John the Baptist, are disregarded, beaten, and killed (12:4-5) by the societal leaders (9:13).[133] Just as Jesus' sonship has been established (1:1, 9-11) and affirmed (9:2-9) as it is in the parable (12:6), he has also predicted his own death (8:31; 9:31; 10:32-34) as it occurs in the parable at the hands of the societal leaders who reject this authority. In the nexus between Christology and discipleship in terms of kinship, the son represents the interests of the father in seeking what is due from the tenants. It results in his death for the sake of the vineyard and for the sake of the household estate and the extended kinship network.

Jesus concludes the parable with the consequences for the tenants supported by another reference to the Hebrew Bible. Jesus says the vineyard owner will destroy the tenants and give the vineyard to others (12:9). Jesus has been establishing the empire of God throughout Galilee and now in Jerusalem by calling a core kinship group of disciples and providing hospitality, teaching, and healing to an extended kinship network. This extended kinship network will be the heirs of the vineyard/empire, those whom Jesus has designated as his family (3:31-35) and to whom he promises kinship, homes, and farms because they have followed him (10:29-30).[134] This time Jesus quotes Ps 118:22-23, further utilizing his authority of scripture

132. Marcus, *Mark 8-16*, 811.

133. The reference to John the Baptist is clear because John came before Jesus (1:4-8) and was killed by the same leaders (Herodians) who seek Jesus' life. Moreover, the language for the beating, being struck on the head (κεφαλιοῦν), is akin to John's actual execution of beheading (ἀποκεφαλίζειν). See Collins, *Mark*, 546 and Tolbert, *Sowing the Gospel*, 238. A one-to-one correspondence of slaves and the descriptions of their rejection is not necessary to make the connection with John the Baptist.

134. Iverson, "Jews, Gentiles," 305-35, has claimed that the "others" referenced in the parable refer to the Gentiles, thus supporting the work of several scholars who contend the same. See Jeremias, *Parables of Jesus*, 70; Carlston, *Parables of the Triple Tradition*, 189; Painter, *Mark's Gospel*, 162; Hooker, *Mark*, 276; Schweizer, *Good News according to Mark*, 241. I argue that the empire of God (vineyard) is established for those who believe in God (1:15) and do God's will (3:31-35). This group is not limited to the Gentiles, but includes all those who have entered into Jesus' extended kinship network and thus are his brothers and sisters and children, Gentile or Jew.

as God's Son to demonstrate his ultimate victory, even in death, over the Jerusalem societal leaders (and the Romans with whom they are aligned). Jesus the beloved Son of God is the cornerstone that is rejected by the builders/tenants/societal leaders, but who becomes the chief cornerstone for the building/household/empire of God. It is at this moment (12:12) that Mark explicitly indicates that the tenants are the Jerusalem societal leaders in their recognition that the parable is against them. Once more, in a display of violence that indicates their complete loss of honor, the societal leaders want to arrest him.[135] In order to save face again due to their fear of the crowds (11:32), they depart (12:12).

The nexus between Christology and discipleship in terms of kinship is evident in this parable through the explicit kinship relationships Jesus uses to tell the story as well as the continued confirmation of the outcome of the story. The Son comes to establish the empire of God, procuring a family of disciples and extended kinship network of followers. As he continues to establish his authority and provide teaching to those who receive it, he threatens the local societal leaders (both in Galilee and Jerusalem) as he questions their authority and power since they are often in line with the Roman imperial elite who ultimately rule and occupy the land. Although Jesus will be arrested and crucified, he remains the most honorable Son and agent of God as he goes toward this end knowingly and for the sake of his kinship group, modeling the way of discipleship he has taught to his core kinship group of disciples.

16. 12:13-17 SHOULD THE SON HONOR GOD OR CAESAR?

The heightened action in the Jerusalem temple continues and the Jerusalem societal leaders have not given up trying to trap Jesus by means of an honor challenge. Once more some Pharisees and Herodians come to challenge Jesus.[136] A parade of elite and allied Jerusalem leaders takes turns and ask Jesus if it is legal to pay taxes to the emperor. The Pharisees and Herodians address Jesus as "teacher" (διδάσκαλε, 12:14), much in the same way that the

---

135. Malina and Rohrbaugh provide a discussion on the relationship between honor and violence where they conclude, "In a sense, then, the over-quick resort to violence in a challenge-response situation was not only dangerous, it was frequently an unintended public admission of failure in the game of wits. The death of a challenger was sometimes a worthy response to public dishonor, but an over-quick resort to violence was an inadvertent admission that one had lost control of the challenge situation. Wits have failed and bully tactics have taken over" (*Social-Science Commentary*, 372).

136. The Pharisees and the Herodians are the ones who conspire to kill Jesus in 3:6.

disciples and those who seek a benefit from Jesus address him (4:38; 9:17; 9:38; 10:17, 20, 35; 13:1), those who are a part of his extended kinship network. They also offer a compliment that honors Jesus as a teacher, but since they are trying to trap him (12:13) and they are later identified as hypocrites (12:15), this compliment is false, but ironic as it accurately describes Jesus as a teacher of the way of God. "He takes no heed of the opinions or status of any others except God. He has engaged the powerful and the lowly equally with beneficial power ([Matt] 8:1-13), though the powerful are generally resistant."[137] The Pharisees and Herodians falsely ingratiate themselves with Jesus; they try to enter into his extended kinship network by honoring him and addressing him as their teacher in order to ask their question. Moreover, Pharisees' and Herodians' public flattery "raises the stakes by forcing Jesus to 'save face' before the crowd by opposing the payment of tribute."[138]

The Pharisees and the Herodians have already proven that they fail at proper kinship boundaries (6:14-29; 10:2-12). In the nexus between Christology and discipleship in terms of kinship, the Pharisees and the Herodians demonstrate their false kinship and discipleship with Jesus in an effort to trap him rather than to honor him as the Son of God that he is. Moreover, they use the competing kinship system of the Roman Empire to trap Jesus in their challenge. If one does not pay taxes to Rome, he or she dishonors by treason the Roman Empire, which ultimately rules over Jerusalem and the surrounding territories. If Jesus encourages the payment of taxes, then he aligns himself with Rome.[139] The Roman Empire itself was an extended kinship network with the emperor as the *pater patriae* and *paterfamilias* of the household of Rome.[140] The Roman Empire extracted honor and fidelity through taxes and tribute, "a means of subjugation, of establishing authority ... the source of Rome's wealth and a means of sustaining its people and militarily imposed peace."[141] Mark's gospel has demonstrated Jesus establishing an alternative empire (1:14-15), the empire of God that is both contestive and imitative of the Roman Empire. The primary means for establishing this empire is the recruitment of a kinship group of disciples and followers who give their honor and fidelity to God through his agent and Son, Jesus.

---

137. Carter, *Matthew and the Margins*, 438. An equivalent story of Jesus healing both the lowly and the powerful in Mark would be the healings of the synagogue leader's daughter and the woman with the flow of blood (5:21-43).

138. Herzog, "Onstage and Offstage," 53.

139. Carter, *Matthew and the Margins*, 439.

140. See chapter 2.

141. Carter, *Matthew and the Margins*, 439. See also Marcus, *Mark 8-16*, 817.

Jesus responds to the challenge by requesting a denarius, a Roman coin with a picture of the emperor, Tiberius, and the inscription (ἐπιγραφή, 12:16) of his title, which would have included "son of a god."[142] The coin itself represents the presence and power of the Roman Empire in its occupied territories. Moreover, it was propaganda that proved the legitimacy of Rome's power and authority. "It legitimated Tiberius by relating him to Augustus and asserted that the 'peace of Rome' was mediated by the gods through their high priest who was a member of the ruling family. The coin reinforced the ideological basis of Roman domination."[143] The fact that Jesus does not have a coin and requests it from the Herodians and Pharisees, who are already aligned with Rome, allows Jesus to take control of the challenge and to move the focus of the conversation to the tribute, rather than the Torah.[144]

When they identify the image as the emperor's, Jesus tells them, "Give to Caesar what is Caesar's and give to God what is God's" (12:17). At surface value, the response seems non-committal and ambiguous and his challengers are amazed (ἐξεθαύμαζον, 12:17).[145] Jesus wins the challenge because "he has succeeded in saying something that neither gives a pretext for reporting him to the Romans nor undermines his popularity by endorsing foreign rule unequivocally."[146] However, in the nexus between Christology and discipleship in terms of kinship, his response is not ambiguous. Jesus has come to establish an alternative empire, which, while it does not require tax and tribute, does require honor, faith, sacrifice, and service for those who are in the extended kinship network, much in the same way that the Roman Empire requires honor and fidelity. The Roman Empire, however, appropriated this honor and fidelity by means of taxation. All things belong to God, "the land, the earth and the fullness thereof, the heavens and the riches of the earth. What then can belong to Caesar? One thing only. The coin which he minted in his image and likeness."[147] The things of God do not equal the

---

142. Malina and Rohrbaugh, *Social-Science Commentary*, 201; Myers, *Binding the Strong Man*, 311; and Marcus, *Mark 8–16*, 824, suggest that the coin in question was a denarius produced during Tiberius' reign (14–37 CE). "On the obverse of this coin, Tiberius' laurel-crowned head is portrayed surrounded by the inscription *TI[BERIVS] CAESAR DIVI AVG[VSTI] F[ILIUS] AVGVSTVS* ('Tiberius Caesar, son of the deified Augustus, [himself] Augustus')." See also Herzog, "Onstage and Offstage," 54.

143. Herzog, "Onstage and Offstage," 54.

144. Ibid., 54.

145. Moore, *Empire and Apocalypse*, 33, notes the ambiguity both in Jesus' response in 12:17 and in its interpretation.

146. Marcus, *Mark 8–16*, 825.

147. Herzog, "Onstage and Offstage," 58.

things of Caesar. Jesus states that one may give to Caesar what belongs to him, a coin with his image and title whose intrinsic value lies only in those who "buy into" the Roman imperial system of exploitation and taxation. Jesus, as God's Son, has come to establish an alternative empire of God consisting of mothers, brothers, and sisters (3:31–35) who demonstrate their faith and honor to God in service and sacrifice for their superior kinsman, Jesus (8:35), and for each other (9:35; 10:43–44).

17. 12:18–27 KINSHIP IN THE RESURRECTION

In the third challenge presented to Jesus by the alliance of Jerusalem leaders in the Jerusalem temple, a group of Sadducees challenges Jesus on the issue of marriage in the resurrection. This encounter continues to demonstrate the heightened tensions between Jesus and his opponents.[148] The Sadducees, mentioned only here in the Gospel of Mark, were a Jewish sect and "a wealthy, elite group associated with the high priesthood."[149] Mark reveals their folly and intent to dishonor Jesus immediately when Mark states that they do not believe in the resurrection (12:18) and defines them as opponents since he has declared he will rise (8:31; 9:31; 10:33–34). Thus their question holds no validity from their perspective. Just the same, they ask Jesus, in the form of a story, about the practice of levirate marriage (Deut 25:5–10) in the resurrection. They ask whose husband will a woman be after death and in the resurrection (12:19–23) if she has seven husbands in her lifetime, six by levirate marriage. The practice of levirate marriage ensured the perpetuation of a family through patriarchy. Not only do the Sadducees question Jesus about the resurrection, but they also raise issues of kinship boundaries and relationships.

In the nexus between Christology and discipleship in terms of kinship, Jesus utilizes his authority as God's Son to demonstrate once more his superior interpretation of scripture in order to strengthen the kinship boundaries and relationships of his own kinship group of disciples and followers. The Sadducees' question tries to point out the absurdity of the resurrection by the example of these kinship relationships of marriage that seem impossible in the resurrection.[150] Jesus tells them they are wrong, states that marriage

---

148. Meier, "Debate on Resurrection," 4–5.

149. Marcus, *Mark 8–16*, 1121. Josephus confirms Mark's description of them concerning resurrection. Josephus states that the Sadducees' doctrine claims that souls (τὰς ψυχὰς) die along with bodies and that they have no concern except for that of the law (*Ant*. 18.16).

150. Collins, *Mark*, 560.

contracts and relationships are not made in the resurrection, and provides a biblical reference to support his teaching (12:24–27). Jesus' reference to Moses and the burning bush (Exod 3:1–12) and the identification of God as the God of Abraham, Isaac, and Jacob, appears to be a non sequitur. However, Jesus utilizes the kinship relationship of father-son, specifically fathers and sons who are intimately connected with God, to prove the existence of the resurrection. God promised lives and a great nation to Abraham, Isaac, and Jacob (Gen 12:2–3; 26:2–5; 28:1–4). "That promise was a type of immortality in that their offspring would continue and multiply and fill the earth. Thus the patriarchs live because their progeny live."[151] Moreover, Jesus has already promised to his kinship group of followers kinship relationships restored both now and eternal life in the age to come (10:30). Akin to his encounter with the Pharisees and the legality of divorce (10:1–12), Jesus pits Moses (Exod 3:14) against Deuteronomy 25 to demonstrate that Deuteronomy 25 does not apply in the resurrection. The covenant promise between God and fathers and sons is the proof of the resurrection and proof that God is a God of the living (12:27). Moreover, the father-son relationship between God and Jesus will also result in the defeat of death through resurrection. The resurrection will not only benefit Jesus, but in the nexus between Christology and discipleship in terms of kinship, all followers and disciples who are bound to Jesus through kinship have also been given the promise of the resurrection (8:35).

18. 12:28–34 LOVING GOD AND NEIGHBOR AS KIN

Jesus' final encounter with the Jerusalem societal leaders is not a hostile honor challenge as the others have been (11:27–33; 12:13–17; 12:18–27). Rather, a scribe, on his own,[152] approaches Jesus and asks a question regarding the commandments, and which is the greatest.[153] Jesus responds immediately with a citation of Deut 6:4–5 and Lev 19:18. Jesus states that God commands people to love God with their whole being and to love their neighbors as themselves. In the nexus between Christology and disciple-

---

151. Neyrey, *Render to God*, 18.

152. Up to this point, all the honor challenges have been presented to Jesus by a group of opponents. Kozar, "Complementary Insight," 36, notes that the scribe seems to be going outside his cultural and social group boundaries by approaching Jesus alone and without intent to trap or dishonor him.

153. Myers notes three significant aspects of this story in the Gospel of Mark. "1. It is the climax to the series of debates with Jesus in the temple; 2. it is the only place in which Jesus' interaction with a scribe is not wholly hostile; 3. it deals with a central ideological issue: the 'greatest commandment'" (Myers, *Binding the Strong Man*, 317).

ship in terms of kinship, the Son of God demonstrates the centrality of relationship (kinship) to God and to others. "His recitation of monotheistic faith functions as commitment and loyalty to his Patron [father]. It serves to bind him to that Patron [father] and to declare to scribes, Sadducees, Pharisees and chief priests his orthodoxy."[154] Moreover, in tying the two commandments together, Jesus demonstrates how kinship with God extends to kinship with neighbor.[155] For the nexus between Christology and discipleship in terms of kinship, Jesus as the Son of God extends kinship with God to his disciples and neighbors so that they may follow these biblical commandments.

The setting of this encounter remains in the temple precincts. While Jesus' statement of the commandments is not overtly antitemple, the scribe's response questions the relative value of the Jerusalem temple and its sacrificial system. The scribe acknowledges Jesus' authority publicly and honors him with the title, "Teacher," not falsely as Jesus' opponents did previously (12:14). The scribe affirms Jesus' statement and then adds that to love God and to love neighbor as oneself is more important than the entire temple system (12:33). "His implicit denigration of temple worship, made more poignant because he is listening to Jesus' teaching in the temple itself (11:27), coincides with, and develops Jesus' earlier disruption of the business of sacrifice in the temple (11:15-16) and his condemnation of the temple for failing to become God's house of prayer for all peoples (11:17)."[156] This conclusion echoes the extended kinship network Jesus has established as part of the empire of God. The extended kinship network consists of members who give their faith and fidelity to God (3:31-35) in their service and sacrifice for each other and for the sake of the gospel (8:35; 9:35; 10:43-44). Jesus' kinship network does not require the type of sacrifice that has been appropriated and exploited by the ruling elite groups who are aligned with Roman imperial leaders.[157] In the nexus between Christology and discipleship in terms of kinship, loving God and neighbor exhibits the

---

154. Neyrey, *Render to God*, 18.

155. Kozar recognizes the neighbor Jesus refers to as a part of the extended kinship network. "The neighbor may be, in fact, that fictive community which replaces family because the Markan faction is 'hated by all' (13:13) because of Jesus' name" (Kozar, "Complementary Insight," 37).

156. Heil, "Narrative Strategy," 85.

157. That is not to say that every act of sacrifice in the temple was exploited by the Roman imperial rulers and the priests aligned with them, but that there was exploitation of the temple system by the Romans and the temple elite. See Borg and Crossan, *The Last Week*, 15-17, for a summary of the exploitative nature of the Roman Empire through the Jerusalem temple.

sacrifice and service of those who are a part of the empire of God, those who are a part of the extended kinship network of Jesus, the Son of God.

For Jesus' response, the scribe commends Jesus and publicly honors him, publicly affirming his authority as the Son of God and his understanding of the law. In return Jesus extends honor to the scribe, and entrance into his kinship group,[158] by telling him he is not far from the empire of God (οὐ μακρὰν εἶ ἀπὸ τῆς βασιλείας τοῦ θεοῦ, 12:34).[159] This exchange of mutual honor and reverence in addition to Jesus' continued demonstration of authority and power over scripture and his opponents brings the series of honor challenges to an end. At Jesus' mention of the empire of God, with authority to establish it, even in the temple precincts under the competing authority of the Roman Empire, his opponents are silenced. No one tries to challenge Jesus any longer (12:34). "Indeed, it is Jesus' very last direct confrontation with his opponents until he is arrested and prosecuted by them–and in it he silences them once and for all."[160] As in Galilee (3:6), Jesus has won all the honor challenges presented to him.[161] It will still lead to crucifixion and death, but in the nexus between Christology and discipleship in terms of kinship, it will be the most honorable Son of God who willingly goes forward to that death as a demonstration of the service, sacrifice, and love of neighbor Jesus commands of his kinship group of disciples and followers.

---

158. This claim is made because the remark is an example of litotes, a figure of speech that uses understatement to intensify. Collins notes, "The understated emphasis is on the scribe's nearness to the kingdom of God, not the fact that he does not yet belong to the kingdom" (Collins, *Mark*, 577).

159. Malbon remarks that this statement echoes 1:15 where Jesus proclaims the kingdom [empire] of God is coming near. The presence of God's empire is experienced in Jesus' healing and exorcising power. "Another is Jesus' powerful teaching 'as one having authority, and not as the scribes' (1:22)–except for the present scribe who teaches in harmony with Jesus" (Malbon, *Mark's Jesus*, 228).

160. Myers, *Binding the Strong Man*, 317.

161. Myers notes: "The debating section of the Jerusalem narrative closes with a declaration of 'victory' for Jesus: Mark tells us that no one had the courage to challenge Jesus thereafter (12:34c). He has thrown the commercial special interests out of the temple and in their place assumed a role as 'teacher.' He has met challenges and foiled plots with brilliant rhetorical skill. He has gone nose to nose with the political leaders and the intellectuals, questioning the legitimacy of their respective vocations insofar as they are based upon privilege and exploitation. And in the end he has silenced his social and political opponents, and done it on their own home ground: the temple. In other words, Jesus appears to have 'bound the strong men,' and ransacked their house" (Myers, *Binding the Strong Man*, 318).

19. 12:35-37 THE SON OF DAVID

Upon defeating his opponents, the Jerusalem leaders, and their honor challenges and gaining public affirmation (12:12), Jesus continues to teach with authority in the Jerusalem temple. He offers his own honor challenge to the scribes. In the nexus between Christology and discipleship in terms of kinship, Jesus the Son of God challenges the authority and scribes' teaching that the Messiah is the Son of David and disputes this sonship as a means of instructing his own family of disciples and followers. By citing Ps 110:1, Jesus declares that the Messiah is not the Son of David because David, to whom the Psalms are attributed, himself calls him "Lord." Within this declaration Jesus implies that the Messiah is equivalent, at least in authority and power, with God (εἶπεν κύριος τῷ κυρίῳ μου· κάθου ἐκ δεξιῶν μου, 12:36). Moreover, Jesus argues "that the authority of Messiah 'preexists' the authority of David...rejecting both of the earlier messianic acclamations, 10.47f. and 11:9f."[162] In Jesus' response to the scribal teaching, "the Messiah cannot be David's son (since a son cannot be greater than a father). Rather, he must be greater than David, since David calls him Lord (thus David cannot be his father!)."[163] This statement provides a corrective to the scribal teaching that the Messiah would be a "Son of David." Furthermore, as Joel Marcus points out, the imagery in the psalm that Jesus quotes further emphasizes the Messiah as superior to David. It "implies that 'my lord' stands in a relation of near-equality with God, and the inference for Mark would seem to be that Jesus is not (just) the Son of David but (also) the Son of God."[164] Within the intersection of Christology and discipleship, Jesus instructs his disciples that the title Son of David, and perhaps any connection with David, is not an appropriate descriptor or role for Jesus, Son of God and Christ (1:1; 8:29).[165]

Jesus also indicates that it is the Holy Spirit (12:36) who directs David in the writing of the psalm. The Holy Spirit functions as the unifying life force for the divine family, compelling Jesus, and David, to do the will of

---

162. Myers, *Binding the Strong Man*, 319. Myers is arguing from a political and ideological perspective, not one of genealogy. Power and authority exhibit agency of, not identity with, God.

163. Malina and Rohrbaugh, *Social-Science Commentary*, 203.

164. Marcus, *Mark 8–16*, 850–51.

165. Kieffer, "Christology of Superiority," 66. Marcus notes the problem with the interpretation of this passage and the fact that Jesus does not explicitly refute the two times he is linked with the Davidic Messiah (10:47-48 and 11:9-10). Marcus concludes that "the Markan Jesus is not denying the Messiah's physical descent from David but the adequacy of the Davidic image to express his full identity" (Marcus, *Mark 8–16*, 847–48).

God.¹⁶⁶ At the least, this relationship with the Holy Spirit places Jesus and David on par with one another because Jesus has also been directed by the Spirit (1:12). However, Jesus also receives the Holy Spirit (1:10) which is the same moment when he is identified as God's Son which equates Jesus with God by means of an intimate kinship relationship. Furthermore, Jesus is prophesied as one who will baptize with the Holy Spirit (1:8). In the nexus between Christology and discipleship in terms of kinship, Jesus will give the Holy Spirit he has received to his family of disciples. Moreover, Jesus indicates that it was the Holy Spirit who directed David to write the psalm that indicates that the Messiah is equivalent in authority and power to God and therefore cannot be the Son of David.¹⁶⁷ This reference to the Spirit further emphasizes the corrective to the scribal teaching that the Messiah is the Son of David since Jesus is the Messiah and he is the Son of God, but he is not the Son of David.

Once more, Jesus has garnered a large following (πολὺς ὄχλος, 12:37) as he had in and around Galilee (3:7; 4:1; 5:21, 24; 6:34; 8:1; 9:14) and on his way to Jerusalem (10:46). Jesus' wit, wisdom, and authority as God's Son impress the crowd (12:37). In the nexus between Christology and discipleship in terms of kinship, this crowd enters into Jesus' extended kinship network since they recognize and honor his teaching as authoritative. This is the same crowd that Jesus' opponents, the Jerusalem societal leaders fear (11:18; 11:32; 12:12), further emphasizing the strength of the (kinship) relationship between Jesus and the crowd. For now, the crowd has no relationship with the Jerusalem societal leaders since their honor and allegiance is pointed toward Jesus. If the Jerusalem societal leaders arrested Jesus, they could incite a riot (14:2), or some sort of agitation, when the crowd would try to defend their superior kinsman, Jesus.¹⁶⁸

---

166. See discussion on the Holy Spirit in chapter 3. See also Peppard, *Son of God in Roman World*, 114.

167. Although he argues for a Davidic messianic interpretation of Jesus based upon Mark's use of Pss 2, 118, 110, and 22 throughout the gospel, Watts does acknowledge, "More than the Melchizedekian David priest-king who is responsible for the Lord's house [Ps 110:4], Jesus looks remarkably like David's Lord and thus the very Lord of the house" (Watts, "Lord's House," 320). This supports the argument that Jesus *is not* a Davidic Messiah, but rather superior to the Davidic Messiah as the Son of God.

168. Collins, *Mark*, 532; Myers, *Binding the Strong Man*, 303.

20. 12:38-44 THE SON DISHONORS THE SCRIBES AND HONORS A WIDOW

Jesus further criticizes and challenges the scribes in the latter part of his teaching in this satellite. He accuses them of only seeking honor and acquiring it by any means possible, even by defrauding vulnerable widows. Honor was the most valuable possession in ancient Mediterranean societies.[169] In Jesus' accusation, he implies that the scribes demonstrated their honorable status by their dress, their social interactions, and where they were seated (in places of honor) at social gatherings (12:38-39). He suggests that they will receive greater judgment (περισσότερον κρίμα, 12:40) rather than honor for their actions, especially for their treatment of others. In the nexus between Christology and discipleship in terms of kinship, Jesus, the most honored Son of God, instructs his family of disciples and extended kinship network in the form of the crowd by a negative example. The scribes demonstrate the inappropriate pursuit for honor which results in the exploitation of those more vulnerable. Rather, as Jesus has most recently taught (12:27-33), honor and obedience to the law is derived through service and sacrifice of oneself for the sake of another. Just as Jesus, the Son of God, provides for and cares for all those who seek healing and instruction, so to does he expect his family of disciples and followers to love their neighbors as themselves (12:31). Not only do the scribes require correction in their teaching, but their ethics, including their kinship boundaries in recognizing their neighbors as those whom they should love and with whom they should be in relationship, prove that they are far removed from the empire of God (12:34). In the nexus between Christology and discipleship in terms of kinship, Jesus, the most honorable Son provides the corrective teaching through his indirect reference that he is the Messiah and Son of God who teaches that honor is derived from service and sacrifice among his kinship group of followers.[170]

As soon as Jesus finishes challenging and discrediting the scribes and their dishonorable behavior, he sits down opposite the treasury (γαζοφυλακίου) and observes people placing their offerings (12:41).[171] In his

169. See discussion on honor in chapter 2.

170. Malina and Rohrbaugh further conclude, "Having bested his opponents in the long series of honor challenges (11:27–12:34) and then publicly insulting them in this fashion, the Markan Jesus has demonstrated his honor in the highest degree" (*Social-Science Commentary*, 203).

171. There has been some dispute as to the interpretation of γαζοφυλακίου. Marcus notes that it "would normally refer to the treasury storerooms, which lay behind the walls of the inner court and therefore were not accessible to laypeople (see, e.g., 1 Macc 14:49; 2 Macc 3:6; Josephus, *War* 5.200; 6.282; *Ant*. 19.294). Because of this difficulty

act of sitting, Jesus as God's Son places himself in a position of authority in the temple evaluating its processes (11:15–17) and continues his role as a teacher, echoing his teaching with authority, not as the scribes in the synagogue in Capernaum (1:22).[172] After he observes several wealthy people giving large amounts of money, he notices a widow who gives two *lepta*, a *quadrans*, the smallest coins in circulation.[173] At this moment, Jesus calls his disciples and instructs them by using the widow as an example of discipleship. It could be argued that Jesus identifies her as a victim of the scribes' exploitative activity and of the temple's exploitation by requiring offerings even from the poor and destitute.[174] In a patriarchal society, women were defined and held their social place by the men to whom they were related. A woman whose husband had died and was unable either to return to her father's family or had no son to support her would be socially destitute and vulnerable.[175] The poor widow, as Jesus defines her, is the exact opposite of the scribes whom Jesus just criticized (12:38–40). Without a kin group to provide for her, the woman would not be treated with respect, she would have no place of honor, and she would have no means to exploit anyone else. Within the intersection of Christology and discipleship in terms of kinship, however, Jesus provides her with a place in his kinship group by lamenting the exploitation she experiences.

It is also possible that Jesus is honoring the widow as exemplary in her behavior; she is the exact opposite of the scribes in her humility and generosity. Even as a victim of the scribes' exploitation and the temple's corrupt practices, the woman demonstrates great faith in giving her whole life to the temple treasury. Faith has been a central component to discipleship and kinship with Jesus (1:15; 2:5; 5:34; 9:24). By honoring her and appointing her an example of discipleship, Jesus as God's Son provides her a place of honor and a place in his extended kinship group, restoring to her what she has lost in her widowhood. In the nexus between Christology and discipleship

---

exegetes usually interpret our verse as a reference to one of the thirteen trumpet-shaped offering boxes that stood in the Women's Court, six of which were designated for freewill offerings (Marcus, *Mark 8-16*, 857–58).

172. Malbon notes, "Sitting was the authoritative position of the rabbis while teaching. Jesus is sitting in the boat on the sea (4:1) as he speaks to the crowd in parables in chap. 4, an extended teaching discourse with interesting parallels to chap. 13, where Jesus is sitting on the Mount of Olives (13:3) as he speaks to four of the disciples about the eschaton" (Malbon, "Poor Widow in Mark," 600).

173. Marcus, *Mark 8-16*, 858.

174. Malina and Rohrbaugh, *Social-Science Commentary*, 204; Myers, *Binding the Strong Man*, 321–22. Wright, "Widow's Mites," 256–65; Sugirtharajah, "Widow's Mites Revalued," 42–43.

175. Malina and Rohrbaugh, *Social-Science Commentary*, 204.

in terms of kinship, Jesus the Son honors the widow in her action since she displays the behavior that he expects from his family of disciples. Jesus notes that many gave out of their abundance, but the widow, a woman without a kinship group to support her, gives her whole life (ὅλον τὸν βίον αὐτῆς) in those two insignificant coins.[176]

Jesus the Son of God and teacher to his kinship group of followers on the way of the discipleship once more utilizes his authority within the temple precincts to offer instruction to his family. He calls the disciples to him (προσκαλεσάμενος τοὺς μαθητὰς αὐτοῦ, 12:43) in the same way that he has called his disciples and followers to offer instruction on discipleship (8:34; 9:35; 10:42).[177] Moreover, as Malbon observes, each of these instances of calling and instruction on discipleship is in terms of self-giving. Jesus calls his disciples to renounce him or herself to take up the cross and follow (8:34), to be last and servant of all (9:35), and to be slave of all (10:44). Moreover, Jesus upholds this instruction in his conversation with the scribe with the greatest commandment which is to love God with one's whole heart, soul, mind, and strength and to love one's neighbor as oneself (12:30-31). Furthermore, Jesus prefaces his teaching with "Amen, I tell you . . . " (12:43) indicating the significance of this teaching and that he offers "a solemn proclamation about the kingdom–its coming now and in the future, its Messiah, and the demands and rewards that fall to the followers of such a Messiah of such a kingdom."[178] In the nexus between Christology and discipleship in terms of kinship, the widow gives her whole life as will the Son of God (10:45). Moreover, the family of disciples may be required to give their lives as well. At the end of Jesus' time in the temple, the example of the widow who gives her whole life as an offering (for her neighbor) summarizes his teaching and demonstrates to the family of disciples the requirement of service and sacrifice that is characteristic of the kinship group of the Son of God.

---

176. Malbon, "The Poor Widow," 589n1, argues that this is an acceptable translation, in addition to "her whole living," based on her interpretation of the story that understands Jesus' teaching on discipleship and the expectation that disciples are required to give their lives just as Jesus will give his life in Mark 14–15.

177. Collins, *Mark*, 589; Malbon, "The Poor Widow," 600.

178. Malbon, "The Poor Widow," 601. Jesus has prefaced other teaching on discipleship with the "Amen" formula including 3:28; 8:12; 9:1, 41; 10:15; 10:29; and 11:23.

21. 13:1-37 THE SON INSTRUCTS THE DISCIPLES ON THE TEMPLE'S DESTRUCTION

As Jesus and the disciples depart from the Jerusalem temple, one of his disciples admires the temple buildings and foundation, refurbished by Herod the Great and his building campaign. Jesus responds to the disciple with a word of prophecy that none of the stones will be left standing and it will all be destroyed (13:2). Once more Jesus demonstrates his authority as the Son of God by offering a prophecy to his family of disciples about the temple. In the nexus between Christology and discipleship, the Son of God gives certain knowledge only to his disciples, extending his intimate relationship with God to them. Not only has the temple been corrupted by the Jerusalem societal leaders as allies of the Roman Empire, but Jesus now instructs the disciples about its destruction.

As in the early days of his ministry in Galilee (1:29; 5:37), it is the initial band of brothers who speak with Jesus about his statement regarding the temple's destruction. In an extended discourse akin to his teaching in parables in 4:1-34, Jesus gives the four brothers a private explanation on the destruction of the temple and Jerusalem. Primarily, their discipleship with Jesus remains central. Jesus warns about many who will purport to be him and try to lead them astray (13:6). These false leaders will identify themselves in the same way that Jesus identified himself to the disciples while walking on the sea of Galilee (ἐγώ εἰμι, 6:50), implying that they are the ones who have an intimate relationship with God and can invoke God's name. Unlike those who were casting out demons and doing the work of Jesus in his name (9:38-40), these false leaders seek to lead the disciples astray (πλανήσουσιν, 13:6).

In addition to false leaders, the disciples will face internal threats as well as a sign of the coming destruction. As much as Jesus the Son has extended kinship with his disciples and established an extended kinship group as part of the empire of God, these kinship relationships will be threatened. Just as Jesus has predicted his own arrest and death (8:31; 9:31; 10:33-34), he now predicts that the disciples will face similar consequences because of their discipleship in the nexus between Christology and discipleship in terms of kinship. Not only will the societal and political leadership arrest, beat, and try the disciples because of Jesus and their proclamation of God's empire (13:9-11), but close kinship relationships, brothers, father and child, children and parents, will be destroyed because of their discipleship with Jesus. "The contextualization of this possible persecution within the paradigm of Jesus' life gives the disciples' suffering meaning. Just as Jesus' suffering and death paradoxically won the mythological and eschatological battle over evil, so through suffering and death will the disciples participate in this reality."[179]

In a further extension of kinship from Jesus to the disciples, also illuminating the nexus between Christology and discipleship, Jesus extends the power of the Holy Spirit to the disciples (13:11). Just as the Spirit functioned as the unifying life force of the family of God and Jesus at Jesus' baptism and inauguration of his ministry (1:9-11), and just as John the Baptist prophesied that Jesus would baptize with the Holy Spirit (1:8), now that life force is extended to the family of disciples.[180] Jesus assures them that when they are on trial they do not need to worry about what they say. By its very nature as the unifying life force, the Holy Spirit will speak for them. Even with the destruction of kinship relationships and under these dire circumstances, Jesus promises salvation to those who endure (13:13). Part of discipleship and membership in the kinship group of the Son of God requires suffering (8:34-35).

The Son of God also provides for his family of disciples a prophetic vision surrounding the destruction of the temple and Jerusalem. As Mark was composed after the destruction of Jerusalem by the Romans in 70 CE, then this vision of destruction could very well be Mark's interpretation of the events for his readers.[181] In the nexus between Christology and discipleship in terms of kinship, the Son of God prophesies for his disciples the events of the Jerusalem temple's destruction by another father-son dynasty and their empire, granting them knowledge about future events as he has given them instruction previously. The reference to the "abomination of desolation" (τὸ βδέλυγμα τῆς ἐρημώσεως, 13:14) is language that echoes Daniel and a reference to the statue of a god that was placed on the altar in the Jerusalem temple by Antiochus IV Epiphanes, the Seleucid emperor who ruled Israel from 175 until 164 BCE (Dan 11:31; 12:11; 1 Macc 1:54).[182] This "abomination of desolation" has been reinterpreted as the statue of the Roman emperor Caligula that he attempted to place in the temple in 40 CE.[183]

---

179. Ahearne-Kroll, "'Who Are My?,'" 18-19.

180. See the discussion on the Holy Spirit in chapter 3. See also Peppard, *Son of God*, 114.

181. I argue for a post-70 date of composition as I discussed in chapter 1. There are several theories regarding the composition of chapter 13 and its purpose. See Marcus, *Mark 8-16*, 889-91, for a helpful summary of those theories.

182. Ibid., 889-90.

183. Zuntz, "Wann wurde das Evangelium?" 47-48; Taylor, "Palestinian Christianity," 121-22.

These events however did not precipitate the destruction of the Jerusalem temple. However, at the time of the temple's destruction by the Romans in 70 CE, Josephus observes Titus, under the command of his father Vepsasian, as central to the events.[184] Titus enters into the holy part of the temple, originally in an effort supposedly to stop the fire that was started and then to view its splendor.[185] Moreover, Titus, the son, enters into the Holy of Holies, literally standing where no one should stand except for the high priest on the Day of Atonement (Lev 16:32–33).[186] Jesus has most recently designated the temple as his house (11:17) and thus Jesus and God are the only legitimate father-son dynasty in association with the Jerusalem temple. The presence of Titus, as son and agent to his father, Emperor Vespasian, signifies that those who follow Jesus (and God) must flee (13:14–16).[187] Shortly after the destruction of the temple, Titus is declared imperator (αὐτοκράτορα, *Jewish War* 6.316) and offered sacrifices by his troops within the temple precincts.[188] Once more the wrong son stands where he should not because Jesus is the legitimate Son of God who maintains authority in the Jerusalem temple. It appears that Mark provides Jesus' prophecy as a retrospective on the destruction of Jerusalem and its temple, but due to the series of events of the "abomination of desolation," throughout history, the destruction is not the end in itself but a sign of the end. "The exhortation 'let the reader understand' directs the audience's attention to the yet-future and unspecified key event. It is a sign of hope (Rome's downfall is imminent) but also of the community's flight in a time of intensified hardship and suffering."[189] In the nexus between Christology and discipleship in terms of kinship, Jesus

---

184. See Brandenburger, *Markus 13*, 82 and Lührmann, *Das Markusevangelium*, 222.

185. Josephus, *War*, 6.316.

186. Collins, *Mark*, 610, argues that the reference to the "abomination of desolation" must refer to a statue because of the language of "standing" (ἑστηκότα) and that any statue erected would be of a deity. The statue in Daniel and Caligula's statue were both statues of living emperors. I would argue that the statues themselves represent the actual presence of the emperor. Because Titus, as a Roman emperor, will be divinized after his death in 81 CE and honored as one descended from a divine being, there need not be a distinction between the emperor and his effigy. See Price, *Rituals and Power*, 200.

187. Marcus, *Mark 8–16*, 890, states that this reference to flight means that the "abomination of desolation" cannot possibly refer to Titus since Titus's presence in the temple signified the end of the war. I would argue that even at the destruction of the temple, those who were nearby had the possibility to flee lest they be killed or taken as slaves by the Romans (Josephus, *War*, 6.271, 284).

188. Josephus, *War*, 6.316–21.

189. Carter, *Matthew and the Margins*, 473.

instructs the four brothers about a series of signs, one of which is the destruction of Jerusalem, but it is not the only one.

After further warning and signs about the coming tribulation, including more caution about false messiahs and false prophets (13:22) and cosmological calamities (13:24-25), Jesus provides the final sign to his family of disciples. It is one about which they have already heard. Jesus' family of disciples will witness the Son of Man coming in power and glory (13:26) just as he described to them his coming with his father's glory with the angels (8:38) after his first passion prediction and instruction on discipleship that requires self-sacrifice and the taking up of one's cross (8:34). Although Jesus goes toward certain death, he also predicts the redemption of that death in future glory because of his kinship relationship with God as God's Son. The establishment of God's empire will be complete when the Son of Man comes in glory and gathers all those whom he has called (τοὺς ἐκλεκτοὺς, 13:27), his extended kinship group of disciples, who will one day cover heaven and earth. This gathering echoes the work of God gathering God's people who have been dispersed (Deut 30:4; Isa 43:5-6; Zech 2:6), but as Joel Marcus notes, "The Markan Jesus tweaks the biblical scenario by picturing himself, rather than God, as the figure who will do this gathering,"[190] demonstrating the intimacy of the father-son relationship between Jesus and God and Jesus' absolute power and authority as God's agent. In the nexus between Christology and discipleship in terms of kinship, Jesus the Son, by supreme agency of God, will gather his called family of disciples, providing them with the same glory and redemption that he will receive.

By way of conclusion, Jesus instructs the family of disciples that no one knows when these events will take place (13:32). Although Jesus has demonstrated his intimate kinship relationship with God and surprising knowledge of people and situations throughout the gospel (2:8; 5:30, 39; 11:2-6), not even the Son knows the knowledge of the father in this instance (13:32). As Warren Carter notes, Jesus' ignorance is surprising, but it is "consistent with other declarations in apocalyptic texts that only God knows the time of the coming of the Messiah (*Pss. Sol.* 17:21) or of the end (*2 Bar* 21:8; 54:1; contrary to Daniel's updating efforts to identify the time; cf. Dan 7:25; 8;13; 9:27; 12:7, 11, 12)."[191] Moreover this warning helps "to proclaim the good news that the sufferings of the present are almost over and to warn against a pretension to eschatological knowledge too precise that it compromises the sovereignty of God."[192] Jesus is the Son and powerful agent of God, but even

---

190. Marcus, *Mark 8-16*, 909.
191. Carter, *Matthew and the Margins*, 480.
192. Marcus, *Mark 8-16*, 918.

he is limited for the sake of the gospel and the establishment of God's empire for the sake of the family of disciples. Nonetheless, Jesus requires that the disciples be aware and keep alert for these signs and events.

In this final warning to keep awake and alert, Jesus utilizes the imagery of the household in another parable (13:34). As the vineyard owner was absent in the parable (12:1), so too is the lord of the household occasionally gone. It is the work of the members of the household to remain vigilant for his return and to be ready to serve him (13:35). Jesus has predicted his own death and ultimate separation from his family of disciples, even with the promise of resurrection and a triumphant return. But, no one knows when that return will occur and so there will be a time that the family of disciples is without their superior kinsman, Jesus. In the nexus between Christology and discipleship in terms of kinship, the parable of the servants of the household to keep awake reminds the family of disciples that although they will be without Jesus, who is the presence of God for them as God's Son and agent, after his crucifixion, they must still remain faithful to him and prepare for his imminent return. These warnings are focused on the end times, about which the disciples are keen to understand (13:4), but they also prepare the disciples (and the reader) for the events of Jesus' crucifixion and death about to take place in the narrative of the gospel. Marcus concludes:

> But it is also significant that this concluding call to attention immediately precedes the final section of the Gospel, which contains the narratives of Jesus' passion (chapters 14–15) and of the discovery of the empty tomb (16:1–8). For these events of passion and resurrection are at least a partial fulfillment of the eschatological prophecies in chapter 13: in them the end has come. The elect fall asleep (14:37, 40–41) and go astray (14:50–52, 66–72), the sun is dimmed (15:33), the Temple suffers damage that portends its destruction (15:38), and the Son of Man passes through an all-night vigil until finally, on the other side of cosmic death, he returns as the herald of new life and a new age.[193]

In the nexus between Christology and discipleship in terms of kinship, the Son's final instructions to the core kinship group of disciples by means of the four brothers requires faith and vigilance for the establishment of God's empire. Jesus foretells of ultimate victory for himself and for his disciples, but it is not without trial and tribulation, through which the disciples must wait and be alert until the end. Even in the prediction of eschatological events, discipleship will require service, sacrifice, suffering, and faith for the Son.

---

193. Ibid., 923.

22. 14:1-11 A WOMAN DOES THE WORK OF A KINSWOMAN FOR THE SON

Two days before the Passover festival, the Jerusalem societal leaders are still looking for a way to arrest and kill Jesus (14:1) as their previous attempts (11:27-33; 12:13-17, 18-27, 28-34) have all been thwarted by Jesus' ability to win every honor challenge presented to him. Instead, they resort to stealth (δόλῳ, 14:1), which will begin with the bribery of Judas at the close of this satellite (14:10-11). The Jerusalem societal leaders utilize their elite status to get what they want since they have been unable to defeat Jesus publicly.[194] In the nexus between Christology and discipleship in terms of kinship, Jesus, as the Son of God, continues to pose a threat to the Jerusalem societal leaders in his ability to teach with such authority that the crowds follow him and enter into Jesus' extended kinship group. Moreover, the content of his teaching appears to threaten their honorable status in Jerusalem as well as the Jerusalem temple whose cultic tradition and practice provides them with the authority and honor they claim to possess.

While Jesus has been visiting Jerusalem during the day, the evenings are spent in Bethany (11:11, 12, 19; 14:3). This evening, he is in the house of Simon the leper at a banquet. The language of reclining (κατακειμένου, 14:3) is indicative of a special meal or feast in a wealthy person's home.[195] Moreover, the reference to the host as a leper echoes the host of another banquet Jesus attended at the home of Levi the tax collector (2:15). Once more Jesus chooses to keep company and be at home with (ἐν τῇ οἰκίᾳ, 14:3) those who were perceived as socially dishonorable. Part of the custom of a festive meal was for servants and slaves to wash the hands and feet of the guests and to anoint them with oils. Jesus is not anointed by a servant, but rather by a woman with an entire alabaster jar of nard (14:3). Initially, his fellow banqueters respond in disgust at her profligacy and perhaps at

---

194. Malina and Rohrbaugh, *Social-Science Commentary*, 208, note that this stealth is just the beginning of the means that the Jerusalem cultural leaders will use to kill Jesus. Following their stealth, they bribe Judas (14:10-11), produce false witnesses (14:56-58), give fallacious accusations before Pilate (15:3), incite the crowd against Jesus (15:11), and finally participate in his public and shameful crucifixion (15:31-32).

195. Ibid., 209. Marcus notes, "With the exception of the outdoor scene in Mark 6:39, however, the Gospel references presume that the meal under discussion is a special feast and/or taking place in a rich person's home; common people did not have the space or the money for banqueting couches and usually ate sitting on the floor" (Marcus, *Mark 8-16*, 933). Jesus reclines with Levi the tax collector in 2:14. Also, the guests at Herod's birthday banquet in 6:22 are referred to as "those who reclined with him" (συνανακειμένοις).

her very presence at the banquet as anyone but of questionable reputation.¹⁹⁶ The other guests scold the woman and suggest that her perfume could have been sold and the profits given to the poor (14:4–5), thus clamoring for the more honorable position of doling out charity instead of doing the work of a slave in anointing a person.

In the nexus between Christology and discipleship in terms of kinship, the Son of God extends kinship to this woman, first by publicly honoring her and claiming that her work of anointing is good (καλὸν ἔργον, 14:6), and second by suggesting that the work she does, she does as Jesus' kinswoman.¹⁹⁷ Jesus reinterprets her anointing as preparing him for his burial (14:8). Jesus has already predicted his passion and death at the hands of his opponents and enemies (8:31; 9:31: 10:33–34). This story is introduced with a description of the active intent for Jesus' death by his opponents indicating that the climax of the narrative is drawing near (14:1–2). Jesus draws this woman into his kinship group by designating her as one who helps to prepare him for death (14:8). The woman who anoints Jesus anticipates the women who go to Jesus' tomb to anoint him (16:1) after his death and burial. These women are also described as witnesses to the crucifixion and as women who followed him and served him (ἠκολούθουν αὐτῷ καὶ διηκόνουν αὐτῷ, 15:41), essentially functioning as disciples and as a part of his kinship network, preparing to do the work required of families in burial customs.

Although Jesus interprets her anointing as anointing for death (14:8), the act of pouring the nard on Jesus' head is reminiscent of the anointing of priests and kings (Exod 29:7; Lev 21:10; 1 Sam 10:1; 16:6; 24:7).¹⁹⁸ "Anointing by pouring liquid on the head expresses a commission to perform a special role in God's service."¹⁹⁹ The reader understands, then, that this kinswoman anoints Jesus as the messiah, as Son and heir to God's empire, just as he was anointed by the Spirit in his baptism (1:9–11) which designated him as Son and precipitated the establishment of God's empire (1:14–15). If her anointing is in line with that of a prophet anointing priests and kings, then her act (and Jesus' interpretation) serves to reiterate the type of messiah Jesus is and the purpose of his sonship. Jesus is anointed a messiah and

---

196. Malina and Rohrbaugh, *Social-Science Commentary*, 209.

197. Burial and funeral customs were duties that belonged to the deceased's family. In Roman society, if the family could not afford it, funerary societies known as *collegia* existed to aid with funeral and banquet expenses. See Tulloch, "Women Leaders," 167–71.

198. D'Angelo, "(Re)Presentations of Women," 143, suggests that the woman functions as a prophet in the like of Samuel by anointing Jesus and that her prophetic act is extended by prophesying Jesus' death as he interprets her act.

199. Carter, *Matthew and the Margins*, 502.

emperor in order to die. In the nexus between Christology and discipleship, Jesus explicitly moves toward the enactment of the type of discipleship he requires of his followers (8:31–34). The Son of God has come to be a servant and to give his life (10:45), just as he has asked his disciples to be servants (10:43), last of all (9:35), and to lose their lives for his sake (8:35).

Not only does the woman become Jesus' kin by anointing him for burial and doing the work that would normally be done by a kinswoman at a death, but she also demonstrates the behavior expected of Jesus' disciples. Like the widow who gave her whole life (12:44) in the temple and is held up as exemplary, this woman breaks open an entire jar of costly perfume to give to Jesus in the manner of a slave. "She cannot prevent what she believes will happen, but she does what she can (14:8a), and such loving generosity with no prospect of material or even moral return (unlike giving money to the poor, 14:5) prompts Jesus to commend her action to all who hear the gospel preached 'in memory of her' (14:9)."[200] Elisabeth Schüssler Fiorenza notes that "the unnamed woman who names Jesus with a prophetic sign-action in Mark's Gospel is the paradigm for the true disciple."[201] In her act of discipleship, kinship, and anointing, the woman recognizes the definition of Jesus' sonship and what he asks of his disciples in order to follow. In the nexus between Christology and discipleship in terms of kinship, Jesus the anointed Son of God honors the woman as a disciple, as a member of his family and kinship group, and as one deserving of memorial wherever the gospel is proclaimed.

In contrast and in a breaking of the kinship boundaries Jesus has established with his disciples, Judas departs the banquet in order to betray Jesus (14:10). "The narrator reports that 'Judas Iscariot, who was one of the twelve' (14:10), hands over Jesus for money, in contrast to the unnamed woman who hands over money for Jesus."[202] Judas acts in direct opposition to the exemplary discipleship just displayed in both the poor widow in the temple and now the woman who has anointed Jesus. Instead of giving his life and all that he has (as Jesus expected of the young man, 10:21), Judas instead literally and figuratively departs from the kinship group of disciples to betray his superior kinsman to the Jerusalem societal leaders. In the nexus between Christology and discipleship in terms of kinship, Judas's betrayal represents a break in the kinship structures established between Jesus and the disciples. However, it also highlights Jesus' continued honor and power as God's Son since he has already predicted his handing over ($\pi\alpha\rho\alpha\delta\acute{\iota}\delta o\tau\alpha\iota$,

---

200. Tolbert, *Sowing the Gospel*, 274.
201. Schüssler Fiorenza, *In Memory of Her*, xliv.
202. Malbon, *Mark's Jesus*, 226.

9:31; 10:33), which is precipitated by Judas's betrayal (παραδοῖ, 14:10). Judas's action serves to move the narrative closer to the climax of Jesus' death and crucifixion, the service and gift of life that Jesus gives to his family of disciples just as he expects their service and self-sacrifice as part of membership in his kinship network.

23. 14:12–25 THE SON GIVES HIS BODY AND BLOOD FOR HIS FAMILY

Following the banquet at Simon the leper's, and after Judas's betrayal, Jesus and the disciples prepare for and observe the Passover feast in Jerusalem. Jesus knows the location of the meal ahead of time and instructs the disciples to follow a set of directions so that they may arrive and prepare the meal (14:13–16). Once more, Jesus demonstrates his honor and authority as God's Son in his knowledge of events before they occur.[203] Jesus and the disciples arrive in the evening to participate in the Passover meal, again in the context of a household (14:14). In the nexus between Christology and discipleship in terms of kinship, Jesus the Son acts as host and *paterfamilias* for his core kinship group of disciples. Jesus has provided the location and will also provide the meal for his disciples. The celebration of Passover and the Passover meal were both kinship events. Exodus 12 instructs each household will share a meal of one lamb to observe the Passover. K. C. Hanson and Douglas Oakman characterize the Passover festival as a communion sacrifice and the least holy "because they were partaken of substantially by lay offerers in familial solidarity or communion with God and one another."[204] The meal shared between Jesus and his disciples suggests that they are a family and cohesive kinship group.[205] In the nexus of Christology and discipleship in terms of kinship, Jesus the Son extends hospitality to and participates in kinship with his disciples in the form of a meal, just as he has done in his ministry in Galilee (6:30–44; 8:1–10).

Before they share in the meal, however, Jesus demonstrates his honor and authority as God's Son by once more predicting what will happen to

203. Marcus, *Mark 8–16*, 946–48, indicates that this scene parallels the triumphant entry (11:1–6) and Jesus' instructions to the disciples regarding the colt, which further emphasizes Jesus' sovereignty and his knowledge of events before they occur. Jesus' sovereignty and knowledge of events before they occur serve to maintain Jesus' identity and role as God's Son in light of the events of his betrayal, arrest, and crucifixion. Everything will occur exactly as Jesus had told the disciples it would (14:16).

204. Hanson and Oakman, *Palestine*, 136.

205. Hellerman, *Ancient Church as Family*, 67; Malina and Rohrbaugh, *Social-Science Commentary*, 211.

him. Jesus foretells his betrayal by one in his core kinship group of disciples (14:18). In a continued illustration of Judas's break in the kinship structures Jesus has established, the Son further divides his work and the work of his betrayer in terms of honor. Jesus, identifying himself in kinship terms as the Son of Man, states that he has already predicted and continues to go toward his death willingly and knowingly (14:21). As agent of, and intimately bound with, humanity as the Son of Man, Jesus demonstrates his honor as God's Son and as the *paterfamilias* of the disciples. He has maintained the kinship structures he has established with the disciples, primarily those of service and the willingness to lose one's life for the sake of the gospel.

Jesus' betrayer, on the other hand has not observed those kinship structures and has acted dishonorably in his betrayal. Jesus condemns Judas and his action suggesting that it would have been better he had never been born (14:21). Jesus' statement about Judas "is an indication of a total unconcern for reputation, a total lack of honor, of being situated off the scale of human beings."[206] Judas maintains a total lack of honor for kinship and discipleship with Jesus and acts in complete opposition to Jesus' actions. In an effort to deny this allegation and to maintain faith and allegiance toward Jesus as the superior kinsman, the disciples deny that they would betray him (14:19). Jesus reassures them that one of them will indeed betray him and break the kinship bonds he has established (14:20).

During the meal, as the host and *paterfamilias*, Jesus performs the table blessing and distribution of the meal with the bread and the wine.[207] In taking the bread, blessing it, breaking it, and giving it to his family of disciples, Jesus designates the bread as his own body (τὸ σῶμά, 14:22). Jesus also takes a cup of wine, gives thanks (εὐχαριστήσας, 14:23), and gives it to his disciples to drink. He designates it as his blood of the covenant poured out for many (14:24). Not only does Jesus provide food and nourishment for his family of disciples in the meal, but he also interprets the food and nourishment as his very body and blood.[208] The designation of the cup as Jesus' blood combined with the covenant language evokes Exod 24:8 where Moses indicates the sacrificial blood splashed onto the Israelites seals the covenant between God and God's people.[209] Jesus gives the family of disciples his very self and seals the promise with his blood, sacrificial blood that binds him to his family of disciples. Just as Jesus has provided benefactions in the form

---

206. Malina and Rohrbaugh, *Social-Science Commentary*, 211.

207. Jeremias, *Eucharistic Words of Jesus*, 232.

208. This designation of the bread and wine as body and blood is present in the synoptic gospels and 1 Cor (Matt 26:26–29; Luke 22:15–20; 1 Cor 11:23–25).

209. Marcus, *Mark 8–16*, 966; Carter, *Matthew and the Margins*, 506.

of exorcism, healing, teaching, and hospitality, in his interpretation of the bread and the wine, Jesus provides one final benefaction for his family of disciples in the form of his body. Even with the knowledge of his betrayal by one close to him, Jesus demonstrates his honor and worth as God's Son by providing a benefaction for his disciples that puts him at risk and causes him to lose his life.[210] Unlike the household of Rome, unlike the household of the corrupt temple, where people are exploited and subjugated by rulers and leaders, Jesus, as host and *paterfamilias*, gives himself for the sake of his family, giving his body and blood even in the light of betrayal and desertion.

In one last prophetic act during the meal, Jesus foretells his death again by indicating that he will never drink wine until he drinks it in the empire of God (14:25). Although Jesus goes towards a shameful death, he also goes toward ultimate triumph as he has predicted (13:26-27). In the nexus between Christology and discipleship in terms of kinship, Jesus swears an oath to his family of disciples, extending kinship in the form of a promise and word of honor that this ultimate victory will occur.[211] "Against all hope, then, and according to divine necessity, the Messiah must suffer and die; but against all expectation, this demise will signal not defeat but victory."[212] As God's son, Jesus will be victorious in the establishment of God's empire for his family of disciples and extended kinship network of followers in imitation and contest to the present imperial establishment of Rome. Although Jesus has prophesied his betrayal and death, and goes toward it knowingly, he also predicts his ultimate victory and that of the empire of God. Once more in the nexus between Christology and discipleship in terms of kinship, the family meal and designations of bread and cup as body and blood bind Jesus to his disciples in ultimate victory in the empire he has established as agent and Son of God, even as he goes forward to desertion and death.

24. 14:26-31 THE SON PREDICTS PETER'S DENIAL OF AFFILIATION

After the meal and the hymn, Jesus and the core kinship group of disciples go outside of Jerusalem to the Mount of Olives (14:26). Jesus predicts the desertion of the disciples in the same place where he predicted the demise of the Jerusalem temple (13:3). Jesus instructs his disciples that they will

---

210. DeSilva notes, "It was considered the height of generosity to give one's life for the good of another (hence the extreme honor showed to those who died in battle to protect a city)" (DeSilva, *Honor*, 136).

211. Malina and Rohrbaugh, *Social-Science Commentary*, 212.

212. Marcus, *Mark 8-16*, 968.

all desert him citing Zech 13:7–9. The language of the shepherd and the sheep evokes imagery from the meal Jesus provided for the five thousand in Galilee (6:34). There the crowds were like sheep without a shepherd and required a leader and a kinsman to provide for them. Here, following the predictions of Jesus' betrayal, Jesus indicates that the kinship group will be destroyed, temporarily. Jesus will be removed as the head of the household and the family of disciples will not maintain its kinship bonds (14:27), so much so that Peter will deny even knowing Jesus (14:30). However, Jesus also predicts his resurrection and return to Galilee (14:28). Although the covenant is disrupted by the kinship group of disciples and those who will arrest and kill Jesus, his sacrifice maintains the covenant. Jesus will be deserted and killed, but he will also be raised as God's Son and the kinship group will be reconciled in his resurrection.[213] Once more Jesus demonstrates that he knows everything that is going to happen to him. Even with the knowledge of a shameful death, Jesus goes toward it willingly as the most honorable Son for the sake of his family of disciples.

In an effort to maintain faith and fidelity toward Jesus and to demonstrate his own honor, especially as the first-called member of Jesus' band of brothers (1:16–17), Peter speaks up and declares that he will not desert Jesus (14:29) and if he has to, he will die with Jesus (14:31). As the superior kinsman, Jesus gives a precise prediction of Peter's betrayal which will entail three denials before the rooster crows twice (14:30). The prediction is prefaced with the language, "Amen, I tell you," indicative of Jesus' sincerity and authority in his speech (3:28; 8:28; 9:1; 9:41; 10:15, 29; 11:23; 12:43; 13:30; 14:9, 18, 25). In an ironic turn due to Peter's imminent denial, his "vehement protest of his loyalty (14:31) exegetes perfectly the meaning of Jesus' call to discipleship (8:34): to stand with Jesus indeed would require that he deny himself, and consequently share Jesus' death."[214] Not only does Peter deny his desertion and promise to die with Jesus, but the entire core kinship group of disciples says the same thing (14:31). In the nexus between Christology and discipleship in terms of kinship, Peter and the disciples claim to adhere to the requirement of discipleship and kinship with Jesus. Just as Peter had a partial view of Jesus' identity as God's Son in 8:29, so now he has only a partial understanding of discipleship and Jesus' death.[215] Jesus remains faithful and maintains the kinship structures by continuing toward his crucifixion and speaking to the ultimate victory in his resurrection that

---

213. Kinship renewal in the resurrection echoes 2 Macc 7:29. See the discussion above.

214. Myers, *Binding the Strong Man*, 365.

215. See discussion on Peter's confession in chapter 3. See also Perkins, *Peter*, 64.

will be for both him and the disciples. Jesus, as the superior kinsman, goes before the disciples both in suffering and in death, but also in resurrection and in victory ("I will go before you to Galilee," 14:28). Even though the kinship group of disciples will be unable to remain faithful to Jesus, Jesus as the Son of God has the power and authority to renew the kinship group in his resurrected return to Galilee, once more extending kinship to the disciples in the nexus between Christology and discipleship.²¹⁶

25. 14:32–52 KINSHIP TIES UNRAVEL: THE SON IS BETRAYED INTO HUMAN HANDS

Jesus and the core kinship group of disciples enter the Garden of Gethsemane so that Jesus might pray (14:32). In the nexus between Christology and discipleship in terms of kinship, the Son extends kinship to his initial band of brothers, Peter, James, and John when he asks them to accompany him in his time of distress.²¹⁷ Jesus reveals to his band of brothers that he is grieving, even to death (14:34). He evokes the lament psalms (Pss 42:5, 11; 43:5) which look for God's deliverance from oppressive enemies.²¹⁸ Although Jesus knowingly goes toward his arrest, suffering, and death, he does not do it calmly. Just as Jesus called the band of brothers initially (1:16–20), brought them to a healing within a household (5:37), had them as witnesses to his transfiguration (9:2–8), so now he asks them to accompany him (14:33–34). Each previous event emphasized Jesus' identity and role as God's Son, bringing the band of brothers into kinship with God through Jesus' kinship with God. It is not clear if Peter, James, and John heard Jesus' prayer, Mark only indicates that they were sleeping when he returned to them (14:37). However, in the prayer, Jesus prays to God as his father (ἀββᾶ ὁ πατήρ, 14:36), once more demonstrating the kinship relationship that

---

216. Hurtado, *Mark*, 242.

217. One of the requirements of discipleship when Jesus called the twelve was to accompany him, literally "be with him" (ὦσιν μετ' αὐτοῦ, 3:14) (Kelber, "Mark 14.32–42," 176), notes that the focus within the pericope is on both Jesus and the disciples since "they went" (ἔρχονται) into Gethsemane which helps to emphasize the intersection of Christology and discipleship in Mark. He concludes that as Jesus realizes and accepts the necessity of his death (Christology), the disciples also have a chance to embrace the passion and follow Jesus (discipleship theology). However, the disciples fail and thus "lose everything" (184). Kelber goes on to conclude that the disciples' failure stems from a conflict within the Markan community. Kelber fails to recognize the continued faithfulness of Jesus that sustains discipleship, as well as those other followers who exhibit discipleship even though they are not the twelve. He does mention the women who witness the crucifixion and resurrection but claims that they have failed also.

218. Carter, *Matthew and the Margins*, 510.

exists between Jesus and God and the source of kinship between Jesus and the disciples. Jesus establishes a family of disciples because he is the Son of God establishing God's empire. In the disciples' vigil and accompaniment, the kinship relationship between Jesus and God is extended to the disciples because the disciples are with Jesus (14:33).

Although Jesus often functions as the *paterfamilias* among his disciples and in his ministry, Jesus' primary identity is that of *God's* Son (1:1; 1:9–11).[219] Even though Jesus' identity is found in his sonship, God as "father" directly does not occur very often in the Gospel of Mark (8:38; 11:25; 13:32; 14:36). Of the four occurrences of God as "father," three of them refer specifically to God as Jesus' father. The other occurrence refers to God as father in the context of prayer and the forgiveness of sins (11:25). In the context of this prayer of Jesus to his father, it becomes apparent that the kinship relationship between Jesus and God has been the defining marker of Jesus' ministry. Up to this point, Jesus has been compelled by his designation as God's Son to establish God's empire, to call disciples, to perform exorcisms, to preach, and to prophesy and to endure his suffering and death. It also becomes clear that although Jesus would rather not endure the suffering and death he is about to endure, he acts as an honorable Son toward his father and respects the will of his father (14:35–36). Moreover, Jesus as God's Son remains faithful to his kinship relationship with God in acknowledging God's will and going forward toward his crucifixion. In the nexus between Christology and discipleship in terms of kinship, Jesus demonstrates the faithfulness in his kinship relationship with God that he requires of his disciples in their kinship relationship with him, doing "the will of God" (3:35).

The disciples fail at accompanying Jesus in his vigil three times,[220] further illustrating the breaking down of the kinship ties between Jesus and the disciples as he approaches his death, but also highlighting Jesus' continued faithfulness toward the disciples and the maintenance of the kinship group. At one point, Jesus warns Peter that he not enter into a time of temptation and testing, but Jesus acknowledges that even with the spirit willing, the flesh is weak (14:38). This evokes Jesus' own time of testing driven by a different spirit after he was identified as God's Son at his baptism (1:12–13).[221]

---

219. For Jesus as *paterfamilias* see chapter 2.

220. Mark utilizes series of three for emphasis on their subject matter. Here Mark emphasizes the fact that disciples fail at their vigil keeping and subsequently fail in their discipleship, illustrating that the disciples behave exactly the way Jesus predicted they would. See chapter 2 for a discussion on the rhetorical device of series of three in Mark.

221. Marcus, *Mark 8–16*, 980, suggests that although the human spirit referred to in 14:38 is not the same as the Holy Spirit, the line of demarcation between the two grows thin through Mark, especially with the reference to the Holy Spirit speaking for

Just as Jesus must remain faithful to God's purposes for the establishment of God's empire, so too Jesus exhorts the family of disciples to maintain their faithfulness to him and to God, even when they will fail.

After the present failure of the disciples' to maintain their vigil, Jesus once more predicts what will happen to him (14:41). While the predicted event occurs immediately after the prediction, Jesus identifies himself in kinship terms as the Son of Man and indicates that he is about to be betrayed (14:41). Although Jesus is about to be arrested and to undergo suffering and death, as God's most honorable Son, Jesus knows about the events before they occur and he willingly accepts them (8:31; 9:31; 10:33-34). Jesus as Son of God and Son of Man, intimately bound with God and intimately bound with human beings, is betrayed by one member of his core kinship group of disciples (14:43-45). In the nexus between Christology and discipleship in terms of kinship, it is the kinship relationship between Jesus and Judas that allows for the betrayal. Judas identifies Jesus as his teacher and kissed him, signs that he has a close relationship with Jesus.

Judas arrives with a crowd holding clubs and swords who have been sent by the Jerusalem leaders (14:43). Judas no longer maintains his kinship bonds with Jesus; rather he has now aligned himself with the Jerusalem societal leaders. Not only are the kinship ties broken, but Judas and the crowd come with symbols of violence, further evidence of their misunderstanding and incomprehension of Jesus, his identity, and his role and purpose as God's Son. In contrast to Jesus and his call to suffering and service, "the elite typically resorts to violence to impose its will, assert control, and secure its resources."[222] Moreover, the Jerusalem elite use intermediaries to arrest Jesus and demonstrate no deference or honor toward Jesus as the Son of God.

After they have laid hands on him and arrested him (14:46),[223] one of the disciples draws a sword and cuts off the ear of a slave of the high priest (14:47). Even in the midst of his arrest, Jesus acts as the most honorable Son and demonstrates his honor by pointing out the folly of his opponents. He suggests they had several opportunities to arrest him while he was teaching in the temple, yet they did not. Instead, they resort to stealth (14:1) to arrest Jesus at night away from the city and treat him as a bandit suggesting that he

---

the disciples in 13:11. Even in an echo, the Holy Spirit remains the unifying life force of the family of God.

222. Carter, *Matthew and the Margins*, 513. See Josephus, *Ant.* 20.181, 206-207.

223. Carter, *Matthew and the Margins*, 513. Carter notes the differences between the hands laid on Jesus in arrest by his opponents and enemies (14:46) and how Jesus laid hands on those who required healing (1:31, 41; 5:41; 6:5; 7:33; 8:23; 9:27) and blessing (10:16).

was hiding out and would rise up against them in violence.²²⁴ Furthermore, the crowd's description and actions identify Jesus as a bandit (ὡς ἐπὶ λῃστὴν, 14:48), demonstrating that they do not discern or accept his identity as a Son, thereby rejecting his kinship with God. With the exception of the one who cut of the slave's ear, Jesus and his disciples do not react in violence against the crowd from the chief priests, scribes, and elders. Rather, Jesus maintains his honorable status and aligns himself with scripture, further indicating his honor and authority as God's Son. In the nexus between Christology and discipleship in terms of kinship, the Son predicts for his family of disciples everything that has started to happen to him leading up to his death. Moreover, the core kinship group of disciples behave exactly as Jesus predicted they would (14:27) and desert him (14:50). In order to emphasize the complete desertion of Jesus by his followers, Mark includes a reference to a young man who followed Jesus (συνκολούθει, 14:51). He was almost arrested along with Jesus, but he managed to run away by abandoning his linen cloth. Marcus notes that the young man gives up everything he has to flee away from Jesus, as opposed to the disciples who have left everything (10:28) and Bartimaeus who abandons his garment to follow Jesus (10:50).²²⁵ The disciples do not maintain their faithfulness and appear to erode the kinship relationships Jesus has established. In the nexus between Christology and discipleship in terms of kinship, however, Jesus maintains faithfulness and goes toward his death willingly for the sake of God's empire and his family of disciples. He maintains his status as the most honorable Son because he has the knowledge of all that will happen to him and fulfills the predictions. Jesus has been handed over and now everyone has abandoned him, just as he said.

26. 14:53-65 JESUS CONFESSES HIS IDENTITY IN KINSHIP TERMS AS THE SON OF THE BLESSED ONE

Jesus is brought before the Jerusalem societal leaders, his opponents, where they will bring charges against him (14:55). In the nexus between Christology and discipleship in terms of kinship, Jesus does not go by himself, but he is followed by one of his disciples, Peter (14:54). Even though Peter maintains his distance, betrayed Jesus, and ran away (14:50), the kinship ties the Son has established with his disciples have not been completely severed. Ultimately, this satellite is sandwiched by the scene in the courtyard with Peter (14:54, 66-72), who will deny Jesus three times. Several witnesses are

224. Malina and Rohrbaugh, *Social-Science Commentary*, 213-14.
225. Marcus, *Mark 8-16*, 1000.

brought forward to provide testimony against Jesus, but in continued illustration of Jesus' honor as God's Son, none of the testimony is deemed valid because it was false or did not agree with other testimony (14:56). Although there is no valid testimony, the high priest still demands Jesus to answer for himself. Jesus says nothing until he is asked about his identity. The high priest asks Jesus if he is "the Christ, the Son of the Blessed One" (ὁ χριστὸς ὁ υἱὸς τοῦ εὐλογητοῦ, 14:61) using kinship language that accurately expresses (i.e., from God's perspective) Jesus' identity. "Son of the Blessed One" is equivalent to "Son of God;" the high priest offers a circumlocution for God.[226] Mark places the first accurate identification of Jesus by a human on the lips of Jesus' primary opponent in Jerusalem.[227] Moreover, that Jesus' opponents name him as such, "even against their will, is one of the subtle signs in the Markan passion narrative that, despite Jesus' apparent subjection to their power, God is still in control and his victory march ongoing."[228]

Jesus responds to the question of the high priest with the simple answer, "I am" followed by a statement about his ultimate victory as the Son of Man seated at the right hand of God (14:62).[229] Not only has Jesus been identified in public as the Christ, the Son of God, but he augments the identification in his own response. Jesus echoes the very name of God in his statement "I am." Just as Jesus identified himself in this way to the disciples when he was walking on the sea (6:50), he now upholds the kinship relationship with God by using God's name (Exod 3:14; Deut 32:39; Isa 41:4). Moreover, Jesus further refers to himself in kinship terms as the Son of Man when he speaks of his ultimate victory. Evoking Dan 7:12–14, Jesus will receive vindication in the resurrection. The eternal establishment of God's empire, inaugurated by Jesus, predicts the end of the Roman imperial world. In the nexus between Christology and discipleship in terms of kinship, Jesus, intimately bound with God, identifies himself intimately bound to human beings. Regardless of his current state of arrest, the suffering that he is about to endure, and the abandonment of his family of disciples, Jesus

---

226. Marcus provides evidence from a synagogue inscription of 41 CE on the Black Sea that is dedicated to "the Most High God, Almighty, Blessed One." Moreover, "some manuscripts, indeed, combine the two terms (e.g., A, Y, K, Π, 1346) or follow the lead of Matt 26:63 in substituting 'God' for "the Blessed One' (e.g., ℵ, 579)" (Marcus, *Mark 8–16*, 1004).

227. Unclean spirits have already identified Jesus as the Son of God (3:11; 5:7).

228. Marcus, *Mark 8–16*, 1016.

229. Ibid., 1005. Marcus argues for the longer reading of 14:62 which includes, "You say that . . ." based on Origen and Matt 26:64. I stand by the shorter reading based on the larger narrative context of Mark and Jesus' use of "I am" in 6:50 and 13:6 and also the fact that the majority of texts (ℵ B C L W Ψ D OL Sy¹ Syᶜ Ir Heges Clem) maintain the shorter reading. See also Huizenga, "Confession of Jesus," 244–66.

remains faithful to God and to his disciples as he proceeds through death to the promised victory.

Jesus' affirmation of his identity and description of his glory at the right hand of God is interpreted as blasphemy by the high priest. Just as Jesus was accused of blasphemy by the scribes for maintaining authority to forgive sins (2:7), now he is accused of blasphemy by equating himself with God. Jesus is condemned by the Jerusalem societal leaders (14:64). In spite of his identity as the Son of God and in spite of the honor and authority that he maintains because of that identity, the societal leaders try to destroy any honor Jesus has left by publicly shaming him. This may also offer a solution as to why the disciples are never pursued for their affiliation with Jesus. If the Jerusalem societal leaders deny Jesus' kinship with God, his kinship with the disciples is of no consequence and, thus, they are no threat. Some begin to spit on him and blindfold him and tell him to prophesy (14:65). "It is the first of the public attempts to get honor satisfaction by destroying the honor status of Jesus as the story moves toward his total condemnation."[230] The nexus between Christology and discipleship in terms of kinship is evident when the Son begins to endure the same suffering that he will require of his family of disciples (8:34). The establishment of the empire of God and being faithful to the gospel will result in suffering. Even though Jesus endures public humiliation and shaming for his identity as God's Son, he remains the faithful and honorable Son of God who will receive ultimate victory at God's right hand (14:62) which he will extend to his kinship group of disciples and followers (13:27).

27. 14:66–72 PETER DENIES HIS KINSHIP AFFILIATION WITH THE SON

While Jesus is before the Jerusalem societal leaders, Peter is outside in the courtyard. Up to this point, Peter maintains his status as Jesus' disciple and kinsman by following him after he was arrested, even though he had fled (14:50). However, when a servant-girl and a bystander recognize him and claim that he was with Jesus (σὺ μετὰ τοῦ Ναζαρηνοῦ ἦσθα τοῦ Ἰησοῦ, 14:67) three times, Peter denies their claims, three times. In the nexus between Christology and discipleship in terms of kinship, the Son knows exactly how Peter will behave and has accurately predicted that Peter would deny him three times (14:30). Peter would have denied association with Jesus in an effort at self-preservation and to avoid his own arrest and public shaming. Unfortunately, Peter had claimed to Jesus that he would remain faithful

---

230. Malina and Rohrbaugh, *Social-Science Commentary*, 215.

to death (14:31), pledging an oath to Jesus.²³¹ Even as Jesus demonstrates his kinship relationship with Peter by his intimate knowledge of his behavior, that kinship relationship falls apart by Peter's denial.²³² Peter mourns the realization that Jesus was correct (14:72). He has dishonored Jesus and their kinship relationship by failing to uphold the oath that he swore to Jesus to stand by him until death (14:31) and instead cursing and swearing an oath that he does not know Jesus at all (14:71).

The nexus between Christology and discipleship in terms of kinship is evident in the descriptions given to Peter when the bystanders identify him. The servant-girl states that Peter was *with* Jesus (σὺ μετὰ τοῦ Ναζαρηνοῦ ἦσθα τοῦ Ἰησοῦ, 14:67). When Jesus appointed the disciples, one of their responsibilities was to accompany him; they were to be with him (ὦσιν μετ' αὐτοῦ, 3:14).²³³ Furthermore, Peter is identified as a Galilean (14:70). He is associated ethnically and culturally with Jesus, as a kinsman. Their ministry and large following began in the region of Galilee.

Jesus' predictions about Peter keep coming true (14:27, 30) and continue to demonstrate his honor and authority as God's Son even in light of his betrayal, arrest, and public dishonor. Bookended by Peter's denial of Jesus' identity (14:54, 66–72) is the public confirmation of Jesus' identity as God's Son. In effect, Peter's denial serves to highlight Jesus' identity as God's Son.²³⁴ The denial occurs because of and was predicted by the Son. In the nexus between Christology and discipleship in terms of kinship, these accurate predictions maintain Jesus' honor and extend hope and honor to Jesus' disciples. Moreover, alongside those predictions, Jesus also promised that he would go before the disciples back to Galilee (14:28). Even if they endure suffering and rejection, even as they flee from and deny the Son of God, his kinship group of disciples, like Jesus, will receive ultimate victory.

---

231. Malina and Rohrbaugh note that oaths function as words of honor, "to make known as clearly as possible the sincerity of an honorable person's intentions. Oaths, which are critically important in oral societies, are necessary when persons with whom the person of honor interacts find the behavior or claims of that person ambiguous or incredible" (Malina and Rohrbaugh, *Social-Science Commentary*, 207).

232. Mark emphasizes the separation between Peter and Jesus by Peter's physical movement away from Jesus and the high priest's house in each successive denial (14:68). See Marcus, *Mark 8–16*, 1023–24. In terms of Jesus' knowledge of Peter, Mark has presented Jesus with knowledge about future events that are fulfilled in the gospel narrative (8:31; 9:31; 10:32–33; 15:1–16:8) and in his perception of other people (2:8; 3:5).

233. Marcus, *Mark 8–16*, 1022.

234. Huizenga, "Confession of Jesus," 260–61.

28. 15:1-20 THE SON OF GOD BEFORE THE ROMANS

In the morning, the Jerusalem leaders bring Jesus before the Roman governor, Pilate. Apparently the chief charge against Jesus is that he has declared himself the "King of the Jews," (ὁ βασιλεὺς τῶν Ἰουδαίων, 15:2). The charge poses a threat to the Roman rulers because Jesus would be establishing sovereignty over and against Rome without their permission or knowledge. The only other king mentioned in the Gospel of Mark is Herod (6:14–29), whose use of the title was not officially sanctioned by the Romans.[235] His brother, Archelaus, ethnarch of Judea, had been promised the title king, but was removed and replaced by a Roman prefect in 6 BCE.[236] If Jesus claims to be king then he denies that Rome is the only power who can legitimately sanction kings (as they did for Herod the Great).[237] Jesus does not deny the charge, but simply replies to Pilate, "You say so." As the honorable Son of God, Jesus still is able to utilize his power and authority when he offers no response to any of the other charges brought against him (15:5). Pilate is amazed (θαυμάζειν, 15:5), much in the same way that Jesus' kinship group of disciples and followers have responded to him throughout his ministry (1:27; 2:12; 5:20; 10:32; 12:17).

Pilate recognizes that Jesus has been arrested because of the Jerusalem leaders' envy (φθόνον, 15:10). "Pilate knows that Jesus is being accused to satisfy the honor of his accusers, the chief priests."[238] Pilate is also allied with the Jerusalem leaders, and they hand Jesus over intending that Pilate will uphold this alliance and execute Jesus.[239] In addition to witnessing Jesus before Pilate, the crowd also calls for a prisoner's release (15:8). Pilate polls the crowd, giving the crowd some semblance of control, but actually maintaining complete power and control over the situation as the highest ranking official of the Roman Empire in Jerusalem in order to test the crowd and determine any support Jesus might have. Pilate suggests the release of Jesus, referring to him as "The King of the Jews." "By using this title Pilate shrewdly presents the question as a test of loyalty to Rome and the emperor. The title reminds the crowd of Pilate's power as Rome's representative and their status as a subjugated people."[240] The crowd, under the direction of the Jerusalem societal leaders (15:11), calls for the release of the rebel

---

235. See chapter 3.
236. Josephus, *War*, 2.167.
237. Josephus, *Ant*.14.384–85.
238. Malina and Rohrbaugh, *Social-Science Commentary*, 217.
239. Carter, *Pontius Pilate*, 60.
240. Ibid., 69–70.

Barabbas. Unlike Jesus, Barabbas is identified as a rebel (τῶν στασιαστῶν, 15:7) who has used violence (murder) in revolt against the Romans. Barabbas's very name is composed of kinship terms, the Aramaic words for "son" and "father." In the nexus between Christology and discipleship in terms of kinship, the crowd, ironically, calls for the release of the "son of the father" as opposed to the Son of God, the Father. Adela Yarbro Collins states, "Since Jesus addresses God as 'Abba' in Gethsemane, the name 'Barabbas (bar Abba)' suggests that Jesus and this other prisoner are rival claimants to be the Son of God, that is the messiah, and that they are to be compared and contrasted as such."[241] When they call for the false son's release, Pilate asks what should be done with Jesus. The crowd, manipulated by the leaders (15:11) and by Pilate's line of questioning to secure Jesus' execution, calls for his death by crucifixion (15:13). Pilate "will act for himself and his allies. But with his questions he has managed to secure the crowd's loyalty, assent, and support while disguising his own interests!"[242] In one last assurance of their loyalty to Rome, Pilate asks the crowd what evil Jesus has done. But they still cry for his crucifixion, implicitly identifying Jesus as a rebel and disloyal to Rome.

Doing Roman justice under the guise of the "manipulated" crowd's will, Pilate hands Jesus over to be crucified (15:15). Captured, imprisoned, subject to a mock trial, and now handed over for crucifixion, Jesus appears to be completely powerless at the hands of the Jerusalem societal leaders and the Roman leaders. However, Jesus' predictions continue to be fulfilled. As he said in 10:33–34, he has been brought by the Jerusalem societal leaders and handed over to the Gentiles who will mock him and kill him. Jesus continues to be the most honorable Son of God's empire, enduring what is happening to him with the promise of ultimate victory. On the other hand, Pilate, the bastion of Roman authority in Jerusalem, should hold ultimate power. "To him belong oversight of the tasks of provincial government: military occupation, tax collection, supervision of public order, which includes the power of life and death."[243] Pilate demonstrates his implicit power over his allies and the crowd and secures an end to Jesus' threat and his execution. Although Pilate condemns Jesus to death and has him killed, the Romans will not have the power to keep the Son of God dead (16:6).

The soldiers take Jesus to the courtyard of the governor's palace to humiliate and mock him. In the nexus between Christology and discipleship in terms of kinship, Jesus' knowledge of this event as he predicted it

---

241. Collins, *Mark*, 718.
242. Carter, *Pontius Pilate*, 72.
243. Carter, *Matthew and the Margins*, 522.

to his family of disciples corroborates Jesus' honor and authority as God's Son. Ironically, the soldiers, and their whole cohort (15:16) which would consist of around six hundred men,²⁴⁴ pay homage to Jesus as he is dressed in a purple cloak, greeting him as the King of the Jews. This satellite evokes images of the victory of Titus in Jerusalem. At the destruction of Jerusalem, the Roman soldiers bring their flags and banners to the eastern gate of the Jerusalem temple where they offer sacrifices and greet Titus as imperator (αὐτοκράτορα).²⁴⁵ In imitation and mockery, Jesus is hailed by a troop of Roman soldiers as King of the Jews in imitation of and contest against the son of Emperor Vespasian and future emperor of Rome. Even in the midst of Jesus' public humiliation and degradation, Jesus maintains his identity as the most honorable Son of God, inciting wonder (15:5) and (ironic) honor from his enemies (15:18).

29. 15:21-41 THE SON OF GOD IS CRUCIFIED

The crucifixion scene is the final kernel in the plot of Mark's gospel. The previous kernels of Jesus' baptism (1:9-11) and passion prediction and transfiguration (8:31-9:8) and the surrounding satellites have been leading to this final event. Jesus was inaugurated as God's Son and embarked on his ministry in Galilee to establish God's empire populated by a kinship group of disciples and followers. His identity and work was later affirmed at the transfiguration but with the revelation that the Son will have to suffer and to die, a requirement extended to his family of disciples. Here the narrative has its climax, with the apparent desertion of the family of disciples and the death of the Son of God. The nexus between Christology and discipleship in terms of kinship, though not evident by the disciples' abandonment, is still present in others who enter into Jesus' kinship group by following and serving Jesus at his crucifixion and death.

As they lead Jesus out to be crucified, the soldiers compel a man to carry Jesus' cross (15:21). In the nexus between Christology and discipleship in terms of kinship, this man, Simon of Cyrene, enters into kinship with Jesus by performing an act of discipleship in the carrying of the cross. One of the requirements of discipleship as Jesus instructed his core kinship group was to take up the cross and follow Jesus (8:34). Simon of Cyrene provides the literal example of this discipleship, even under force, carrying

---

244. Marcus, *Mark 8-16*, 1039.
245. Josephus, *War*, 6.136. Suet.*Tit.* 5, notes that the soldiers hailed Titus as "Imperator" when he took Jerusalem.

the cross behind Jesus to his crucifixion.[246] Moreover, Simon is presented in kinship terms, as the father of Rufus and Alexander (15:21), suggesting that Mark's community may have known these two sons. The kinship relationship between Jesus and Simon is thus extended to the community through Rufus and Alexander.

Once they reach Golgotha, they crucify Jesus (15:24). Jesus is derided while he is on the cross with calls for him to save himself and to come down from the cross to prove his identity as the King of the Jews (15:29–32). Ironically, Jesus' crucifixion stands as the witness to his identity as God's Son since he predicted to his kinship group of disciples what would happen. In the nexus between Christology and discipleship in terms of kinship, Jesus endures the suffering and death that he requires of his disciples in order to demonstrate his faithfulness and honor as God's Son. Ironically, Jesus does not save himself from crucifixion because in giving up his life he will save it (8:35). Moreover, the proof of Jesus' sonship will be in his death as he predicted. To prove his identity to the Jerusalem societal leaders by doing what they ask for would not allow him to maintain his faithfulness to God or to the family of disciples. He will suffer and die, and be raised on the third day (10:34).

Like the events of the baptism (1:9–11) and the transfiguration (9:2–9), the crucifixion takes on cosmic aspects. As the heavens are torn at Jesus' baptism and a cloud covers the sky at the transfiguration, darkness covers the earth for three hours at the crucifixion (15:33). Right before he dies, Jesus calls out from the cross, "Eloi, eloi, lema sabachthani," which is translated, "My God, my God, why have you forsaken me?" Jesus evokes Ps 22, a lament psalm, previously evoked by the dividing of Jesus' garments (15:24) and the mockery he endured (15:29–32). The first line of the psalm and Jesus' cry indicate the experience of total abandonment by God. However, as God's Son, Jesus has predicted that he will achieve victory and be raised from the dead. The experience of abandonment should not be negated, but as Ps 22 itself ends triumphantly, there is the knowledge that Jesus' crucifixion will also result in triumph.[247] When the people witness Jesus' cry, they once more associate him with Elijah (8:28), misunderstanding the necessity of Jesus' death for the establishment of the empire of God and to demonstrate his faithfulness to his family of disciples.

At the moment of Jesus' death, the cosmic events continue. In an echo of the tearing (σχιζομένους, 1:10) of the heavens and the covering over of the heavens where Jesus' sonship was revealed, the curtain of the Jerusalem

---

246. Marcus, *Mark 8–16*, 1048.

247. Ibid., 1063.

temple is torn (ἐσχίσθη, 15:38) in two. The temple curtain is described as a representative of the night sky by Josephus;[248] thus the heavens are symbolically torn open.[249] Immediately after, Mark describes a centurion who was watching Jesus die declare him to be the (a) Son of God (15:39). Once more, in an ironic turn, the Roman occupying forces recognize Jesus' identity as God's Son. There is debate as to whether this is a genuine confession or acerbic mockery.[250] Even if the centurion is mocking Jesus, he speaks the truth of Jesus' identity. Akin to God's voice at the baptism and transfiguration, the sky, in the form of the temple curtain, opens up and a voice declares Jesus to be God's Son. Even in the suffering death, even in the abandonment of Jesus by all, Jesus remains the honorable and faithful Son of God. In the nexus between Christology and discipleship in terms of kinship, Jesus upholds the kinship boundaries of faithfulness and honor in the form of service and sacrifice even as some of his disciples have abandoned him.

At the end of the crucifixion scene, Mark notes that there were other witnesses to the events. There was a group of women, including Mary Magdalene, Mary the mother of James the younger and of Joses, and Salome, who watched from a distance (15:40). Mark also states that these women followed him (ἠκολούθουν, 15:41) and provided for him (διηκόνουν). That is, they functioned as disciples (1:17).[251] Like the core kinship group of the twelve disciples, these women followed him in Galilee, served him, and even followed him to Jerusalem, and thus entered into kinship with Jesus.[252] Edwin Broadhead suggests that these women maintain the central character

---

248. Josephus, *War*, 5.212, 214.

249. See Ulansey, "The Heavenly Veil Torn," 125.

250. See Shiner, "Ambiguous Pronouncement," 3–22; Iverson, "Centurion's 'Confession,'" 329–50.

251. See Munro, "Women Disciples in Mark?," 225–41; Malbon, "Fallible Followers," 40–46.

252. Kinukawa, "Women Disciples of Jesus," 171–90, argues that although the women are not designated as disciples they become disciples in their actions according to the descriptions of discipleship (8:34–38; 9:35–37; 10:42–45). She implies because they are women that their membership in the group of disciples is more difficult to prove since the twelve designated disciples were men (and the context of a patriarchal society). If the group of disciples and followers of Jesus are viewed in terms of kinship, the presence and activity of the women followers are not problematic at all and, in fact, follows the example of all the women and men (named and unnamed) who have become followers by their receipt of benefits from Jesus and doing the will of God (3:31–35). Kinukawa concludes that the true disciples of Jesus are those that serve as these women did. I do not think it is necessary to suggest that the "true" discipleship depicted by these women nullifies the discipleship of any other follower of Jesus in the Gospel of Mark. In fact, this demonstrates a limited view of discipleship, especially when she ignores the fact that these women flee just as the twelve did in 16:8.

trait of discipleship. "The destiny of the Son of Man is to serve (10:45), and followers of Jesus can accomplish greatness only through service (10:43-44) ... Only three characters are called servants in the Gospel of Mark: the Son of Man (10:45), angels (1:13) and women (1:31; 15:40-41)."[253] In the nexus between Christology and discipleship in terms of kinship, these women upheld the kinship structures and followed Jesus to his death, allowing the kinship group of disciples to maintain their faithfulness to Jesus.

30. 15:42-47 THE SON IS BURIED BY A DISCIPLE AND KINSMAN

The crucifixion of Jesus concludes with his burial. Those executed by crucifixion normally would not have been allowed to receive a proper burial.[254] However, a member of the council and a Jerusalem societal leader whom Mark describes as anticipating the empire of God (προσδεχόμενος τὴν βασιλείαν τοῦ θεοῦ, 15:43), Joseph of Arimathea, boldly goes to Pilate (τολμήσας) to request the body of Jesus. Once more, in the nexus between Christology and discipleship in terms of kinship, Joseph's act of kinship and discipleship by burying Jesus, extends kinship to him as the Son of God.[255] Moreover, Joseph himself is described in association with the empire of God. It is not only his act that demonstrates his discipleship and kinship with Jesus, but he already holds faith in the empire that Jesus has come to establish. Some scholars argue that Joseph's act should be seen as dishonorable toward Jesus and that Joseph was interested in avoiding the scandal of Jesus' crucifixion.[256] However, with the association of the empire of God in 15:43 and the fact that he associates himself at all with Jesus after the council's condemnation demonstrates Joseph's entrance into the kinship group of Jesus.[257] Joseph functions as a disciple and kinsman to Jesus by providing Jesus with a burial, doing the work that would be expected of Jesus' family of followers.

In addition to Joseph of Arimathea, two of the women disciples are still following Jesus (15:47). In the nexus between Christology and discipleship

---

253. Broadhead, *Teaching with Authority*, 63n1. See also Schüssler Fiorenza, *In Memory of Her*, 139; Malbon, "Fallible Followers," 40-46.

254. Malina and Rohrbaugh, *Social-Science Commentary*, 218. See also Myers, *Binding the Strong Man*, 395.

255. Hellerman, *Ancient Church as Family*, 67.

256. See Myers, *Binding the Strong Man*, 395 and Brown, *Death of the Messiah*, 2:1214-19.

257. Marcus, *Mark 8-16*, 1075.

in terms of kinship, the women maintain their kinship with Jesus as his disciples in their faithfulness in following him to his burial place. As the Son of God, Jesus has predicted his betrayal, arrest, and death. He has also predicted that he will rise again after three days. Thus far, he has proven faithful and honorable and his predictions have come true. In their own act of faithfulness toward Jesus, perhaps the women continue to follow to see if his final prediction of victory over death will also be true. If not this, the women maintain their faithfulness as Jesus' kin because they will complete the burial of Jesus by anointing his body after the Sabbath is over (16:1).[258] They will anoint Jesus in death akin to the woman who demonstrated discipleship and was honored for anointing Jesus ahead of time (14:3-9). Even in death, the nexus between Christology and discipleship in terms of kinship is present in the faithfulness of Joseph and the women toward the Son of God.

31. 16:1-8 THE SON IS RESURRECTED

The resurrection of Jesus is the final satellite and concludes the Gospel of Mark. After the Sabbath is over, the women who followed Jesus to his crucifixion and burial make their way back to the tomb to anoint the body of Jesus (16:1). The women act as disciples just as the woman who did anoint Jesus, functioning as his kinswoman and being honored and remembered for her actions (14:3-9). When they arrive at the tomb, the stone that Joseph placed in front had been rolled away. Upon entering the tomb, they discover a young man dressed in white sitting on the right hand side. They are amazed (ἐξεθαμβήθησαν, 16:5), akin to the way many have responded to Jesus (1:27; 9:15; 10:24; 10:32). He tells them not to be astounded (μὴ ἐκθαμβεῖσθε, 16:6) and reveals the fulfillment of the final prediction regarding Jesus' death and crucifixion (8:31; 9:31; 10:34). On the third day after Jesus' death, the young man informs the women that Jesus has been raised (16:6). In the nexus between Christology and discipleship in terms of kinship, the message of the Son's triumph over death is given to his women

---

258. Malbon notes that the women are faulted for not expecting Jesus' resurrection and instead preparing to anoint Jesus in his burial. Malbon concludes, "But the Markan narrative makes no mention of the presence of the women followers at Simon the leper's house and explicitly states that the predictions of Jesus' passion and resurrection are presented to the disciples, the twelve (8:31; 9:31; 10:33-34; cf. 9:9; contrast Luke 24:5-8). Those at Simon the leper's house do not understand the implications of the anointing (14:4-5; τινες at 14:4 is ambiguous), and the twelve do not understand the reference to the resurrection (9:32; cf. 9:10). It seems unlikely, then, that the Markan narrator and implied reader would expect the women followers to anticipate or understand the resurrection with no forewarning" (Malbon, "Fallible Followers," 44).

disciples, women who are a part of his kinship group of followers. The message of resurrection brings with it the pronouncement of justice and vindication for Jesus and the promise of reunion for Jesus and the family of disciples (14:28). Moreover, the young man echoes the very words of Jesus when he offers comfort to his disciples (5:36; 6:50) providing these women with care and concern in the same way Jesus offered care and concern to his kinship group of disciples and followers.

In a final call of discipleship, the young man instructs the women to go and tell the disciples and Peter what he predicted on the Mount of Olives (16:7). This command to "go" is also the command that Jesus most often gives to those who have received his benefaction of healing (1:44; 2:11; 5:19, 34; 7:29; 10:52).[259] Jesus has gone ahead of them to Galilee and he will see them as he said (14:28). In the nexus between Christology and discipleship in terms of kinship, the women are called by Jesus as his kinship group of disciples to proclaim the message of his resurrection. They have the opportunity to pronounce the triumphant victory Jesus has had over his execution and death at the hands of the Jerusalem societal leaders and the Roman occupying forces. The most honorable Son has fulfilled all the predictions he made about himself and now plans to reunite with the kinship group of disciples and followers in Galilee where he began the establishment of God's empire.

The women went out, but rather than bringing this message to Peter and the disciples, they flee in fear and say nothing to anyone. This response by the women is sometimes interpreted in the same light as the core kinship group of disciples' abandonment of Jesus at his arrest.[260] However, the women continue to remain faithful even after the core kinship group has abandoned Jesus and they follow him to the cross and to the tomb. Fear and amazement are common responses to the Son of God from his core kinship group of disciples (4:41; 6:51; 9:6; 9:32; 10:24, 26, 32), those who witness his teaching and ministry (1:27; 2:12; 9:15), and his opponents (11:18; 12:17; 15:5). Moreover, the disciples have also responded to a question or statement of Jesus with silence (9:6; 9:34). Although the women appear to fail at proclaiming the message of Jesus' resurrection to the other disciples, in the nexus between Christology and discipleship in terms of kinship, they function in a manner akin to the other disciples. "Such a reiteration of major themes fulfills one of the necessary functions of an epilogue, reminding

259. Tolbert, *Sowing the Gospel*, 295.

260. Dewey, "Gospel of Mark," 506; Perrin, *Resurrection*, 30; Tannehill, "Disciples in Mark," 386–405.

the audience in brief of the foregoing plot."[261] They have followed faithfully, but they have also responded with fear and abandonment. David Catchpole suggests that their reaction is a typical response to an epiphany,[262] leading Elizabeth Struthers Malbon to conclude, "Thus the women's fear and silence are as much signs of the limits of humanity in the presence of divinity as signs of fallibility as followers in the usual sense."[263] Just as Peter was at a loss for words when he witnessed the wonder of the transfiguration (9:6), a prefiguring of Jesus' resurrection glory, so too do the women fail to speak at the reality of Jesus' resurrection.

Regardless of the women's response, they have served as the witnesses to Jesus' death, burial, and resurrection.[264] The proclamation of the raising of the Son of God concludes the Gospel of Mark and fulfills the final prediction Jesus made. Jesus is the vindicated and triumphant Son of God who has inaugurated the empire of God and established a family of disciples and followers. Jesus has remained faithful and he maintains the kinship boundaries that he established in Galilee by promising to return there to meet his core kinship group of disciples. The message of the Son's resurrection has the power and authority to uphold the kinship relationships established by Jesus among his family of disciples and followers in spite of the women's apparent failure.

The Son of God has been triumphant over those who arrested him and executed him. The Son of God who came to establish the empire of God and to build a family of disciples and followers has remained faithful through to the fulfillment of all the predictions and prophecies about him. In imitation and contest, Jesus has established an eternal father-son dynasty that cannot be destroyed, even by the powerful Roman father-son dynasties that maintain political and military might. The Son of God has provided the benefits of hospitality, teaching, exorcism, and healing to those who follow akin to the benefits that Rome could provide for its (elite) citizens. Jesus also has promised a place in his empire for eternity to those who do God's will, who become servants of all, and who lose their lives. In the nexus between

---

261. Tolbert, *Sowing the Gospel*, 295.
262. Catchpole, "Fearful Silence," 9.
263. Malbon, "Fallible Followers," 44-45.

264. Jong, "Mark 16:8 as a Satisfying Ending," 130-38, argues that the thrust of the scene of 16:1-8 is the proclamation of the resurrection, reiterating what Jesus already told the disciples in 14:28. The women's response simply ends the scene and is irrelevant since their primary purpose was to witness the proclamation of resurrection as they witnessed Jesus' crucifixion and burial. De Jong suggests that the empty tomb is an innovation in the resurrection story (since Paul does not attest it) and another proof of Jesus' resurrection, though no one has heard of it since the witnesses remained silent about it (16:8).

Christology and discipleship in terms of kinship, the Son of God embodies the call to faithful discipleship, extending kinship in light of abandonment and fear, and promising to maintain the kinship group with the promise of his triumphant vindication in his resurrection.

5

Conclusion

IN CHAPTER 1, I provided an historical and thematic survey of Markan studies in Christology and discipleship, their contributions, and their limitations. I highlighted the importance of the Markan narrative context when determining Markan Christology. Moreover, within the arena of discipleship, I pointed out that scholarship focuses much more on the function of discipleship rather than identity in relation to Jesus. After a review of Howard Clark Kee, John R. Donahue, and Suzanne Watts Henderson and their attempts to provide an intersection of Christology and discipleship in Mark, I demonstrated that there has not been sufficient work in approaching Christology and discipleship as connected or integrated categories. In this study I have proposed that kinship language and structures in the Gospel of Mark draw Christology and discipleship together. I also provided an overview of the significant contributions made in the study of Mark and its Roman imperial context as a means to locate my argument of the intersection of Christology and discipleship in terms of kinship contextually.

Chapter 2 presents the methodology that I used to examine Christology and discipleship in terms of kinship in the Gospel of Mark. In the discussion on narrative criticism, I provided an analysis of plot, character, setting, and point of view. Utilizing the work of Seymour Chatman, I determined Mark's plot was arranged into four narrative blocks based on three kernels, or central plot events, Jesus' baptism (1:9–11), Jesus' first prediction of his passion and the transfiguration (8:31–9:10), and Jesus' crucifixion (15:21–41). The kernels function as hinge points within the plot where the rest of the plot leads to or leads from these main events. The kernels raise and answer questions in the arrangement of events. Each kernel is supported by and/or elaborated through satellites, or minor plot events, which help to flesh out the skeleton of the kernels. Central to the plot development in the Gospel of Mark is the fact that before any of the events take place, Mark introduces Jesus as the Son of God in 1:1. What it means for Jesus to be the Son of God will be revealed through the plot, in the turn of events, actions, and encounters with other characters.

Character is a paradigm of traits through which the audience builds knowledge and understanding of traits and accounts for the actions of a character throughout the plot events. Jesus functions as the main character in the Gospel of Mark; subsequently I paid particular attention to the way he developed throughout the narrative and to his interactions with other characters. Jesus is initially identified as a Son, and through the narrative his sonship is revealed to its full extent where kinship leads to suffering and death for Jesus and, as he instructs his disciples, for them as well. Other characters in the Gospel of Mark, particularly the disciples and followers of Jesus, develop traits through their interactions with Jesus. Disciples and other followers of Jesus become characterized through their kinship relationships with Jesus, being designated as family members and receiving benefactions of exorcism, healing, hospitality, and teaching from their superior kinsman, Jesus.

Both plot and characterization serve to emphasize the sonship of Jesus in the Gospel of Mark. Furthermore, the author's point of view does the same thing. Point of view is the perspective from the author, narrator, or any character in a narrative. For Mark, the author, narrator, and Jesus exhibit the point of view that Jesus is the Son of God based on 1:1 and the first kernel of Jesus' baptism (1:9–11) where Jesus hears the designation that he is God's Son. Moreover, the perspective of Jesus as the Son has implication for kinship as it relates to discipleship. Jesus the Son calls disciples to follow him and extends kinship to them and to others because he is God's Son and has the authority to establish a new kinship group of those who do the will of God.

Setting functions as the context in which the plot and characters emerge. Setting has a variety of dimensions including social, political, geographical, and religious, which may affect the plot and characters. In addition to the geographical settings of Galilee and Jerusalem, in the synagogue, beside the sea, and in the temple, many satellites within in the Gospel of Mark occur in a house. The setting of the household highlights the kinship relationships Jesus establishes with his disciples and those who follow him. I also consider the Gospel of Mark in its Roman imperial setting since both the Galilee and Jerusalem were under Roman occupation in the first century CE. In addition to the pervasive implicit setting of the Roman Empire, there are also explicit references to Rome including the man possessed by "Legion" (5:1–20) and Jesus' response to a question about paying taxes to

Caesar (12:13–17). Against the setting of the Roman Empire, the character of Jesus, his identity as a Son, and his relationships with others, especially his disciples and followers in terms of kinship, stand in both contrast to and imitation of the Roman Empire's own claim on kinship, discipleship, and sonship concerning their subjects.

The second methodology I utilized concerns social-scientific critical approaches to the New Testament. I focused on anthropological and cultural models of kinship and honor. Kinship is the means by which human cultures organize themselves, most often according to sexual relationships and reproduction through birth. Kinship is also organized around meals, working together, living together, and sharing the same code of conduct. The Gospel of Mark utilizes kinship language as a means to define the primary relationships of both Jesus and the disciples. Patrilineal descent, tracing the line of descent through male descendants, is a primary aspect of kinship in the first-century Mediterranean region. In the identity of Jesus as God's Son, patrilineal descent becomes the primary means of establishing and maintaining the kinship group of Jesus and the disciples in Mark. Jesus' character, actions, and interactions are based upon his primary identity as a Son which in turn provides a kinship characterization to those whom Jesus encounters, particularly his disciples and followers. In addition to kinship, the social structure of the household is also considered in relation to kinship, particularly the roles and functions that kinship members may hold within the household. Within the setting of the household in the Gospel of Mark, Jesus, in addition to his identity as a Son, also functions in a particular role as the head of the household, as the *paterfamilias*, among his disciples and followers.

Honor, the status one claimed in a community and the public recognition of that status, is a central value in the first-century Mediterranean world. In the identification of Jesus in terms of kinship with God, his actions, and even in his suffering and death, the Gospel of Mark presents Jesus as the most honorable man. Throughout the gospel, Jesus' honor is challenged and threatened by his adversaries and those who do not believe he is honorable by means of the public game of challenge-riposte. In each challenge-riposte, Jesus wins the challenge by his authority, his teaching, and his ability to heal and exorcise, honorable attributes that have been ascribed to him because of his kinship relationship with God. In the nexus between Christology and discipleship in terms of kinship, Jesus then extends this honor to his family of disciples and those who follow him.

As a means of locating the narrative of Mark and understanding the use of kinship and honor, I utilize empire studies as the final methodological approach. Of primary importance is the theory that Rome established itself as a centralized historical bureaucratic empire. The emperor did this by weakening conventional political and ideological ties based on kinship, clan, territory, and religion by creating an alternative kinship system where he functioned as the *pater patriae*, father of the fatherland. The emperor becomes the father of the kinship network of Rome conceiving of the empire as a household overwhich he exercised fatherly rule. The empire is able to maintain power and control of its vast territories and many subjects, but at the same time, groups exist who negotiate hegemonic control by forming alternative communities or households within the imperial structure. The kinship relationships and group established by Jesus' sonship and discipleship is one example of such a group. Mark portrays Jesus, as the Son of God, and his family of disciples, as an imitative, yet contesting group who provide an alternative empire and kinship group to that of the reigning dynasty of Vespasian and his son, Titus at the time of Mark's composition in 71 or 72 CE. Of primary importance to the Gospel of Mark becomes the legitimation of Vespasian's ascendancy through imperial propaganda, chiefly the divine prophecies concerning his reign and the miracle stories where he is portrayed as a healer. Imperial inscriptions and imagery on coins establish the hereditary Flavian dynasty and identify Titus in terms of his sonship, *Caesar Augusti filius*. Vespasian is posited as the primary means of success for the Roman Empire and his first born son, Titus, plays a central role, both in the legitimation of his reign and his military prowess, as well as being the son, the anticipated ruler who will follow in his father's footsteps and continue the success and prosperity that Vespasian has achieved.

In addition to the Roman emperor and his dynasty, it is also important to consider the social stratification that existed within the empire and its kinship system. Utilizing Gerhard Lenski's theory of social stratification, the Roman elite, including the emperor and his household, stood at the top of the top tier while merchants, peasants, and artisans, the majority of the population, found themselves in the bottom strata.[1] Among the lowest strata, the majority of folks would have lived at the subsistence level and would have been far removed from the ruling elite and any benefit their reigning kinship system could provide.[2] Besides the frequently self-destructive act of

1. Lenski, *Power and Privilege*, 243–85.
2. Elliott, "Household/Family," 63.

blatant rebellion, those who resisted the Roman Empire and its exploitation and subjugation, did so through hidden transcripts of resistance. According to James Scott, subordinated groups utilize disguised, muted, and veiled means in order to safely express their resistance to the powerful.[3] The Gospel of Mark functions as concrete evidence of resistance and negotiation of the dominant discourse and power of the Roman Empire. Mark designates Jesus as Son; Jesus then inaugurates the empire of God by establishing a kinship group of disciples and followers as a means of resisting, competing with, and negotiating the Flavian hereditary dynasty and rule of the Roman Empire.

Chapters 3 and 4 of this study provide an analysis on the Gospel of Mark in terms of my thesis that the nexus between Christology and discipleship is in terms of kinship. I addressed each kernel and satellite episodically, applying my methodologies, and tracing the characterization of Jesus and the disciples as they developed through the plot events in terms of kinship. I also addressed those places where Jesus' identity or the empire of God echoed in imitation or contest the Roman Empire and its rulers, especially Vespasian and Titus. The gospel presents Jesus as the Son of God (1:1) and inaugurates his ministry by his baptism where his identity is declared and then tested in the wilderness (1:9–13). After the first kernel, the hinge point that embarks Jesus' ministry, the subsequent satellites consist of the establishment of an alternative empire of God by means of a kinship group of disciples, stories of teaching, exorcism, and healing, and public honor challenges by opponents and adversaries. These satellites demonstrate the honor and authority ascribed to Jesus through his kinship relationship with God. Moreover, Jesus extends this honor and kinship relationship by means of benefactions in the form of teaching, exorcism, healing, and feeding. Jesus' identity as a Son is affirmed and developed in the encounters he has with disciples, followers, recipients of his benefactions, and his opponents. In addition to the twelve disciples specifically called by Jesus (3:13–16), those who receive benefactions also enter into a kinship relationship with Jesus. This kinship relationship is explicit in the healing of the paralytic (2:1–12) and the healing of the woman with the flow of blood (5:25–34) by the kinship language Jesus uses.

Throughout the first two narrative blocks, Jesus' popularity increases with the people in the Galilee and the surrounding regions (6:55). As Jesus continues to exercise his authority and power as the Son, he calls his kinship group of disciples to faith and fidelity, to follow him, and to do the will of God. As the disciples witness Jesus' teaching and ministry, they struggle

---

3. Scott, *Domination and Resistance*, 137.

to comprehend his identity and to maintain their fidelity. This incomprehension along with the increasing conflict with the local societal leaders foreshadows the disciples' ultimate abandonment of Jesus at his betrayal, arrest, and crucifixion. As Jesus and the disciples journey away from Galilee toward Jerusalem, Jesus, as the most honorable Son, will remain faithful to his family of disciples and followers and continue to provide for them.

The second kernel of the first passion prediction and transfiguration (8:31–9:10) affirms Jesus' identity but offers new information regarding Jesus' sonship. Not only is Jesus the most honorable Son of God establishing an alternative empire of God, but this most honorable Son will be arrested, tried, and crucified by the empire of Rome and its Jerusalem allies. Moreover, in the nexus between Christology and discipleship in terms of kinship, Jesus' family of disciples will be required to follow Jesus by taking up their crosses and losing their lives for his sake and the sake of the gospel (8:34–35). In addition to offering continued benefits of healing and exorcism to followers, Jesus teaches his disciples two more times that he will be arrested, tried, and crucified, but also raised on the third day (9:31; 10:32–33). Jesus and his family of disciples and followers make their way toward Jerusalem where Jesus will encounter opposition from the Jerusalem societal leaders and the Roman government. Not only does Jesus continue to be presented as the most honorable Son of God, who willingly goes toward certain suffering and death, but he is presented in imitation and contest to the reigning father-son dynasty of the Flavian rulers. Jesus enters into the city triumphantly, echoing, and yet mocking, a Roman triumph (11:1–11). Jesus establishes his authority within the Jerusalem temple precincts against the priestly authorities who are aligned with the Roman ruling elite (11:15–19). Jesus responds to a challenge from the Pharisees and Herodians regarding the payment of taxes to the emperor (12:13–17).

As the most honorable Son, Jesus also displays knowledge about future events. In addition to predicting his own suffering, death, and resurrection three times, Jesus predicts the destruction of the Jersualem temple (13). He also demonstrates foreknowledge of his disciples' betrayal (14:18), abandonment (14:27), and denial (14:30). All of these are fulfilled within the narrative of the gospel (14:43; 14:50; 14:67–72). Although the disciples will ultimately abandon Jesus and deny affiliation with him, Jesus' own honor and fidelity will maintain the kinship group he has established. The women followers of Jesus remain faithful until his crucifixion (15:40–41) and witness the proclamation of the resurrection (16:1–8). And Jesus promises that he will be reunited with the disciples in Galilee (14:28; 16:7) and will achieve ultimate victory in the resurrection.

The final kernel in the Gospel of Mark consists of Jesus' crucifixion (15:21–41). The Jerusalem societal leaders with the Roman authorities condemn and crucify Jesus, apparently destroying the possibility of an alternative empire of God. And yet, at the time of Jesus' crucifixion, once more, there is a cosmic event in the tearing of the temple curtain (symbolizing the sky) and Jesus' identity as God's Son is proclaimed, albeit ironically (15:38–39). Even at his crucifixion and death, Jesus remains the Son of God. The crucifixion is followed by Jesus' burial and resurrection. The resurrection serves as the final satellite in the gospel's narrative. Here the women receive the news that Jesus has been raised from the dead and has gone to Galilee. They are called, like disciples, to go and tell the other disciples and Peter about the resurrection (16:7). Even as the women fail in this task, all that Jesus predicted about himself has come to pass. Jesus is the vindicated and triumphant Son of God who has established an alternative empire of God in the establishment of a family of disciples and followers.

The nexus between Christology and discipleship in terms of kinship has been evident throughout the Gospel of Mark by means of Jesus' identity as God's Son and his establishment of a kinship group of disciples and followers. It is Jesus' kinship relationship with God that inaugurates, authorizes, and compels Jesus to establish an alternative empire of God by means of a family of disciples. As the Son of God, Jesus also requires his disciples to follow God's will, to serve others, to bear a cross, and to give their lives for the sake of the gospel. Just as Jesus will give his life for the sake of his family of disciples and followers, Jesus expects the same of his kinship group. Although Jesus' kinship relationship with God is challenged, although the family of disciples are not able to maintain faith and fidelity toward Jesus, his kinship relationship with God vindicates Jesus in the resurrection and promises reconciliation to the family of disciples and followers. The Son of God embodies the call to discipleship, extending kinship to all, and maintaining the kinship group through crucifixion and death in the promise of triumph and vindication in the resurrection.

Bibliography

Achtemeier, Paul J. "Exposition of Mark 9:30-37." *Int* 30/2 (April 1976) 178-83.
———. *Mark*. Proclamation Commentaries. Philadelphia: Fortress, 1986.
———. "Mark as Interpreter of the Jesus Traditions." *Int* 32/4 (1978) 339-52.
Ahearne-Kroll, Stephen P. "'Who Are My Mother and My Brothers?' Family Relations and Family Language in the Gospel of Mark." *JR* 81/1 (January 2001) 1-25.
Allison, Dale C., Jr. "Elijah Must Come First." *JBL* 103/2 (1984) 256-58.
Aristotle. *The Poetics*. Edited and translated by Stephen Halliwell. LCL 199. Cambridge, MA: Harvard University Press, 1939.
———. *Politics*. Translated by H. Rackham. LCL 264. Cambridge, MA: Harvard University Press, 1932.
Barr, Steve. "The Eye of the Needle–Power and Money in the New Community: A Look at Mark 10:17-31." *Andover Newton Review* 3/1 (1992) 31-44.
Barton, Stephen. *Discipleship and Family Ties in Mark and Matthew*. SNTSMS 80. Cambridge: Cambridge University Press, 1994.
Bauer, Walter, William F. Arndt, F. Wilbur Gingrich, and Frederick William Danker. *A Greek-English Lexicon of the New Testament and Other Early Christian Literature*. 3rd ed. Chicago: University of Chicago Press, 2000.
Beard, Mary. *The Roman Triumph*. Cambridge, MA: Belknap, 2007.
Beavis, Mary Ann. *Jesus and Utopia: Looking for the Kingdom of God in the Roman World*. Minneapolis: Fortress, 2006.
Best, Ernest. *Disciples and Discipleship: Studies in the Gospel according to Mark*. Edinburgh: T. & T. Clark, 1986.
———. *Following Jesus: Discipleship in the Gospel of Mark*. JSNTSup 4. Sheffield, UK: JSOT, 1981.
Betsworth, Sharon. *The Reign of God Is Such as These: A Socio-Literary Analysis of Daughters in the Gospel of Mark*. Library of New Testament Studies 422. London: T. & T. Clark, 2010.
Betz, Hans Dieter. "Jesus as Divine Man." In *Jesus and the Historian: Written in Honor of Ernest Cadman Colwell*, edited by F. Thomas Trotter, 114-33. Philadelphia: Westminster, 1968.
Blackburn, Barry. *Theios Anēr and the Markan Miracle Traditions: A Critique of the Theios Anēr Concept as an Interpretive Background of the Miracle Traditions Used by Mark*. Tübingen: Mohr, 1991.
Borg, Marcus J., and John Dominic Crossan. *The Last Week: What the Gospels Really Teach about Jesus' Final Days in Jerusalem*. New York: HarperCollins, 2006.

Boring, M. Eugene. "Mark 1:1-15 and the Beginning of the Gospel." *Semeia* 52 (1990) 43-81.

———. *Mark: A Commentary*. NTL. Louisville: Westminster John Knox, 2006.

Brandenburger, Egon. *Markus 13 und die Apokalyptik*. Göttingen: Vandenhoeck & Ruprecht, 1984.

Broadhead, Edwin K. *Teaching with Authority: Miracles and Christology in the Gospel of Mark*. JSNTSup 74. Sheffield, UK: Sheffield Academic Press, 1992.

Bromiley, Geoffrey W. *Theological Dictionary of the New Testament*. Edited by Gerhard Kittel and Gerhard Friedrich. Abbr. in one vol. ed. Grand Rapids: Eerdmans, 1985.

Brower, Kent E. "The Holy One and His Disciples: Holiness and Ecclesiology in Mark." In *Holiness and Ecclesiology in the New Testament*, edited by Kent E. Brower and Andy Johnson, 57-75. Grand Rapids: Eerdmans, 2007.

Brown, Raymond E. *The Death of the Messiah: From Gethsemane to the Grave: A Commentary on the Passion Narratives in the Four Gospels*. 2 vols. New York: Doubleday, 1994.

Brown, Raymond E., et al., eds. *Mary in the New Testament*. Philadelphia: Fortress, 1978.

Burkett, Delbert. *The Son of Man Debate: A History and Evaluation*. Cambridge: Cambridge University Press, 1999.

Cadwallader, Alan H. "The Markan/Marxist Struggle for the Household: Juliet Mitchell and the Challenge to Patriarchal/Familial Ideology." In *Marxist Feminist Criticism of the Bible*, edited by Roland Boer and Jorunn Økland, 151-81. BMW 14. Sheffield, UK: Sheffield Phoenix, 2008.

Cargal, Timothy B. "'If Your Salt Should Become Non-salt' (Mark 9:33-50): Exclusion in an Inclusive Community. In *Reading Communities, Reading Scripture: Essays in Honor of Daniel Platte*, edited by Gary A. Phillips and Nicole Wilkinson Duran, 134-46. Harrisburg, PA: Trinity, 2002.

Carlston, Charles E. *The Parables of the Triple Tradition*. Philadelphia: Fortress, 1975.

Carradice, Ian. "Towards a New Introduction to the Flavian Coinage." *BICS* 42/S71 (February 1998) 93-117.

Carter, Warren. "James C. Scott and New Testament Studies: A Response to Allen Callahan, William Herzog, and Richard Horsley." In *Hidden Transcripts and the Arts of Resistance: Applying the Work of James C. Scott to Jesus and Paul*, edited by Richard A. Horsley, 81-94. SemeiaSt 48. Atlanta: Society of Biblical Literature, 2004.

———. *John and Empire: Initial Explorations*. New York: T. & T. Clark, 2008.

———. "Matthew 4:18-22 and Matthean Discipleship: An Audience-Oriented Perspective." *CBQ* 59/1 (January 1997) 58-75.

———. *Matthew and the Margins: A Sociopolitical and Religious Reading*. The Bible and Liberation. Maryknoll, NY: Orbis, 2000.

———. *Matthew: Storyteller, Interpreter, Evangelist*. Rev. ed. Peabody, MA: Hendrickson, 2008.

———. *Pontius Pilate: Portraits of a Roman Governor*. Collegeville, MN: Liturgical, 2003.

———. *The Roman Empire and the New Testament: An Essential Guide*. Abingdon Essential Guides. Nashville: Abingdon, 2006.

Casey, Maurice. *The Solution to the 'Son of Man' Problem*. London: T. & T. Clark, 2009.

———. *Son of Man: The Interpretation and Influence of Daniel 7*. London: SPCK, 1979.

Catchpole, David. "The Fearful Silence of the Women at the Tomb: A Study in Markan Theology." *JTSA* 18 (1977) 3–10.

Chatman, Seymour. *Story and Discourse: Narrative Structure in Fiction and Film*. Ithaca, NY: Cornell University Press, 1978.

Chilton, Bruce D. "An Exorcism of History: Mark 1:21–28." In *Authenticating the Activities of Jesus*, edited by Bruce D. Chilton and Craig A. Evans, 2:215–46. NTTS 28. Leiden: Brill, 2002.

Collins, Adela Yarbro. *Mark: A Commentary*. Edited by Harold W. Attridge. Hermeneia. Minneapolis: Fortress, 2007.

———. "Mark and His Readers: The Son of God among Greeks and Romans." *HTR* 93 (2000) 85–100.

———. "The Worship of Jesus and the Imperial Cult." In *The Jewish Roots of Christological Monotheism*, edited by Carey C. Newman, James R. Davila, and Gladys S. Lewis, 234–57. Journal for the Study of Judaism Supplements 63. Leiden: Brill, 1999.

Collins, Adela Yarbro, and John J. Collins. *King and Messiah as Son of God: Divine, Human, and Angelic Messianic Figures in Biblical and Related Literature*. Grand Rapids: Eerdmans, 2008.

Corbier, Mireille. "Child Exposure and Abandonment." In *Childhood, Class and Kin in the Roman World*, edited by Suzanne Dixon, 52–73. London: Routledge, 2001.

Cotter, Wendy J. *The Christ of the Miracle Stories: Portrait through Encounter*. Grand Rapids: Baker Academic, 2010.

———. "Mark's Hero of the Twelfth-Year Miracles: The Healing of the Woman with the Hemorrhage and the Raising of Jairus's Daughter (Mark 5.21–43)." In *A Feminist Companion to Mark*, edited by Amy-Jill Levine, 2:54–78. Feminist Companion to the New Testament and Early Christian Writings. Sheffield, UK: Sheffield Academic Press, 2001.

Cranfield, C. E. B. *The Gospel according to St. Mark*. New York: Cambridge University Press, 1959.

Crossan, John Dominic, and Jonathan L. Reed. *Excavating Jesus: Beneath the Stones, Behind the Texts*. San Francisco: HarperSanFrancisco, 2001.

———. *In Search of Paul: How Jesus' Apostle Opposed Rome's Empire with God's Kingdom*. San Francisco: HarperSanFrancisco, 2004.

Cummins, S. Anthony. "Integrated Scripture, Embedded Empire: The Ironic Interplay of 'King' Herod, John and Jesus in Mark 6:1–44." In *Biblical Interpretation in Early Christian Gospels*, edited by Thomas R. Hatina, 1:31–48. Library of New Testament Studies 304. New York: T. & T. Clark, 2006.

D'Angelo, Mary Rose. "Abba and 'Father': Imperial Theology and the Jesus Traditions." *JBL* 111/4 (1992) 611–30.

———. "(Re)Presentations of Women in the Gospels: John and Mark." In *Women and Christian Origins*, edited by Ross Shepard Kraemer and Mary Rose D'Angelo, 129–49. New York: Oxford University Press, 1999.

———. "Roman Imperial Family Values and the Gospel of Mark: The Divorce Sayings (Mark 10:2–12)." In *Women and Gender in Ancient Religions: Interdisciplinary Approaches*, edited by Stephen P. Ahearne-Kroll, Paul A. Holloway, and James A. Kelhoffer, 59–83. WUNT 263. Tübingen: Mohr Siebeck, 2010.

Danove, Paul L. *The End of Mark's Gospel: A Methodological Study*. BIS 3. Leiden: Brill, 1993.

Deissmann, Adolf. *Licht vom Osten: Das Neue Testament und die neuentdeckten Texte der hellenistisch-römischen Welt.* Tübingen: Mohr, 1909.

Derrett, J. Duncan M. "Contributions to the Study of the Gerasene Demoniac." *JSNT* 3 (1979) 2–17.

DeSilva, David A. *Honor, Patronage, Kinship and Purity: Unlocking New Testament Culture.* Downers Grove, IL: InterVarsity, 2000.

Dewey, Joanna. "The Gospel of Mark." In *Searching the Scriptures: A Feminist Introduction*, edited by Elisabeth Schüssler Fiorenza, 2:470–509. New York: Crossroad, 1997.

Dio Cassius. *Roman History: Books 61–70.* Translated by Earnest Cary. Vol. 8. LCL 176. Cambridge, MA: Harvard University Press, 1925.

Donahue, John R. *The Theology and Setting of Discipleship in the Gospel of Mark.* The Père Marquette Theology Lecture. Milwaukee: Marquette University Press, 1983.

Donahue, John R., and Daniel J. Harrington. *The Gospel of Mark.* SP 2. Collegeville, MN: Liturgical, 2002.

Duling, Dennis. "Empire: Theories, Methods, Models." In *The Gospel of Matthew in its Roman Imperial Context*, edited by John Riches and David C. Sim, 49–74. JSNTSup 276. Early Christianity in Context. London: T. & T. Clark, 2005.

———. "Matthew's Plurisignificant 'Son of David' in Social Science Perspective: Kinship, Kingship, Magic, and Miracle." *BTB* 22/3 (Fall 1992) 99–116.

———. "Solomon, Exorcism, and the Son of David." *HTR* 68/3–4 (July–October 1975) 235–52.

Dunstan, William E. *Ancient Rome.* Lanham, MD: Rowman & Littlefield, 2011.

Edwards, James R. *The Gospel According to Mark.* Pillar New Testament Commentary. Grand Rapids: Eerdmans, 2002.

———. "Markan Sandwiches: The Significance of Interpolations in Markan Narrative." *NovT* 31/3 (1989) 193–216.

Elliott, John H. "Household/Family in the Gospel of Mark as a Core Symbol of Community." In *Fabrics of Discourse: Essays in Honor of Vernon K. Robbins*, edited by David B. Gowler, Gregory Bloomquist, and Duane F. Watson, 36–63. Harrisburg, PA: Trinity, 2003.

———. "The Jesus Movement was Not Egalitarian but Family Oriented." *BibInt* 11/2 (2003) 173–210.

Evans, Craig A. "The Beginning of the Good News and the Fulfillment of Scripture in the Gospel of Mark." In *Hearing the Old Testament in the New Testament*, edited by Stanley E. Porter, 83–103. Grand Rapids: Eerdmans, 2006.

———. "Did Jesus Predict His Death and Resurrection?" In *Resurrection*, edited by Stanley E. Porter, Michael A. Hayes, and David Tombs, 82–97. JSNTSup 186. London: T. & T. Clark, 1999.

———. "Mark's Incipit and the Priene Calendar Inscription: From Jewish Gospel to Greco-Roman Gospel." *The Journal of Greco-Roman Christianity and Judaism* 1 (2000) 67–81.

Eve, Eric. "Spit in Your Eye: The Blind Man of Bethsaida and the Blind Man of Alexandria." *NTS* 54/1 (2008) 1–17.

Faierstein, Morris M. "Why Do the Scribes Say that Elijah Must Come First?" *JBL* 100/1 (1981) 75–86.

Fitzmyer, Joseph A. "More about Elijah Coming First." *JBL* 104/2 (June 1985) 295–96.

Friesen, Steven. "Poverty in Pauline Studies: Beyond the So-called New Consensus." *JSNT* 26/3 (March 2004) 323–61.
Fuller, Reginald H. *The Foundations of New Testament Christology*. New York: Scribner, 1965.
Garnsey, Peter. *Famine and Food Supply in the Graeco-Roman World*. Cambridge: Cambridge University Press, 1988.
———. *Food and Society in Classical Antiquity*. Cambridge: Cambridge University Press, 1999.
Garnsey, Peter, and Richard Saller. *The Roman Empire: Economy, Society, and Culture*. Berkeley: University of California Press, 1987.
Garroway, Joshua. "The Invasion of a Mustard Seed: A Reading of Mark 5.1–20." *JSNT* 32/1 (2009) 57–75.
Gibson, Jeffrey B. "Jesus' Wilderness Temptation in Mark." *JSNT* 53 (March 1994) 3–34.
Glancy, Jennifer A. "Jesus, the Syrophoenician Woman, and Other First Century Bodies." *BibInt* 18 (2010) 342–63.
———. *Slavery in Early Christianity*. Minneapolis: Fortress, 2006.
Goodacre, Mark. "Mark, Elijah, the Baptist and Matthew: The Success of the First Intertextual Reading of Mark." In *The Gospel of Matthew*, edited by Thomas R. Hatina, 2:73–84. Library of New Testament Studies 310. London: T. & T. Clark, 2008.
Goodman, Martin. *Judaism in the Roman World: Collected Essays*. Ancient Judaism and Early Christianity 66. Leiden: Brill, 2007.
Guijarro, Santiago. "Why Does the Gospel of Mark Begin as It Does?" *BTB* 33 (2003) 28–38.
Gundry, Robert H. *Mark: A Commentary on His Apology for the Cross*. Grand Rapids: Eerdmans, 1993.
Gundry-Volf, Judith M. "Children in the Gospel of Mark." In *The Child in the Bible*, edited by Marcia J. Bunge, 143–76. Grand Rapids: Eerdmans, 2008.
———. "The Least and the Greatest: Children in the New Testament." In *The Child in Christian Thought*, edited by Marcia J. Bunge, 29–60. Grand Rapids: Eerdmans, 2001.
Gutierrez, Gustavo. "Mark 1:14–15." *RevExp* 88/4 (1991) 427–31.
Guttenberger, Gudrun. "Why Caesarea Philippi of All Sites? Some Reflections on the Political Background and Implications of Mark 8:27–30 for the Christology of Mark." In *Zwischen den Reichen: Neues Testament und Römische Herrschaft: Vorträge auf der Ersten Konferez der European Association for Biblical Studies*, edited by Michael Labahn, 119–31. Tübingen: Francke, 2002.
Hahn, Ferdinand. *The Titles of Jesus in Christology: Their History in Early Christianity*. Translated by Harold Knight and George Ogg. Cambridge: James Clark, 1963.
Hanson, K. C. "The Galilean Fishing Economy and the Jesus Tradition." *BTB* 27 (1997) 99–111.
———. "Kinship." In *The Social Sciences and New Testament Interpretation*, edited by Richard L. Rohrbaugh, 62–79. Peabody, MA: Hendrickson, 1996.
Hanson, K. C., and Douglas E. Oakman. *Palestine in the Time of Jesus: Social Structures and Social Conflicts*. 2nd ed. Minneapolis: Fortress, 2008.
Harris, W. V. "Child-Exposure in the Roman Empire." *The Journal of Roman Studies* 84 (1994) 1–22.

Hawkin, David. "The Incomprehension of the Disciples in the Marcan Redaction." *JBL* 91/4 (1972) 491–500.

Heil, John Paul. "The Narrative Strategy and Pragmatics of the Temple Theme in Mark." *CBQ* 59/1 (January 1997) 76–100.

Hellerman, Joseph H. *The Ancient Church as Family*. Minneapolis: Fortress, 2001.

———. "Challenging the Authority of Jesus: Mark 11:27–33 and Mediterranean Notions of Honor and Shame." *JETS* 43/2 (June 2000) 213–28.

Henderson, Ian H. "'Salted with Fire' (Mark 9:42–50): Style, Oracles and (Socio) Rhetorical Gospel Criticism." *JSNT* 80 (2000) 44–65.

Henderson, Suzanne Watts. *Christology and Discipleship in the Gospel of Mark*. SNTSMS 135. Cambridge: Cambridge University Press, 2006.

Hengel, Martin. *Judaism and Hellenism: Studies in Their Encounter in Palestine during the Early Hellenistic Period*. 2 vols. Translated by J. Bowden. Philadelphia: Fortress, 1974.

Herzog, William R, II. "Onstage and Offstage with Jesus of Nazareth: Public Transcripts, Hidden Transcripts, and Gospel Texts." In *Hidden Transcripts and the Arts of Resistance: Applying the Work of James C. Scott to Jesus and Paul*, edited by Richard A. Horsley, 41–60. SemeiaSt 48. Atlanta: Society of Biblical Literature, 2004.

———. "Temple Cleansing." In *Dictionary of Jesus and the Gospels: A Compendium of Contemporary Biblical Scholarship*, edited by Joel B. Green and Scot McKnight, 817–21. Downers Grove, IL: InterVarsity, 1992.

Hodge, Caroline Johnson. *If Sons, then Heirs: A Study of Kinship and Ethnicity in the Letters of Paul*. New York: Oxford University Press, 2007.

Holzner, Burkart. *Reality Construction in Society*. New York: Schenkman, 1972.

Homer. *Iliad: Books 13–24*. Vol. 2. Translated by A. T. Murray. Revised by William F. Wyatt. LCL 171. Cambridge, MA: Harvard University Press, 1925.

Hooker, Morna D. *The Gospel according to Saint Mark*. Black's New Testament Commentaries. Peabody, MA: Hendrickson, 1991.

———. "Mark's Parables of the Kingdom (Mark 4:1–34)." In *The Challenge of Jesus' Parables*, edited by Richard N. Longenecker, 79–101. Grand Rapids: Eerdmans, 2000.

———. "'What Doest Thou Here, Elijah?' A Look at St. Mark's Account of the Transfiguration." In *The Glory of Christ in the New Testament: Studies in Christology in Memory of George Bradford Caird*, edited by L. D. Hurst and N. T. Wright, 59–70. Oxford: Clarendon, 1987.

Horsley, Richard A. *Galilee: History, Politics, People*. Valley Forge, PA: Trinity, 1995.

———. *Hearing the Whole Story: The Politics of Plot in Mark's Gospel*. Louisville: Westminster John Knox, 2001.

———. "Introduction—Jesus, Paul, and the 'Arts of Resistance': Leaves from the Notebook of James C. Scott." In *Hidden Transcripts and the Arts of Resistance*, edited by Richard A. Horsley, 1–26. SemeiaSt 48. Atlanta: Society of Biblical Literature, 2004.

Huizenga, Leroy Andrew. "The Confession of Jesus and the Curses of Peter: A Narrative-Christological Approach to the Text-Critical Problem of Mark 14:62." *NovT* 53 (2011) 244–66.

Hurtado, Larry W. *Lord Jesus Christ: Devotion to Jesus in Earliest Christianity*. Grand Rapids: Eerdmans, 2003.

———. *Mark*. Grand Rapids: Baker, 1989.

Hutchinson, John C. "Servanthood: Jesus' Countercultural Call to Christian Leaders." *BSac* 166 (January 2009) 53–69.

Iersel, Bastiaan van. *Reading Mark*. Translated by W. H. Bisscheroux. Edinburgh: T. & T. Clark, 1989.

Incigneri, Brian J. *The Gospel to the Romans: The Setting and Rhetoric of Mark's Gospel.* BIS 65. Leiden: Brill, 2003.

Iverson, Kelly R. "A Centurion's 'Confession': A Performance-Critical Analysis of Mark 15:39." *JBL* 130/2 (2011) 329–50.

———. "Jews, Gentiles, and the Kingdom of God: The Parable of the Wicked Tenants in Narrative Perspective (Mark 12:1–12)." *BibInt* 20 (2012) 305–35.

Jeffers, James S. *The Greco-Roman World of the New Testament Era: Exploring the Background of Early Christianity*. Downers Grove, IL: InterVarsity, 1999.

Jeremias, Joachim. *Die Kindertaufe in den ersten vier Jahrhunderten*. Göttingen: Vandenhoeck & Ruprecht, 1958.

———. *The Eucharistic Words of Jesus*. London: SCM, 1966.

———. *The Parables of Jesus*. Rev. ed. New York: Scribner, 1963.

Jong, Matthijs J. de. "Mark 16:8 as a Satisfying Ending to the Gospel." In *Jesus, Paul and Early Christianity: Studies in Honour of Henk Jan de Jonge*, edited by Rieuwerd Buitenwerf, Harm W. Hollander, and Johannes Tromp, 123–49. Leiden: Brill, 2008.

Josephus. *Jewish Antiquities*. Translated by H. St. J. Thackery et al. 9 vols. LCL 242, 281, 326, 365, 410, 433, 456, 489, and 490. Cambridge, MA: Harvard University Press, 1930–1965.

———. *The Jewish War*. Translated by H. St. J. Thackeray. 2 vols. LCL 203, 487. Cambridge, MA: Harvard University Press, 1997.

Juel, Donald. *Messiah and Temple: The Trial of Jesus in the Gospel of Mark*. SBLDS 31. Missoula, MT: Scholars, 1977.

Keck, Leander. "Introduction to Mark's Gospel." *NTS* 12/4 (1966) 352–70.

———. "Mark 3:7–12 and Mark's Christology." *JBL* 84/4 (1965) 341–58.

———. "Toward the Renewal of New Testament Christology." *NTS* 32/3 (1986) 362–77.

Kee, Howard Clark. *Community of the New Age: Studies in Mark's Gospel*. Philadelphia: Westminster, 1977.

Kelber, Werner H. "Mark 14.32–42: Gethsemane; Passion Christology and Discipleship Failure." *Zeitschrift für die neutestamentliche Wissenschaft und die Kunde der älteren Kirche* 63/3–4 (1972) 166–87.

———. *Mark's Story of Jesus*. Philadelphia: Fortress, 1979.

———. *The Oral and Written Gospel: The Hermeneutics of Speaking and Writing in the Synoptic Tradition, Mark, Paul, and Q*. Philadelphia: Fortress, 1983.

Kieffer, René. "A Christology of Superiority in the Synoptic Gospels." *Religious Studies Bulletin* 3/2 (May 1983) 61–75.

Kim, Tae Hun. "The Anarthrous υἱὸς θεοῦ in Mark 15.39 and the Roman Imperial Cult." *Biblica* 79/2 (1998) 221–41.

Kingsbury, Jack Dean. *The Christology of Mark's Gospel*. Philadelphia: Fortress, 1983.

———. "The Spirit and the Son of God in Mark's Gospel." In *Sin, Salvation, and the Spirit: Commemorating the Fiftieth Year of the Liturgical Press*, edited by Daniel Durken, 195–202. Collegeville, MN: Liturgical, 1979.

Kinukawa, Hisako. "Women Disciples of Jesus (15:40–41; 15:47; 16:1)." In *A Feminist Companion to Mark*, edited by Amy-Jill Levine, 2:171–90. Feminist Companion to the New Testament and Early Christian Writings. Sheffield, UK: Sheffield Academic Press, 2001.

Koester, Helmut. "Jesus the Victim." *JBL* 111/1 (1992) 3–15.

Kozar, Joseph Vlcek "Complementary Insight: A Scribe's Approval of the 'Most Important' Commandment in mark 12:28–34." *Proceedings: Eastern Great Lakes and Midwest Biblical Societies* 22 (2002) 35–45.

———. "Forsaking Your Mother-in-law to Go Fishing: The Call of the First Disciples in Mark and the Abandonment of Family Ties as Exemplar of Markan Discipleship (Mark 1:9–39)." *Proceedings: Eastern Great Lakes and Midwest Biblical Societies* 29 (2009) 37–49.

Kunst, Christiane. *Römische Adoption: Zur Strategie einer Familienorganisation*. Hennef, Ger.: Marthe Clauss, 2005.

Laes, Christian. *Children in the Roman Empire: Outsiders Within*. Cambridge: Cambridge University Press, 2011.

Larsen, Kevin W. "A Focused Christological Reading of Mark 8:22–9:13." *TJ* 26/1 (2005) 33–46.

———. "The Structure of Mark's Gospel: Current Proposals." *Currents in Biblical Research* 3/1 (October 2004) 140–60.

Lathrop, Gordon W. *The Four Gospels on Sunday: The New Testament and the Reform of Christian Worship*. Minneapolis: Fortress, 2012.

Leander, Hans. "With Homi Bhabha at the Jerusalem City Gates: A Postcolonial Reading of the 'Triumphant' Entry (Mark 1:1–11)." *JSNT* 32/3 (2010) 309–35.

Lenski, Gerhard. *Power and Privilege: A Theory of Social Stratification*. New York: McGraw-Hill, 1966.

Levick, Barbara. *Vespasian*. New York: Routledge, 2005.

Levine, Amy-Jill. "Discharging Responsibility: Matthean Jesus, Biblical Law, and Hemorrhaging Woman." In *Treasures Old and New: Recent Contributions to Matthean Studies*, edited by David R. Bauer and Mark Allen Powell, 379–97. Atlanta: Scholars, 1996.

Liddell, H. G., and Robert Scott. *An Intermediate Greek-English Lexicon*. Oxford: Oxford University Press, 1889.

Lindars, Barnabas. *Jesus Son of Man: A Fresh Examination of the Son of Man Sayings in the Gospels in the Light of Recent Research*. London: SPCK, 1983.

Longacre, Robert E. "A Top-Down, Template-Driven Narrative Analysis, Illustrated by Application to Mark's Gospel." In *Discourse Analysis and the New Testament: Approaches and Results*, edited by Stanley E. Porter and Jeffrey T. Reed, 140–68. JSNTSup 170. Studies in New Testament Greek 4. Sheffield, UK: Sheffield Academic Press, 1999.

Lührmann, Dieter. *Das Markusevangelium*. Tübingen: Mohr Siebeck, 1987.

MacAdam, Henry Innes. "Domus Domini: Where Jesus Lived (Capernaum and Bethany in the Gospels)." *ThR* 25/1 (April 2004) 46–76.

Malbon, Elizabeth Struthers. "Disciples/Crowds/Whoever: Markan Characters and Readers." *NovT* 28/2 (1986) 104–30.

———. "Fallible Followers: Women and Men in the Gospel of Mark." *Semeia* 28 (1983) 29–48.

———. *In the Company of Jesus: Characters in Mark's Gospel*. Louisville: Westminster John Knox, 2000.

———. *Mark's Jesus: Characterization as Narrative Christology.* Waco, TX: Baylor University Press, 2009.

———. "The Poor Widow in Mark and Her Poor Rich Readers." *CBQ* 53/4 (1991) 589–604.

———. "Reflected 'Christology:' An Aspect of Narrative 'Christology' in the Gospel of Mark." *PRSt* 26/2 (Summer 1999) 127–45.

———. "Texts and Contexts: Interpreting the Disciples in Mark." *Semeia* 62 (1993) 81–102.

Malina, Bruce J. *The New Testament World: Insights from Cultural Anthropology.* 3rd ed. Louisville: Westminster John Knox, 2001.

Malina, Bruce J., and Richard L. Rohrbaugh. *Social-Science Commentary on the Synoptic Gospels.* 2nd ed. Minneapolis: Fortress, 2003.

Maloney, Elliott C. *Jesus' Urgent Message for Today: The Kingdom of God in Mark's Gospel.* New York: Continuum, 2004.

Marcus, Joel. *Mark 1–8: A New Translation with Introduction and Commentary.* AB 27. New Haven, CT: Yale University Press, 2000.

———. *Mark 8–16: A New Translation and Commentary.* AB 27A. New Haven, CT: Yale University Press, 2009.

———. "Mark 14:61: Are you the Messiah-Son-of-God?" *NovT* 31/2 (1989) 125–41.

———. *The Way of the Lord: Christological Exegesis of the Old Testament in the Gospel of Mark.* London: T. & T. Clark, 1992.

Martin, Dale B. "Slave Families and Slaves in Families." In *Early Christian Families in Context: An Interdisciplinary Dialogue,* edited by David L. Balch and Carolyn Osiek, 207–30. Grand Rapids: Eerdmans, 2003.

Martin, Martina. "It's My Prerogative: Jesus' Authority to Grant Forgiveness and Healing on Earth." *JRT* 59–60 (2006–2007) 67–74.

May, David M. "Leaving and Receiving: A Social-Scientific Exegesis of Mark 10:29–31." *PRSt* 17/2 (1990) 141–51, 154.

McInery, William F. "An Unresolved Question in the Gospel Called Mark: 'Who is This Whom Even Wind and Sea Obey?' (4:41)." *PRSt* 23/3 (Fall 1996) 255–68.

Meier, John P. "The Debate on the Resurrection of the Dead: An Incident from the Ministry of the Historical Jesus?" *JSNT* 77 (2000) 3–24.

Melbourne, Bertram L. *Slow to Understand: The Disciples in Synoptic Perspective.* Lanham, MD: University Press of America, 1988.

Mercer, Joyce Ann. *Welcoming Children: A Practical Theology of Childhood.* St. Louis: Chalice, 2005.

Moloney, Francis J. "Mark 6:6b–30: Mission, the Baptist, and Failure." *CBQ* 63/4 (2001) 647–63.

———. *Mark: Storyteller, Interpreter, Evangelist.* Peabody, MA: Hendrickson, 2004.

Moore, Stephen D. *Empire and Apocalypse: Postcolonialism and the New Testament.* BMW 12. Sheffield, UK: Sheffield Academic Press, 2006.

———. "Why There Are No Humans or Animals in the Gospel of Mark." In *Mark as Story: Retrospect and Prospect,* edited by Kelly R. Iverson and Christopher W. Skinner, 71–94. Resources for Biblical Study 65. Atlanta: Society of Biblical Literature, 2011.

Mowery, Robert. "Son of God in Roman Imperial Titles and Matthew." *Biblica* 83 (2002) 100–110.

Moxnes, Halvor. *Putting Jesus in His Place: A Radical Vision of Household and Kingdom*. Louisville: Westminster John Knox, 2003.

———. "What is Family? Problems in Constructing Early Christian Families." In *Constructing Early Christian Families: Family as Social Reality and Metaphor*, edited by Halvor Moxnes, 13–41. London: Routledge, 1997.

Muddiman, John. "The Glory of Jesus, Mark 10:37." In *The Glory of Christ in the New Testament: Studies in Christology in Memory of George Bradford Caird*, edited by L. D. Hurst and N. T. Wright, 51–58. Oxford: Oxford University Press, 1987.

Munro, Winsome. "Women Disciples in Mark?" *CBQ* 44 (1982) 225–41.

Myers, Ched. *Binding the Strong Man: A Political Reading of Mark's Story of Jesus*. 20th anniv. ed. Maryknoll, NY: Orbis, 2008.

Naluparayil, Jacob Chacko. *The Identity of Jesus in Mark: An Essay on Narrative Christology*. Analecta/Studium Biblicum Franciscanum 49. Jerusalem: Franciscan, 2000.

Neyrey, Jerome H. *Render to God: New Testament Understandings of the Divine*. Minneapolis: Fortress, 2004.

Nineham, Dennis E. *The Gospel of St. Mark*. Penguin New Testament Commentaries. London: Penguin, 1992.

Oldenhage, Tania. *Parables for Our Time: Rereading New Testament Scholarship after the Holocaust*. American Academy of Religion Cultural Criticism. Oxford: Oxford University Press, 2002.

Painter, John. *Mark's Gospel: Worlds in Conflict*. New Testament Readings. London: Routledge, 1997.

———. "When Is a House Not Home? Disciples and Family in Mark 3:13–35." *NTS* 45/4 (1999) 498–513.

Parkin, Robert. *Kinship: An Introduction to Basic Concepts*. Oxford: Blackwell, 1997.

Peppard, Michael. *The Son of God in the Roman World: Rethinking Divine Sonship in Its Social and Political Context*. Oxford: Oxford University Press, 2011.

Perkins, Pheme. *Peter: Apostle for the Whole Church*. Minneapolis: Fortress, 2000.

Perkinson, Jim. "A Canaanitic Word in the Logos of Christ; or the Difference the Syro-Phoenician Woman Makes to Jesus." *Semeia* 75 (1996) 61–85.

Perrin, Norman. "The Creative Use of the Son of Man Traditions by Mark." *USQR* 23/4 (1968) 357–65.

———. *The Resurrection According to Matthew, Mark and Luke*. Philadelphia: Fortress, 1977.

Plevnik, Joseph. "Honor/Shame." In *Handbook of Biblical Social Values*, edited by John J. Pilch and Bruce J. Malina, 106–15. 2nd ed. Peabody, MA: Hendrickson, 2000.

Poetker, Katrina M. "You Are My Mother, My Brothers, and My Sisters: A Literary-Anthropological Investigation of Family in the Gospel of Mark." PhD diss., Emory University, 2001.

Pomeroy, Sarah. "Some Greek Families: Production and Reproduction." In *The Jewish Family in Antiquity*, edited by S. J. Cohen, 155–63. Atlanta: Scholars, 1993.

Powell, Mark Allen. *What is Narrative Criticism?* GBS New Testament. Minneapolis: Augsburg Fortress, 1990.

Price, S. R. F. *Rituals and Power: The Roman Imperial Cult in Asia Minor*. Cambridge: Cambridge University Press, 1984.

Rawson, Beryl, ed. *A Companion to Families in the Greek and Roman Worlds*. Blackwell Companions to the Ancient World. Malden, MA: Blackwell, 2010.

Rhoads, David. *Reading Mark, Engaging the Gospel*. Minneapolis: Fortress, 2004.
Rhoads, David, Donald Michie, and Joanna Dewey. *Mark as Story: An Introduction to the Narrative Gospel*. 2nd ed. Minneapolis: Fortress, 1999.
Ringe, Sharon. "A Gentile Woman's Story Revisited: Rereading Mark 7.24–31a." In *A Feminist Companion to Mark*, edited by Amy-Jill Levine, 2:79–100. Feminist Companion to the New Testament and Early Christian Writings. Sheffield, UK: Sheffield Academic Press, 2001.
Robbins, Vernon K. "The Healing of Blind Bartimaeus (10:46–52) in the Marcan Theology." *JBL* 92/2 (June 1973) 224–43.
———. "Summons and Outline in Mark: The Three-Step Progression." *NovT* 23/2 (1981) 97–114.
Rohrbaugh, Richard. "Honor: Core Value in the Biblical World." In *Understanding the Social World of the New Testament*, edited by Dietmar Neufeld and Richard E. DeMaris, 109–25. London: Routledge, 2010.
Roller, Duane W. *The Building Program of Herod the Great*. Berkley: University of California Press, 1998.
Salyer, Gregory. "Rhetoric, Purity, and Play: Aspects of Mark 7:1–23." *Semeia* 64 (1993) 139–69.
Samuel, Simon. "The Beginning of Mark: A Colonial/Postcolonial Conundrum." *BibInt* 10/4 (2002) 405–19.
Schnelle, Udo. *The History and Theology of the New Testament Writings*. London: SCM, 1998.
Schüssler Fiorenza, Elisabeth. *In Memory of Her: A Feminist Theological Reconstruction of Christian Origins*. 2nd ed. London: SCM, 1994.
Schwartz, Seth. *Imperialism and Jewish Society: 200 B.C.E. to 640 C.E.* Princeton: Princeton University Press, 2001.
Schweizer, Eduard. *The Good News According to Mark*. Translated by D. H. Madvig. Richmond, VA: John Knox, 1970.
Scott, James C. *Domination and the Arts of Resistance: Hidden Transcripts*. New Haven, CT: Yale University Press, 1990.
———. "Prestige as the Public Discourse of Domination." *Cultural Critique* 12 (Spring 1989) 145–66.
Scott, Kenneth. *The Imperial Cult under the Flavians*. Stuttgart: W. Kohlhammer, 1936.
Setzer, Claudia. "Three Odd Couples: Women and Men in Mark and John." In *Mariam, the Magdalen, and the Mother*, edited by Deirdre Good, 75–92. Bloomington: Indiana University Press, 2005.
Shepherd, Tom. *Markan Sandwich Stories: Narration, Definition, and Function*. Berrien Springs, MI: Andrews University Press, 1993.
Shiner, Whitney Taylor. "The Ambiguous Pronouncement of the Centurion and the Shrouding of Meaning in Mark." *JSNT* 78 (2000) 3–22.
———. *Follow Me! Disciples in Markan Rhetoric*. SBLDS 145. Atlanta: Scholars, 1995.
Smith, Dennis E. *From Symposium to Eucharist: The Banquet in the Early Christian World*. Minneapolis: Fortress, 2003.
Smith, Morton. "Prolegomena to a Discussion of Aretalogies, Divine Men, the Gospels and Jesus." *JBL* 90 (1971) 174–99.
Smith, Stephen H. *A Lion with Wings: A Narrative-Critical Approach to Mark's Gospel*. Biblical Seminar 38. Sheffield, UK: Sheffield Academic Press, 1996.

Spitaler, Peter. "Welcoming a Child as a Metaphor for Welcoming God's Kingdom: A Close Reading of Mark 10:13–16." *JSNT* 31 (2009) 423–46.

Stevenson, Seth William, C. Roach Smith, and Frederick W. Madden. *Dictionary of Roman Coins: Republican and Imperial*. London: George Bell, 1889.

Suetonius. *The Lives of the Caesars*. Translated by J. C. Rolfe. 2 vols. LCL 31, 38. Cambridge, MA: Harvard University Press, 1914.

Sugirtharajah, R. S. "The Widow's Mites Revalued." *Expository Times* 103/2 (1991) 42–43.

Tacitus. *Histories: Books 4–5. Annals: Books 1–3*. Vol. 3. Translated by Clifford H. Moore. LCL 249. Cambridge, MA: Harvard University Press, 1956.

Tait, Michael. *Jesus, The Divine Bridegroom, in Mark 2:18–22: Mark's Christology Upgraded*. AnBib 185. Rome: Gregorian & Biblical, 2010.

Tannehill, Robert C. "Disciples in Mark: The Function of a Narrative Role." *JR* 4 (1977) 386–405.

———. "The Gospel of Mark as Narrative Christology." *Semeia* 16 (1979) 57–95.

Taylor, Nicholas H. "Palestinian Christianity and the Caligula Crisis: Social and Historical Reconstruction." *JSNT* 61 (1996) 101–24.

Taylor, Vincent. *The Gospel According to St. Mark*. London: MacMillan, 1952.

Telford, William R. *The Barren Temple and the Withered Tree: A Redaction-Critical Analysis of the Cursing of the Fig-tree Pericope in Mark's Gospel and its Relation to the Cleansing of the Temple Tradition*. JSNTSup 1. Sheffield, UK: JSOT, 1980.

———. *Writing on the Gospel of Mark*. Guides to Advanced Biblical Research 1. Blandford Forum, UK: Deo, 2009.

Theissen, Gerd. *The Gospels in Context: Social and Political History in the Synoptic Tradition*. Translated by Linda M. Maloney. Minneapolis: Fortress, 1991.

Todd, Emmanuel. *The Explanation of Ideology: Family Structures and Social Systems*. Translated by D. Garrioch. Family, Sexuality, and Social Relations in Past Times. Oxford: Blackwell, 1985.

Tolbert, Mary Ann. "Mark." In *Women's Bible Commentary, Expanded Edition*, edited by Carol A. Newsom and Sharon H. Ringe, 350–62. Louisville: Westminster John Knox, 1998.

———. *Sowing the Gospel: Mark's World in Literary-Historical Perspective*. Minneapolis: Fortress, 1996.

Trainor, Michael F. *The Quest for Home: The Household in Mark's Community*. Collegeville, MN: Liturgical, 2001.

Trocmé, Etienne. *The Formation of the Gospel according to Mark*. Translated by Pamela Gaughan. Philadelphia: Westminster, 1975.

Tulloch, Janet H. "Women Leaders in Family Funerary Banquets." In *A Woman's Place: House Churches in Earliest Christianity*, by Carolyn Osiek and Margaret Y. MacDonald, 164–93. Minneapolis: Fortress, 2006.

Tyson, Joseph. "Blindness of Disciples in Mark," *JBL* 80/3 (1961) 261–68.

Ulansey, David. "The Heavenly Veil Torn: Mark's Cosmic *Inclusio*." *JBL* 110/1 (Spring 1991) 123–25.

Van Eck, Ernest, and Andries G. Van Aarde. "A Narratological Analysis of Mark 12:1–2: The Plot of the Gospel of Mark in a Nutshell." *HvTSt* 45 (November 1989) 778–800.

Wasserman, Tommy. "The 'Son of God' Was in the Beginning (Mark 1:1)." *JTS* 62/1 (April 2011) 20–50.

Watts, Rikk E. "The Lord's House and David's Lord: The Psalms and Mark's Perspective on Jesus and the Temple." *BibInt* 15/3 (2007) 307–22.
Weeden, Theodore J. *Mark: Traditions in Conflict*. Philadelphia: Fortress, 1971.
Wefald, Eric K. "The Separate Gentile Mission in Mark: A Narrative Explanation of Markan Geography, the Two Feeding Accounts and Exorcism." *JSNT* 60 (1995) 3–26.
Wegener, Mark I. *Cruciformed: The Literary Impact of Mark's Story of Jesus and His Disciples*. Lanham, MD: University Press of America, 1995.
Wilson, Carol B. *For I was Hungry and You Gave Me Food: Pragmatics of Food Access in the Gospel of Matthew*. Eugene, OR: Pickwick, 2014.
Wilson, John F. *Caesarea Philippi: Banias, the Lost City of Pan*. London: Tauris, 2004.
Winn, Adam. *The Purpose of Mark's Gospel*. WUNT 245. Tübingen: Mohr Siebeck, 2008.
Wrede, William. *The Messianic Secret*. Translated by J. C. G. Greig. Cambridge: J. Clarke, 1971.
Wright, Addison G. "The Widow's Mites: Praise or Lament? A Matter of Context." *CBQ* 44/2 (1982) 256–65.
Zuntz, Günther. "Wann wurde das Evangelium Marci geschrieben?" In *Markus-Philologie: historische, literargeschichtliche und stilistische Untersunchungen zum zweiten Evangelium*, edited by Hubert Cancik, 47–71. Tübingen: Mohr Siebeck, 1984.

Ancient Document Index

HEBREW BIBLE

Genesis

1:1—2:3	92, 158
1:2	92
1:26	93
1:27	186
1:31	158
2:1–3	116
2:24	186
3:6–7	93
6:2	86
9:26–27	190
12:2–3	217
15:1	151n212
19:8	146n193
22:2	192n72
25:28	192n72
26:2–5	217
27:1–40	190
28:1–4	190, 217
35:13–15	151n211
37:3	192n72
44:20	192n72
48:10	190
48:14	190

Exodus

3:1–12	217
3:10	93, 151n211
3:14	151n213, 217, 241
4:22	92
12	233
12:11	143
14:13	151n212
14:19	93
16	148
17:1–7	161n238
19–24	170
19:3–7	122, 123n123
20:1–17	155
20:12	154, 155
20:14	186, 187
20:20	151n212
21:23–25	183
23:20	93
23:23	93
24:8	234
24:9–11	122
29:7	231
32	175
32:34	93
33:2	93
33:19	151n210
33:22	151n210
34:6	151n210
34:21	115
34:29–30	175

Leviticus

4	85
13:17	106n80
16:29	113
16:31	113
16:32–33	227
18:16	145
19:18	217
20:21	145
21:10	231
22:7	106n80

Leviticus *(continued)*

24:19–20	183

Numbers

11:17	151n211
11:29	89n20

Deuteronomy

6:4–5	217
6:4	95, 191, 192n69
6:5–9	192n69
17:6	143
18:15	171
18:18	171
19:15	143
19:21	183
23:25	115
24:1–4	186
25	217
25:5–10	216
29:5	143
30:4	228
32:8	133n146
32:39	151n213, 241

Joshua

1:1–9	200
2	200
5:13—6:26	200
8:1	151n212

Judges

6:17	151n211
11:7	91n32
14:1	146n193
14:3	146n193
14:7	146n193

1 Samuel

2:10	85
2:35	85
10:1	231
12:12	95n39
16:6	231
21	116
24:7	231

2 Samuel

7:13–14	86
7:13	85
12:16	113
23:1–2	89n20
23:4	151n210

1 Kings

1:13	201
2:1	201
17:8–16	148
17:17–24	139
19	170
19:5–7	93
19:11	151n210
19:16	85

2 Kings

2:1–12	171n7
4:1–7	148
4:9	100
4:18–37	139
4:42–44	148, 149

1 Chronicles

23:1	201
28:5	95n39
29:22	201

2 Chronicles

13:8	95n39
24:19	142
36:15–16	142

Nehemiah

9:26	142

Esther

2:4	146n193
2:9	146
5:3	146
6:14—7:10	147n198
9	146n193

Job

9:11	151n210

Ancient Document Index 277

31:10	146n193

Psalms

2	85, 221n167
2:7	32, 86
5:2	95n39
10:16	95n39
22	221n167, 247
23:5	198
29:1	86
35:13	113
42:5	237
42:11	237
43:5	237
44:4	95n39
45	85
47:7–8	95n39
68:24	95n39
89	85
89:26–27	86
93:1	95n39, 96
96:10	95n39
99:1	95n39
103:19	95, 95n39
106:16	100
110	85, 221n167
110:1	85n5, 220
110:4	221n167
118	202n102, 221n167
118:22–23	212
132	85
146:10	95n39

Proverbs

1:1	201
1:8	108
31:2	108

Ecclesiastes

1:1	201

Isaiah

5	211
5:1–7	210
5:2	211
5:7	211n129, 212
6:5	95n39
9	85
11:1–2	89n20
25:6–10	148, 162
33:22	95n39
35	158n229
35:5–6	158
40	88
41:4	151n213, 241
42:1	32
43:5–6	228
44:6	95n39
50	196
51:17	198
51:22	198
52:7	95n39
53	196
53:4–5	196
56:7	206
61:1	89n20

Jeremiah

7:11	206
7:30–34	184
19:6–9	184
23:5–6	85
49:12	198

Ezekiel

2:1	110
2:3	110
2:6	110
34:23–24	85

Daniel

2:37–45	95n42
3:25	86
7	5, 110
7:12–14	241
7:13–14	110
7:13	5
7:25	228
8:13	228
9:27	228
10:12	151n212
10:19	151n212
11:31	226
12:7	228

Daniel (continued)

12:11	226, 228
12:12	228

Hosea

11:1	92

Joel

3:1–2	89n20

Amos

7:8	151n210
8:2	151n210

Jonah

1:15	131

Zephaniah

3:15	95n39
3:16	151n212

Zechariah

2:6	228
9:9	202, 204
12:8	85
13:7–9	236
14:9	95n39
14:16	95n39

Malachi

1:14	95n39
3	88
3:2–3	184
3:22–23	171
4:5–6	173

APOCRYPHA

Tobit

12:17	151n213

Wisdom

2:18	86
10:10	94

Sirach

2:1	108
3:1	108
3:9	190
4:10b	86

4 Ezra

13	85

1 Maccabees

1:6	95n42
1:16	95n42
1:41	95n42
1:51	95n42
1:54	226
13:51	203
14:49	222n171

2 Maccabees

3:6	222n171
7	169
7:9	169
7:14	169
7:23	169
7:29	169, 236n213

PSEUDEPIGRAPHA

The Assumption of Moses

10:1–3a	95

2 Baruch

21:8	228
54:1	228

1 Enoch

49:3	89n20
62:2	89n20

The Letter of Aristeas

	91n32

Psalms of Solomon

17	85

17:21	228		206n120, 208, 212, 226, 231, 238, 246, 247, 254, 255
17:37	89n20		
		1:9	144
NEW TESTAMENT		1:10–11	101, 107
		1:10	109, 221, 247
Matthew		1:11	32, 49, 52, 68n93, 71, 100, 126, 130, 131, 141, 165, 208
9:15	114n104		
9:18–26	48n45		
13:55	49n47	1:12–13	42, 238
13:57	142n181	1:12	221
15:22–28	157n225	1:13	249
17:13	174n16	1:14—8:26	40
18:1–13	214	1:14—5:43	42
19:1	185n45	1:14–20	63
20:25	204	1:14–15	45, 68, 82, 94, 94–97, 106, 107, 122, 142, 165, 176, 176n22, 214, 231
21:33	211n130		
26:26–29	234n208		
26:63	56n50, 241n226	1:14	144, 196
		1:15	65, 68n94, 108, 137, 143, 176, 201, 212n134, 219n159, 223
Mark			
1:1—8:30	83		
1:1–8	82	1:16—8:26	39
1:1–3	88n18	1:16—3:19	46n43
1:1	39, 40, 42, 43, 43n35, 44, 45, 50, 59, 62, 68n93, 71, 84–88, 89, 90n24, 93, 94, 100, 120, 122, 126, 130, 165, 182, 196, 207n120, 208, 212, 220, 238, 255, 258	1:16—3:12	120
		1:16–20	21, 23, 45, 62, 82, 87, 97–99, 103, 112, 122, 124, 192, 237
		1:16–17	236
		1:16	126
		1:17–28	120, 132
1:2–15	39	1:17	248
1:2–13	40, 88–94	1:19	68, 181, 197n82
1:2–8	42, 45n39	1:20	193
1:2–3	62, 94	1:21–28	45, 99–102
1:4–8	62, 212n133	1:21–27	113, 140
1:4–5	250n258	1:21–22	45
1:4	144	1:21	63, 115, 140
1:6	174	1:22	115, 206n119, 219n159, 223
1:7–9	189n60		
1:7–8	144	1:23–26	60
1:8	221, 226	1:23	68n93
1:9—8:30	82	1:24	103, 105
1:9–20	34	1:25	131
1:9–13	42, 43n35, 44, 45–50, 51, 59, 258	1:27	140n174, 195, 244, 250, 251
1:9–11	32, 42, 62, 82, 98, 101n68, 120, 126, 165, 170, 198,	1:28	106n80
		1:29–34	156

Ancient Document Index

Mark (continued)

1:29–31	45, 59, 63, 69, 99, 102–104, 112n99, 113, 137, 140, 157
1:29	99n58, 112, 155, 225
1:31	153, 177, 239n223, 249
1:32–34	3, 104–105, 106n80, 153
1:32	63, 188
1:33	107, 185
1:34	49, 153, 158, 205n116
1:35–45	106–107, 119
1:39	205n116
1:40–45	45, 113, 140
1:41	153, 176, 239n223
1:44	251
1:45	111
2:1—3:6	118, 208
2:1–12	45, 63, 70, 70n101, 107–12, 113, 118, 119, 140, 176n22, 178, 258
2:1	106n80
2:2	106n80
2:3	188, 189
2:4	185
2:5	116, 190n62, 201, 205, 223
2:7	51, 178, 191, 242
2:8	113, 228, 243n232
2:10	171
2:11	251
2:12	140n174, 206n119, 244, 251
2:13–28	119
2:13–22	116
2:13–17	45, 112–13, 115
2:13–15	122
2:13–14	62
2:13	63, 87, 185
2:14	68, 230n195
2:15–17	70n101
2:15	230
2:16–28	49
2:16	154n218, 178
2:17	190
2:18–22	46, 70n101, 113–15
2:18	144, 154n218, 178, 194
2:19	82, 83, 92, 97, 105, 113, 116, 122, 123, 129, 133, 192n72
2:23–28	46, 70n101, 115–18, 143, 148n199
2:24	51, 154n218, 178, 194
2:28	110n92, 171
3:1–6	46, 70n101, 118–20, 140, 162, 163
3:1	63
3:2	51, 194
3:5	151, 243n232
3:6	51, 122, 142, 147, 153, 172, 178, 188, 194, 196, 198, 200, 206, 213n136, 219
3:7–12	3, 46, 120–21, 140n174, 143, 153
3:7	221
3:8	185
3:9	63
3:10	153
3:11	68n93, 100, 100n60, 132, 191n68, 241n227
3:13–19	21, 23, 46, 62, 87, 121–23, 123n123, 127n135, 142
3:13–18	94
3:13–16	258
3:14–15	122, 127n135, 130, 158
3:14	135, 136, 144, 237n217, 243
3:15	102, 135, 175, 182, 188, 205n116
3:16–35	60
3:17	68
3:18	68
3:20–35	34, 46, 64, 123–27
3:20–34	70n101
3:20–25	22, 123
3:20	185
3:21	140
3:22–30	60
3:22–23	205n116
3:22	178, 194
3:28	224n178, 236
3:31–35	15, 62, 87, 94, 98, 99, 135, 140, 141, 142–44, 182,

Ancient Document Index   281

	193, 199, 212, 212n134,	5:42	140n174, 206n119
	216, 217, 248n252	6:1—8:26	42
3:33–35	82, 97, 105, 191n67	6:1–14	160n233
3:33		6:1–6	48, 140–42
3:34–35	71, 135, 193	6:2	206n119
3:35	61, 69, 83, 91, 97, 133,	6:3	48n47, 90
	137, 141, 155, 157, 238	6:5	239n223
4	47, 135n157	6:6b–13	21
4:1–34	23, 127–30, 132, 210, 224	6:7–13	23, 49
4:1–20	131	6:7	175, 182, 188
4:1	51, 185, 221, 223n172	6:13	175
4:10–20	193	6:14–29	49, 65, 135n158, 144–47,
4:11	68n94		174, 187, 196, 214, 244
4:26	68n94	6:14–17	174
4:30	68n94	6:14–16	164
4:35–41	47, 130–31, 132, 140, 143,	6:17	95, 187, 194
	149, 150, 151, 205	6:18	187
4:38	214	6:21–22	148n201
4:40	142, 176n23, 177, 184	6:21	181, 189
4:41	47, 140n174, 151, 174,	6:22–25	189
	251	6:22	189, 194, 230n195
5:1–20	65, 101n67, 102n71,	6:24	189
	132–36, 140, 151, 158,	6:30–44	24, 92, 147–49, 160, 180,
	196, 255		193, 233
5:7	47, 68n93, 100, 100n60,	6:30–32	49
	241n227	6:30	144
5:13	206n116	6:33–34	49
5:19	251	6:34	160, 176, 185, 221, 236
5:20	140n174, 244	6:39	230n195
5:21–43	136–40, 151, 156, 157,	6:41	190n62
	158, 181, 188, 214n137	6:45–52	24, 149–52, 205
5:21	185, 221	6:50	225, 241, 241n229, 251
5:22–43	47	6:51–52	176n23, 177
5:22–23	48, 175	6:51	206n119, 251
5:22	191n68	6:52	184
5:24	185, 221	6:53–56	3, 153
5:25–34	140, 258	6:54–56	51, 188, 189
5:28	153	6:55	258
5:30	228	7	50
5:33	121, 191n68	7:1–37	163
5:34	47, 48, 153, 190n62, 201,	7:1–23	49, 154–56, 183
	205, 223, 251	7:1–8	70n101
5:35–43	64, 140	7:5	194
5:35	176, 191, 197	7:10	141n5
5:36	251	7:17–23	157
5:37	197n82, 225, 237	7:18	184
5:39	228	7:21–22	183
5:41	153, 177, 239n223	7:24–37	155n221

Mark (continued)

7:24–30	156–58, 181, 188
7:25	121, 175, 191n68
7:29	251
7:31–37	158–59
7:32–37	163
7:33	239n223
7:37	206n119
8	50
8:1–10	92, 155n221, 160–61, 180, 193, 233
8:1	185, 221
8:2	176
8:11–21	161–63
8:11	194
8:12	224n178
8:14–21	165
8:15	172
8:17–21	193
8:17	176n23, 177, 184
8:18	163
8:22—10:52	199
8:22–26	50, 159, 163–64, 199
8:23	239n223
8:27—10:52	39, 40
8:27—9:50	42
8:27–31	174
8:27–30	44n37, 164–67
8:27	50, 178n28
8:28	236, 247
8:29	170, 179, 182, 191, 220, 236
8:31—15:20	168
8:31—9:10	44, 50–56, 59, 89, 168, 195, 254, 259
8:31—9:8	163, 168–73, 246
8:31–38	52, 179
8:31–34	232
8:31	52, 53, 162, 173, 174, 177, 180, 196, 198, 212, 216, 225, 231, 239, 243n232, 250, 250n258
8:32	176n23, 177, 184, 188
8:34–38	174, 193, 248n252
8:34–35	182, 195, 226, 259
8:34	179, 180, 184, 224, 228, 236, 242, 246
8:35	179, 199, 205, 216, 217, 232, 247
8:38	68n93, 179, 228, 238
9:1	68n94, 95, 224n178, 236
9:2–10	52
9:2–9	89, 133n147, 212, 247
9:2–8	173, 208, 237
9:2	197n82
9:3–4	52
9:4	173
9:6	251
9:7	52, 68n93, 166
9:9–13	173–74
9:9	250n258
9:10	250n258
9:13	212
9:14–29	174–77, 181, 188
9:14	221
9:15	185, 250, 251
9:17	214
9:18	177, 182
9:24	205, 223
9:25	185
9:27	239n223
9:30–32	177–79
9:30–31	53
9:31	169, 180, 196, 198, 212, 216, 225, 231, 233, 239, 243n232, 250, 250n258, 259
9:32	184, 250n258, 251
9:33–37	64, 179–81
9:33–34	184, 184
9:33	178n28
9:34	182, 189, 251
9:35–50	193
9:35–37	182, 248n252
9:35	184, 189, 190, 191n67, 192, 194, 204, 205, 216, 217, 224, 232
9:36–37	188, 189
9:37	53, 183
9:38–50	181–85
9:38–40	225
9:41	224n178, 236
9:47	68n94
10:1–52	42
10:1–45	195

10:1–12	53, 70n101, 185–88, 217	11	54
10:1	178n28	11:1—16:8	42
10:2–12	214	11:1—15:41	39, 40
10:2	194	11:1–11	42, 202–205, 259
10:10	64, 191	11:1–10	178n28
10:13–16	181, 188–91	11:1–6	233n203
10:13	201	11:1	185n45
10:14–15	68n94	11:2–6	228
10:15	186, 191n67, 192, 224n178, 236	11:7–10	54
		11:9–10	220n165
10:16	239n223	11:9	220
10:17–31	191–94	11:11	230
10:17	178n28, 197, 214	11:12—13:37	42
10:19–31	195	11:12–25	205–208
10:20	214	11:12	230
10:21	186, 232	11:15–19	259
10:24–25	68n94	11:15–17	208, 223
10:24	190, 195, 250, 251	11:15–16	217
10:26	251	11:17	217, 227
10:28	155, 240	11:18	221, 251
10:29–31	22	11:19	230
10:29–30	212	11:23	224n178, 236
10:29	224n178, 236	11:25	68, 68n93, 238
10:30	15, 197n82, 217	11:27—12:34	208, 222n170
10:32–45	195–99	11:27–33	70n101, 208–209, 217, 230
10:32–34	53, 54, 199, 212		
10:32–33	243n232, 259	11:27	217
10:32	178n28, 244, 250, 251	11:32	213, 221
10:33–34	169, 216, 225, 231, 239, 245, 25n258	12	54
		12:1–12	38, 209–13
10:33	233	12:1	229
10:34	247, 250	12:12	220, 221
10:35–45	54	12:13–17	65, 213–16, 217, 230, 256, 259
10:35	68, 214		
10:42–45	22, 184, 191n67, 199, 248n252	12:13–16	19
		12:13	172, 200, 209
10:42	224	12:14	217
10:43–44	64n74, 186, 209, 216, 217, 249	12:17	244, 251
		12:18–27	55, 70n101, 216–17, 230
10:43	232	12:18	209
10:44	64, 201, 224	12:27–33	222
10:45	224, 232, 249	12:28–34	217–19, 230
10:46–52	54, 163n241, 199–202	12:30–31	224
10:46	68, 178n28, 221	12:31	222
10:47–48	220n165	12:34	68n94, 222
10:47	220	12:35–37	220–21
10:50	240	12:38–44	222–24
10:52	178n28, 190n62, 251	12:43	236

Mark (continued)

12:44	232
13	55, 72, 259
13:1–37	225–29
13:1	214
13:3	223n172, 235
13:6	241n229
13:11	93, 239n221
13:12	151
13:13	217n155
13:21	68n93
13:26–27	68, 235
13:26	55
13:27	242
13:30	236
13:32	238
13:33–36	22
13:55	22
14	56
14:1—16:8	42
14:1–11	230–33
14:1	239
14:2	221
14:3–9	250
14:4	250n258
14:7	203
14:9	236
14:12–26	56
14:12–25	233–35
14:14	64
14:17–26	64
14:18	236, 259
14:25	68n94, 236
14:26–31	235–37
14:27	240, 243, 259
14:28	243, 251, 252n264, 259
14:30	242, 243, 259
14:31	243
14:32—15:20	178
14:32–52	237–40
14:33	197n82
14:36	68n93, 198
14:37	229
14:40–41	229
14:43	259
14:50–52	229
14:50	131, 162, 170, 179, 184, 194, 240, 242, 259
14:53–65	240–42
14:54	243
14:56–58	230n194
14:61–64	101n69
14:61	68n93, 85n5, 182
14:62	85n5
14:63–64	85n5
14:66–72	229, 240, 242–43
14:67–72	259
15:1—16:8	243n232
15:1–39	65
15:1–20	135n158, 244–46
15:1	196n79, 200
15:2–15	196n79
15:3	230n194
15:5	251
15:11	230n194
15:20	178
15:21—16:8	168
15:21–41	44, 52, 56–58, 59, 89, 168, 246–49, 254, 259
15:21	68
15:27	197n81
15:31–32	230n194
15:33–39	89
15:33	229
15:38–39	57, 259
15:38	229
15:39	68n93, 203n107
15:40–41	259
15:41	231
15:42—16:8	39, 40
15:42–47	249–50
15:43	68n94
15:46	147
16:1–8	229, 250–53, 259
16:1	231, 250
16:6	245
16:7	259
16:8	58n53, 248n252

Luke

4:24	142n181
5:34	114n104
13:33	142n181
18:12	113n102
22:15–20	234n208
24:5–8	250n258

John
4:44	142n181

Romans
1:1	94n37
15:16	94n37

1 Corinthians
7:33–34	146n193
11:23–25	234n208

2 Corinthians
11:7	94n37

1 Thessalonians
2:2	94n37
2:8	94n37
2:9	94n37

DEAD SEA SCROLLS
1QapGen 21:2	133n146
4Q174	86
4Q246	86, 133n146

RABBINIC WRITINGS
b. Ta'an 12a	113n102
m. Gittin 9:10	186
m. Ned. 9:1	154n219

GRECO-ROMAN WRITINGS

Aristotle
Poetics
	36

Politics
	186n47

Dio Cassius
Roman History
53.18.3	78n140
65.15	75n120
65.8	75n121, 163n243
65.8.1	119n117, 159n231, 159n232

Homer
Iliad
	150n206

Josephus
Jewish Antiquities
4.325–26	171n7
6.51	180n31
9.28	171n7
14.384–85	244n237
14.410	200n91
15.259	187n51
15.363–64	165n246
17.146	146n196
17.311–17	144n186
17.344	144n186
17.354	144n186
18.16	216n149
18.110	145n187
18.136	145n187
18.240–41	146n196
19.294	222n171
20.181	239n222

Jewish War
1.40	95n42
1.392	95n42
1.396	95n42
1.398	95n42
1.404–6	165n246
1.457–58	95n42
2.93–94	95n42
2.167	200n92, 244n236
2.197	204n114
2.215	95n42
2.220	95n42
3.444	165n248

Jewish War (continued)

3.399–404	73n112
3.446–47	133n149
3.462–531	152n215
4.614–19	87n16
4.623	73n112
5.200	222n171
5.212	57n52, 248n248
5.214	57n52, 248n248
5.409	95n42
6.136	227, 227n185, 246n245
6.271	227n187
6.282	222n171
6.316–21	227n188
6.316	227, 227n185
7.40	95n42
7.117–59	74n113, 203n104
7.121–57	152n216, 165n249
7.126–27	204n111
7.154	74n116

Lucian

De Dea Syria

14	91n32
33	91n32
54	91n32

Philostratus

Life of Apollonius

1.354.12	142n181

Plutarch

De Exilio 604D

	142

Suetonius

Caligula

19	150n208

Titus

5	74n117, 246n245

6	74n119

Vespasian

4	73n111
7.2	75n121, 159n231, 159n232, 163n243, 201n99

Tacitus

Histories

2.2	75n120
2.78	133n147
4.81	75n121, 75n122, 159n231, 159n232, 163n243, 201n99
5.8.3	73n112

Tibullus

Elegiae

1.17.18	91n32

Xenophon

Memorabilia

	180n31

EARLY CHRISTIAN WRITINGS

Didache

8:1	113n102

Dio Chrysostum

Discourses

47.6	142n181

Gospel of Thomas

31	142n181

Papyrus Oxyrhynchus

31:1	142n181

www.ingramcontent.com/pod-product-compliance
Lightning Source LLC
Chambersburg PA
CBHW061433300426
44114CB00014B/1669